The Impact of Private Sector Participation in Infrastructure

The Impact of Private Sector Participation in Infrastructure
Lights, Shadows, and the Road Ahead

Luis A. Andrés, J. Luis Guasch,
Thomas Haven, and Vivien Foster

THE WORLD BANK
Washington, D.C.

ISBN: 978-0-8213-7409-2
eISBN: 978-0-8213-7410-8
DOI: 10.1596/978-0-8213-7409-2

Library of Congress Cataloging-in-Publication Data
The impact of private sector participation in infrastructure: lights, shadows, and the road ahead / Luis A. Andrés ... [et al.].

  p. cm.—(Latin American development forum series)
Includes bibliographical references.
ISBN 978-0-8213-7409-2 (print)—ISBN 978-0-8213-7410-8 (electronic)
1. Infrastructure (Economics)—Latin America. 2. Public-private sector cooperation—Latin America. 3. Public utilities—Finance. 4. Public utilities—Latin America—Finance. 5. Privatization—Latin America. I. Andrés, Luis. II. World Bank.
HC130.C3I47 2008
363.6098—dc22

                                                                    2008014496

Cover design: ULTRAdesigns.

Latin American Development Forum Series

This series was created in 2003 to promote debate, disseminate information and analysis, and convey the excitement and complexity of the most topical issues in economic and social development in Latin America and the Caribbean. It is sponsored by the Inter-American Development Bank, the United Nations Economic Commission for Latin America and the Caribbean, and the World Bank. The manuscripts chosen for publication represent the highest quality in each institution's research and activity output and have been selected for their relevance to the academic community, policy makers, researchers, and interested readers.

Advisory Committee Members

Alicia Bárcena Ibarra, Executive Secretary, Economic Commission for Latin America and the Caribbean, United Nations

Inés Bustillo, Director, Washington Office, Economic Commission for Latin America and the Caribbean, United Nations

José Luis Guasch, Senior Advisor, Latin America and the Caribbean Region, World Bank; and Professor of Economics, University of California, San Diego

Santiago Levy, General Manager and Chief Economist, Research Department, Inter-American Development Bank

Eduardo Lora, Principal Advisor, Research Department, Inter-American Development Bank

Luis Servén, Research Manager, Development Economics Vice Presidency, World Bank

Augusto de la Torre, Chief Economist, Latin America and the Caribbean Region, World Bank

Other Titles in the Latin American Development Forum Series

New and Forthcoming Titles

China's and India's Challenge to Latin America: Opportunity or Threat? (2008) by Daniel Lederman, Marcelo Olarreaga, and Guillermo E. Perry, editors

Does the Investment Climate Matter? Microeconomic Foundations of Growth in Latin America (2008) by Pablo Fajnzylber, José Luis Guasch, and J. Humberto López, editors

Job Creation in Latin America and the Caribbean: Trends and Policy Challenges (2009) by Carmen Pagés, Gaëlle Pierre, and Stefano Scarpetta

Innovative Experiences in Access to Finance: Market-Friendly Roles for the Visible Hand? (2009) by Augusto de la Torre, Juan Carlos Gozzi, and Sergio L. Schmukler

Published Titles

Remittances and Development: Lessons from Latin America (2008) by Pablo Fajnzylber and J. Humberto López, editors

Fiscal Policy, Stabilization, and Growth: Prudence or Abstinence? (2007) by Guillermo Perry, Luis Servén, and Rodrigo Suescún, editors

Raising Student Learning in Latin America: Challenges for the 21st Century (2007) by Emiliana Vegas and Jenny Petrow

Investor Protection and Corporate Governance: Firm-level Evidence Across Latin America (2007) by Alberto Chong and Florencio López-de-Silanes, editors

The State of State Reform in Latin America (2006) by Eduardo Lora, editor

Emerging Capital Markets and Globalization: The Latin American Experience (2006) by Augusto de la Torre and Sergio L. Schmukler

Beyond Survival: Protecting Households from Health Shocks in Latin America (2006) by Cristian C. Baeza and Truman G. Packard

Natural Resources: Neither Curse nor Destiny (2006) by Daniel Lederman and William F. Maloney, editors

Beyond Reforms: Structural Dynamics and Macroeconomic Vulnerability (2005) by José Antonio Ocampo, editor

Privatization in Latin America: Myths and Reality (2005) by Alberto Chong and Florencio López-de-Silanes, editors

Keeping the Promise of Social Security in Latin America (2004) by Indermit S. Gill, Truman G. Packard, and Juan Yermo

Lessons from NAFTA: For Latin America and the Caribbean (2004) by Daniel Lederman, William F. Maloney, and Luis Servén

The Limits of Stabilization: Infrastructure, Public Deficits, and Growth in Latin America (2003) by William Easterly and Luis Servén, editors

Globalization and Development: A Latin American and Caribbean Perspective (2003) by José Antonio Ocampo and Juan Martin, editors

Is Geography Destiny? Lessons from Latin America (2003) by John Luke Gallup, Alejandro Gaviria, and Eduardo Lora

About the Authors

Luis Alberto Andrés is an infrastructure economist in the Sustainable Development Department for the Latin America and the Caribbean Region of the World Bank. His work at the World Bank involves analytical and advisory services, and economic input, with a focus on infrastructure, mainly in water and energy sectors, impact evaluations, and empirical microeconomics. He worked with numerous Latin American governments on issues on infrastructure and impact evaluation. Before joining the World Bank, he was the chief of advisors for the secretary of fiscal and social equity, and for the government of Argentina and held other top positions in the chief of cabinet of ministries and the Ministry of Economy. He holds a doctorate in economics from the University of Chicago.

José Luis Guasch, a Spanish national, is currently senior regional advisor in the Latin America and Caribbean Region of the World Bank in Washington, D.C., responsible for the areas of competitiveness, regulation, infrastructure, innovation, and technological development; he is also Head of the World Bank Infrastructure Regulation Thematic Group. He has been a professor of economics at the University of California, San Diego, since 1980. He holds a doctorate in economics from Stanford University, California, and an engineering degree from the Polytechnic University of Barcelona in Spain. He has written extensively in leading economic journals. Among his most recent books are: *Managing the Regulatory Process: Design, Concepts, Issues and the Latin America and Caribbean Story*; *The Challenge of Designing and Implementing Effective Regulation: A Normative Approach and an Empirical Evaluation*; *Labor Markets: The Unfinished Reform in Latin America and Caribbean*; *Closing the Gap in Education and Technology in Latin America*; *Granting and Renegotiating Concessions: Doing it Right*; and *Quality and Standards Matter for Trade and Competitiveness Initiatives*.

Thomas Haven is a private sector development specialist focused on the Latin America and the Caribbean Region of the World Bank. His work at the Bank involves lending operations related to competitiveness, innovation, and energy. His analytical work has dealt primarily with infrastructure privatization, investment climate assessments, and energy sector strategies. Before joining the World Bank, he was a business-strategy consultant in the private sector. He holds a master's degree in international development from Harvard University and a degree in economics from Dartmouth College.

Vivien Foster is lead economist in the Office of the Director for Sustainable Development in the Africa Region of the World Bank. She is responsible for coordinating a major knowledge program known as the Africa Infrastructure Country Diagnostic. Her work at the World Bank involves analytical and advisory services, and economic input into the design and supervision of projects, with a focus on the impacts of infrastructure reform and privatization on the poor. Before joining the World Bank, she was a managing consultant of Oxford Economic Research Associates Ltd. in the United Kingdom, where she advised private and public sector clients in the water and energy industries, and worked with numerous Latin American governments on issues relating to water sector reform. She holds a doctorate in economics from University College London.

Contents

Preface   xxiii

Acknowledgments   xxv

Abbreviations   xxvii

1   INTRODUCTION   1

2   SETTING THE STAGE   7

    Why Infrastructure Matters   7
    Trends in Infrastructure Financing   10
    Distribution   17
      Sectoral Distribution   17
      Geographic Distribution   19
      Modal Distribution   21
      Investor Type: Geographic Location   26
    Limitations   28
    Achievements and Moving Forward   35

3   LEARNING FROM EXISTING LITERATURE   43

    Employment and Wages   44
    Prices of Services   45
    Quality of Services   45
    Access to Services and Coverage   46
    Asset Ownership   46
    Impact on Investors   47
    Fiscal Flows   48
    Productivity and Financial Solvency   49
    Distributional Impact and Consumer Welfare   50

4   FILLING GAPS WITH NEW DATA SETS AND
    METHODOLOGIES   57

    Data Sets   58
       Performance Indicators Data Set   58
       Contract and Regulatory Characteristics Data Set   60
       LAC Electricity Benchmarking Database   60
    New Methodology: Separating Transition
       versus Long-Run Effects   67
    New Methodology: Distinguishing Levels from Trends   68
    Means and Medians Analysis   70
    Econometric Analysis   71
       Adding Contract and Regulatory Characteristics   73
       Endogeneity and Selection Bias   74

5   THE IMPACT ON ELECTRICITY DISTRIBUTION   79

    Introduction   79
       The Privatization Process   79
       Data   90
    Impact on Output and Coverage   90
       Electricity Distribution: Output and Coverage Summary   90
       Energy Sold   90
       Number of Connections   93
       Coverage   95
    Impact on Employment   98
       Electricity Distribution: Employment Summary   98
    Impact on Labor Productivity and Efficiency   101
       Electricity Distribution: Labor Productivity
          and Efficiency Summary   101
       Labor Productivity   101
       Distributional Losses   102
    Impact on Prices   106
       Electricity Distribution: Price Summary   106
    Impact on Quality   109
       Electricity Distribution: Quality Summary   109
    Conclusion   114

6   THE IMPACT ON FIXED-LINE TELECOMMUNICATIONS   117

    Introduction   117
       The Privatization Process   118
       Data   120

Impact on Output and Coverage 122
  Telecommunications: Output and Coverage Summary 122
  Number of Connections 122
  Number of Minutes 124
  Coverage 126
Impact on Employment 129
  Telecommunications: Employment Summary 129
Impact on Labor Productivity and Efficiency 131
  Telecommunications: Labor Productivity and Efficiency
    Summary 131
  Labor Productivity 132
  Incomplete Calls 136
Impact on Prices 138
  Telecommunications: Price Summary 138
Impact on Quality 141
  Telecommunications: Quality Summary 141
Liberalization and Competition 144
  Telecommunications: Liberalization and Competition
    Summary 144
  Liberalization 148
  Competition from Mobile Service Providers 149
Conclusion 151

7 THE IMPACT ON WATER AND SEWERAGE 153

Introduction 153
  The Privatization Process 153
  Data 155
Impact on Output and Coverage 157
  Water and Sewerage: Output and Coverage
    Summary 157
  Number of Connections 159
  Water Production 159
  Coverage 161
Impact on Employment 165
  Water and Sewerage: Employment Summary 165
Impact on Labor Productivity and Efficiency 166
  Water and Sewerage: Labor Productivity and Efficiency
    Summary 166
  Labor Productivity 166
  Distributional Losses 171
Impact on Prices 173
  Water and Sewerage: Price Summary 173

Impact on Quality   176
    Water and Sewerage: Quality Summary   176
    Service Continuity   178
    Potability   178
Conclusion   180

8   AN ASSESSMENT OF THE ELECTRICITY DISTRIBUTION
    PERFORMANCE OF PRIVATE AND PUBLIC UTILITIES   185

Introduction   185
Main Findings   186
    Coverage   187
    Output   187
    Labor Productivity   187
    Operating Performance   190
    Tariffs   190
    Quality of Service   195
Top 10 Percent and Bottom 10 Percent Performers   199
    Output   199
    Labor Productivity   199
    Operating Performance   203
    Quality of Service   203
Conclusion   203

9   DETERMINANTS OF IMPACT: REGULATORY AND
    CONTRACT VARIABLES   207

Introduction   207
Sale Method   209
Autonomy of Regulatory Body   211
Duration of Regulatory Body Appointments   212
Investor Nationality   214
Award Criteria   215
Tariff Regulation   218
Conclusion   219

10 CONCLUSION   223

Key Methodological Contributions   223
Main Findings   224
Moving Forward   228

Critical Elements to Be Introduced in Moving Forward
to Secure Success and Maximum Benefit of Private
Participation Programs   233
Improved Institutionality   233
Improved Contract and Concession Design   233
Regulatory Framework   235
Regulatory Instruments   235
Conflict Resolution Mechanism   236
Addressing Social Issues   236
Transparency and Communications   236
Evaluation and Monitoring   236

APPENDIXES

1   EXISTING LITERATURE   239

2   DETAILS OF ECONOMETRIC APPROACH   253

Adding Contract and Regulatory Characteristics   255
Estimation   256
Endogeneity   257

3   DETAILED RESULTS OF EMPIRICAL ANALYSIS   259

4   SUMMARY OF POWER MARKET REFORMS IN LATIN
    AMERICA AND THE CARIBBEAN   303

5   UTILITY COMPANIES   315

Bibliography   321

Index   329

BOXES
2.1   Hidden Failures and Perception Management:
      Explanations for Social Discontent
      about Privatization   36
2.2   Public Perceptions of Infrastructure Privatization
      in Peru   38
5.1   A Failed Electricity Privatization in Peru   89

FIGURES
2.1   Growth Improvement if Infrastructure Stocks and
      Quality Improved to Costa Rican Levels   8
2.2   Logistics Costs as a Percentage of Product Value, 2004   9
2.3   The Rise and Fall of Private Finance for Infrastructure 11

2.4	Investment in Infrastructure Projects with Private Participation by Region, 1990–2004	12
2.5a	Evolution of Private Participation in Electricity Distribution	13
2.5b	Evolution of Private Participation in Fixed Telecommunications	14
2.5c	Evolution of Private Participation in Water Distribution	14
2.6a	Public Infrastructure Investment	15
2.6b	Private Infrastructure Investment	15
2.6c	Total Infrastructure Investment	16
2.7	Investment in LAC by Sector, 1990–2001	16
2.8	Sectoral Concentration of Private Participation	17
2.9	PPI in LAC by Country, 1990–2004	20
2.10	Types of Private Participation in Infrastructure	22
2.11	Modal Breakdown by Sector in Latin America, by Number of Projects, 1990–2004	24
2.12	Modal Breakdown of Private Participation	26
2.13	Modal Trends for Private Participation, 1990–2004	27
2.14	Cumulative Private Investment in LAC by Investor Type and Sector, 1998–2004	28
2.15	Private Investment in LAC by Investor Type	29
2.16	Population Expressing Dissatisfaction with Privatization in Latin America	33
2.17	Survey Probing Public Opinion	34
2.2.1	Negative Results of Privatization in Peru	39
3.1	Internal Rate of Return and Weighted Average Cost of Capital	48
3.2	Fiscal Capture of Benefits	49
3.3	Increase in Household Earnings from Access to Infrastructure Public Services	51
3.4	Increase in Household Earnings from Access to Markets through Rehabilitated Rural Roads	51
3.5	Joint Welfare Effect of Price and Access Changes on Consumers Expressed as a Percentage of per Capita Total Household Expenditure	52
3.6	Joint Welfare Effect of Price and Access Changes on Consumers Expressed as a Percentage of per Capita Total Household Expenditure	53
4.1	Transitional Effects on Employment: Electricity Distribution	68
4.2	Transition versus Nontransition Period Comparison	69
4.3	Steady Trend	70
5.1	Electricity Distribution, MWh	92

5.2	Before and After Comparison of Electricity Distribution Levels, GWh	93
5.3	Electricity Distribution: Connections	94
5.4	Before and After Comparison of Electricity Distribution Levels: Connections	95
5.5	Electricity Distribution: Coverage	96
5.6	Before and After Comparison of Electricity Distribution: Coverage Levels	97
5.7	Electricity Distribution: Employment	99
5.8	Before and After Comparison of Electricity Distribution: Employment Levels	100
5.9	Electricity Distribution: Labor Productivity	103
5.10	Before and After Comparison of Electricity Distribution: Labor Productivity Levels	104
5.11	Electricity Distribution: Distributional Losses	105
5.12	Before and After Comparison of Electricity Distribution: Distributional Losses	106
5.13	Electricity Distribution: Average Prices	108
5.14	Before and After Comparison of Electricity Distribution: Prices	109
5.15	Electricity Distribution: Quality	111
5.16	Before and After Comparison of Electricity Distribution: Quality	112
6.1	Telecommunications: Number of Connections	123
6.2	Before and After Comparison of Telecommunications: Number of Connections	124
6.3	Telecommunications: Number of Minutes	125
6.4	Before and After Comparison of Telecommunications: Number of Minutes	126
6.5	Telecommunications: Coverage	127
6.6	Before and After Comparison of Telecommunications: Coverage Levels	128
6.7	Telecommunications: Employment	130
6.8	Before and After Comparison of Telecommunications: Employment Levels	131
6.9	Telecommunications: Connections per Employee	133
6.10	Telecommunications: Minutes per Employee	134
6.11	Before and After Comparison of Telecommunications: Labor Productivity Levels	136
6.12	Telecommunications: Percentage of Incomplete Calls	137
6.13	Before and After Comparison of Telecommunications: Efficiency Levels	138

6.14	Telecommunications: Three-Minute Call Prices	140
6.15	Before and After Comparison of Telecommunications: Three-Minute Call Prices	141
6.16	Telecommunications: Residential Monthly Service Charges	142
6.17	Before and After Comparison of Telecommunications: Residential Monthly Service Charges	144
6.18	Telecommunications: Installation Charges	145
6.19	Before and After Comparison of Telecommunications: Installation Charges	146
6.20	Telecommunications: Quality	147
6.21	Before and After Comparison of Telecommunications: Quality Levels	148
7.1	Water and Sewerage: Number of Connections	160
7.2	Before and After Comparison of Water and Sewerage: Number of Connections	161
7.3	Water and Sewerage: Water Production	162
7.4	Before and After Comparison of Water and Sewerage: Cubic Meters per Year	163
7.5	Water and Sewerage: Coverage	164
7.6	Before and After Comparison of Water and Sewerage: Coverage Levels	167
7.7	Water and Sewerage: Employment	168
7.8	Before and After Comparison of Water and Sewerage: Employment Levels	169
7.9	Water and Sewerage: Connections per Employee	170
7.10	Before and After Comparison of Water and Sewerage: Connections per Employee	171
7.11	Water and Sewerage: Distributional Losses	172
7.12	Before and After Comparison of Water and Sewerage: Distributional Losses	173
7.13	Water and Sewerage: Water Prices	175
7.14	Before and After Comparison of Water and Sewerage: Water Prices	176
7.15	Water and Sewerage: Sewerage Prices	177
7.16	Water and Sewerage: Service Continuity	179
7.17	Before and After Comparison of Water and Sewerage: Service Continuity	180
7.18	Water and Sewerage: Potability	181
7.19	Before and After Comparison of Water and Sewerage: Potability	182
8.1	Electricity Coverage	188
8.2	Energy Sold per Connection per Year	189

8.3	Residential Connections per Employee	191
8.4	Energy Sold per Employee	192
8.5	Distributional Losses	193
8.6	Average Residential Tariffs	194
8.7	Average Industrial Tariffs	196
8.8	Average Frequency of Interruptions per Connection	197
8.9	Average Duration of Interruptions per Connection	198
8.10	Energy Sold per Connection per Year, Public versus Private	200
8.11	Residential Connections per Employee, Public versus Private	201
8.12	Energy Sold per Employee, Public versus Private	202
8.13	Distributional Losses, Public versus Private	204
8.14	Average Frequency of Interruptions per Connection, Public versus Private	205

TABLES

1.1	Private Sector Participation in Electricity, Telecommunications, and Water	5
2.1	Concentration of Investment with Private Participation by Country, 1990–2004	21
2.2	Jurisdictions and Responsibilities under Different Types of Private Participation	23
2.3	Canceled or Distressed Investments in Private Infrastructure Projects in Latin America	31
2.4	Renegotiation Incidence and Average Time until Renegotiation, 1988–2001	31
2.5	Common Outcomes of the Renegotiation Process	32
2.6	Illustration of Fiscal Cost of Guarantees from Colombia	33
2.7	Civil Disturbances	35
3.1	Summary of Theoretical and Actual Impacts of Private Participation	53
4.1	Variable Definitions	61
4.2	Summary Statistics	63
4.3	Contract and Regulatory Variables	65
4.4	Example of Means and Medians Analysis in Levels Output—Electricity Distribution	72
4.5	Example of Econometric Analysis—Electricity Distribution	74
5.1	Power Sector Reform in Latin America and the Caribbean	81

5.2	LAC Wholesale Electricity Markets: Extent of Unbundling and Retail Competition	82
5.3	Electricity Market in LAC	84
5.4	Chronology of the Privatizations of Electricity Distribution in LAC by Country	86
5.5	Description of Electricity Distribution Variables	91
5.6	Electricity Distribution: Output and Coverage Results	98
5.7	Electricity Distribution: Employment Results	101
5.8	Electricity Distribution: Labor Productivity and Efficiency Results	107
5.9	Electricity Distribution: Price Results	110
5.10	Electricity Distribution: Quality Results	113
5.11	Electricity Distribution Impact Summary	113
6.1	Privatization Chronology of Fixed Telecommunications in LAC	118
6.2	Privatization Chronology of Fixed Telecommunications in LAC: Liberalization and Competition	119
6.3	Description of Telecommunications Variables	121
6.4	Telecommunications: Output and Coverage Results	129
6.5	Telecommunications: Employment Results	132
6.6	Telecommunications: Labor Productivity and Efficiency Results	135
6.7	Telecommunications: Price Results	143
6.8	Telecommunications: Quality Results	146
6.9	Fixed Telecommunications Impact Summary	150
7.1	Overview of Water Sector Reform	155
7.2	Privatization Chronology of Water and Sewerage in LAC	156
7.3	Description of Water and Sewerage Variables	158
7.4	Water and Sewerage: Output Results	163
7.5	Water and Sewerage: Coverage Results	166
7.6	Water and Sewerage: Employment Results	169
7.7	Water and Sewerage: Labor Productivity and Efficiency Results	174
7.8	Water and Sewerage: Price Results	178
7.9	Water and Sewerage: Quality Results	182
7.10	Water and Sewerage Impact Summary	183
9.1	Base Case for Regulatory and Contract Variables	209
9.2	Impact of Sale Method	210
9.3	Impact of Autonomy of Regulatory Body	213
9.4	Impact of Duration of Regulatory Body Appointments	214

9.5	Impact of Investor Nationality	216
9.6	Impact of Award Criteria	218
9.7	Impact of Tariff Regulation	220
A1.1	Infrastructure Privatization in Selected Cross-Country and Latin American Country Studies	243
A3.1	Means and Medians Analysis in Levels—Electricity Distribution	260
A3.2	Means and Medians Analysis in Growth—Electricity Distribution	264
A3.3	Econometric Analysis—Electricity Distribution	268
A3.4	Means and Medians Analysis in Levels—Fixed Telecommunications	270
A3.5	Means and Medians Analysis in Growth—Fixed Telecommunications	275
A3.6	Econometric Analysis—Fixed Telecommunications	280
A3.7	Econometric Analysis—Fixed Telecommunications, Liberalization	282
A3.8	Econometric Analysis—Fixed Telecommunications, Mobile Competition	284
A3.9	Econometric Analysis—Fixed Telecommunications, Instrumental Variables	286
A3.10	Means and Medians Analysis in Levels—Water and Sewerage	288
A3.11	Means and Medians Analysis in Growth—Water and Sewerage	293
A3.12	Econometric Analysis—Water Distribution and Sewerage	298
A3.13	Summary of Minimum and Maximum Changes Disaggregated by Regulatory and Contract Variables	300
A4.1	Latin America and the Caribbean Region Summary of Power Market Reforms	304

Preface

As numerous countries in Latin America and the Caribbean and elsewhere are moving toward a second phase of private participation in infrastructure programs—mostly through public–private partnership schemes—and other countries are just beginning the process, several concerns remain from the outcomes of the first phase. These concerns are making governments cautious in moving forward. *The Impact of Private Sector Participation in Infrastructure* addresses these concerns and brings clarity to the debate on the impact of private participation in infrastructure. The assessment of this impact may be one of the most emotional policy issues in economics, as it is clouded in a mist of myths, perceptions, and reality.

A fairly large body of literature has been published on this topic, but most of it has been based on case studies and, too often, on anecdotes rather than on facts and robust economic analysis. This book analyzes the impact and sorts out the truth from the myths. The authors take a systematic and hard look at the facts (i.e., data) in Latin America, where starting in the late 1980s, many governments brought private sector participation into the delivery of essential utilities services. Although there are many assessments of this experience, none was able to rely on systemic, cross-country, and time-series data, and practically all of them did not—save rare exceptions—account for what would have happened in the absence of interventions (the counterfactual). This book does just that. It brings together an all-encompassing database from the 1980s to the first decade of this century and develops an effective and robust methodology, accounting for the counterfactual, which tests and estimates the impact of reform on an exceptionally wide set of outcome indicators. As a result, this book presents the most in-depth study to date of the private sector participation experience in Latin America, and it substantially advances the existing literature by offering robust econometric analysis.

The Impact of Private Sector Participation in Infrastructure presents compelling arguments to isolate the impacts and effects of private participation in the electricity, telecommunications, and water sectors. The authors examine and evaluate the determinants of that impact in terms of the characteristics of the regulatory environment and private participation contracts to help governments improve the design of the coming programs of private participation in infrastructure.

The robust results of this analysis show that the benefits of those programs are quite large, particularly in terms of productivity gains, quality of service, and coverage. It highlights the fact that the benefits can be even larger with better design and implementation, and an appropriate institutional capacity and legal and regulatory framework. By separating the facts from the perceptions, this book will help governments to secure broader support for those types of programs and to improve the outcomes of the second phase and overall sector performance, much-needed objectives to support sustained growth and poverty alleviation.

Acknowledgments

In the production of this book we benefited from the comments and suggestions of many people, whose contributions have improved the book significantly. In particular, we acknowledge the vision and leadership of Makhtar Diop and Laura Tuck in supporting the conception of this book. In addition, the comments and suggestions of Marianne Fay, Philippe Marin, Carolina Czastkiewicz, Alejandro Zentner, Tomas Serebrisky, Makhtar Diop, Jordan Schwartz, Julio Gonzalez, Sebastian Lopez Azumendi, Georgeta Dragoiu, Jose Guilherme Reis, Pablo Spiller, Miguel Castilla, Jon Stern, Antonio Estache, Austan Goolsbee, Sam Peltzman, and Chad Syverson were very useful. We are also very grateful to Denise Bergeron and Andrés Meneses for their help in the printing process, to Dina Towbin for her excellent editorial assistance, and to Shana Wagger for her leadership in securing an efficient and timely production process.

Abbreviations

ANEEL	Agência Nacional de Energia Elétrica
ARIAE	Asociación Iberoamericana de Entidades Reguladores de Energía
BOO	build-own-operate
BOT	build-operate-transfer
CARICOM	Caribbean Community
CIER	Comisión de Integración Energética Regional
CORFO	Corporación de Fomento de la Producción
CTC	Compañía de Teléfonos de Chile
EAP	East Asia and Pacific
ECA	Europe and Central Asia
ECLAC	Economic Commission for Latin America and the Caribbean
ENDESA	Empresa Nacional de Electricidad S.A.
ENTel	Empresa Nacional de Telecomunicaciones (National Telecommunications Company)
ESEBA	Empresa Social Eléctrica de Buenos Aires
FGLS	feasible generalized least square
GDP	gross domestic product
GLS	generalized least square
GWh	gigawatt hour
IEA	International Energy Agency
IPP	independent power producer
IRIS	Integrated Records and Information System
IRR	internal rate of return
ITU	International Telecommunication Union
IV	instrumental variable
kW	kilowatt
LAC	Latin America and the Caribbean
MENA	Middle East and North Africa
MWh	megawatt hour

OECD   Organisation for Economic Co-operation and
              Development
OFWAT   Water Services Regulation Authority
OLADE   Organización Latinoamericana de Energía
OLS   ordinary least square
ONS   Operador do Nacional do Sistema Elétrico
OSINERG   Organismo Supervisor de Inversión en Energía
POLS   pooled ordinary least square
PPI   private participation in infrastructure
PPIAF   Public–Private Infrastructure Advisory Facility
PSP   private sector participation
SA   South Asia
sd   standard deviation
SEGBA   Servicios Eléctricos del Gran Buenos Aires
SIN   Sistema Nacional Interconectado (National Interconnected
              System)
SOE   state-owned enterprise
SSA   Sub-Saharan Africa
TFP   total factor productivity
WACC   weighted average cost of capital

1

Introduction

Infrastructure plays a critical role in fostering growth and productivity and reducing poverty and inequality. Numerous studies have found a positive economic and social impact of infrastructure, especially in developing countries. Calderón and Servén (2003) found that Latin America's slow infrastructure accumulation in the 1980s and 1990s relative to East Asia explains much of why it has lagged behind economically, as measured by growth rates. Another study found that if all Latin American countries caught up with Costa Rica—the region's leader in terms of infrastructure quantity and quality—their long-term per capita growth gains would range between 1.4 and 1.8 percent per year (Calderón and Servén 2004a). Good infrastructure contributes to making firms more productive and hence more competitive internationally (see, for example, Escribano, Guasch, and Pena 2007; Escribano, Guasch, Pena, and de Orte 2007a, 2007b). Infrastructure allows countries to reap the benefits of trade liberalization and is critical for improving economic opportunities for the poor (Escobal and Torero 2004). Infrastructure development has been linked to improved health and education levels for the poor and reduced income inequality in Latin America.[1]

Perhaps the most comprehensive work showing the impact of infrastructure on growth for developing countries is Straub (2008a, 2008b), in which the author identifies direct and indirect channels from infrastructure to growth and addresses largely unexplored issues regarding the composition—new investments versus maintenance; operational versus capital expenditures; private versus public investments; and the sequencing of reforms. The author reviews 64 papers with various specifications and reports that in more than two-thirds of those works a positive and significant link is found between infrastructure investments and growth. In particular, the findings show that the infrastructure impact on more disaggregated variables, or intermediate themes, is even stronger. Nearly 90 percent of the studies that evaluated the infrastructure impact on themes such as poverty, inequality, individual earnings, child height, export, investments, and so on showed strongly significant and positive effects.

The 1990s were characterized by a massive policy redirection toward private participation in infrastructure (PPI).[2] This reflected the disappointment with ineffective state-operated utilities, the promise of private funding, and the greater flexibility offered by technological change and regulatory changes. In Latin America, private participation went from roughly US$17 billion in 1995 to a peak of more than US$70 billion in 1998, dropping back to US$20 billion by 2002 (World Bank 2007a).

Private sector participation has since become unpopular in Latin America, and investors' appetites have waned.[3] In November 2000, 36 percent of Argentines believed that infrastructure services should come back under government control; five years later, 78 percent did (*El Cronista* April 18, 2005). This reflects a general trend in Latin America: with the exception of Panama, about 40 percent of the population expressed discontent with private sector participation in 1998. Today, the average is closer to 75 percent (see figure 2.17). Public opposition has become a real constraint on PPI in some countries, both politically and operationally. At the same time, the private sector seems to have lost its appetite for infrastructure: the average number of bidders for power distribution privatizations in Latin America fell from more than four in 1998 to less than two in 2000 and 2001 (Harris 2003).

Latin America is currently faced with the dangerous combination of relatively low public *and* private infrastructure investment. Increases in private financing in the 1990s were not enough to offset the collapse in public funding, which occurred in the late 1980s in many countries in Latin America and the Caribbean (LAC). Indeed, public investment in infrastructure dropped from 3 percent of gross domestic product (GDP) in 1980 to less than 1 percent in 2001 in Latin America (De Ferranti, Perry, Ferreira, and Walton 2004). Low levels of infrastructure investment are a concern because of the widely documented link between infrastructure and growth, productivity, and poverty reduction (see Briceño-Garmendia, Estache, and Shafik 2004; Calderón and Servén 2004a; Fay and Morrison 2006).

To move forward, a solid understanding of the true impacts of private sector participation in LAC, as well as an understanding of the determinants of those impacts, is necessary. If Latin American governments are to increase infrastructure investment in politically feasible ways, it is critical that they learn from past experience, have an accurate idea of what kind of future impacts to expect, and correct the errors of the past. This book contributes to that aim by producing what is arguably the most comprehensive and systemic private sector participation impact analysis in LAC to date.

The book looks at what happened before, during, and after private sector participation in three sectors—electricity, water, and telecommunications—by focusing on a range of performance variables. It is necessary to look at all three periods, because often the most dramatic effects of private sector participation are found in the transition period, when the enterprise is overhauled as part of the transaction process. These transitions constitute a one-time adjustment, however, and present a pace of improvement that is not necessarily sustained in the long run. The book focuses on changes and rates of changes in the three different periods, rather than on absolute numbers, because in many cases, the performance variables exhibit natural changes over time (with or without private sector participation). Hence, the analysis controls for such naturally occurring rates of change. Having looked at changes "before, during, and after" private sector participation, "with and without" private sector participation scenarios are then examined. Because of data limitations, however, such "with and without" comparisons can be made only for one sector: electricity.

The book draws on an extremely comprehensive data set and range of empirical methodologies:

- **Data.** The data set is comprehensive in terms of types of indicators, sectoral coverage, and time. It is a cross-country time series, covering 181 infrastructure firms in Latin America that changed from public to private sector participation during the 1990s. Many studies look at the financial performance of private sector participation companies, which is just part of the story; this analysis considers changes in output, labor, efficiency, labor productivity, quality, coverage, and prices. In terms of sectors, this analysis includes the often-neglected water and electricity distribution sectors, in addition to fixed telecommunications. The data also have a relatively long time span, starting five years before the introduction of private sector participation and continuing five years after the private participation. The time span allows for the separation of short-run or transitional effects from long-run results.

- **Methodologies.** The long time span of the data enables the private sector participation experience to be divided into three distinct periods: pre–private sector participation, a three-year transition period, and post–private sector participation. Means, medians, and growth rates across periods are then compared and tested for statistical significance. A separate econometric analysis controls for firm-specific fixed effects as well as time trends across periods. Time trends refer to the natural rate of change of certain variables, such as the number of connections. In cases in which there is such a natural rate of change, the analysis controls for it, allowing deviations from the natural rate caused by private sector participation to be measured. This range of methodologies allows for comparison with the "internal counterfactual"—that is, what presumably would have happened in the absence of the private sector participation—in terms of levels and trends. It also produces a richness of results that has not been possible with previous studies and allows for fairly sophisticated predications about the impacts of future private sector participations.

The analysis also considers the "external counterfactuals,"—that is to say the evaluation of enterprises that have remained in public control and the contrasting their performance with those that were transferred or concessioned to the private sector. In the case of electricity, it was possible to assemble such a control sample of Latin American distribution utilities that had remained in public hands throughout the study period.

In sum, this book provides the most comprehensive analysis to date of the impact of private sector participation in the electricity, telecommunications, and water sectors in Latin America. It makes two important methodological contributions, both of which are designed to avoid any overstatement of the benefits of private sector participation. First, it makes the distinction between transition period effects and longer-term changes in performance. Second, it provides a comparison of pre- and post-private sector participation trends rather than levels. By providing a rigorous quantitative analysis of past private participation impacts, the book will hopefully help policy makers make more informed and nuanced decisions going forward.

The main results of this analysis, accounting for the counterfactual, are that the changes associated with private sector participation had a significant positive effect on labor productivity, efficiency, and quality. There were significant reductions in the workforce. For telecommunications, private sector participation had significant effects on output and coverage. There were not conclusive results with respect to prices, although care should be exercised in any price impact analysis, because most prices were highly distorted—did not represent cost recovery—before the private sector participation programs (see table 1.1).

The differences between publicly and privately operated distribution utilities showed up primarily with regard to labor productivity, distribution losses, quality of service, and tariffs. In contrast, other indicators such as coverage and operation expenditures exhibit similar trends or do not present significant changes between the groups. Nevertheless, there is significant variation in performance within both groups. The top 10 percent of performers in the public utility group outperformed the average private utility, and the average public utility outperformed the bottom 10 percent of the private utility group.

The analysis also addresses the determinants of performance. By pooling all the cases available across sectors, and adding a new set of variables to capture the transactional and regulatory environment, it was possible to measure the impact of each of these factors. The main findings can be summarized by the following points. First, regulatory and contract characteristics matter: the way privatizations are undertaken can generate significant performance differences. Second, each regulatory and contract characteristic affects each performance variable differently. In other words,

Table 1.1 Private Sector Participation in Electricity, Telecommunications, and Water

	Electricity distribution		Fixed telecommunications		Water and sewerage distribution	
	Transition	Post-transition	Transition	Post-transition	Transition	Post-transition
Number of connections[a]	=	=	↑	=	=	=
Output[a]	=	↓	↑	↑	=	↓
Coverage[a]	=	=	↑	=	=	=
Employment	↓	↓	↓	↓	↓	↓
Labor productivity[a]	↑	↓	↑	↑	↑	↓
Distributional losses	↓	↓	=	↓	↓	↓
Average prices	↑	↑	↑	=	↑/?	↑/?
Monthly service charge	—	—	↑	↑	—	—
Installation charge	—	—	↓	↓	—	—
Quality	↑	↑	↑	↑	↑	↑

Source: Authors' elaboration.

Note: Up and down arrows indicate that a positive or negative change occurred in addition to the natural change that would be expected in the absence of privatization. An equal sign indicates that the trend perceived during the previous period was sustained but not substantially exceeded or diminished. A question mark indicates that insufficient observations were available to reach a conclusion. The arrow size represents the size of the change. — = not available.

a. Results are shown after controlling for time trends.

a certain contract characteristic could have a positive influence on one performance variable while also having a negative or insignificant impact on another. Third, some regulatory and contract variables have bigger impacts than others. For instance, in some cases, the changes attributed to having a fully autonomous regulatory body are much larger than changes attributed to other regulatory variables.

The book concludes by showing the way forward for future and ongoing private sector participation programs, incorporating the lessons learned through near 20 years of experience.

The book is organized as follows. Chapter 2 sets the stage by discussing why infrastructure matters as well as trends and patterns in PPI. Chapter 3 briefly reviews what kind of private sector participation impacts would be expected and have been realized according to existing literature (a more complete literature review can be found in Appendix 1). Chapter 4 covers the data sets, methodologies, and analytical techniques used. Chapters 5 through 7 analyze the impacts of privatization on the electricity distribution, telecommunications, and water sectors, respectively. Chapter 8 complements chapters 5 through 7 by comparing the performance of public and private electricity distribution companies. Chapter 9 adds another layer to the analysis by introducing a number of regulatory and privatization contract and process variables and by identifying their impacts on the performance variables. Chapter 10 summarizes the conclusions and discusses implications for policy makers moving forward.

Notes

1. For a comprehensive review of why infrastructure matters, see World Bank (1994), Guasch (2004), and Fay and Morrison (2006).

2. The four main types of PPI are (i) management and lease contracts; (ii) concessions; (iii) greenfield projects; and (iv) divestitures. In this book, PPI and privatization are used interchangeably to cover all four types.

3. This paragraph draws on Fay and Morrison (2006).

2

Setting the Stage

Why Infrastructure Matters

Infrastructure plays a key role in increasing economic growth. Numerous studies have found that infrastructure has a positive impact on output, especially in developing countries. Calderón and Servén (2003) found that Latin America's slow infrastructure accumulation in the 1980s and 1990s relative to East Asia explains much of why it has lagged behind economically. In fact, they found that the differing evolution of infrastructure assets in Latin America and East Asia widened the cross-regional gap in gross domestic product (GDP) by some 30 percent between 1980 and 1997. Calderón and Servén (2004a) found that if all Latin American countries caught up with Costa Rica—the region's leader in terms of infrastructure quantity and quality—their long-term per capita growth gains would range between 1.4 and 4.8 percent per year (figure 2.1). The impact would be even larger if Latin American countries caught up to the Republic of Korea (the median East Asian country). In Bolivia, Guatemala, Honduras, Nicaragua, and Peru, growth would increase by at least 5 percentage points per year.[1]

Many studies at the micro level have illustrated the effect of infrastructure on unit costs. For example, infrastructure levels and quality are strong determinants of inventory levels. U.S. businesses typically hold inventories equal to about 15 percent of GDP; however, inventories in many developing countries are often twice as large, and raw materials are often more than three times as large (Guasch and Kogan 2001, 2003). The impact of those inventory levels on firm unit costs and on country competitiveness and productivity is extraordinarily significant. The financial costs associated with inventories can be quite high because the cost of capital in developing countries is usually well above 15 percent. The other associated costs of inventories—such as taxes, insurance, obsolescence, and storage—can add

7

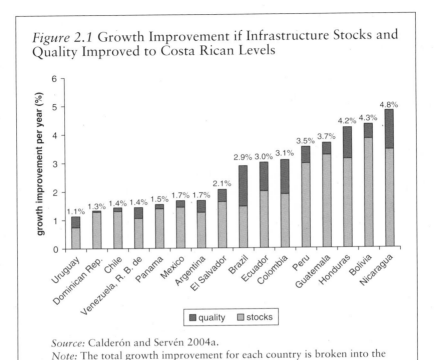

Figure 2.1 Growth Improvement if Infrastructure Stocks and Quality Improved to Costa Rican Levels

Source: Calderón and Servén 2004a.
Note: The total growth improvement for each country is broken into the percentage point gain from an improvement in infrastructure *quality* and an improvement in infrastructure *stocks* compared with Costa Rican levels.

another 5 percentage points. Putting things into perspective, if the interest rate for financing inventory holdings is 15–20 percent—a conservative estimate in most developing countries—then the cost to the economy of the additional inventory holdings is greater than 2 percent of GDP. Given the high cost of capital in most Latin American countries, the impact of that quasi-dead capital—the value of those inventories on unit costs and productivity or competitiveness—is enormous. And a key determinant is not interest rates, as classical models predict, but poor infrastructure (roads and ports). A 1 standard deviation (sd) improvement in infrastructure decreases raw material inventories by 20–40 percent (Guasch and Kogan 2003).

Logistics costs are quite high in Latin America because of poor infrastructure. Logistics costs range from a low of 18 percent of product value in Chile to a high of 34 percent in Peru (see figure 2.2). In comparison, the Organisation for Economic Co-operation and Development (OECD) average hovers around 9 percent (Guasch and Kogan 2005). A key determinant of high logistics costs is poor infrastructure, especially roads, ports, and telecommunications (Guasch and Hahn 1999). Thus, infrastructure matters significantly for productivity, competitiveness, and growth.

Latin American firms rank infrastructure as a serious problem that negatively affects their productivity. According to the World Bank's investment climate assessments, 55 percent of survey respondents in Latin America and the Caribbean (LAC) considered infrastructure to be a major or severe obstacle to the operation and growth of their business. That level, which is shared by the Middle East and North Africa (MENA), is the highest in the world (World Bank 2004b). Infrastructure is also a major determinant of total factor productivity (TFP) and affects firms' ability to export or attract foreign investments.[2] Estimates of the percentage contribution of infrastructure to labor productivity and TFP range between 25 and 50 percent per country (see Escribano, Guasch, and Pena 2007; Escribano, Guasch, Pena, and de Orte 2007a, 2007b). Infrastructure variables with the highest impact on average productivity include poor electricity and transport services.

Infrastructure can improve economic opportunities, as well as health and education levels, for the poor. As poorer individuals and underdeveloped areas become connected to core economic activities, they can access additional productive opportunities. Likewise, infrastructure development

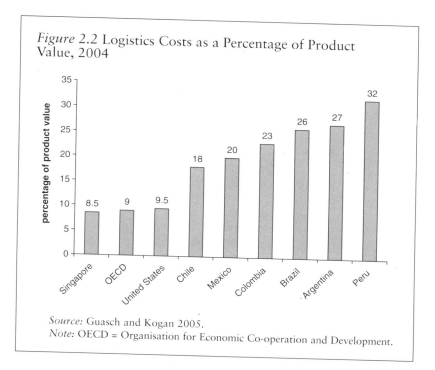

Figure 2.2 Logistics Costs as a Percentage of Product Value, 2004

Source: Guasch and Kogan 2005.
Note: OECD = Organisation for Economic Co-operation and Development.

in poorer regions reduces production and transaction costs (Gannon and Liu 1997). In Argentina, a recent study by Galiani, Gertler, and Schargrodsky (2005) found that child mortality fell by 8 percent in areas that had privatized water utilities (and hence experienced improved coverage and quality), with most of the reduction occurring in low-income areas where the water network expanded the most. More generally, Fay and Morrison (2006) found that allowing the poorest quintile in developing countries the same access to basic services as the richest quintile would reduce child mortality by 8 percent and stunting by 14 percent. Perhaps as a result of the effects of infrastructure on the poor, Calderón and Servén (2004a) found a significant positive impact of infrastructure access and quality on overall inequality. If all Latin American countries caught up with Costa Rica in terms of infrastructure quantity and quality, their Gini coefficients would decline between 0.02 and 0.10.[3]

Trends in Infrastructure Financing

During the 1990s, a major shift took place in the prevailing model of infrastructure service provision. Up until the 1980s, infrastructure services in Latin America and the rest of the world were exclusively operated and financed by public sector entities. This situation began to change in the 1990s, as a growing number of countries turned to a new approach for the infrastructure sectors. This phenomenon was based on the coincidence of two distinct but complementary trends.

On the one hand, governments began to see the private sector as an attractive and manageable solution to the problems posed by infrastructure services. Many governments facing heavy fiscal burdens associated with the support of inefficient state-owned enterprises (SOEs) began to be open to the idea of delegating infrastructure service provision to the private sector. The notion was that the private sector could both improve managerial efficiency and provide access to additional capital for service expansion and improvement. Of course, most governments continued to be concerned about safeguarding the strategic and socially sensitive character of the infrastructure sectors. New thinking, however, suggested that this could be achieved through judicious use of policy and regulatory instruments, without the state needing to be involved directly in service provision. The pioneering experiences of countries such as Chile and the United Kingdom—which demonstrated earlier successes with private participation in telecommunications and electricity—fueled wider interest in this new approach.

On the other hand, the private sector began to see the commercial attraction of investing in emerging economies. The large growth potential of developing country markets appeared to offer attractive commercial opportunities, relative to the mature and relatively stagnant markets of the industrial world. Moreover, traditional private sector fears about government expropriation of investments were allayed by the adoption of new laws and regulations that promised a more stable investment climate.

As a result, private capital flows to infrastructure projects in developing countries grew sixfold during the mid-1990s, but they declined sharply thereafter. From a baseline of US$20 billion in 1990s, investments swelled to a peak of US$131 billion in 1997 (figure 2.3).[4] The increase was primarily driven by the rapid adoption of the new model in Latin America and East Asia. The countries of Eastern Europe and Central Asia are partly responsible for the increase, as the transition economies launched mass privatization programs. From 1997 until recently, private capital flows have been in marked decline. Triggered by the financial crises—and resulting currency devaluations—in East Asia and Latin America, this fall coincided with various corporate crises. Some of the major global energy and telecommunications companies were investing in emerging economies. These companies saw their average share prices fall by 90 percent and 70 percent, respectively (World Bank 2004a). This decline was not so strongly felt in such regions as Africa, the Middle East, and South Asia, because they had barely participated in the initial surge.

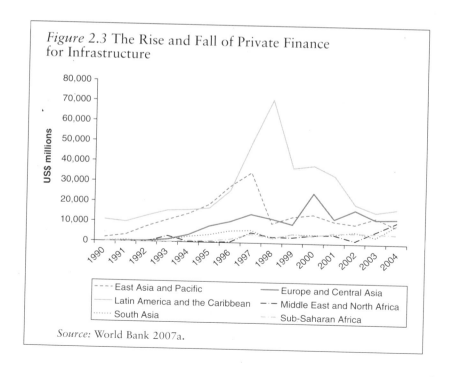

Figure 2.3 The Rise and Fall of Private Finance for Infrastructure

Source: World Bank 2007a.

Latin America has consistently led the way in terms of private participation in infrastructure (PPI). Even against the backdrop of large private investments in East Asia and the transition economies, the privatization record of Latin America seems remarkable. In 1990, for example, investment flows in projects with private participation in LAC were more than 5 times the flows in East Asia and the Pacific. Over the period 1990–2004, LAC accounted for 36 percent of the total number of projects in the world with private participation (figure 2.4, panel A). The LAC share jumps to 45 percent when considering project investment values (figure 2.4, panel B). In recent years, however, privatization has slowed dramatically in Latin America.

The share of households served by private companies has increased dramatically since 1990 in Latin America. Figure 2.5a uses shading to depict the percentage of total households in each Latin American country that was served by private companies in 1990 and 2003. In electricity distribution, only 3 percent of households in the region were served by a private company in 1990, and all of these households were in Chile. In contrast, this number exceeded 60 percent in 2003 (figure 2.5a). Fixed telecommunications saw even more dramatic changes: the percentage of households served by the private sector leapt from 3 percent in 1990 to more than 86 percent in 2003 (figure 2.5b). In water distribution, virtually

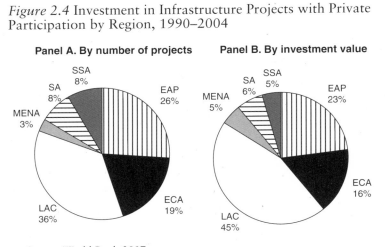

Figure 2.4 Investment in Infrastructure Projects with Private Participation by Region, 1990–2004

Panel A. By number of projects

SSA 8%
SA 8%
MENA 3%
EAP 26%
ECA 19%
LAC 36%

Panel B. By investment value

SSA 5%
SA 6%
MENA 5%
EAP 23%
ECA 16%
LAC 45%

Source: World Bank 2007a.
Note: EAP = East Asia and Pacific; ECA = Europe and Central Asia; LAC = Latin America and the Caribbean; MENA = Middle East and North Africa; SA = South Asia; SSA = Sub-Saharan Africa.

no households were served by the private sector in 1990, while more than 11 percent were served in 2003 (figure 2.5c).

Private participation was followed by a substantial reduction in public infrastructure investment in most cases in Latin America.[5] The decline in public spending on infrastructure was a result of the fiscal austerity forced by the region's macroeconomic crises over the last 20 years. In fact, public investment in infrastructure and the primary deficit followed remarkably similar paths over the last 25 years (Fay and Morrison 2006). In most countries, *the decline in public finance was larger than the increase in private finance*, leading to a net reduction in financing for the infrastructure sectors overall. Calderón and Servén (2004b) charted the evolution of public, private, and total infrastructure investment in Latin America's six biggest economies (figure 2.6a). In all but one of the countries, *public infrastructure investment declined sharply in the late 1980s* (figure 2.6a). The exception is Colombia, where the decline was slight and, on average, public investment levels remained roughly unchanged (albeit with major fluctuations) throughout the period.

In five of the six countries, *private* investment took off in the late 1980s or early 1990s (figure 2.6b). The exception is Brazil, where private sector

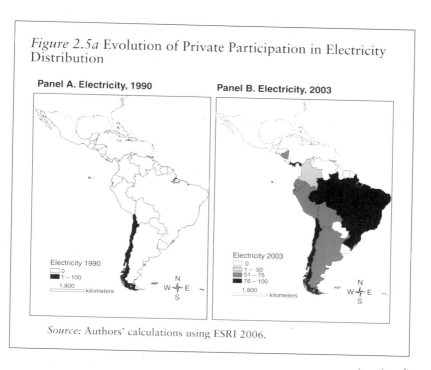

Figure 2.5a Evolution of Private Participation in Electricity Distribution

Panel A. Electricity, 1990

Panel B. Electricity, 2003

Source: Authors' calculations using ESRI 2006.

(continued)

Figure 2.5b Evolution of Private Participation in Fixed Telecommunications

Panel A. Teledensity, 1990

Panel B. Teledensity, 2003

Source: Authors' calculations using ESRI 2006.

Figure 2.5c Evolution of Private Participation in Water Distribution

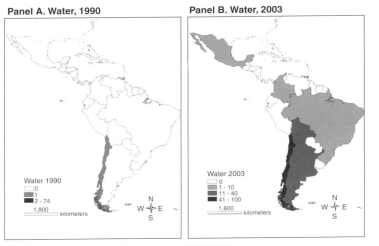

Panel A. Water, 1990

Panel B. Water, 2003

Source: Authors' calculations using ESRI 2006.

investment hovered around 1 percent of GDP over the last two decades, with a small rise after 1995. Chile exhibited the earliest and largest rise in private investment, while Colombia also saw a sizeable increase, although with a slight decline at the end of the 1990s. After peaks in the mid-1990s, private investment in Argentina and Mexico was close to 1 percent of GDP annually during the second half of the 1990s. The increase in private investment was only great enough to offset the drop in public investment in Chile, as shown through *total* investment in figure 2.6c. In Colombia, total investment increased because of a combination of steady public investment and increases in private investment, as mentioned above (Calderón and Servén 2004b).

When broken down by sector, Calderón and Servén's (2004b) data show that electricity accounted for the largest share of public spending during the period from 1990 to 2001. Meanwhile, the majority of private investment went into telecommunications (figure 2.7). These numbers only account

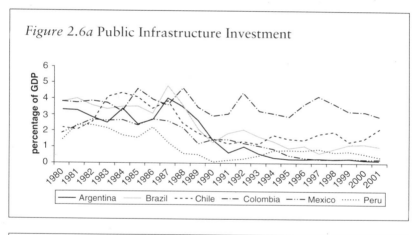

Figure 2.6a Public Infrastructure Investment

Figure 2.6b Private Infrastructure Investment

(continued)

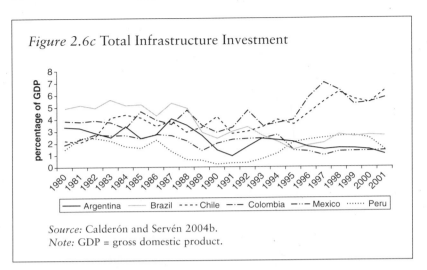

Figure 2.6c Total Infrastructure Investment

Source: Calderón and Servén 2004b.
Note: GDP = gross domestic product.

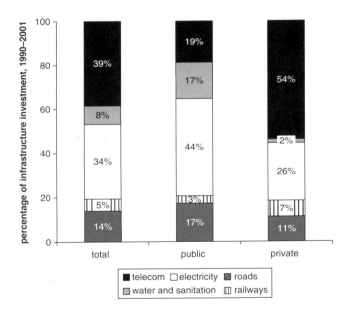

Figure 2.7 Investment in LAC by Sector, 1990–2001

Source: Data set from Calderón and Servén (2004b).
Note: Data are for the nine largest economies in Latin America.
LAC = Latin America and the Caribbean.

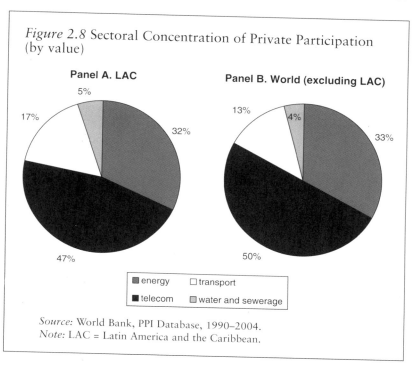

Figure 2.8 Sectoral Concentration of Private Participation (by value)

Panel A. LAC

5%
17%
32%
47%

Panel B. World (excluding LAC)

13%
4%
33%
50%

■ energy　　□ transport
■ telecom　　▩ water and sewerage

Source: World Bank, PPI Database, 1990–2004.
Note: LAC = Latin America and the Caribbean.

for actual investment—they do not include operating and maintenance expenditures or money spent to purchase existing government assets. Hence, they differ from the World Bank PPI database numbers shown in figure 2.8, which include divestiture expenditures for existing assets.

Distribution

The following sections look at the composition of PPI by (i) sectoral distribution (telecom, energy, transport, and water); (ii) geographic distribution within Latin America and the rest of the world; (iii) modal distribution, or modes or types of investment (concessions, divestitures, management contracts, etc.); and (iv) investor types (local and regional investors versus industrial-country investors).

Sectoral Distribution

Investments with private participation have been disproportionately concentrated in the telecommunications and energy sectors. In many countries,

PPI began in the telecommunications sector, spreading later to the energy sector, and sometimes reaching the transport and water sectors. The reasons behind this are straightforward. Private participation proved easiest to apply in sectors characterized by realistic tariffs, strong demand growth potential, a rapid payback period, and relatively limited social sensitivity and government interference. Telecommunications satisfied these basic criteria to a much greater extent than the other infrastructure sectors. In addition, the desire of governments to benefit from the rapid technological progress experienced by the telecommunications sector during the 1990s offered a powerful incentive to invite private participation. Given these considerations, it is hardly surprising that aggregate investment flows in Latin America are so highly concentrated in the telecommunications sector (47 percent), and to a lesser extent in the electricity (26 percent) sector (see figure 2.8, panel A). The breakdown is almost identical for the rest of the world (see figure 2.8, panel B).

The picture differs considerably if the number of projects is considered, rather than investment values. In Latin America, the energy sector accounted for 42 percent of the number of projects. Transport accounted for 32 percent, water and sewerage 13 percent, and telecom only 12 percent. The difference between the number of projects and investment values is due to the nature and size of private participation in each sector. Telecommunications tended to involve divestitures of large, nationwide companies or greenfield projects.[6] Divestitures and greenfield projects were popular in energy, but often at the subnational level. In contrast, concessions were heavily favored in transport and water and sewerage. These concessions often were made at the subnational level, and the concession selection criteria did not necessarily require large amounts of private investment.

Within the electricity sector in Latin America, the majority of investment with private participation has gone into electricity generation projects. Over the period 1990–2004, about 50 percent of investment with private participation in electricity went to pure electricity generation projects, while projects combining generation and transmission and distribution accounted for another 19 percent. Pure distribution projects absorbed 24 percent of electricity sector investment, and pure transmission projects only 5 percent.[7] The focus on electricity generation has proved attractive both for governments and private investors. From the government's perspective, private participation in generation has made it possible to meet growing demand for power without necessitating a wholesale reform of the electricity sector and an immediate adjustment of end-consumer tariffs. From the private sector's perspective, involvement in the generation sector makes it possible to avoid the commercial and operational risks associated with managing a large distribution network. Private participation in electricity generation typically has been achieved through Power Purchase Agreements with downstream public utilities that provide private investors with a revenue stream that is largely guaranteed, irrespective of the outturn level of demand.

Within the Latin America transport sector, most investment has gone into toll road projects. During the period 1990–2004, 54 percent of investment with private participation in transport went to toll road projects, compared with 25 percent for railways, 10 percent for sea ports, and 11 percent for airports.[8] This largely reflects the fact that the roads sector accounts for the bulk of investment needs in transport. Private participation has tended to be confined to the highest traffic corridors for which toll revenues had the potential to cover the full costs of investment and operation. Nevertheless, uncertainty regarding traffic flows on tolled segments, together with the risks entailed in road construction and rehabilitation, have made such projects risky, with the result that worldwide only 55 percent of proposed projects have succeeded in reaching financial closure (Public Works Financing 1995, 1998, 2003). A common government response has therefore been to incorporate various kinds of guarantees into the design of toll road concessions.

In telecommunications, investment has been evenly split between mobile and fixed-line projects. Specifically, both mobile and fixed-line (including long distance) projects accounted for 28 percent of telecommunications investment (by value) with private participation in Latin America over the period 1990–2004. Projects with a mix of fixed access, long distance, and mobile access accounted for the remaining 45 percent.[9] In the early 1990s, investments in fixed-line projects exceeded mobile investments. A substantial spike in mobile investments in 1997 and 1998, however, offset initial fixed-line advantage.

Geographic Distribution

The bulk of infrastructure investment with private participation in Latin America has gone to Brazil, Argentina, and Mexico. During the period 1990–2004, Brazil, Argentina, and Mexico captured 76 percent, of the region's total investment by value. Chile, Colombia, Peru, and República Bolivariana de Venezuela were responsible for another 16 percent, and the remaining 21 countries (including the Caribbean) accounted for the rest (figure 2.9). When considering PPI as a share of GDP, however, the picture is not so skewed. In most LAC countries, cumulative PPI during 1990–2004 was equivalent to roughly 15–30 percent of average GDP over the same period. Bolivia is the big outlier, garnering 74 percent of its average GDP in investment with private participation.

Private investment has been disproportionately concentrated in certain regions of the developing world. Not all regions have been equally successful in attracting private finance for infrastructure. Indeed, the bulk

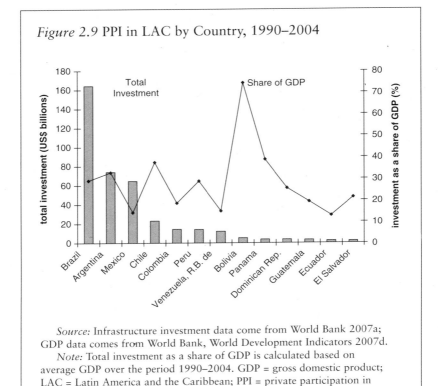

Figure 2.9 PPI in LAC by Country, 1990–2004

Source: Infrastructure investment data come from World Bank 2007a;
GDP data comes from World Bank, World Development Indicators 2007d.
   Note: Total investment as a share of GDP is calculated based on
average GDP over the period 1990–2004. GDP = gross domestic product;
LAC = Latin America and the Caribbean; PPI = private participation in
infrastructure.

of infrastructure investment with private participation has been captured
by Latin America (45 percent) and East Asia (23 percent).[10] However,
adjusting for population and income levels, Latin America and Europe
and Central Asia emerge as the two regions with the greatest success in
attracting private finance. These differences across regions reflect two
underlying factors. On the one hand, there was the greater openness to
private participation among these governments, which was reflected in
supportive policies and legislation. On the other hand, the relatively high
incomes and positive growth prospects offered by these regions during the
1990s made them more attractive investment locations.

Within successful regions, a handful of countries have captured the lion's
share of private finance. Not only have private capital flows been concentrated in certain regions, but certain countries within each region have
been disproportionately successful in attracting private capital flows (table
2.1). Across all regions, the three most successful countries have captured

Table 2.1 Concentration of Investment with Private
Participation by Country, 1990–2004

Region	Top three countries	Share of total investment (%)
East Asia and Pacific	China, Malaysia, Philippines	69
Europe and Central Asia	Poland, Russian Federation, Hungary	47
Latin America and Caribbean	Brazil, Argentina, Mexico	76
Middle East and North Africa	Morocco, Saudi Arabia, Egypt, Arab Rep. of	69
South Asia	India, Pakistan, Bangladesh	96
Sub-Saharan Africa	South Africa, Nigeria, Mozambique	65

Source: World Bank 2007a.

47–96 percent of investment. Worldwide, the four most successful countries—
Brazil, Argentina, China, and Mexico, in that order—accounted for 43 percent of global private investment in infrastructure over the period 1990–
2004. Finally, although it has not been rigorously documented, it is known
anecdotally that what is true across countries is also true within countries.
That is to say that private investment tends to concentrate itself in the larger
cities and economically more prosperous regions of countries, largely bypass-
ing smaller towns, rural areas, and depressed provinces.

Modal Distribution

Many types or modes of private participation occur in the provision of
infrastructure services (figure 2.10). Each type differs in terms of government participation levels, risk allocations, investment responsibilities, operational requirements, and incentives for operators (table 2.2). The most
common types are privatizations and concessions and, to a much lesser
extent, management contracts.

In service or management contracts, the private party takes on varying
degrees of responsibility for the operation and maintenance of the infrastructure service in return for some kind of fixed or performance-related fee
paid directly by the state. In lease contracts (often known by their French
name *affermage*), the private party additionally takes on responsibility
for collecting service revenues directly from customers and retaining a

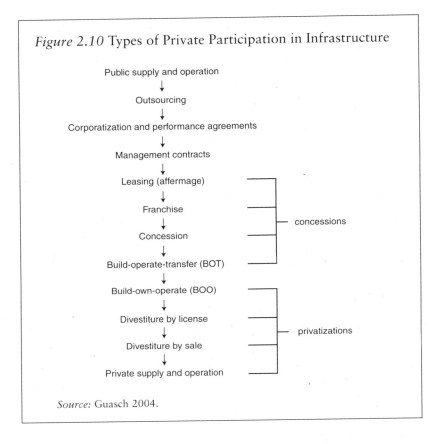

Figure 2.10 Types of Private Participation in Infrastructure

Source: Guasch 2004.

portion of these revenues before the remainder is passed on to the state. Under this approach, the private contractor relies directly on customers for its remuneration. None of these three approaches entails any investment obligations on the part of the private sector. These can be incorporated through concession contracts, whereby the private operator takes over the management of the assets for a fixed period and performs associated investments, while ultimate ownership remains with the state. Alternatively, under build-operate-transfer (BOT) contracts, the private sector may build a new infrastructure asset and hold ownership of it for a temporary period, before transferring it to the state. Under divestiture arrangements, asset ownership may be permanently transferred to the private sector.

The choice of private participation modes varies by sector. In sectors such as telecommunications, and to some extent electricity generation and natural gas (the usual pioneer sectors), private sector participation generally has been achieved through outright privatization—that is,

Table 2.2 Jurisdictions and Responsibilities under Different Types of Private Participation

Variable	Management contracts	Concessions	Privatizations
Ownership of physical and land assets	Government	Government	Private operator
Ownership of vehicles	Government	Government/ private operator	Private operator
Investment responsibilities	Government	Private operator	Private operator
Service control	Government	Government/ private operator	Government/ private operator
Tariff control	Government	Government/ private operator	Government/ private operator
Revenue risk	Government	Private operator	Private operator
Cost risk	Government	Private operator	Private operator
Labor risk	Government	Private operator	Private operator
Management cost risk	Private operator	Private operator	Private operator

Source: Guasch 2004.

divestiture accompanied by structural reforms of market structures and regulations. But in other sectors—ports, airports, roads, railroads, water and sanitation, and segments of the electricity sector—legal, political, and constitutional restraints have impeded the sale of public utilities to private parties (which are often foreign companies, making the issue even more complicated politically).

Moreover, in some countries that have no legal or constitutional impediments to full privatization of infrastructure services, concerns about performance have led governments to retain some control in various sectors. Thus, in many countries where the state could not or did not want to transfer ownership of public assets to the private sector, innovative strategies have been used to introduce PPI. Among the alternatives to outright privatization, concessions for the right to operate a service for a defined period have emerged as the leading approach. In the water and transport sectors in Latin America, private participation has come predominantly through concessions when measured by both number of projects (figure 2.11) and investment values. For energy and telecommunications, greenfield projects have been the most popular (by number), while divestitures have accounted for the majority of investment values.

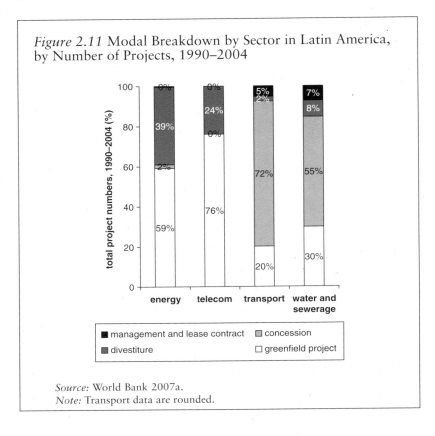

Figure 2.11 Modal Breakdown by Sector in Latin America, by Number of Projects, 1990–2004

Source: World Bank 2007a.
Note: Transport data are rounded.

Although concessions and privatizations tend to achieve the same objectives—securing private sector managerial and operational expertise and investments—they differ in three key respects. First, concessions do not involve the sale or transfer of ownership of physical assets, only the right to use the assets and to operate the enterprise. Second, concession contracts last for a limited period—usually 15 to 30 years, depending on the context and sector. Third, the government, as owner of the assets, retains much closer involvement and oversight in concessions.

Concessions of quasi-natural monopolies offer several advantages. First, they allow private participation in sectors in which private ownership is constitutionally, legally, or politically untenable. Second, if awarded competitively (which tends to be the case), concessions enable competition for the market (as opposed to competition in the market) and ought to dissipate monopoly rents—ensuring the most efficient operator and, in principle, facilitating regulatory oversight. Third, concessions can encourage cost-efficiency, particularly when granted under price-cap regulation or rate-of-return regulation if cost referential benchmarks are used. Under price-cap regulation, concession contracts specify maximum prices for set quantities of goods or services, permitting cost savings to accrue to the concessionaire, at least between tariff reviews. Finally, concessions can achieve optimal pricing even when sunk costs rule out contestability, because competition occurs before firms commit to investment programs.

Disadvantages of concessions include the need for complex design and monitoring systems when multiple targets are involved, the inability to cover every conceivable contingency, the difficulty in enforcing contracts (and limiting incentives to renegotiate), the need to account for poor service quality, and the lack of investment incentives toward the end of the concession period because of the fixed-term nature of contracts and the inability to commit to price adjustments over the life of the concession. Government's inability to be credible in its commitment to no renegotiation creates opportunities to use and abuse renegotiation, raising doubts about the initial price bid on which a concession is awarded (Spiller 1993; Mueller 2001). Incentives for concessionaires to maintain transferred assets properly can be strengthened by compensating them at the end of the concession period with an amount linked to the winning bid for the next concession period or to investments not yet depreciated. Bidding for concessions remains an attractive approach if properly designed—and if abuses after the award are contained, enforcement is appropriate—and (especially) if repeated bidding is practical.[11]

The prevalence of different modalities has varied significantly over time. In particular, the number of greenfield projects and (more recently) management and lease contracts have been on the rise, while the number of concessions and asset divestitures have been falling. This partly reflects the fact that once a firm is privatized or a concession is granted, the privatization or concession cannot be done again (at least for some time), whereas new greenfield projects can always be created.

Latin America shows a bias toward divestitures, whereas all the other regions have relied predominantly on greenfield project vehicles. Divestitures accounted for 53 percent of private infrastructure investment (by value) during 1990–2004 in Latin America, compared with only 31 percent in the rest of the world (see figure 2.12, panel B). When looking at the number of projects, the bias toward divestitures in LAC disappears, while the number of concessions projects in LAC is roughly twice as large as the rest of the world (see figure 2.12, panel A).

The divestiture boom in the region peaked in 1998, reaching $40 billion that year.[12] In contrast, divestitures in the rest of the world amounted to just $9 billion in 1998. In recent years, Latin America has seen a sharp drop in all modes of private investment, while levels of both greenfield projects and divestitures in the rest of the world have remained substantial (figure 2.13).

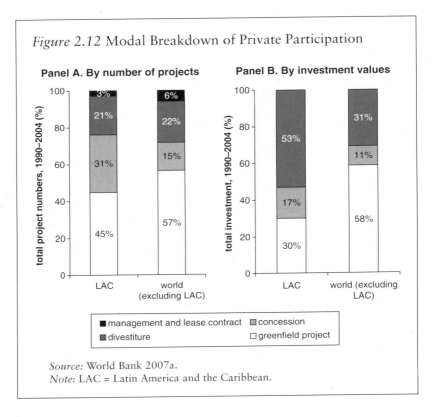

Figure 2.12 Modal Breakdown of Private Participation

Panel A. By number of projects

Panel B. By investment values

■ management and lease contract   ▨ concession
▨ divestiture   □ greenfield project

Source: World Bank 2007a.
Note: LAC = Latin America and the Caribbean.

Investor Type: Geographic Location

Investors from within Latin America have become an important factor in private infrastructure projects, supplying 40 percent of investment funding over the period 1998–2004. The greatest part of this came from local investors (28 percent), though a substantial proportion came from investors in neighboring LAC countries (12 percent).[13]

The share of local private investment varies by sector. Although the total number of developed country and local investors are about the same in LAC, the value of investments from developed countries is more than twice as much. A major factor for this difference is the sector distribution. More than half of the local investments (by number) are in transport, where the average value of investments is $79 million. Yet, the largest number of industrial country investments are made in the energy sector, for which the average value is $160 million. Industrial country investors are dominant in energy and water, and the largest category is in telecommunications. Local investors are dominant in transport, and together with foreign investors from other LAC countries, have been

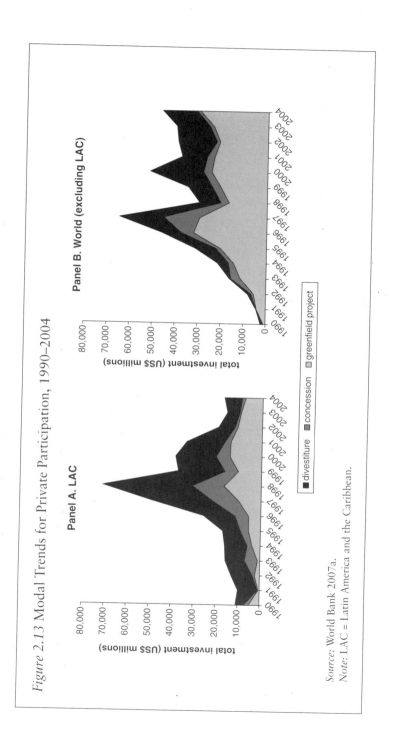

Figure 2.13 Modal Trends for Private Participation, 1990–2004

Source: World Bank 2007a.
Note: LAC = Latin America and the Caribbean.

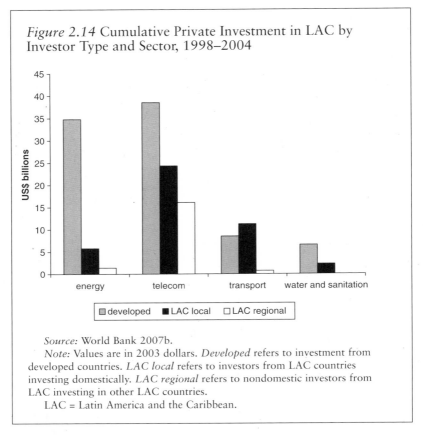

Figure 2.14 Cumulative Private Investment in LAC by Investor Type and Sector, 1998–2004

Source: World Bank 2007b.

Note: Values are in 2003 dollars. *Developed* refers to investment from developed countries. *LAC local* refers to investors from LAC countries investing domestically. *LAC regional* refers to nondomestic investors from LAC investing in other LAC countries.

LAC = Latin America and the Caribbean.

important players in telecommunications as well. Figure 2.14 shows the share of investment in each sector in the LAC by category of investor (Ettinger, Schur, von Klaudy, Dellacha, and Hahn 2005).

Figure 2.15, panel A, shows the amount of investment by the three geographic investor types over the period 1998–2004. While investment by all three types has been decreasing, there is a slight trend in terms of investment share shifting from industrial country investors to local LAC investors over the period. Whether this is a temporary phenomenon or the start of a major shift remains to be seen. Figure 2.15, panel B, presents this time series in percentage terms.

Limitations

After more than a decade of experience, private sector participation has raised a number of concerns. From a public policy perspective, those concerns

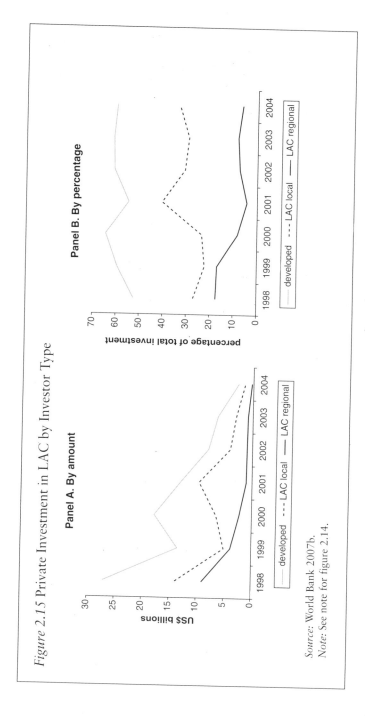

Figure 2.15 Private Investment in LAC by Investor Type

Panel A. By amount

Panel B. By percentage

Source: World Bank 2007b.
Note: See note for figure 2.14.

include a limited private sector interest in some areas of infrastructure, the limited sustainability of some arrangements for private participation, the high fiscal cost sometimes associated with private participation, and the backlash of public opinion in some parts of the world. Moreover, from the private sector perspective, participation in infrastructure projects has not always proved to be as profitable as had been originally envisaged.

There are major areas of infrastructure in which private finance has not proved capable of making a significant contribution. As noted above, private capital flows have been highly concentrated in certain sectors and geographic regions. Consequently, the initial optimism that private finance could eventually replace public finance for infrastructure proved to be misplaced. Part of the problem has been on the supply side. As long as the public sector does not place projects in the market for private participation, clearly there will not be private participation. And, for a number of reasons, that has been the case for the water sector in a number of countries. As a result, the private sector investments in the water sector are relatively small. The reality is major areas of infrastructure will continue to rely heavily on public finance for the foreseeable future, especially in the water and sanitation sector. In Latin America, private investment has been predicted to cover nearly all investment needs for telecommunications, roughly 20 and 50 percent of investment needs for electricity and transport respectively, and less than 10 percent for water and sanitation (Fay 2001). The same phenomenon arises within countries, such that private investment tends to bypass smaller population centers and more depressed regions.

Private participation by foreign investors is not always sustainable in emerging economy environments. The large currency devaluations experienced in Latin America and elsewhere during the late 1990s and early 2000s created major problems for participation by international private infrastructure operators. These problems were caused by the resulting currency mismatch between dollar-denominated debt and local currency business revenues. Even in cases in which contractual provisions provided for some degree of dollarization of revenues, they often proved politically impossible to implement given the decline in real incomes resulting from the currency shocks. As a result of such problems, about 12 percent of investments committed to infrastructure by the private sector over the period 1990–2004 in Latin America have already been canceled or are currently in distress (table 2.3). These problems affect 8 percent of private infrastructure projects overall in Latin America and are disproportionately concentrated in larger projects. A marked concentration of distressed projects is found in the water sector, in which 41 percent of committed investments in Latin America have been lost or are at risk. Furthermore, Argentina accounts for two-thirds of the value of canceled or distressed investments in Latin America.

Another red flag that has raised concerns and is partially responsible for the backlash has been the high incidence of renegotiated contracts with outcomes generally adverse to the users of the service. Renegotiations of concession contracts have been pervasive. Evidence from Latin America suggests that 81 percent of water concessions and 65 percent of transport concessions with the private sector have been renegotiated within a two-year period (table 2.4). This finding indicates the general contractual instability affecting private participation in such a socially and politically sensitive sector. Common outcomes of the renegotiation process include delays and reductions in investment obligations and tariff increases (table 2.5).

Private investment in infrastructure has often generated unexpected fiscal costs because of the provision of poorly conceived guarantees and generous (to the operator) risk assignments in the concession contract. In many cases, governments had to provide the private sector with various forms of guarantees to attract them into an untested environment or to compensate them for various types of project risk. One of the most common instruments has been the minimum revenue guarantee. These have been extensively used for example, in Power Purchase Agreements for

Table 2.3 Canceled or Distressed Investments in Private Infrastructure Projects in Latin America

	Energy	*Telecom*	*Transport*	*Water and sewerage*	*Total*
Value of investments (US$ millions)	22,272	8,142	8,642	8,692	47,748
Percent of total investment (%)	18	4	13	41	12
Number of projects	45	2	26	12	85
Percent of total projects (%)	10	2	8	9	8

Source: World Bank 2007a.

Table 2.4 Renegotiation Incidence and Average Time until Renegotiation, 1988–2001

	Renegotiated concessions (%)	*Average time (since award until renegotiation, years)*
All sectors	51	2.1
Electricity	22	2.3
Transport	65	3.1
Water and sanitation	81	1.7

Source: Guasch 2004, with updated numbers.

Table 2.5 Common Outcomes of the Renegotiation Process

	Renegotiated concession contracts with that outcome (%)
Delays on investment obligations targets	69
Acceleration of investment obligations	18
Tariff increases	62
Tariff decreases	19
Increase in the number of cost components with automatic pass-through to tariff increases	59
Extension of concession period	38
Reduction of investment obligations	62
Adjustment of canon-annual fee paid by operator to government	
Favorable to operator	31
Unfavorable to operator	17
Changes in the asset-capital base	
Favorable to operator	46
Unfavorable to operator	22

Source: Guasch 2004.

electricity generation plants and in the design of concession contracts for toll roads. In many cases, the demand forecast for these new infrastructures proved to be unduly optimistic, leading to the activation of minimum revenue guarantees and substantial fiscal liabilities for the state. For example, a study of 32 toll road concessions worldwide found that traffic levels averaged only 73 percent of initial forecasts in 88 percent of cases (Bain and Wilkinson 2002). Colombia provides a particularly interesting example of this problem. In the early phases of the privatization program, the Colombian government provided generous guarantees for private participation in electricity generation, toll roads, and telecommunications. These guarantees were eventually called, resulting in fiscal costs in excess of US$4 billion, just over half the amount that the private sector had invested in return for receiving these guarantees (table 2.6).

There has been a backlash of public opinion against PPI in Latin America. Public opinion became increasingly negative toward PPI the late 1990s. According to the regional Latinobarómetro survey, the percentage of the population who agreed that privatization had been beneficial for their country declined from 45 percent in 1998 to 25 percent in 2002 (figure 2.16). Typical concerns raised by opponents include layoffs

Table 2.6 Illustration of Fiscal Cost of Guarantees from Colombia

	Electricity generation	Toll roads	Telecom	Total
Estimated total cost of guarantees (US$ millions)	3,000	450	936	4,386
Value of guarantees as share private investment (%)	90	45	25	54

Sources: World Bank 2004c.

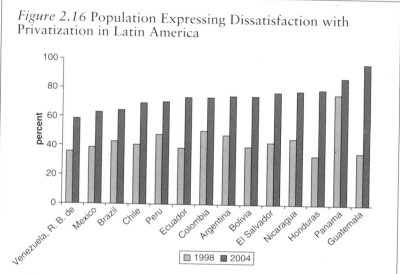

Figure 2.16 Population Expressing Dissatisfaction with Privatization in Latin America

Source: Latinobarómetro 1998 and 2004.

Note: The 1998 results reflect survey respondents who disagreed or strongly disagreed with the statement, "privatizations of state companies have been beneficial for the country." The 2004 numbers are of those who were less satisfied or much less satisfied with public services after privatization, in terms of price and quality.

of employees of former SOEs, tariff increases faced by the general public, lack of transparency in the transaction process, and the magnitude of returns made by private investors. In some extreme cases, public unrest led to the cancellation of contracts (such as the water concession in Cochabamba, Bolivia) or the abandonment of plans for new private sector projects (such as the privatization of the national telephone company in Paraguay).

Several surveys with focus groups from different countries in Latin America provide more details about public opposition. For instance, opposition was often higher among groups of a lower socioeconomic status. Moreover, some focus groups consisted of individuals who did not have access to electricity, water, or telecommunications services before the private participation programs, but they got the service as a result of the program (Andrés, Diop, and Guasch 2008). One would hope that such individuals would support the programs considering their individual benefits. Yet, the surveys do not reflect this hope. In fact, their opinions are negative and are statistically equivalent to those who did not benefit from the programs. When these individuals were interviewed, they explained, "although I benefited, the process was unjust, we do not understand the purpose and my neighbor lost his work" (Andrés, Diop, and Guasch 2008). Such responses seem to be reactions caused by the perceived lack of fairness and transparency of the process. Focus groups identified the following concerns about private sector participation: (i) transactions lacked transparency; (ii) multinationals made excess profits; (iii) tariffs increased; (iv) labor conditions worsened; (v) people's lives did not improve; (vi) the poor were overlooked; and (vii) there were no regulatory controls (Andrés, Diop, and Guasch 2008).

Surveys were conducted to determine whether any conditions or process and design elements would make private sector participation more palatable to the users. Figure 2.17 summarizes the results of a survey conducted in Peru shortly after the riots in Arequipa (table 2.7 notes some civil disturbances—in Arequipa and elsewhere—associated with private

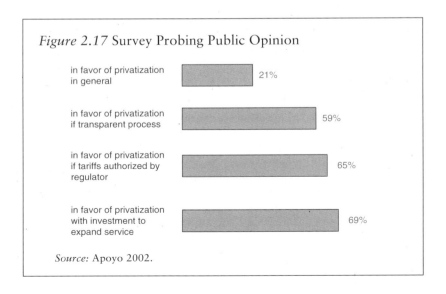

Figure 2.17 Survey Probing Public Opinion

in favor of privatization in general — 21%

in favor of privatization if transparent process — 59%

in favor of privatization if tariffs authorized by regulator — 65%

in favor of privatization with investment to expand service — 69%

Source: Apoyo 2002.

Table 2.7 Civil Disturbances

	Casualties	Issue	Outcome
Arequipa 2002	12 (state of emergency)	Electricity tariffs, jobs, corruption	Sale abandoned
Cochabamba 2000	130 (state of emergency)	Water tariffs, community wells	Concession cancelled
Dominican Rep. 2002	50	Blackouts, electricity tariffs	Bailout of utility
Ecuador 2002	Unknown	Electricity tariffs	Sale abandoned
Paraguay 2002	20	Unemployment, corruption	Sale postponed

Source: Apoyo 2002.

participation). This survey was conducted to understand the nature of the public opposition to privatization, through general questions. The results show that the percentage of the population supporting private sector participation increased from 20 percent to 60–70 percent when private sector participation was conducted in a transparent way, when tariffs were controlled, and the expansion of the service supported.

Box 2.1. examines the possible reasons for the social discontent with privatization. Box 2.2. dissects public perceptions surrounding PPI in Peru.

Achievements and Moving Forward

The phenomenon of private participation has undoubtedly led to major achievements in infrastructure service provision. These include the broader policy reforms that were adopted as a result, additional financial resources captured, and improvements in firm performance, quality, and coverage. Measuring these improvements (or lack thereof) is the subject of the rest of this book. Chapter 3 looks briefly at existing evidence regarding the impacts of private participation and later chapters describe this book's contribution to that body of evidence.

Private participation prompted governments to make important complementary reforms with potentially wider ramifications. To provide the institutional environment needed to attract private finance, governments

Box 2.1 Hidden Failures and Perception Management:
Explanations for Social Discontent about Privatization

There is a remarkable contrast between generally positive evaluations of privatization and the extreme public disaffection of it. Martimort and Straub (2005) review the literature for possible explanations for this paradox. This review leads them to the conclusion that either important failures have gone unreported (although clearly not unnoticed by those who suffered) or there has been a major problem with perceptions (and therefore a massive communication failure):

Hidden failures
While estimates of the impact of PPI on service coverage and quality and on redistribution are generally positive, it is possible that some negative aspects were underreported. First, the evidence on quality improvement is partial, and it is conceivable that quality may have deteriorated or at least failed to improve as much as expected. Some cases have reported dissatisfaction with quality (Mexico; electricity in Brazil and Chile). In addition, in some cases quality improvements were insufficient to compensate for price increases.

Second, the redistributional impact of price increases may not have been sufficiently mitigated by subsidies (which are often inefficiently administered). The modality and speed of price adjustments have also generated criticisms.

Third, the record on job losses is clearly negative, although the argument is that losses tended to be reversed in the medium term. It is possible, however, that for all but the most skilled, the job transition resulted in lower quality of employment. There is indeed some evidence that stable or increased wages were the consequences of longer hours worked.

Perceptions and the political economy of privatizations
Negative public perception of privatization may be due to the downturn in the economic cycle, as Boix (2005) documents. First, and in particular, it is not clear how the public distinguishes job losses caused by recessions from those caused by the privatization process as they may all be lumped together in a source of discontent.

Second, perception may have suffered from a gap between actual and expected performance. Many of the points about hidden failures can be rephrased from that point of view, as public discontent may be linked to a disappointment with outcomes that did not match initial expectations.

Third, it is unclear what the public perception of frequent renegotiations and (rare but well-publicized) cancellations have been, but they must have been significant.

Fourth, the perceived transparency of the privatization process is likely to be crucial in shaping public perceptions. Boix (2005) confirms the Lora and Panizza (2002) finding that negative opinions on privatization are stronger in cases in which corruption is perceived as more common.

(continued)

Box 2.1 Hidden Failures and Perception Management:
Explanations for Social Discontent about Privatization
(continued)

Corruption has a destructive effect on privatization, because it affects
competitive bidding and results in the allocation of rent toward a specific
group. Corrupt deals may also be used to maintain monopoly power and
impede the introduction of competition in privatized sectors—in which
case postprivatization profits may be the result of monopoly rent rather
than efficiency gains. Manzetti (2000) argues that this was the case in
telecom in Argentina and in the electricity sector in Chile. Overall, it is
unclear whether corruption has in fact increased or decreased as a result
of the privatization process. One argument is that petty corruption is
easier in public utilities, but that privatization offers the opportunity for
grand-level corruption.

Fifth, privatizations have often been perceived as unfair—rightly or
wrongly. Game theory's ultimatum game shows that individuals would
rather gain nothing at all rather than agree to a deal in which they feel
they gain less than their fair share. This seemingly irrational result, combined with a frequent perception that concessionaires or governments
may have benefited disproportionately, may be a key part of the privatization paradox (Shirley 2004).

More generally, it is difficult to determine the gains and losses from
any given privatization, as neither the population nor researchers have
a proper counterfactual against with which to judge performance. The
implication then for governments is that perceptions of fairness must
be carefully managed. That means not only that transactions must be
transparent and aboveboard, but that the use made of the proceeds of
privatization must offset the possible sense of injustice. In many cases in
which transactions were in fact clean, governments directed the proceeds
of privatization to the general fiscal account, making them "disappear"
rather than using them for direct and visible redistribution.

Source: Fay and Morrison 2006 (based on Boix 2005; Martimort and Straub
2005).

---

often undertook a major overhaul of the legal, regulatory, and institutional framework for infrastructure in their countries. These measures
included the passage of modern legislation, restructuring and liberalization of industry, creation of a regulatory system to safeguard service
quality and promote the accountability of service providers, and adoption of tariff policies more closely aligned with cost-recovery objectives.
Although often prompted by the desire to attract private capital, these
reforms have had a broader impact on the efficiency and transparency of

Box 2.2 Public Perceptions of Infrastructure Privatization in Peru

To uncover more details about deteriorating public perceptions of privatization, the World Bank commissioned a survey of 1,808 households in Peru. The Peruvians polled generally viewed the privatization process negatively, especially with regard to its impact on daily life. Participants indicated that the precarious economic conditions in which most live mean their most serious worries were the rising cost of living and lack of employment. Privatization was thought to adversely affect both of these concerns by affecting both layoffs and increased tariffs for services. While the public felt that private companies had a series of virtues absent from state-run enterprises—such as efficiency and the ability to offer better quality service—the fear of the abovementioned adverse effects was stronger than any perceived benefits offered by privatization.

When asked who benefited from privatization, the perception was that the government received the most benefits and the workers of a company that was privatized benefited the least. The most popular reason given for the recent privatization trend was that government authorities sought personal gain (47 percent of respondents). The second reason was that state-run companies were losing too much money (38 percent). Others attributed privatization to (i) the need to raise money to pay foreign debts (23 percent); (ii) pressure from the World Bank and the International Monetary Fund (20 percent); (iii) the need to modernize the country and undertake public works (20 percent and 16 percent, respectively); and (iv) pressure from foreign governments (8 percent).

On the whole, positive perceptions of privatization were fewer than negative ones. Participants did not discuss the positive aspects spontaneously or explicitly, and interviewers often inferred them from participants' answers. Modernization (of public services and the state), better quality of services, and wider access were considered the principal positive outcomes of privatization. More than 60 percent of those surveyed disagreed with privatization. The negative perceptions included government corruption, unemployment, higher tariffs, and others (box figure 2.2.1).

Almost half of those polled felt that the public had not benefited from the sale of public companies. Instead, the perception was that profits were used for political ends and personal gain by officials. When specifically asked whether the funds garnered from the sales were reinvested adequately by the state, an overwhelming 88 percent of participants thought funds had been misspent. Of those, 76 percent felt that part of the profits fed corruption; more than half thought they had helped the reelection campaign of former President Alberto Fujimori; and roughly 20 percent felt the government bought unnecessary equipment and carried out unnecessary public works projects.

(continued)

Box 2.2 Public Perceptions of Infrastructure Privatization in Peru *(continued)*

Figure 2.2.1
Negative Results of Privatization in Peru

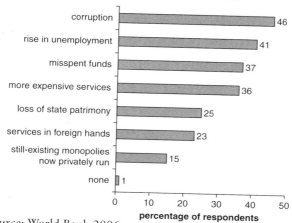

Source: World Bank 2006.

Note: The survey was conducted for the World Bank based on 1,808 interviews. Survey respondents were asked to choose the principal negative results of privatization.

   Though concessions were not fully understood or supported, the concept did garner more support than privatization. If the state were compelled to give some business to the private sector, 72 percent preferred it be given in form of concessions. But when asked how agreeable they were to concessions in general, only 38 percent agreed. Negative perceptions were based on the assumptions that a private company would have a rental agreement over a service or company, whereby the company could act in its own interests, raising the price of services (with the idea of recuperating their investment quickly) and not worry about how they would leave the service or business once their contract ended. Participants perceived that the concession process was without regulations or controls and thus allowed a firm to do as it pleased, a situation which could result in the service or company returning to the state in worse condition. On the other hand, some thought concessions were positive for the country, but only exclusively if there was an agreement that the state would not lose important assets.

   These perceptions suggest that future private participation efforts will require greater transparency and public awareness campaigns that are candid about expected costs and benefits.

Source: World Bank 2006.

infrastructure service provision, often affecting the behavior of operators that were not directly touched by private participation.

The private sector has made a significant contribution to the financing of infrastructure investment. The overall contribution of private finance to infrastructure may have fallen short of initial expectations in the early 1990s, particularly when the resources associated with divestitures are netted out of the total (figure 2.12 and figure 2.13 show divestitures share of private participation). Nevertheless, it has represented a significant addition to total infrastructure finance, particularly for the sectors and countries in which it has been concentrated. In Latin America, the private sector was contributing around 50 percent of estimated annual investment needs at its peak in the late 1990s.

But private investment has fallen well short of estimated investment needs. PPI as a percentage of GDP in Latin America has fallen steadily from 0.9 percent of GDP in 2000 to 0.4 percent in 2004.[14] Yet, according to recent World Bank estimates, annual expenditures of about 3 percent of GDP would be necessary to respond to expected growth in demand from firms and individuals, maintain existing infrastructure and achieve universal service for water, sanitation, and electricity over 10 years. This 3 percent figure is based on adding projections for new investment (1.4 percent of GDP) to maintenance expenses (1 percent of GDP) and to the estimated cost of universal coverage (0.24 percent of GDP). A much higher amount of investment in infrastructure (4 to 6 percent of GDP per year) would be required to bring LAC to the Republic of Korea's level of coverage over 20 years and fund adequate maintenance. This 4–6 percent figure is based on the estimated cost of bringing LAC to the Republic of Korea's level (2.4 to 4.7 percent of GDP[15]), plus the estimated cost of maintenance (about 1 percent of GDP) and universal coverage (0.24 percent of GDP). This does not include the cost of rehabilitation, nor does it cover urban transport, ports, and airports (Fay and Morrison 2006).

While ambitious, reaching the Republic of Korea's level of infrastructure development is not unrealistic. Similar increases were achieved by the Republic of Korea (as well as China, Indonesia, and Malaysia) over the 20-year period from the late 1970s to the late 1990s. Indeed, the Republic of Korea's infrastructure endowments 25 years ago were substantially worse than Mexico's, Argentina's, or Brazil's at the time. And if Calderón and Servén (2004a) are right, the payoffs in terms of growth and decreased inequality would be substantial.

To advance, the experience of the last decade calls for a new perspective on PPI. A new balance between public and private sector roles is emerging for infrastructure financing and service provision. Clearly, the optimism of the early 1990s—which saw private finance entirely replacing public finance—was unfounded. Public sector funding will remain central in many countries and for many types of infrastructure needs. Nevertheless, private investment is likely to remain an important component of infrastructure development in the years ahead, particularly as the available fiscal space in many countries remains limited. The important thing will be to channel private initiative where it has the greatest likelihood of being successful and to have realistic expectations as to what it can achieve.

Some of the problems experienced in the last decade may be avoided through greater reliance on the local private sector. In the early days, PPI was synonymous with large multinational corporations. In many countries, however, the local private sector may have significant resources to invest and may be better equipped to deal with currency devaluation and political interference.

The lessons of experience provide important guidance for future experiments with private participation. Some of the problems experienced with private participation reflect basic errors in the design and implementation of such contracts. Private participation should be focused on those aspects of infrastructure that present the most appropriate risk-reward characteristics, accepting that public finance will remain necessary in other areas. Guarantees for infrastructure projects can be more carefully designed to avoid some of the large payouts experienced in the past. Greater thought needs to be given to the distributional impacts of private participation to ensure that benefits are fairly distributed across different stakeholder groups (including the government, customers, employees, and investors).

Notes

1. There is a debate over the robustness and credibility of such cross-country analyses. See for example Straub (2008b). It is also worth noting that the infrastructure-growth connection is likely a two-way street. Although investment in infrastructure leads to growth, growth likely leads to more investment in infrastructure.

2. TFP is the residual output not explained by capital or labor. Similarly, growth in TFP is the growth of output not attributable to the growth in capital or labor.

3. For a comprehensive review of why infrastructure matters, see World Bank (1994) and Fay and Morrison (2006). For more on the impact of infrastructure on poverty see Brook and Irwin (2003); Chisari, Estache, and Romero (1999); and Estache, Foster, and Woodon (2002). Other evidence on the microeconomic impact of infrastructure can be found in Thomas and Strauss (1992), Gibson and Rozelle (2003), and Fan, Nyange, and Rao (2005). Using investment climate survey data, Reinikka and Svensson (2002) analyzed how the investment behavior of Ugandan firms is affected by poor infrastructure. Previous results on Indonesia, Nigeria, and Thailand come from Anas, Lee, and Murray (1996) and Lee, Anas, and Oh (1996).

4. The numbers reported in this section from the World Bank's Private Participation in Infrastructure database are for commitments, rather than disbursements.

5. Latin America is the one region for which comprehensive data on both public and private finance for infrastructure are available.

6. Although the World Bank's PPI Database categorizes greenfield projects separately, greenfield projects can fall under both the concession and privatization

categories in figure 2.10. In the PPI Database, build-operate-transfer (BOT) and build-own-operate (BOO) projects (both of which usually involve government revenue guarantees) are considered greenfield. "Merchant" projects, in which a private sponsor builds a new facility in a liberalized market in which the government provides no revenue guarantees, are also considered greenfield projects.

7. The equivalent investment with private participation numbers for all countries are as follows: 70 percent of electricity investment went to electricity generation; 15 percent went to distribution, 2 percent to transmission, and 11 percent to projects involving generation and transmission and/or distribution (World Bank, PPI Database, 2007a).

8. The equivalent global percentages are as follows: 52 percent of investment with private participation in transport went to toll road projects, compared with 21 percent for railways, 17 percent for seaports, and 10 percent for airports (World Bank, PPI Database, 2007a).

9. The equivalent global percentages are as follows: 35 percent of investment with private participation in telecommunications went to mobile access, 27 percent went to fixed access and long distance, and the remaining 38 percent went to some combination of the three (World Bank, PPI Database, 2007a).

10. This is for the period 1990–2004 (World Bank, PPI database, 2007a).

11. For an in-depth discussion of concession characteristics, see Guasch (2004).

12. Investments are assigned to their financial closing year.

13. This data comes from the Public-Private Infrastructure Advisory Facility Working Database, PPIAF (World Bank 2007b), which is derived from the World Bank PPI Database (2007a). PPIAF data are not directly comparable to PPI data because the PPIAF data only include investments by private sector sponsors, whereas the PPI database records total investment in the projects. Earlier studies have shown that, on average, 10 to 15 percent of the total equity in PPI came from the public sector. In addition, the PPIAF data only include investments from investors with at least a 15 percent share in any given project (Ettinger, Schur, von Klaudy, Dellacha, and Hahn 2005).

14. PPI data come from World Bank, PPI Database (2007a); GDP data comes from World Bank, World Development Indicators (2007d).

15. This includes costs for telephones (fixed and cellular), electricity generating capacity, and roads. The 2.4 percent estimate is based on road density of total roads. The 4.7 percent estimate is based on road density of paved roads. The total or paved road density target is equal to one-third that of the Republic of Korea because the Republic of Korea's population density is much higher than that of countries in Latin America and the Caribbean (LAC). This assumes an annual growth of GDP of 2.7 percent per year over the next 20 years.

3

Learning from Existing Literature

Chapter 2 outlined the tremendous scope of private participation in infrastructure (PPI) in Latin America. This chapter briefly reviews what has been learned from the experience regarding impacts according to the existing literature. It breaks down the different types of possible impacts, highlighting identified trends and representative studies (a more complete overview of the existing literature is provided in appendix 1). The chapter provides background on previous analyses of themes and indicators similar to those discussed in chapters 5–9 of this book. It briefly discusses themes and indicators that are beyond the scope of the book, including impacts on investors, government budgets, and consumer welfare and poverty.

It should be well understood that private sector participation is often part of a broader reform package. Other reforms that could occur (or have occurred) independently or simultaneously include public sector reform, regulatory reform, horizontal or vertical sector unbundling and restructuring, market liberalization, tariffs, subsidy, and access policy reforms.[1] Hence, it is worth keeping in mind that the impact of private sector participation alone is often hard to disentangle from other reforms. Moreover the actual impact will depend on the quality of implementation, regulatory capacity, and effective and overall contract and concession design. Typical reform combinations in the sectors considered in this book are described below.

Electricity. In the electricity sector, it has been typical to restructure the sector along the different sector activities. That is, it has been common the break up of the historical vertically integrated state-owned firm into separate generation, transmission, and distribution activities. In generation, the market has been typically liberalized to allow for the entry of new independent power producers (IPPs), although existing generation assets may be privatized, sometimes following horizontal restructuring measures designed to increase the number of market players. Electricity distribution, and to a much lesser extent transmission, are sometimes privatized by asset sale or concession, or sometimes reformed within the public sector. Tariff and subsidy reforms have often been part of the overall reform program. The regulatory framework usually has been established through a sectoral energy law leading to the establishment of a national regulatory agency (and sometime state agencies for some of the federated countries).

Telecommunications. In the telecom sector, private participation has become the norm, often entailing the sale of the national monopoly provider. In some cases, however, there were horizontal or vertical restructuring breakups of the integrated state firm (Argentina, Brazil, and Chile). The long-distance market and mobile market are typically liberalized, although a transition period of exclusivity, or sometimes duopoly, may have been granted. In parallel, licenses for cellular telephony are usually bid out to private operators. Also here, tariff reforms, such as the rebalancing of tariffs, have been part of the program. The regulatory framework is invariably established through a telecommunications law leading to the establishment of a national regulatory agency, which sometimes shares responsibility with the antitrust agency.

Water. In the water sector, it is increasingly typical for utilities to be decentralized to the state (provincial) or municipal level structure of the country (unitary or federal). While there have been numerous cases of private sector participation, it remains comparatively unusual overall and rarely, if ever, involves transfer of ownership (Chile has been the exception). Contractual forms have included management contracts, lease contracts (mainly in Africa), concessions (mainly in Latin America), and build-operate-transfer (BOT) schemes as a vehicle for financing new drinking water and wastewater treatment plants. On occasion, sectoral laws have been passed, but that has not been the norm. Contracts have been the salient legal instrument for regulation, and often included tariff reforms. Regulatory agencies have been occasionally created, particularly for larger cities.

PPI and related reforms affect a number of key variables. Reforms can affect employment and wages, prices of services, quality of services, access and coverage, asset ownership, fiscal flows, productivity, financial solvency, and overall welfare; they also can have distributional impacts. The theoretical impacts are discussed below, complemented by actual findings from the existing literature. The theoretical and actual impacts are derived from a survey of more than 60 country and cross-country studies.[2] Table 3.1 at the end of the chapter summarizes the impacts, and appendix 1 contains a more detailed overview of existing studies.

Employment and Wages

Public utilities have traditionally been characterized by labor hoarding; therefore, any reform measure designed to promote efficiency is likely to lead to an immediate and often significant reduction in employment. The evidence indicates that workforce reductions on the order of 30–50 percent can be typical. Although this is a substantial labor market shock to one sector of the economy, as a whole, infrastructure services rarely employ more than 1–2 percent of the workforce, so the overall impact on employment may be much more modest. While the immediate employment effects are typically negative, these may be offset to some degree in the medium term, either by increased employment among subcontractors to the utility (as services are contracted out), or because of faster sectoral growth triggered by the reforms (particularly in sectors such as telecommunications, in which liberalization often triggers rapid market expansion). For instance, looking at privatizations in Argentina in the 1990s, Ennis and Pinto (2003) found that employment fell but has since recovered. Alcázar, Xu, and Zuluaga (2002) found that water and sanitation privatizations in Lima, Peru, caused workers to lose employment through forced early retirement. And based on telecom reforms in 86 developing countries, Fink, Mattoo, and Rathindran (2003) found that privatization was associated with employment decreases.

Prices of Services

Reforms affect both the average level of tariffs and the tariff structure. Regarding tariff levels, the impacts can be major, although the direction of change is ambiguous and may evolve over time. In situations in which tariffs have historically been kept artificially low for political reasons, reform will typically necessitate tariff increases to restore the financial sustainability of the utility. This situation is most typical in the water sector. In situations in which tariffs have historically covered costs, but enterprises have been inefficiently run, reform probably will lead to tariff reductions as consumers benefit from improved efficiency. This situation is more typical in sectors such as electricity and telephony, which have a history of greater commercial management within the public sector and in which some degree of competition may be possible. Substantial changes in tariff structures are often necessary because utilities have historically tended to cross-subsidize, either among services provided by a given utility or among different consumers of the same service. Impacts of price changes on the poor depend on how well subsidies (if any) are targeted. In Côte d'Ivoire (Plane 1999) and the Arab Republic of Egypt (Galal 1999), studies found that telecom privatization led to reduced prices for consumers. Looking at water privatization in Mexico City, Haggarty, Brook, and Zuluaga (2002) found that with the introduction of metering, the number of low-income consumers receiving a water bill rose, while water bills for high-income consumers fell or stayed the same.

Quality of Services

Deficient quality of service provided by utilities imposes major coping costs on consumers. These costs usually take the form of investments in alternative supplies (water storage tanks, water treatment equipment, electricity generators, candles, and batteries) to deal with supply interruptions and inadequacies. If consumers are not able to mitigate the consequences of inadequate supplies, they may also suffer from lost production or reduced household welfare. Successful reforms potentially can have a major impact on quality of service parameters, with consequent improvements in economic productivity and quality of life. Improvements that are typically observed following utility reform include greater service continuity, reduced service interruptions, better customer service, more stable pressure or voltage, more accurate billing, and shortened waiting times for new connections. Quality gains have been found from multisectoral privatizations in Argentina (Benitez, Chisari, and Estache 2003); telecom privatizations in Peru (Torero, Schroth, and Pascó-Font 2003); and water privatizations in Guinea (Ménard and Clarke 2000). However, a survey of telecom regulatory reforms and privatizations in 26 developing countries by Petrazzini and Clark (1996) found no consistent impact on quality.

Access to Services and Coverage

To the extent that reforms improve the availability of investment finance for utility operators, reforms should also pave the way for more rapid expansion of services. However, operators will only voluntarily expand into market segments when they face a clear commercial incentive to do so. Underserved market segments are often associated with low-income neighborhoods, or isolated rural communities, which often present a commercially unattractive combination of low demand and high cost of service provision. In these cases, reforms will need to incorporate special policy measures to encourage service expansion in these areas. Potential instruments include universal service obligations, connection targets, connection subsidies, amended regulations to allow for the use of low-cost technologies, and financing facilities to amortize connection costs. In Chile, Paredes (2003) found that multisectoral privatizations yielded significant increases in coverage. In Guatemala, Foster and Tré (2003) and Foster and Araujo (2004) found that new connections to water, electricity, and sanitation services increased significantly after privatizations and restructuring.

Asset Ownership

Some types of reform can lead to major changes in asset ownership. Given the scale and value of the assets concerned, this situation can have a significant effect on the ownership structure of the economy. The two key changes in ownership occur in decentralization reforms, in which assets are transferred to subnational tiers of government, and in divestitures, in which assets are sold to the private sector. For instance, in Mexico, Galal, Jones, Tandon, and Vogelsang (1994) found that telecom privatization led to a high proportion of foreign ownership, suggesting that benefits leaked abroad. In the United Kingdom, Newbery and Pollitt (1997) found that electricity privatization and restructuring led shareholders to benefit disproportionately more than consumers.

Impact on Investors

Rhetoric is increasing regarding the "great gains of the privatized companies," but empirical evidence on this theme has been limited until recently. The only study to date is by Sirtaine, Pinglo, Guasch, and Foster (2005), who analyzed the rate of return to the investors in private infrastructure companies in Latin America. The study assesses the adequacy of these returns relative to the risks taken (cost of capital) and the impact that the quality .of regulation had on the closeness of alignment between returns and costs of capital. This impact is assessed by estimating both historical and projected future returns earned on a sample of representative private infrastructure concessions, across a number of Latin American countries and infrastructure sectors, and comparing them against expected returns given the level of risk taken. The study shows that the internal rate of return (IRR) from the mid-1990s is below the weighted average cost of capital (WACC). But if standard accounting adjustments are made (for example, to add to the utilities the high rates of management fees and transfers to subsidiaries through purchases), the rate of return surpasses the costs of capital, especially in the telecommunications, transport, and energy sectors. The only sector in which IRR does not surpass cost, on average, is water and sewerage (figure 3.1).

Sirtaine, Pinglo, Guasch, and Foster (2005) found that the variance of returns across concessions and countries is considerable and can be partially explained by the quality of regulation: the better the quality of regulation, the closer the alignment between financial returns and costs of capital. Regulated companies have an incentive to reduce their gains, thus allowing them to increase prices. For that reason, the estimated rates of return are very likely below the actual rates.

Estache and Pinglo (2004) found that returns on equity were marginally negative over the period from 1998 to 2002 in Latin America. East Asia was the only region where returns on equity were commensurate with the cost of equity during that period. Looking across sectors, returns on equity for energy projects were barely a third of the cost of equity, and returns on equity for water projects were close to zero. Reasons for the relatively low returns include slower-than-expected demand growth, regulatory interference in contractual terms, and macroeconomic shocks (such as currency devaluations).

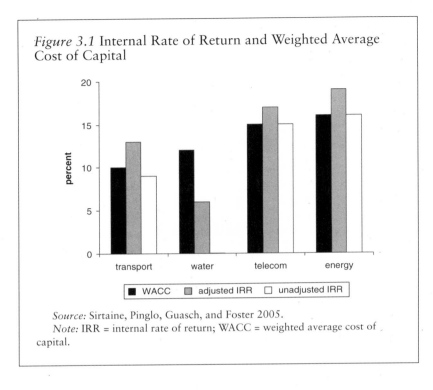

Figure 3.1 Internal Rate of Return and Weighted Average Cost of Capital

Source: Sirtaine, Pinglo, Guasch, and Foster 2005.
Note: IRR = internal rate of return; WACC = weighted average cost of capital.

Fiscal Flows

Infrastructure reform can have a major positive impact on public finances. In this context, it is important to distinguish between one-time windfall gains and ongoing fiscal flows. In cases in which asset sales are involved, there may be major fiscal windfalls in terms of sale revenues. Although of lesser financial importance, concession contracts can sometimes be designed to generate a canon or royalty payment. A key issue is the treatment of the historic debt of public utilities. This may be written off against privatization revenues, transferred to the balance sheet of the private operator, or reabsorbed into the public sector balance sheet. After utilities become commercially viable, governments often start to regard them as an interesting tax base, given their broad reach and relatively low price elasticity. As a result, utilities may begin to generate substantial tax revenues in the medium term.

During the 1990s, private capital investments in infrastructure in Latin America attracted US$290 billion, representing about half of the private capital flows to infrastructure in the world during this period. Nearly 60 percent of these resources, or US$174 billion, were allocated to the state (treasury) for sales to the private sector. This sum is equivalent

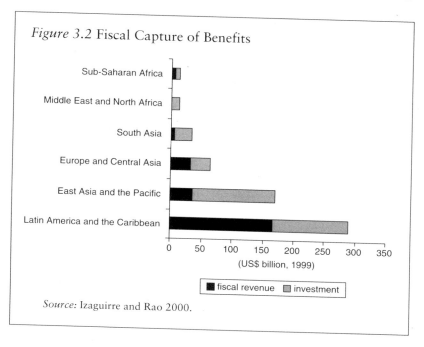

Figure 3.2 Fiscal Capture of Benefits

Source: Izaguirre and Rao 2000.

to 40 percent of the public sector debt stock of the region in 1990, contributing significantly to the reorganization of public finance (figure 3.2). These sale revenues served as unexpected windfalls for governments. Public finance benefited from the recurrent-benefits effect (in many cases even more than the unexpected earnings) reflected in the elimination of recurrent subsidies and the creation of new tax earnings.

Productivity and Financial Solvency

Reforms that increase competition, transparency, accountability, or private sector participation can be reasonably expected to increase the productivity of infrastructure providers. Productivity can improve through any number of means: a reduction in the labor force, more efficient capital investment, improved processes, or smarter management. Operators will have an incentive to increase their efficiency and productivity when doing so will increase their profits. Absent the profit motive, operators can be induced to improve their productivity by a strong, independent regulatory body. Reforms that encourage productivity and efficiency improvements should also improve the bottom connections of infrastructure providers, making them more financially solvent. In a recent book, Chong and López-de-Silanes (2005) built on a variety of Latin American case studies to conclude that improvements in privatized firms' profitability are in line with worldwide evidence.[3] They found that profitability increases typically were accompanied by reductions in unit costs, boosts in output, and reduced or constant levels of employment and investment. Their evidence suggests that higher efficiency, achieved through firm restructuring and productivity improvements, underpins profitability gains.

Distributional Impact and Consumer Welfare

Overall distributional impact depends on how the above effects interact and how they relate to different population groups. For instance, Galal, Jones, Tandon, and Vogelsang (1994) found that electricity privatizations in Chile in 1986 yielded overall welfare gains, but before privatization, nonpaying customers were worse off. Looking at the electricity privatizations in Nicaragua, Freije and Rivas (2002) concluded that the increase in the price of electricity reduced welfare at all expenditure deciles, with larger losses at the top of the distribution. However, households that obtained access during the reform period experienced substantial gains in welfare, with larger gains among poorer households. In Peru, Torero, Schroth, and Pascó-Font (2003) found that the telecom privatization in 1994 improved total consumer welfare, mainly by increasing access to the service. But price increases negatively affected low- and, especially, very-low-income households. Based on studies of four countries—Argentina, Mexico, Nicaragua, and Bolivia—McKenzie and Mookherjee (2003) found no clear pattern of price changes affecting consumers. In fact, in cases in which prices went up, they found that the effects were outweighed by the corresponding increases in access that occurred in the bottom or lower half of the distribution.

With regard to *new consumers*, the initial access entails major welfare effects on the (public) well-being because of access to the service and better quality. In relation to the *existing consumers*, the welfare effect also appears positive. Although the price effect on those consumers was mixed—tariffs increased in some countries and sectors but diminished in others—the quality of service improved significantly. Quality of service improvements appear to more than compensate for tariff increases.

A recent study in Peru by Escobal and Torero (2004) analyzed the impact on household earnings resulting from access to services. The numbers are quite substantial, as seen in figure 3.3. Having access to water and electricity increases earnings by 13 percent; having access to water, electricity, and sanitation increases earnings by 23 percent; and having access to water electricity, sanitation, and telecom increases earnings by 36 percent. An adequate road infrastructure can also have a big impact on poverty, as shown by a number of studies. In the case of Peru, having access to markets through rehabilitated rural roads increases household earnings by 35 percent (figure 3.4).

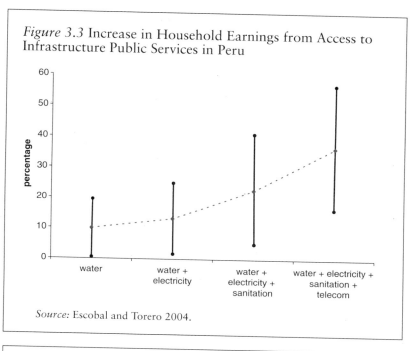

Figure 3.3 Increase in Household Earnings from Access to Infrastructure Public Services in Peru

Source: Escobal and Torero 2004.

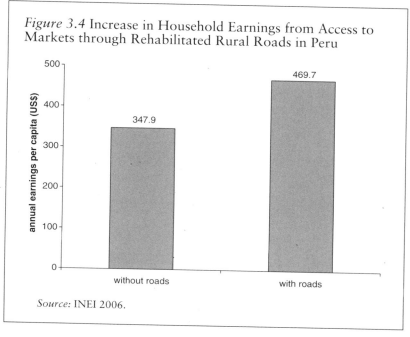

Figure 3.4 Increase in Household Earnings from Access to Markets through Rehabilitated Rural Roads in Peru

Source: INEI 2006.

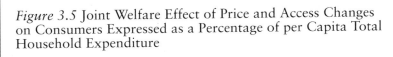

Figure 3.5 Joint Welfare Effect of Price and Access Changes on Consumers Expressed as a Percentage of per Capita Total Household Expenditure

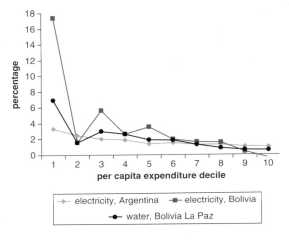

Source: McKenzie and Mookherjee 2003.

Water and Electricity. Figure 3.5 summarizes the conclusions of case studies for Argentina, Bolivia, and Nicaragua. The distinguishing characteristic of these studies is that they develop welfare indicators that account for the impacts of prices on existing consumers (generally negative) with the impact of providing initial access to other consumers (large and positive). The results show that, in Bolivia and Argentina, the privatization of the water and electricity sectors improved the welfare of the consumer, with benefits skewed toward the deciles with lower income. Privatization of electricity in Nicaragua, using the same methodology, hardly produced net benefits, because the gains from the connections were offset by the increase in price (figure 3.6).

Telecommunications. For the telecommunications sector, the situation is quite different. Because of relatively low rates of coverage, most of the gains from connections correspond more closely to the middle class rather than to the poor. This is evident in Bolivia and to a smaller degree in Argentina (figure 3.6).

Table 3.1 summarizes the *theoretical* and *actual* impacts of private participation on the variables discussed above. The descriptions of *actual* impacts provide a rough summary of the findings of past studies; the impacts found in the following chapters of this book are not included.

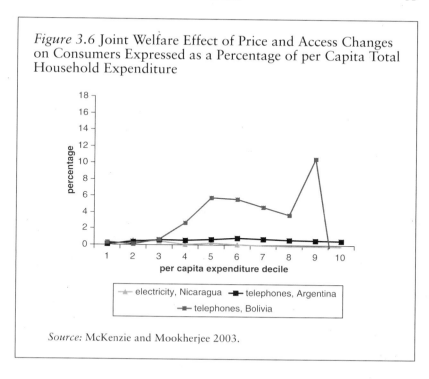

Figure 3.6 Joint Welfare Effect of Price and Access Changes on Consumers Expressed as a Percentage of per Capita Total Household Expenditure

Source: McKenzie and Mookherjee 2003.

Table 3.1 Summary of Theoretical and Actual Impacts of Private Participation

Indicator	Theoretical and actual impacts
Employment	Theoretical: Employment *should*[a] fall because of increased pressure for efficiency. Actual: Studies found substantial employment reductions.
Price of service	Theoretical: Prices *should* adjust upward or downward toward efficient cost-reflective levels, but depend on initial conditions. Actual: Mixed results, with several studies showing price increases.
Quality of service	Theoretical: Quality *should* improve because of better management and know-how. Actual: Quality improvements found in many studies, but others found little impact.

(continued)

Table 3.1 Summary of Theoretical and Actual Impacts of
Private Participation *(continued)*

Indicator	Theoretical and actual impacts
Access to service and coverage	Theoretical: Access *may*[b] improve because of improved finances and reduced cost of service. Actual: Access and coverage improved in most cases.
Asset ownership	Theoretical: Asset sales increase private ownership, concentration depends on design details. Actual: Increased private ownership (by definition); some findings of increased foreign ownership.
Investors	Theoretical: Private investors generally *should*, on average, earn normal profits. Actual: Limited, mixed evidence. Some studies found that returns exceeded the cost of capital, others did not.
Fiscal flows	Theoretical: Subsidies to the sector *should* be reduced, sale revenues *may* be large, and tax revenues *may* increase thereafter. Actual: Fiscal flows did improve in most cases. More than half of private capital flows to infrastructure in LAC went to state treasuries during the 1990s.
Productivity and financial solvency of providers	Theoretical: Productivity and solvency *should* improve because of increased efficiency. Actual: Studies find productivity and profitability improvements.
Distributional impact and consumer welfare	Theoretical: *Should* improve, the extent depends on interaction of above elements. Actual: Studies show varied but largely positive results. New customers tended to gain by attaining access, while existing customers could be hurt by price increases, but enjoyed increased quality of service.

Source: Foster, Tiongson, and Ruggeri Laderchi 2005; authors' elaboration.
Note: LAC = Latin America and the Caribbean.
a. *Should* indicates probable impact.
b. *May* indicates possible impact.

The review of existing evidence identifies shortcomings in the literature. Shortcomings tend to relate to methodology and scope, because most of the literature has focused on case studies or country cases (appendix 1 provides more detail on identified shortcomings). As described in chapter 4, this book addresses these shortcomings by applying new methodologies and a systemic, cross-country approach.

Notes

1. For a discussion of the impacts of these reforms, see Foster, Tiongson, and Ruggeri Laderchi (2005).

2. A summary of the studies can be found in the appendixes of Foster, Tiongson, and Ruggeri Laderchi (2005).

3. Examples of worldwide evidence include Megginson, Nash, and van Randenborgh (1994); Boubakri and Cosset (1998, 2002); and D'Souza and Megginson (1999).

4

Filling Gaps with New Data Sets and Methodologies

The analysis in this book fills a key gap in the literature. Based on the authors' literature review (chapter 3 and appendix 1), no cross-sectoral studies of private participation in Latin America use a rigorous counterfactual approach to holistically measure impact. Existing analyses tend to be narrow (just focusing on one country or sector), are completed ex ante (before the actual reform has taken place), look at too short a time horizon (for example, only one year before and one year after the privatization), or use approaches that do not adequately measure the counterfactual (what would have happened in the absence of the reform) in terms of levels and trends. Privatizations of electricity and water distribution have been relatively underaddressed.

The authors' analysis measures the impact of privatization in telecommunications, electricity distribution, and water distribution by comparing actual outcomes to an estimated counterfactual. To do so, it uses a unique, cross-country time-series data set covering 181 infrastructure firms in Latin America. The data set includes data for five years before the privatization and five years after, where possible. It also includes a variety of indicators that go well beyond traditional financial performance measures. Indicators include changes in output, labor, efficiency, labor productivity, quality, coverage, and prices. The analysis uses a range of statistical measures that account for time trends and firm-level fixed effects.

The analysis in this book relies on a range of approaches to zero in on the true impacts of PPI. In the absence of a control group of comparable firms, the approaches try to estimate the counterfactual—what would have presumably happened in the absence of the privatization—using what is known from before, during, and after the privatization process of each firm. The means and medians approach compares differences between each period in terms of levels and growth rates and tests the differences for statistical significance. The econometric approach essentially tests the same thing, but through a regression analysis that controls for firm-level fixed effects and time trends. The results for each sector are described in the following chapters; the complete results for each approach are shown in appendix 3. The unique data set and range of methodologies produces a richness of results that has not been possible with previous studies. It yields fairly sophisticated predications about the impacts of future privatizations. The data and methodologies used are discussed in the following sections.

Data Sets

Three data sets were merged to create a comprehensive analysis of infrastructure privatization for this book.[1] The first data set is composed of performance indicators for 181 firms in electricity distribution, telecommunications, and water distribution. These data were then matched to a second data set containing details of privatization contract characteristics and the regulatory framework for nearly 1,000 infrastructure projects in Latin America. A third database—the LAC Electricity Benchmarking Database—is discussed in chapter 8. It has detailed data for public and private companies in electricity distribution and is used to complement the findings from the other two data sets.

Performance Indicators Data Set

The performance indicators data set developed for this book is unique because of the comprehensiveness of the indicators and sectoral coverage. It covers 181 infrastructure firms in Latin America that changed from public to private ownership during the 1990s. Many studies look at only the financial performance of privatized companies, which is just part of the story; this analysis considers changes in output, labor, efficiency, labor productivity, quality, coverage, and prices. In terms of sectors, the analysis includes the often-neglected water and electricity distribution sectors, in addition to fixed telecommunications. The analysis focuses on these sectors because of data availability and because they present similar characteristics (in the sense that they all have monopolistic features and are networking markets, allowing for similar interpretations of such indicators as labor productivity, coverage, and distributional losses), a feature that allows for cross-sectoral comparison. For these reasons, other sectors, such as transport, mobile telecommunications, and generation and transmission of electricity, among others, were excluded from the analysis.

The data also have a relatively long time span, starting five years before the change in ownership and continuing five years after the privatization. The time span allows for the separation of short-run or transitional effects from long-run results. How short- and long-run effects are separated is discussed in the following methodology sections. The database targeted utilities privatized mainly in the period from 1990 to 2003—the main privatization wave in the region. The database also includes a few companies privatized during the 1980s (in cases in which preprivatization data were available).[2]

Data came from a variety of sources and was cross-checked, when possible. This research required the construction of an unbalanced panel data set of key indicators for utilities in LAC. For this, official data reported by the firms to their investors and statistical reports of the regulator agencies of each country were used. Information was requested from each of the companies, as well as from each regulatory office. Furthermore, additional sources were used, like ITU (International Telecommunication Union) and OLADE (*Organización Latinoamericana de Energía*, Latin American Energy Organization). A particular effort was made in corroborating the company data with several public sources and with data of the firms provided by different government offices. In addition, the research was particularly cautious about the consistency and comparability of the data across time and across countries.[3]

The analysis will focus on several indicators of outcomes, employment, labor productivity, efficiency, quality, coverage, and prices. Some of these variables have been used by other authors in other samples, such as Ros (1999), who used equivalent indicators for *coverage, labor productivity, quality,* and *prices,* but did so for the telecommunications sector. Ramamurti (1996) used analogous indicators in *output, coverage,* and *labor productivity* for the four Latin American telecommunications firms of his study. Saal and Parker (2001) used similar indicators for *output, employment, quality,* and *prices,* but did so for water and sewerage companies of England and Wales.

The countries analyzed in electricity were Argentina, Bolivia, Brazil, Chile, Colombia, El Salvador, Guatemala, Nicaragua, Panama, and Peru. The sample consists of unbalanced panel data that includes 116 firms and 1,103 firm-year observations. Each of the firms included in the sample contains at least one year of preprivatization data. In fact, 98 of the 116 firms have information for at least the previous three years.

For water and sewerage, the paper reviewed companies in Argentina, Bolivia, Brazil, Chile, Colombia, Mexico, and Trinidad and Tobago. The sample consists of unbalanced panel data that includes 49 firms and 515 firm-year observations. Each of the firms included in the sample contains at least one year of preprivatization data, and 35 of the 49 firms have information for at least the previous two years.

The countries studied for the telecommunications sector were Argentina, Bolivia, Brazil, Chile, El Salvador, Guatemala, Guyana, Jamaica, Mexico, Nicaragua, Panama, Peru, Trinidad and Tobago, and República Bolivariana de Venezuela. The sample consists of an unbalanced panel data that includes 16 firms and 267 firm-year observations. Each of the firms included in the sample contains at least four years of preprivatization data, and 17 out of the 18 firms have information for at least the previous four years.

Table 4.1 presents the definitions of the variables used in the present analysis, and table 4.2 shows the summary statistics of these variables in each sector.

Contract and Regulatory Characteristics Data Set

The performance indicators data set was matched to a novel data set built by the World Bank that describes the characteristics of nearly 1,000 infrastructure projects awarded in Latin American and Caribbean countries from 1989 to 2002 (see Guasch 2004). The data set provides details on the privatization process, including how many bidders participated, the contract process,[4] the award criteria,[5] and the type of concession.[6] The data set covers the regulatory framework, including how the legal framework was established,[7] how tariffs are regulated,[8] if there was a possibility of renegotiation of the contract, and if so, who might be the initiator of the renegotiation.[9]

The data set captures additional privatization contract details, including information about termination clauses, the arbitration process, claim-solving institutions, universal service obligations, contract duration, contract renewal, government guarantees, government subsidies, frequency of tariff review, and how the exchange and commercial risk were borne. If the contract was renegotiated, the reason given and the renegotiation outcome are also known. Characteristics of the regulator—such as an index of the regulator's autonomy, its budget source, the duration of the regulatory board member mandate, and the year of the regulatory board's inceptions—are captured in the data set.

For this book's analysis, not all of the aforementioned variables could be used because of data constraints. Only the variables that had sufficient variation across firms were employed, making it possible to measure the effect of different contract and regulatory characteristics on performance outcomes. Lack of variation also led to the pooling of the three sectors in the analysis of the data set described in chapter 9. Table 4.3 describes the variables that ultimately were used.

LAC Electricity Benchmarking Database

The LAC electricity benchmarking database was built by the World Bank (World Bank 2008) and contains annual information of 250 private and state-owned utilities, using 26 variables indicating coverage, output, input, labor productivity, operating performance, quality, customer services,

Table 4.1 Variable Definitions

	Electricity distribution	Fixed telecommunications	Water distribution
Output	• Total number of subscribers (residential and nonresidential), December of each year • Total energy sold per year (in MWh)	• Total number of active connections. December of each year • Total number of local minutes per year	• Total number of residential water subscribers • Total number of residential sewerage subscribers • Total water production per year
Labor	• Number of employees	• Number of employees	• Number of employees
Labor productivity	• Number of subscribers per employee • Total energy sold each year per employee	• Number of active connections per employee • Local minutes per employee	• Number of water connections per employee • Water production per employee
Efficiency	• Energy lost in the distribution (due to technical losses and illegal connections)	• Percentage of incomplete calls	• Percentage of total water produced that was not charged to the consumers
Quality	• Average duration of interruptions per consumer (hours/year) • Average frequency of interruptions per consumer (number/year)	• Percentage of incomplete calls • Percentage of digital connections in the network	• Average number of hours per day with water service • Percentage of the samples that passed a potability test

(continued)

Table 4.1 Variable Definitions *(continued)*

	Electricity distribution	Fixed telecommunications	Water distribution
Coverage	• Number of residential subscribers per 100 households	• Number of active connections per 100 inhabitants	• Number of residential water subscribers per 100 households • Number of residential sewerage subscribers per 100 households
Prices	• Average tariff for 1 MWh for a residential service in dollars (it includes fixed and variable costs), December of each year • Average tariff for 1 MWh for a residential service in local currency, December 2000	• Average cost for a three-minute, nonpeak local call (dollars) • Average monthly cost for residential service (dollars) • Average cost for the installation of a residential line (dollars) • Average cost for a three-minute, nonpeak local call (real local currency) • Average monthly cost for residential service (real local currency) • Average cost for the installation of a residential line (real local currency)	• Average price per cubic meter of supplied water (in dollars) • Average price per cubic meter of collected waste (in dollars) • Average price per cubic meter of supplied water (in real local currency) • Average price per cubic meter of collected waste (in real local currency)

Source: Authors' elaboration.
Note: MWh = megawatt hours.

62

Table 4.2 Summary Statistics

Variable	N	Mean	Median	SD	Minimum	Maximum
Electricity distribution						
Number of subscribers	98	497,776	225,230	681,698	2,700	3,884,579
Output (thousand of KWhs)	100	2,850	789.5	5282	13.8	34,300
Number of employees	87	1,421	625	2,115	18	13,642
Subscribers per employee	84	558.81	506.67	244.20	210.45	1,523.27
Output per employee	84	2,343.48	2,116.46	1,298.60	663.86	7,323.09
Distributional losses	90	15.3%	13.6%	6.6%	0%	33.9%
Duration of interruptions per subscriber	65	25.26	20.36	21.01	1.75	100.00
Frequency of interruptions per subscriber	67	22.63	16.03	21.24	1.07	100.00
Subscribers per 100 HHs	86	74.6%	81.3%	20.7%	7.0%	100.0%
Average price per KWh (in US$)	92	88.70	85.34	35.43	7.47	323.61
Fixed telecommunications						
Number of subscribers	16	2,423,040	824,594	3,150,005	28,048	9,642,200
Output (million of minutes)	13	20,500	6,200	28,800	774	83,100
Number of employees	16	12,268	9,732	12,097	966	47,949
Subscribers per employee	16	209.30	109.27	241.96	33.81	736.65
Output per employee	13	1,627.35	844.29	1,790.44	257.10	6,419.45
Percentage of digital lines	16	67.0%	70.3%	26.4%	14.6%	100.0%
Percentage of completed calls	12	67.0%	64.8%	20.4%	20.0%	98.8%
Subscribers per 100 inhabitants	16	9.84	8.40	5.83	2.96	22.01

(continued)

63

Table 4.2 Summary Statistics *(continued)*

Variable	N	Mean	Median	SD	Minimum	Maximum
Price of three-minute call (in US$)	14	0.13	0.07	0.25	0.01	0.99
Monthly charge for a residential service (in US$)	15	6.16	6.01	4.52	0.36	19.97
Price for the installation of a line (in US$)	15	343.75	309.51	339.35	1.20	1,102.26
Water and sewerage						
Total subscribers for water	48	147,119	78,864	223,803	1,894	1,282,074
Total subscribers for sewerage	43	107,286	42,991	173,795	435	799,994
Water production	47	91,400	28,900	2,110	145.6	13,700,000
Number of employees	42	528	258	997	9	6,346
Water subscribers per employee	42	312.23	283.10	153.56	43.34	772.36
Water production per employee	33	39.1%	37.3%	12.7%	15.3%	62.8%
Continuity (hours per day)	21	19.40	22.97	6.57	—	24.00
Potability (%)	29	88.5%	98.9%	26.1%	0.0%	100.0%
Water subscribers per 100 HHs	44	74.83	88.29	34.30	0.01	100.00
Sewerage subscribers per 100 HHs	34	64.61	71.99	27.83	0.30	97.70
Average price for water (US$/m³)	27	0.48	0.44	0.16	0.17	0.84
Average price for sewerage (US$/m³)	12	0.40	0.39	0.22	0.07	0.97

Source: Author's calculations.
Note: Each observation is the average for the available information from five years before the change in ownership to five years after that.
HH = households; KWh = Kilowatt hours; N = the number of observations; SD = standard deviation.

Table 4.3 Contract and Regulatory Variables

Variable	Description
Privatization process	
Auction	Dummy with value 1 if the concession was awarded through an auction process
Award: highest price	Dummy with value 1 if the concession was awarded according to the highest price
Award: best investment plan	Dummy with value 1 if the concession was awarded according to the best investment plan
Regulatory board	
Full autonomy	Dummy with value 1 if the regulatory board was fully autonomous
Partial autonomy	Dummy with value 1 if the regulatory board was partially autonomous
Duration	Dummy with value 1 if the duration of appointments to the regulatory board was five or more years
Investors	
Investors: foreign	Dummy with value 1 if the investors were foreign
Investors: mixed	Dummy with value 1 if some of the investors were foreign
Tariff regulation	
Tariffs: rate of return	Dummy with value 1 if the tariffs were regulated according to the rate of return
Tariffs: price cap	Dummy with value 1 if the tariffs were regulated according to price cap

Source: Authors' elaboration.

and prices. The time frame covers data as early as 1990, but the main focus is the period from 1995 to 2005. Data availability and data sources vary by country, often depending on their ownership and means of regulation. While the benchmarking study uses a homogenous set of variables to collect data and measure performance, each country represents a special case; therefore, efforts were made to ensure consistency of the data across time and utility. This database is representative of 88 percent of the electrification in the region.

· The primary means of conducting research was field data collection and in-house data collection. A standard template and set of variables were used by both field and in-house consultants. Field consultants collected data to complement the information in some of the countries. Because of limited information available on the Web for these countries, local consultants were the most resourceful. For these selected countries and utilities, a preliminary feasibility screening was conducted to determine which countries would be likely to provide information. While field workers had direct access to the respective utility and government, the process of data collection was often hindered by unexpected factors, such as political affairs, bureaucracy, unsystematized data, and confidentiality issues, among other elements.

The main sources for the in-house data collection were the World Wide Web, information collected by World Bank staff for other projects, and the internal World Bank databases (Development Data Platform, Integrated Records and Information System [IRIS], and so on). The main sources of information on the Internet were the utilities' Web sites. For some countries, the following sources proved to be useful: regulators, ministries, partnerships, central banks, online financial journals, papers, loan reports, financial reports, annual reports, monthly bulletins, statistics offices, and contacts with the companies and regulators. In addition, the following associations and organizations provided valuable statistics for the region: ARIAE (Asociación Iberoamericana de Entidades Reguladores de Energía), ECLAC (Economic Commission for Latin America and the Caribbean), IEA (International Energy Agency), and CIER (Comisión de Integración Energética Regional). Because regulators, international organizations, and commissions often cover the electricity distribution of the entire region, most of the information provided was aggregated at the country level and not disaggregated by utility. One of the challenges of data collection was the inconsistency of the data provided by utilities or regulators in annual and financial reports. Because of this problem, appropriate calculations and approximations were made to construct missing data points. For example, through the method of interpolation, data were constructed for the earlier years of certain variables, such as number of connections, number of employees, and so on. Interpolation and other means of constructing data were the exceptions based on already concrete data and time trends. Specific methodologies were designed according to the variables at hand to ensure their comparability and consistency across time and utilities.

To best describe the efficiency of the distribution sector of LAC, indicators were selected to determine utility-level performance. The utility-level indicators reflect relevant and feasible measurements in depicting the distribution segment of the electricity sector. The utility-level indicators were computed to measure such factors as technical efficiency, operating efficiency, cost-efficiency, quality of service, and so on. Technical efficiency is defined as the capacity of the utility to achieve maximum output from a given set of inputs. To compute the technical efficiency of a utility, output and input indicators reflecting operating- and cost-efficiency were aggregated.

New Methodology: Separating Transition versus Long-Run Effects

Ideally, to evaluate the impact of privatization, the performance of utilities under private operation should be compared with firms that have similar characteristics and that are still operated by the public sector. These public firms would be assumed to be the counterfactual of the privatized ones. In most cases, it is hard to identify a comparable firm; hence, most of the literature compares the evolution of selected indicators before and after the change in ownership. This analysis uses the same before-and-after comparison with some important innovations that allow for the separation of transition versus long-run effects and control for time trends.

The analysis is separated into three distinct periods:

- The pretransition or preprivatization period, referring to the three years before the transition period;
- The transition period, starting two years before the privatization or concession was awarded—an approximation of when the reform was announced—and ending one year after the awarding;[10]
- The post-transition or postprivatization period, referring to the four years after the transition.

This segmentation helps identify the impact of the reform or transition process on firms. Governments often implemented drastic changes—such as labor force reductions and tariff restructuring—to make public companies more attractive to private bidders before the sale. In other cases, public managers may have had fewer incentives to perform well at the end of their management period. Hence, it is preferable to attribute performance after the reform was announced to a transitional period rather than assume it to be normal behavior for either public or private operators. In addition, it is assumed that some delays in the changes are brought about by private intervention. For instance, it generally takes time for private investments related to quality or coverage enhancements to be designed and executed.

An illustration of the importance of transitional effects can be seen in figure 4.1. The figure shows how the average number of employees in electricity distribution fell faster during the transition period than during both the pretransition and post-transition periods.

Not taking transition effects into account—by simply comparing data from before and after the ownership change—can bias the results. The difference between an analysis with and without a transition period is

Figure 4.1 Transitional Effects on Employment: Electricity
Distribution

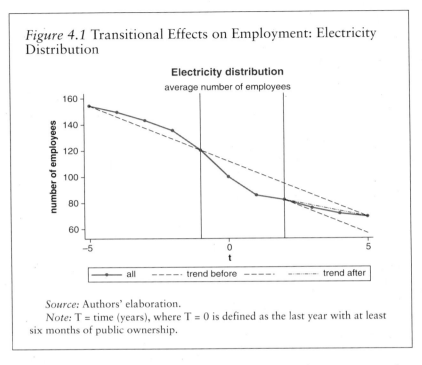

Source: Authors' elaboration.
Note: T = time (years), where T = 0 is defined as the last year with at least
six months of public ownership.

shown in figure 4.2. The figure depicts changes in the average number
of electricity connections in Latin America. T = 0 is defined as the last
year with at least six months of public ownership. Figure 4.2, panel A,
assumes only two periods: public and private ownership. If there actually
were transition effects, however (as shown in panel B), the transition effects
would be split erroneously between the public and private periods shown
in Panel A. Using the example shown, the performance during the public
period is overestimated and performance during the private period is under-
estimated. This is illustrated using the mean values shown in the figure.

For the analysis in this book, the differences across the three periods
are measured and tested for statistical significance using a means and
medians analysis and a separate econometric regression analysis, described
in appendix 2.

New Methodology: Distinguishing Levels from Trends

The previous section was concerned with measuring the changes in levels
of different indicators. However, certain indicators tend to change over
time independent of ownership type. Examples include number of subscribers, output, and coverage.[11] Hence, it is more interesting to look at

Figure 4.2 Transition versus Nontransition Period Comparison

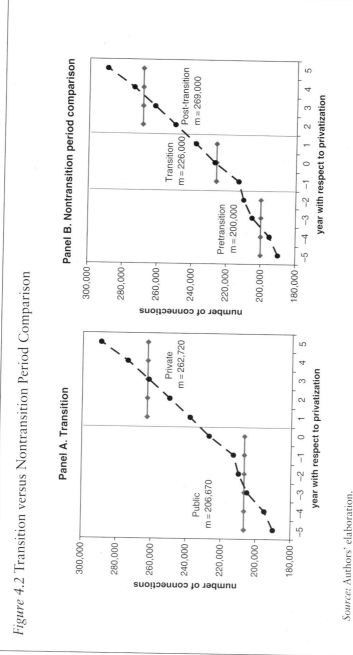

Panel A. Transition

Panel B. Nontransition period comparison

Source: Authors' elaboration.

Note: m = mean; T = 0 is defined as the last year with at least six months of public ownership.

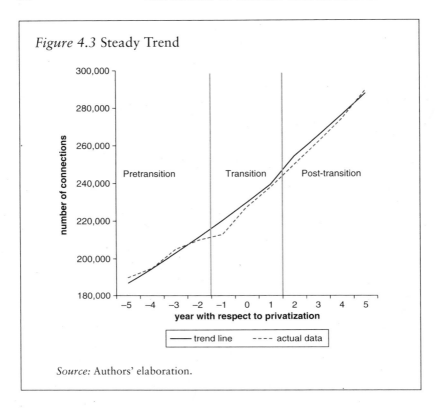

Figure 4.3 Steady Trend

Source: Authors' elaboration.

how the trends of such indicators evolve. Indeed, if trends are not taken into account, then one risks falsely attributing the natural evolution of the indicator to the change in ownership. Figure 4.3 uses the same data as figure 4.2 but adds a trend line. After controlling for the trend, the only change that can be linked to the ownership change is the small jump seen between the transition and post-transition periods. In this case, the jump does not change the slope of the trend line.

Trends are controlled for in both of the approaches described below. The means and medians analysis looks at differences in growth rates across the three periods. The econometric analysis uses a model that analyzes growth rate changes, as well as a model that accounts for firm-specific time trends.

Means and Medians Analysis

This approach compares means and medians of the different variables across the three periods: preprivatization (pretransition), transition, and postprivatization (post-transition).[12] First, changes in the *levels* of the different variables were analyzed. The actual data can be found in table A3.1 (electricity), table A3.4 (telecommunications), and table A3.10 (water and sewage); an example for the electricity distribution output variables is shown in table 4.4. The series was normalized, defining the value 100 for the last year with at least six months of public ownership (T = 0).[13] The average level of each (normalized) indicator for the three periods of analysis is shown in columns (1), (2), and (3) of table 4.4 and the appendix 3 tables. Next, the average change in levels between these three periods was computed: column (4) presents the difference between the transition period average level and the preprivatization period average level. Column (5) presents the average change in levels from the transition to the following period, and column (6) shows the total change in levels from the preprivatization period to the postprivatization period.[14] For each indicator, the tables present the mean, median (p50), standard deviation (sd), and number of firms (N) considered. In columns (7), (8), and (9), the tables show the results of statistical tests for whether the differences presented in columns (4) to (6) are significant. In short, this analysis indicates whether the means or medians of the indicators are truly different across periods with a 90 percent, 95 percent, or 99 percent degree of confidence.

Second, changes in average *growth* of the variables were measured using the same methodology that was used to analyze the change in *levels* described above. The results of the analysis are available in table A3.2 (electricity), table A3.6 (telecommunications), and table A3.11.

Econometric Analysis

A second approach using regression analysis is used to complement the means and medians analysis results. In this approach, the privatization can be thought of as a treatment; and the regression is designed to isolate the effects of the treatment, similar to a drug trial in medicine. In econometric terms, the regression includes dummy variables for the transition and post-transition periods. After controlling for other relevant factors within the regression, the significance of the dummy variables is tested to determine whether or not the treatment has had a demonstrable effect. The size of the coefficient on the dummy variables provides information about the size of the impact. This approach accounts for firm-level fixed effects that are not observable to the econometrician, such as management quality, initial conditions, size, density of the network, and so on. It does so by assuming that these variables are constant for each firm over time; hence, they can be isolated from the privatization effects within the regression. More econometric details behind this approach can be found in appendix 2.[15]

Table 4.4 Example of Means and Medians Analysis in Levels Output—Electricity Distribution

		Mean			Difference in levels			T-stat (Z-stat) for difference in means (medians) in levels		
		Preprivate (1)	Transition (2)	Postprivate (3)	(2)–(1) (4)	(3)–(2) (5)	(3)–(1) (6)	(2)–(1) (7)	(3)–(2) (8)	(3)–(1) (9)
Variable	Statistics									
Outputs										
Residential	mean	85.83	102.26	120.48	17.32	17.11	35.16	−16.209***	−17.493***	−16.809***
connections	p50	85.94	102.00	119.59	17.11	16.55	34.33	−7.843***	−7.306***	−7.459***
	sd	9.20	2.53	10.04	9.68	8.76	16.94			
	N	82	116	74	82	74	71			
MWh sold	mean	82.29	102.67	119.22	20.82	15.60	36.74	−13.119***	−11.882***	−7.554***
per year	p50	82.59	101.20	117.13	19.88	15.17	34.60	−7.399***	−6.945***	−6.128***
	sd	14.11	6.44	21.12	14.28	17.77	25.69			
	N	81	116	74	81	74	69			

Source: Author's calculation.

Note: MWh = Megawatt hour; sd = standard deviation; N = number of observations.
* Significant at 10 percent; ** significant at 5 percent; *** significant at 1 percent.

The results of the econometric analysis are shown in table A3.3 (electricity), table A3.6 (telecommunications), table A3.7 (telecom, including liberalization), and table A3.12 (water). Table 4.5 contains an excerpt from table A3.3 showing four of the electricity distribution variables. A semi-logarithmic functional form is used, meaning that the regressions are run using the logs of each variable. Each column in each model of the tables is from a separate regression for which the log level of each indicator is used as the dependent variable. Two dummy variables are used: one for the transition period, and one for the post-transition (postprivatization) period. The transition dummy variable equals 1 starting two years before the privatization or concession was awarded and continuing for all years thereafter. The post-transition dummy equals 1 for all years after the transition period, that is, starting one year after the privatization was awarded.

Three different model specifications are used. Model 1 does not include firm-specific time trends. Model 2 uses the same specification, but corrects for firm-specific time trends by adding an extra coefficient to the regression equation that captures the time trend of the variable of interest for each firm. Model 3 uses growth in each indicator as the dependent variable, rather than log levels. Standard errors are shown in parentheses beneath the coefficients, and levels of statistical significance are noted with asterisks.

To make sense of the coefficients, they must first undergo a simple transformation. The percentage impact of each indicator is given by $e^{\delta}-1$ where δ is the coefficient.[16] For instance, the transition dummy coefficient for number of connections in Model 1 of table 4.5 is 0.150. The transformation yields an impact of 16.2 percent, meaning that the number of connections was 16.2 percent higher during the transition years than during the preprivatization years. Similarly, the post-transition dummy of 0.176 becomes 19.2 percent, meaning that the number of connections after the transition (postprivatization) was 19.2 percent higher than during the transition period.

The models use Feasible Generalized Least Square (FGLS), which is preferred over Ordinary Least Square (OLS), because it corrects for heteroskedasticity (potential nonspherical errors). For the sake of completeness, the regressions were also run using OLS, although the results are not reported here. The estimates are slightly larger than the FGLS estimates, though qualitatively similar.

Adding Contract and Regulatory Characteristics

A second part of the econometric analysis incorporated the contract and regulatory characteristics described in appendix 2. Specifically, dummies were built for each of the variables described in table 4.3 and then interacted with the transition and post-transition dummies described above. Similar to the first part of the econometric analysis, regression models were run with

Table 4.5 Example of Econometric Analysis—Electricity Distribution

	(1) Number of connections	(2) Energy sold per year	(3) Number of employees
Model 1: Log levels without firm-specific time trend			
Transition	0.150***	0.201***	–0.307***
(t >= –1)	(0.005)	(0.007)	(0.016)
Post-transition	0.176***	0.169***	–0.193***
(t >= 2)	(0.005)	(0.007)	(0.016)
Observations	823	808	586
Model 2: Log levels with firm-specific time trend			
Transition	–0.002	0.040***	–0.054***
(t >= –1)	(0.002)	(0.005)	(0.013)
Post-transition	0.009***	–0.014***	0.047***
(t >= 2)	(0.002)	(0.005)	(0.013)
Observations	823	808	586
Model 3: Growth			
Transition	0.001	–0.002	–0.050***
(t >= –1)	(0.001)	(0.003)	(0.008)
Post-transition	–0.003***	–0.027***	0.064***
(t >= 2)	(0.001)	(0.003)	(0.008)
Observations	803	783	566

Source: Authors' elaboration.

Note: Standard errors in parentheses.

* Significant at 10 percent; ** significant at 5 percent; *** significant at 1 percent.

and without firm-specific time trends. Because of a lack of variation across some of the contract and regulatory characteristics, observations from the three sectors—electricity, telecom, and water—were pooled to achieve more robust results. Chapter 9 contains a detailed explanation of these results, and appendix 2 contains more technical details about how the additional characteristics were added to the original regression specifications.

Endogeneity and Selection Bias

The econometric analysis is potentially subject to endogeneity concerns. Endogeneity means that the independent variables, that is, the transition and post-transition dummies, might be influenced by the dependent variables—for example number of connections, amount of energy sold, and so on—instead of the other way around. This is also known as reverse causality, and it could cause the regression results to be biased. Several hypotheses for endogeneity exist. First, the government could decide to privatize only high-performing firms that have a good chance of being sold. Second, countries with plummeting financial performances may have higher incentives to privatize to acquire much-needed revenue. Third, private investors may be more interested in firms with higher expected rates of return. These factors indicate that the decision to privatize may not be viewed as an exogenous event that can be considered fixed in repeated sampling (Ros 1999).

Endogeneity associated with selection bias—the possibility that only certain types of firms were privatized—should not be a concern in most cases. Most countries opted for widespread privatization, especially in fixed telecommunications and electricity, rather than just picking a few winners to offer to the private sector. The pervasive nature of privatization is shown in the country maps in figure 2.5a and b. In electricity distribution, only 3 percent of households in the region were served by a private company in 1990; by 2003, this number exceeded 60 percent. In fixed telecommunications, the percentage of households served by the private sector leapt from 3 percent in 1990 to more than 86 percent in 2003. For the water sector, this argument may not be assumed, because the number of connections in private hands by 2003 was only 11 percent.

Selection bias potentially could be associated with the sampling technique. For instance, if data were only available for the best-performing privatized firms, then the sample results could be biased. It is argued that sample selection bias is not a problem here—especially in electricity and telecom—because of the comprehensive nature of the database. The database targets all utilities that changed from public to private ownership during the 1990s, plus a few that changed during the 1980s. To the best of the authors' knowledge, data were collected for all telecommunication and electricity distribution companies that fall into that category. In the water sector, the authors believe that most of the privatized utilities with more than 25,000 connections are included in the database. For some utilities in the water sector, however, particularly those with fewer than 25,000 connections, it was not possible to collect information before private participation.

Another endogeneity concern is related to timing. For instance, either higher- or lower-performing firms could have been sold first when an economy was performing poorly. One way to counter that concern is through instrumental variables (IVs). As always, the difficult part of an IV approach is finding proper instruments. In this case, macroeconomic variables were selected. They have properties that are related to privatization decisions, and in general, they are independent of the variables under study. In other words, it is assumed that privatization decisions are driven somewhat by the strength of the economy, yet the strength of the economy does not affect variables like number of electricity connections, quality, and prices.

A problem with the IV approach arises from the fact that, in some sectors, companies in the same country were privatized in different years. This is not a problem for the telecommunications sector, which generally consists of large, national-level companies. For electricity distribution and water and sewerage, however, it would be ideal to have additional instruments to take the country-level variation into account. These instruments should include data at the state or city level, making the collection of the data complex. Because of the unavailability of subnational data, however, the IV approach is run using only national-level variables.

There are two possible explanations if timing endogeneity has indeed occurred: either the best firms were privatized first or the worst firms were privatized first. If the best firms were privatized first, then privatization would be expected to bring a relatively small improvement in performance indicators. Using IVs would be expected to increase the value of the privatization dummy variables, as the bias toward the privatization of better-performing firms is controlled for. Conversely, if the worst firms were privatized first, then a relatively large performance jump would be expected. Instrumental variables would then result in smaller privatization coefficients.

The results of the IV approach are consistent with the FGLS analysis. Only the IV results for telecommunications are presented (see table A3.9) because the telecommunications privatizations tended to occur at the national level—meaning the national-level macroeconomic variables are reasonable instruments. Moreover, most of the IV coefficients resulted in higher absolute values, suggesting that the results of the FGLS analysis are a lower bound for the total effect of the reforms. These results would suggest that, if anything, better-performing firms tend to be privatized first.

Notes

1. Privatization or private ownership in this context refers to private participation in general, particularly divestitures and concession contracts.

2. The database contains 11 companies privatized in the 1980s. Nine of these companies were in the electricity distribution sector (seven in Chile in several years during the decade and two in Brazil in 1988 and 1989) (see table 5.4). The remaining two were telecommunications companies in Chile (privatized in 1987) and Jamaica (privatized in 1989).

3. As quality indexes vary across countries, the most similar indexes were collected to compare their evolution across time, rather than absolute quality levels.

4. Bid, direct adjudication, invitation, petition, or request.

5. Highest canon, highest price, tariff, lowest government subsidy, investment plan, shorter duration of the concession, or multiple criteria.

6. Operation, BOT, BOO, privatization, and so on.

7. Law, decree, contract, or license.

8. Revenue cap, price cap, rate of return, or no regulation.

9. The government, the concessionaire, both, or nobody.

10. A review of this arbitrary period definition was performed with several country analysts, and this criterion seems to respond to most of the cases.

11. In contrast, price and quality might be better analyzed using simple levels, because they probably do not exhibit a natural trend over time.

12. A variety of studies have used a similar means and medians methodology, beginning with Megginson, Nash, and van Randenborgh (1994).

13. When the LAC averages were calculated, each firm received an equal weight. In other words, the data are not weighted by firm size to keep large firms from dominating the results.

14. The values shown in columns (4), (5), and (6) in table 4.4 are the *means of the differences*. In other words, the difference between two time periods is first calculated for each firm with observations in both time periods. Then, the differences are averaged to obtain the mean of the differences. An alternative method, which was not employed, is to (i) first calculate the mean for each time period based on data from all firms with observations in that time period—shown in columns (1), (2), and (3); then (ii) subtract the mean of the first time period from the mean of the second time period. This alternative method takes the *difference of the means* and does not make sense here, because the numbers of observations in each time period is different (due to data limitations). In fact, comparing means from samples of different size would lead to erroneous results. For that reason, subtracting column (2) from (1) does not equal (4), unless the sample of firms used for column (1) is identical to that for (2), which only occurs in the case of an output measure for telecommunications (see table A3.4).

15. This approach follows the program evaluation literature. See Heckman and Robb (1985), Boardman and Vining (1989), and Ros (1999).

16. Coefficients lower than |0.18| can be interpreted as the percentage impact with an error smaller than 10 percent.

5

The Impact on Electricity Distribution

Introduction

This chapter summarizes the elements of the electricity sector reform in the Latin America and Caribbean (LAC) Region and evaluates its impact. It uses an original data set built by the authors, using official documentation from 116 electricity distribution companies in Latin American countries for the years before and after their privatization. Two complementary methodologies were used to learn about the effects of changes in ownership: (i) a means and medians analysis and (ii) an econometric analysis. For a description of these methodologies, see chapter 4. The full results of the means and medians analysis and econometric analysis, including statistical significance, are shown in appendix 3. This chapter synthesizes the results from the two methodologies, presenting summaries of the impact, geared toward policy makers in the following areas: outputs and coverage, employment, labor productivity, efficiency, and prices. As described in chapter 4, the period under analysis is separated into three parts: preprivatization (pretransition), a three-year transition period, and postprivatization (post-transition). This allows for the study of short- versus long-term effects. The main results of the analysis are summarized in each section and in the conclusion of the chapter.

The Privatization Process

The reforms of the electricity sector in most countries in LAC in the 1990s were motivated by poor performance of the public model in which the state was policy maker, regulator, investor, and monopoly provider of electricity supply service. Lack of incentives for efficiency in the operation and expansion of the sector, and the politicization of policy decisions and management of sector utilities resulted in high electricity losses and operations and maintenance costs, investments in generation that did not respond to least-cost principles, relatively low electricity coverage, electricity tariffs that did not reflect economic costs, difficulties in mobilizing the financial resources required for the expansion of the power system, poor reliability of service, and recurrent financial losses of state-owned enterprises (SOEs), which finally were reflected on unsustainable fiscal deficits.

The reform of the electricity sector in LAC, which was part of a broader reform of the public sector based on the introduction of market principles, aimed to solve the main problems that besieged the public sector model: improve the quality, reliability, and efficiency of electricity services; improve the government's fiscal position; and increase affordable access to energy services for the poor. To achieve these objectives, a market-oriented reform promoted the following: (i) the separation of roles of policy making, regulation, and service provider, limiting the role of the state to policy making and regulation, and relying on the private sector to be the main investor and provider of electricity service; and (ii) the introduction of competition wherever possible and of economic regulation in the natural monopolies to improve economic efficiency. This market model would improve the government's fiscal position and ensure the financial sustainability of the sector by promoting the participation of private investment and the establishment of competitive prices for generation and cost-covering tariffs for transmission and distribution. It would be sustainable from a social and political point of view by improving access to energy services by the poor, based on a scheme of efficient subsidies.

All countries in LAC, with the exception of Paraguay, Suriname, and the small island states in the Caribbean Community (CARICOM) introduced or attempted to introduce reforms along these lines. Tables 5.1, 5.2, and 5.3 summarize the characteristics of the power reform in most countries in the region. The differences are notable in the extent of competition and private participation. Three basic market models were used in the region: (i) a vertically integrated monopoly and independent power producers (IPPs) that sell their production or excess generation to the monopoly at avoided cost or at a price determined by competitive bidding; (ii) a single buyer of electricity that purchases the required energy under long-term contracts following competitive bidding procedures; and (iii) a competitive wholesale power market in which generators, distributors, marketers, and large consumers trade electricity in spot transactions and long-term contracts. At the lower end of competition are those countries like Mexico and Costa Rica that maintained a vertically integrated monopoly or countries like República Bolivariana de Venezuela and Uruguay that approved a new law establishing a wholesale market but for different reasons have not implemented the law. The single-buyer scheme is working in some of the large island states of CARICOM, Honduras, and Guyana, which represent a marginal percentage

Table 5.1 Power Sector Reform in Latin America and the
Caribbean

% demand	1%	33%	47%	18%	
Competition ❂❂					
Unbundling, wholesale power market, large consumers		Ecuador	Brazil, Colombia, Guatemala, El Salvador, Nicaragua, Dominican Republic	Argentina, Bolivia, Chile, Peru, Panamá	65%
Single buyer & IPPs		Guyana	Trinidad and Tobago, Honduras	Jamaica	2%
Vertically integrated monopoly and IPPs	Uruguay	Costa Rica, Mexico	Suriname		24%
No competition	Paraguay	Venezuela, R.B. de		Most island states	9%
	SOE	low	medium	high	% demand
			private participation ❂		

Source: World Bank 2007d.
Note: The "% demand" row and column refer to the percentage of total demand
in Latin America and the Caribbean that is associated with the given level of
competition (vertical axis) and private participation (horizontal axis).
IPP = independent power producer; SOE = state-owned enterprise.

of electricity demand in LAC. Most of the countries in Central and South
America, representing about 65 percent of electricity demand in LAC, have
implemented a wholesale power market (see table 5.1).

The extent of private participation is not directly related to the scope
of competition in all cases. For example, the smaller island states in the
Caribbean have high private participation with very limited competition.
On the other extreme, Ecuador adopted a competitive wholesale power
market but failed to attract private participation. In most cases, however, private participation increases as competition increases. At the lower
levels of competition, except for Jamaica, private participation is limited
to generation in IPPs. At the high level of competition, the private sector
has a substantial participation mostly in distribution and generation.

Unbundling does not guarantee effective competition. Effective competition in the wholesale market can be assessed better by the extent of
horizontal unbundling (number of generators and distribution companies

Table 5.2 LAC Wholesale Electricity Markets: Extent of Unbundling and Retail Competition

| | No. of gencos | No. of self-gen. & IPPs | No. of transcos | No. of distcos | No. of marketers | Large consumers | |
						Threshold	No. (market share)
High degree of competition							
Argentina	41		57	62	46	5 MW, reduced to 30 kW	1,496 (21% of demand)
Brazil	25	89	54	43	42	10 MW, reduced to 500 kW	577 (21% demand)
Chile	12	6	4	31	0	2 MW, reduced to 500 kW	30% demand
Colombia	66		11	32	67	2 MW, reduced to 100 kW	4,206 (31% demand)
El Salvador	4	10	1	5 (2 groups)	5	Full retail competition	5 (10% demand)
Guatemala	10	12	1	3 + 13(small municipal)	7	100 kW	32% demand
Peru	18		6	33	0	1 MW	46% demand

Table 5.2 LAC Wholesale Electricity Markets: Extent of Unbundling and Retail Competition *(continued)*

	No. of gencos	No. of self gen. & IPPs	No. of transcos	No. of distcos	No. of marketers	Large consumers	
						Threshold	No. (market share)
Low degree of competition							
Bolivia	8		2	6	0	1 MW	2
Costa Rica	1	4 small cooperatives and municipalities, 30 small renewable IPPs	1	1+6 small municipal and cooperatives	0	No	0
Dominican Republic	11	2	1	3	0	2 MW reduced to 200 kW	
Ecuador	13	16	1	20	0	1 MW	11% of demand
Honduras	1	22	1	1	0	1 MW	1 (2%)
Mexico	1	403 power stations (362 self-generators, 18 IPP, 36 cogen)	1	1	0	No	0
Nicaragua	9	1	1	1	0	2 MW	9 (8% demand)
Panama	8	10	1	3	0	100 kW	5 (2% demand)
Uruguay	2	1	1	1	0	250 kW	0
Venezuela, R. B. de	07 vertically integrated monopolies, 2 distributors, 4 generators				0	No	0

Source: World Bank 2007d.

Note: Gencos = generation companies; self-gen. & IPPs = self-generation and independent power producers; transcos = transmission companies; distcos = distribution companies; kW = kilowatt; MW = megawatt; cogen = combined cycle power generation.

Table 5.3 Electricity Market in LAC

	Regulatory agency	Vertical unbundling	Horizontal generation breakup	Horizontal distribution breakup	Entry of IPPs	Creation of wholesale market	Introduction of competition
Argentina	✓	✓	✓	✓	✓	✓	✓
Bolivia	✓	✓	✓	✓	✓	✓	
Brazil	✓	✓			✓	✓	
Chile	✓	✓	✓	✓	✓	✓	✓
Colombia	✓	✓			✓	✓	✓
El Salvador	✓	✓	✓	✓	✓	✓	✓
Guatemala	✓	✓		✓	✓	✓	✓
Mexico	✓				✓		
Nicaragua	✓	✓	✓		✓	✓	
Panama	✓						
Peru	✓	✓	✓	✓	✓	✓	✓

Source: Authors' elaboration.
Note: IPP = independent power producer; LAC = Latin America and the Caribbean.

participating in the market) and by the number and market share of large consumers that have the option to select the supplier and negotiate the conditions and prices of energy supply. Table 5.2 shows the countries classified in two categories: high and low degrees of competition. Most of the countries with a high degree of competition have implemented substantial horizontal unbundling, have reduced the threshold for large consumers below 500 kilowatts (kW), and have a liberalized market with a market share above 21 percent. In the smaller markets, which have introduced retail competition for large consumers, competition in the market is not effective because the industrial market is small.

Most countries in LAC progressed in the 1990s to the most advanced stages of competition and privatization in a market-oriented reform of the power sector (see table 5.3). Separation or roles, unbundling, competition, and private participation were the main instruments used to increase efficiency, improve the government's fiscal position, and increase access to electricity service for the poor. Even the few countries (Mexico, República Bolivariana de Venezuela, Costa Rica, Uruguay, Paraguay, and the small islands in the Caribbean) that decided to maintain vertically integrated monopolies have introduced reforms to facilitate participation of private IPPs. Power sector reforms based on competitive wholesale markets or single-buyer schemes were effective in mobilizing private capital to expand the generation capacity. Table 5.1 summarizes the extent of electricity market reform in Latin American countries (a more complete description is presented in appendix 4).

Private participation in electricity in Latin America mainly involved vertical unbundling and the privatization or concessioning of electricity generation, transportation, and distribution. Most of the competition arose in the generation stage, and in the bidding for transportation and distribution firms. Once the concessions were awarded, these two subsectors maintained monopolistic characteristics. Meanwhile, all the countries created a regulatory board to set the quality standards, regulate the fares, and monitor the compliance of the privatized firms. The following paragraphs present illustrative examples from Chile, Argentina, Bolivia, Peru, and Brazil. Table 5.4 reviews the chronology of electricity distribution privatizations in LAC.

In Chile, the privatization process started at the beginning of the 1980s and was completed in 1989 when Corporación de Fomento de la Producción (CORFO) sold their share in Empresa Nacional de Electricidad S.A. (ENDESA). The government owned 80 percent of the distribution segment, and ENDESA and CHILECTRA were the main companies. The process consisted of six regional subsidiaries for distribution[1] and two generational subsidiaries from ENDESA. Additionally, CHILECTRA was divided into CHILGENER (generation), CHILQUINTA, and CHILMETRO (see Moguillansky 1997; OLADE 1996). See appendix 5 for a list of the utility company abbreviations.

Table 5.4 Chronology of the Privatizations of Electricity Distribution in LAC by Country

Country	Year	Privatized firms
Argentina	1992	EDENOR, EDESUR, and EDELAP
	1993	EDESAL
	1995	EDELAR, EDET, and EDEFOR
	1996	EDESA, ESJSA, EDEERSA, EDERSA, EJESA, and EDECAT
	1997	EDEA, EDEN, and EDES
	1998	EDEMSA
Bolivia	1996	CESSA, CRE, ELECTROPAZ, ELFEC, ELFEO, SEPSA, and SETAR
Brazil	1985	CAIUA
	1989	CELTINS
	1996	CFLO, FORCEL
	1996	CERJ, LIGHT
	1997	AES SUL, CEMAT, CEMIG, CENF, COELBA, ENERSUL, and ESCELSA
	1998	CELPA, COELCE, COSERN, CPFL, ELEKTRO, ELECTROPAULO, ENERGIPE, and RGE
	1999	BANDEIRANTE, CEB, CELB, CELESC, COCEL, COPEL, CPEE, and SULGIPE
	2000	CELB, CELPA, DEMEI, MUXFELDT, and SAELPA
	2001	CEAL, CEMAR, CEPISA, CERON, ELECTROCAR, MANAUS, and NOVAPALMA
Chile	1980–81	FRONTEL and SAESA
	1984	CGE and CONAFE
	1985	EDELMAG and TIL TIL
	1986	EMEC
	1987	CHILECTRA and CHILQUINTA
	1989	ELECDA, ELIQSA, EMELARI, and EMELAT
	1992	CURICO, COOPREL, and COPELEC
	1996	EDELAYSEN and EEC

(continued)

Table 5.4 Chronology of the Privatizations of Electricity
Distribution in LAC by Country *(continued)*

Country	Year	Privatized Firms
Colombia	1997	CODENSA and EPSA
	1998	ELECTROCosta and ELECTROCaribe
El Salvador	1998	CAESS, DEL SUR, CLESA, EEO, and DEUSEM
Guatemala	1999	EEGSA, DEOCSA, and DEORSA
Nicaragua	2000	DISNORTE and DISSUR
Panama	1998	EDEMET, EDECHI, and ELEKTRA
Peru	1994	EDELNOR and LUZ DEL SUR
	1996	CHANGAY and EDECAÑETE
	1997	ELECTRO SUR MEDIO
	1998	ELECTRO CENTRO, ELECTRO NOROESTE, ELECTRO NORTE, and ELECTRO NORTE MEDIO

Source: Authors' elaboration.
Note: See appendix 5 for a list of the utility company abbreviations.

In the case of Argentina, the process started with the division of Servicios Eléctricos de Gran Buenos Aires (Electrical Services of Greater Buenos Aires, SEGBA) into three areas in 1992. Two of the new companies, EDENOR and EDESUR, each covered half of the city of Buenos Aires and the area of Greater Buenos Aires, while a third one, EDELAP, covered the area of Greater La Plata. These companies covered almost 40 percent of the population of the country. The rest of the distribution in the country was carried out by state public companies and small local cooperatives. The provinces of San Luis, La Rioja, Tucuman, and Formosa were the first to grant concessions for their distribution of electricity. In 1996, ESEBA,[2] the biggest company after SEGBA, was divided into three firms: EDEA, EDEN, and EDES. The provinces of San Juan, Jujuy, Entre Rios, Rio Negro, Salta, Catamarca, and Mendoza later replicated the process. Currently, around 70 percent of the population is served by private companies.[3] See appendix 5 for a list of the utility company abbreviations.

Before 1994, the electrical industry in Bolivia was vertically integrated into the SIN (National Interconnected System), which was composed of two national companies: ENDE (National Enterprise of Electricity), a government enterprise with a generation, transmission, and distribution monopoly, and COBEE (Bolivian Company of Electrical Energy), which had a generation, transmission, and distribution monopoly in the cities of La Paz, Oruro, and El Alto. In 1994, the Congress enacted the Electrical Act that allowed the vertical unbundling of these companies. The new distribution firms that originated from ENDE were CRE, ELFEC, CESSA, and SEPSA; and from COBEE, the new firms were ELECTROPAZ, ELFEO, and SETAR—CENTRAL (Cárdenas 2003). See appendix 5 for a list of the utility company abbreviations.

In Peru, the government approved a law that unbundled power generation from electricity distribution and transmission in 1992. A regulatory body for private investment in energy (*Organismo Supervisor de Inversión en Energía*, OSINERG) was also created. Between 1994 and 1998, privatizations led to 14 private distribution and generation companies, and in 2004, the privatized companies represented 79 percent of the distribution service. Despite performance improvements, public opposition to continuing the privatization process has been considerable (see box 2.2). In fact, an attempt to privatize two generation companies in Arequipa in 2002 failed because of violent public protests. This event has frozen future electricity privatizations, despite the fact that a number of important generation and distribution firms remain in public hands. Furthermore, four regional electricity companies in the north and center of the country that were sold to a local group under favorable credit conditions ended up reverting to state control (box 5.1).

In Brazil, generation and transmission activities were historically the responsibility of the federal company Eletrobras, while distribution was largely undertaken by state utilities. In 1995, a sector reform process initiated the vertical unbundling and privatization of the sector. Because of political resistance, the unbundling process was never completed, so that 58 percent of national generating capacity remained in the hands of vertically integrated Eletrobras subsidiaries. However, 23 percent of generation assets and 64 percent of distribution were successfully privatized. As part of the reform process, the government introduced an independent system operator (*Operador Nacional do Sistema Elétrico*, ONS) to be responsible for central cost-based dispatch, and a new regulatory agency (*Agência Nacional de Energia Elétrica*, ANEEL) to supervise the sector. The incomplete implementation of the original reform model left a variety of structural problems, however. For instance, many distribution companies continued to have significant interests in generation, introducing the danger of uncompetitive self-dealing arrangements for power purchase. Another issue that has since been addressed was restrictions on distributors that prevented them from passing along costs beyond their control to customers.

The important conclusion is that most of the LAC countries, which represent more than 60 percent of the demand in the region, progressed to the most advanced stages of competition and privatization in the 1990s. Therefore, a wealth of experience can be used to assess the progress

Box 5.1 A Failed Electricity Privatization in Peru

In the 1990s, four electric distribution enterprises in the northern and central parts of Peru were included in the privatization process. The state was selling 60 percent of its shares in the enterprises according to the following terms: 30 percent initially, and the remaining 30 percent could be bought by the buyer within the 12th and the 24th month after the contract was signed. The price for the remaining 30 percent was the one offered in the winning bid plus 3 percent annually. There were favorable credit conditions to purchase the initial 30 percent. The buyer could pay 10 percent in cash and the rest in 24 semiannual installments. The interest rate was London Interbank Offered Rate (LIBOR) plus 2 percent and there was a grace period of up to three years during which the buyer only paid interest. As collateral, the buyer put a letter of credit for 20 percent of the debt as well as the enterprises' shares. If the buyer did not exercise its option to buy the remaining 30 percent two years after the contract was signed, the state was free to sell them.

To guarantee that the new buyer could control the enterprises before exercising its option to purchase the remaining 30 percent, a shareholder pact was devised to ensure that the buyer would control the voting decisions of this additional 30 percent. A trust fund with these shares was set up for that purpose. In practical terms, the new buyer was granted voting powers for 60 percent of total shares by paying upfront for only 30 percent of them. Jose Rodríguez Banda S.A. offered the highest bid for all four companies and the contract was signed in December 1998.

The winning bids were considerably above base prices and, as time would confirm, overly optimistic. In fact, the buyer did not exercise the option to buy the remaining 30 percent of the shares within the period stipulated in the contract and hence the state regained the control of the enterprise. This was not a smooth process—the private owner alleged that the state did not honor several of its obligations in the contract. After some legal disputes, a settlement allowed the state to repurchase the shares, although at a lower price than the bidding price. With the proceeds of the shares plus an additional disbursement, the domestic investor canceled the initial debt for 30 percent of the shares. By the end of 2001, the four enterprises were back in full control of the Peruvian state.

Source: World Bank 2006.

made in achieving the reform objectives, namely, to improve the quality, reliability, and efficiency of electricity services; improve the government's fiscal position; and increase affordable access to energy services for the poor. Experience also makes it possible to analyze the main difficulties that threatened the sustainability of the reform, identify the main causes, and draw important lessons for the future.

Data

The countries analyzed were Argentina, Bolivia, Brazil, Chile, Colombia, El Salvador, Guatemala, Nicaragua, Panama, and Peru. The sample consists of unbalanced panel data that includes 116 firms[4] and 1,199 firm-year observations. Each of the firms included in the sample contains at least one year of preprivatization data. In fact, 98 of the 116 firms have information for at least the previous three years. Table 5.5 presents the definitions of the variables used in the authors' analysis.

Impact on Output and Coverage

Electricity Distribution: Output and Coverage Summary

The number of connections, energy sold each year, and coverage levels increased across all three periods—pretransition, transition, and post-transition—but effects were driven by trends. The trend in energy sold declined slightly after privatization.

Energy Sold

Two measures are used to estimate output: the megawatt hours (MWhs) of energy sold each year and the total number of connections at the end of each year. The amount of energy sold increased over all three periods: pretransition, transition, and post-transition (see figure 5.1). These increases were found to be statistically significant by both the means and median analysis (table A3.1) and the econometric analysis (table A3.3). According to the econometric analysis, the average amount of energy sold increased by 22.3 percent during the transition; the average[5] amount sold after the transition was 18.4 percent higher than transition levels. These estimates, as well as figure 5.1, indicate the existence of a time trend. In other words, output levels seem to exhibit a natural rate of growth that must be controlled for to isolate the impacts of privatization. The econometric results show that there was a slight improvement in the growth trend during the transition. After the transition (during the postprivatization phase), however, the growth trend in the number of MWhs sold seems to have slowed slightly.[6] Possible reasons for this include the following:

- An overall decrease in the average consumption per household, perhaps because of the increase in prices (see table 5.9).
- A change in the composition of the average household. Of those households that did receive electricity connections after a concession

Table 5.5 Description of Electricity Distribution Variables

Variable	Description
Output and coverage	
Number of connections	Total number of subscribers (residential and nonresidential), December of each year
Energy sold	Total energy sold per year (in MWh)
Coverage	Percent of houses with electrical connection (number of residential subscribers divided by the number of households in the covered area)
Employment	
Number of employees	Total number of employees
Efficiency	
Connections per employee	Number of connections divided by the number of employees
Energy per worker	Energy sold each year divided by the number of employees
Distributional losses	Energy lost in the distribution (due to technical losses and illegal connections)
Quality	
Duration	Average duration of interruptions per consumer (hours/year)
Frequency	Average frequency of interruptions per consumer (number/year)
Prices	
Average tariff (US$)	Average tariff for 1 MWh for a residential service in dollars (including fixed and variable costs), December of each year Variable was built with original data on nominal tariffs and converted using the exchange rate for each year
Average tariff (real local currency)	Average tariff for 1 MWh for a residential service in local currency of December 2000 Variable was built with original data on nominal tariffs and converted using Consumer Price Indexes

Source: Authors' elaboration.
Note: MWh = megawatt hours.

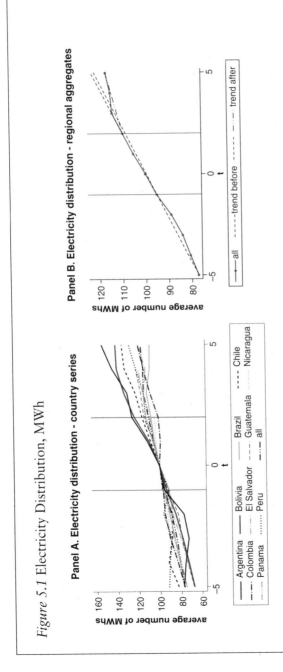

Figure 5.1 Electricity Distribution, MWh

Panel A. Electricity distribution - country series

Panel B. Electricity distribution - regional aggregates

Source: Authors' calculations.

Note: The x axis is time; t = 0 is the last year with at least six months of public ownership. The y axis is normalized at 100 when time = 0. The dotted connections in panel B show the trend; in the post-transition period, the extension of the "trend before" is shown, as well as the "trend after" the privatization. The "trend before" line is also transposed to originate at the same level as the "trend after" line, allowing for easier comparison.

MWh = Megawatt hour.

was awarded, it is very likely that they were mostly low-income families, with a smaller average consumption of energy.

• A reduction in distributional technical and commercial losses (see table 5.8). The data series was built using the total energy supplied to the distributional network, hence a reduction in losses could lead to a drop in MWh.

The results reported above might seem contradictory, so they are worth repeating. Specifically, the absolute amount of energy sold increased during all three periods, but the growth rate of energy sold slowed after privatization.

Figure 5.2 compares actual amounts of energy sold before and after the ownership transition. (In contrast to figure 5.1, the values are not normalized.) The figure shows that electricity distribution companies in Brazil are far larger than those in other countries. Companies in Argentina and Colombia score a distant second and third.

Number of Connections

The number of connections for electricity distribution increased significantly during the three periods.[7] According to the econometric analysis, the average level of connection numbers was 16.2 percent higher

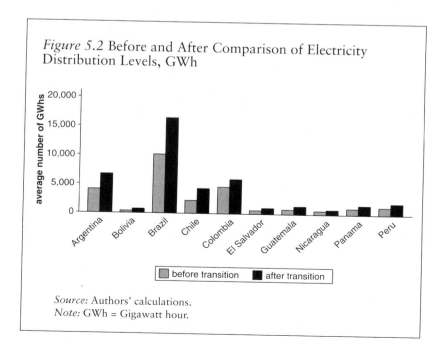

Figure 5.2 Before and After Comparison of Electricity Distribution Levels, GWh

Source: Authors' calculations.
Note: GWh = Gigawatt hour.

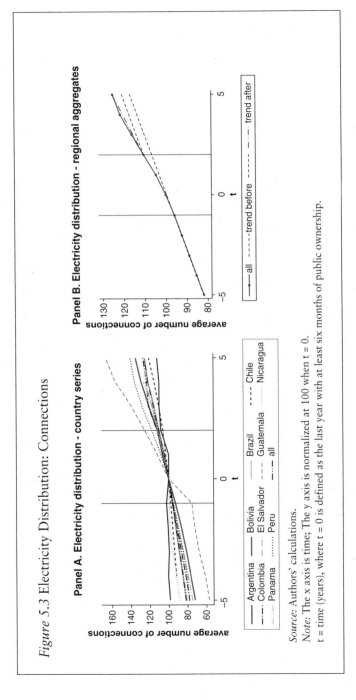

Figure 5.3 Electricity Distribution: Connections

Panel A. Electricity distribution - country series

Panel B. Electricity distribution - regional aggregates

Source: Authors' calculations.

Note: The x axis is time; The y axis is normalized at 100 when t = 0.
t = time (years), where t = 0 is defined as the last year with at least six months of public ownership.

during the transition than in the previous period. The average level after the transition was 19.2 percent higher than during the transition (table A3.3). These increases were found to be statistically significant by both the means and median analysis (table A3.1) and the econometric analysis (table A3.3). An examination of figure 5.3, however, shows that the increases largely followed a trend. The cross-country differences in the evolution of connection numbers potentially could be explained by differences in initial coverage conditions or differences in contract and regulatory characteristics. Contract and regulatory characteristics are explored in detail in chapter 9.

When comparing the actual number of average electricity connections across countries, it is clear that the companies in Brazil are by far the largest. Similar to the energy sold indicator, Argentina and Colombia rank second and third in terms of average connection numbers (figure 5.4).

Coverage

There were improvements in electricity distribution coverage across all three periods: the average increase during the transition was 5.4 percent, and the average increase after that (with respect to transition levels) was 8 percent. Like the output increases, the coverage increases were

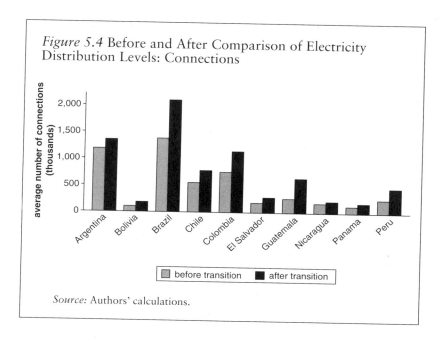

Figure 5.4 Before and After Comparison of Electricity Distribution Levels: Connections

Source: Authors' calculations.

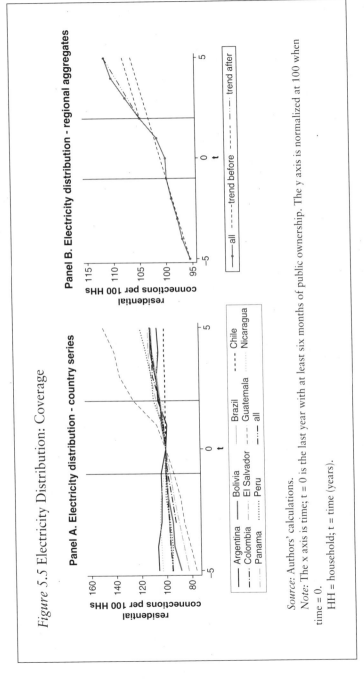

Figure 5.5 Electricity Distribution: Coverage

Panel A. Electricity distribution - country series

Panel B. Electricity distribution - regional aggregates

Source: Authors' calculations.

Note: The x axis is time; t = 0 is the last year with at least six months of public ownership. The y axis is normalized at 100 when time = 0.

HH = household; t = time (years).

statistically significant. But after controlling for time trends or when looking at changes in growth patterns, the impacts of privatization become negligible or difficult to discern (figure 5.5). Actual differences in coverage across countries can be seen in figure 5.6. Brazil overtook Argentina to have the highest coverage level—more than 95 percent—during the post-transition period, and Guatemala experienced the largest jump between the "before transition" and "after transition" periods.

Looking at the coverage rate also yields information about the evolution of the number of connections. One explanation for the increases in connection numbers discussed earlier in the section is that the growth in connections simply kept up with population growth. Analyzing the coverage rate, however, shows that this is not the case. Coverage increases show that the electricity distribution network expanded faster than the growth rate of the population.

Output (number of connections and energy sold each year) and coverage levels increased across all three periods, but effects were driven by trends. In other words, these outcomes would have occurred in the absence of privatization. The trend in energy sold declined slightly after privatization. Table 5.6 presents the results of the econometric analysis mentioned above; the asterisks indicate levels of statistical significance.

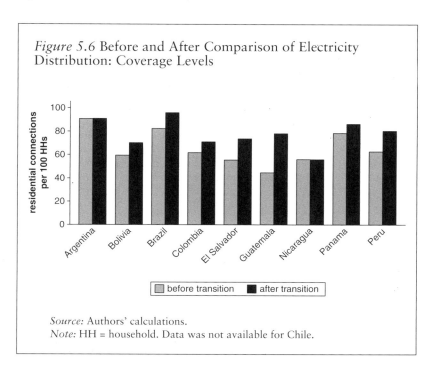

Figure 5.6 Before and After Comparison of Electricity Distribution: Coverage Levels

Source: Authors' calculations.
Note: HH = household. Data was not available for Chile.

Table 5.6 Electricity Distribution: Output and Coverage Results

	Energy sold (MWh)	Number of connections	Coverage
Percentage change in level			
Transition	22.3***	16.2***	5.4***
Post-transition	18.4***	19.2***	8.0***
Percentage change in level after controlling for time trend			
Transition	4.1***	–0.2	–0.7***
Post-transition	–1.4***	0.9***	0.9***
Percentage point change in annual growth rate			
Transition	–0.2	0.1	0.0
Post-transition	–2.7***	–0.3***	0.0

Source: Authors' calculations.

Note: The percentage change for the post-transition period is with respect to the level during the transition period. The annual growth change is the percentage point change in the annual growth rate with respect to the previous period. For example, if the transition annual growth rate for energy sold was 5.8 percent, then the post-transition annual growth rate would be 2.7 percent lower, or 3.1 percent.

*Significant at 10 percent; **significant at 5 percent; ***significant at 1 percent.

Impact on Employment

Electricity Distribution: Employment Summary

Employment levels dropped substantially during the transition, not controlling for time trends. They also fell after the transition, but to a lesser extent.

Most of the SOEs were characterized by having excess personnel. Hence, as expected, significant reductions in the number of employees clearly were observed across the three periods (figure 5.7).[8] Figure 5.8 highlights the tremendous size of the drops in absolute employment numbers, especially in the larger countries like Argentina, Brazil, and Colombia.

The literature found that, in some cases, the government reduced the number of employees before privatization to increase the value of the firms (Chong and López-de-Silanes 2003b). Investors often proved indifferent to these kinds of policies, however, and the value of the firms were unchanged or even reduced when the government applied layoff programs in advance. The basic explanation is selection issues: good employees often have incentives to leave while bad employees remain in the company (Chong and López-de-Silanes 2003a).

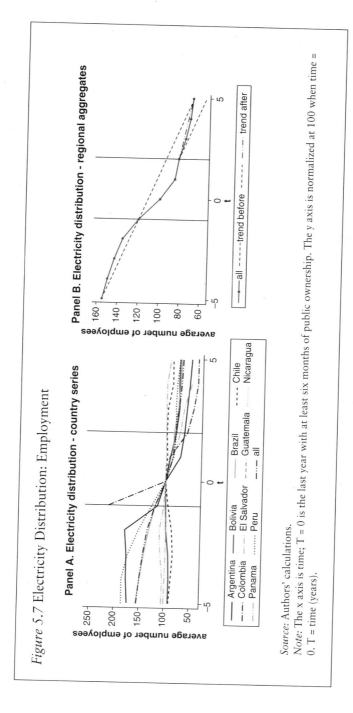

Figure 5.7 Electricity Distribution: Employment

Panel A. Electricity distribution - country series

Panel B. Electricity distribution - regional aggregates

Source: Authors' calculations.

Note: The x axis is time; T = 0 is the last year with at least six months of public ownership. The y axis is normalized at 100 when time = 0. T = time (years).

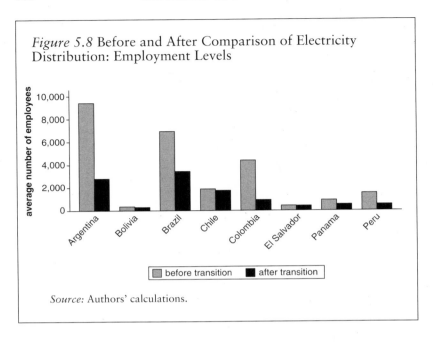

Figure 5.8 Before and After Comparison of Electricity Distribution: Employment Levels

Source: Authors' calculations.

Consistent with the literature, this analysis found that labor force reductions during the transition were substantially larger than those after. Specifically, the econometric analysis found a 26.4 percent drop in the number of employees during the transition; after the transition, there was an additional drop of 17.6 percent.[9]

After controlling for firm-specific time trends, the number of employees fell by 5.3 percent during the transition, and increased by 4.8 percent after the transition (with respect to transition levels).[10] When comparing labor force trends or growth rates before the transition to those after the transition, there is no statistically significant difference.[11] This confirms that the largest changes came during the transition years. Time trends for the employment indicator are *not* controlled for in the outcome summary, as was the case for output and coverage (table 5.6). It is not necessarily assumed that employment should be falling naturally over time. As a result, although the pre- and post-transition growth rates may be similar, the ultimate result is that privatization resulted in a drop in employment levels after the transition period.

Employment levels dropped substantially during the transition; they also fell after the transition, but to a lesser extent. Table 5.7 shows the changes in employment levels found by the econometric analysis.

Table 5.7 Electricity Distribution: Employment Results

	Number of employees
Percentage change in level	
Transition	−26.4***
Post-transition	−17.6***
Percentage change in level after controlling for time trend	
Transition	−5.3***
Post-transition	4.8***
Percentage point change in annual growth rate	
Transition	−5.0***
Post-transition	6.4***

Source: Authors' calculations.
Note: The change for the post-transition period is with respect to the transition period values.
***Significant at 1 percent.

Impact on Labor Productivity and Efficiency

Electricity Distribution: Labor Productivity and Efficiency Summary

Connections per employee and energy sold per employee showed large gains in levels during both the transition and post-transition periods. When looking at growth rates, however, a temporary growth acceleration occurred during the transition, which was followed by a deceleration after the transition. Distributional losses declined in both periods.

Three variables are used to measure labor productivity and efficiency: (i) energy per employee, (ii) connections per employee, and (iii) distributional (technical and commercial) losses. As pointed out by Kumbhakar and Hjalmarsson (1998), while productivity in electricity generation is mainly determined by the technology, productivity in distribution is, to a large extent, driven by management and efficient labor use.

Labor Productivity

With respect to the connections and energy per employee, the results are a composition of the previous comparisons (tables 5.6 and 5.7). These results are driven by the positive trend in the output measures and by the reduction in the number of employees. Although the greatest gains came during the transition period, levels of both connections per employee and energy per employee showed significant improvements during the transition and post-transition periods relative to the previous period (figure 5.9).[12] According to the econometric analysis, connections per employee were 55.6 percent higher during the transition and another 44.5 percent higher after the transition. Equivalent numbers for energy sold per employee are 60.6 percent and 41.3 percent.

Looking at actual labor productivity levels shows that the improvement in Colombia vastly exceeds that seen in other countries both in relative and absolute terms. Peru has the second highest number of connections per employee, while Brazil has the second highest amount of energy sold per employee (figure 5.10).

Given the underlying data—connections and energy sold, which follow natural trends, versus employment, which does not—it is argued that it is more appropriate to analyze labor productivity after controlling for trends. As was the case for the output and labor indicators, controlling for trends dramatically reduces the privatization impacts. With the effect of time trends removed, connections per employee and energy per employee increased by 5 percent and 9 percent, respectively, during the transition. Levels after the transition decreased slightly (–3.6 percent for connections per employee and –7.7 percent for energy per employee, with respect to transition levels). The econometric growth rate analysis produced similar results: the average annual growth rate for both connections per employee and MWh per employee increased during the transition and decreased after the transition.

Distributional Losses

With respect to distributional losses, the situation during public ownership was heterogeneous. Some countries had increasing distributional losses, but others had decreasing losses. After the transition, however, almost all the countries reduced their average distributional losses. The reason for the upturn in losses partway through the post-transition period in some countries is unclear (figure 5.11).

Looking at actual levels of distributional losses shows that Nicaragua stands out as an underperformer. In fact, Nicaragua was one of two countries (the second was Brazil) that had higher losses after the transition compared with before the transition. The country with the largest drop in losses was Colombia, resulting in post-transition levels that were on par with several other countries (figure 5.12).

The transition period saw an average drop in distributional losses of 3.1 percent, according to the econometric analysis. In contrast, distributional losses plunged 13.2 percent during the post-transition period (with respect to the transition period). When looking at the means and medians analysis, results tell a slightly different story. The mean for the transition period was 11.5 percent lower than the mean during the pretransition

Figure 3.9 Electricity Distribution: Labor Productivity

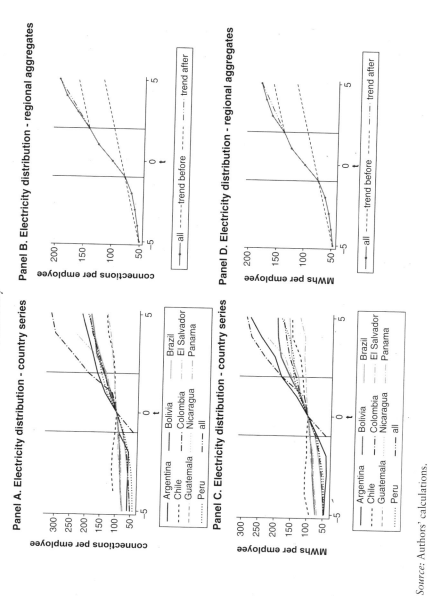

Panel A. Electricity distribution - country series

Panel B. Electricity distribution - regional aggregates

Panel C. Electricity distribution - country series

Panel D. Electricity distribution - regional aggregates

Source: Authors' calculations.
Note: The x axis is time; T = 0 is the last year with at least six months of public ownership. The y axis is normalized at 100 when time = 0.
T = time (years).

103

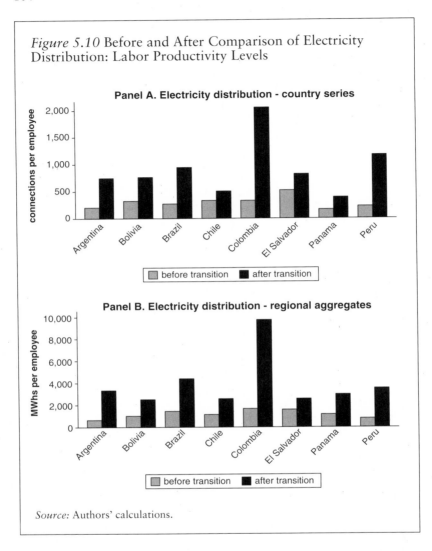

Figure 5.10 Before and After Comparison of Electricity
Distribution: Labor Productivity Levels

period; the mean during the post-transition period was about 10 percent
lower than during the transition period. When considering changes in the
median, the results are more similar to the econometric analysis. The distributional loss median was 6 percent lower during the transition period
and 11 percent lower during the post-transition period with respect to
the previous period (see table A3.1). In this case, it makes more sense to
analyze changes in loss levels, rather than trends, because a natural trend
is not expected.

Figure 5.11 Electricity Distribution: Distributional Losses

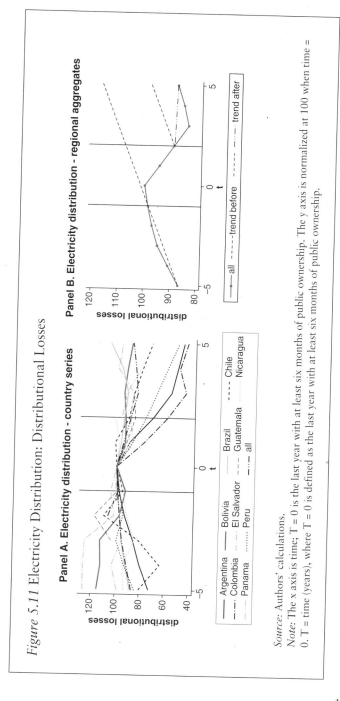

Panel A. Electricity distribution - country series

Panel B. Electricity distribution - regional aggregates

Source: Authors' calculations.

Note: The x axis is time; T = 0 is the last year with at least six months of public ownership. The y axis is normalized at 100 when time = 0. T = time (years), where T = 0 is defined as the last year with at least six months of public ownership.

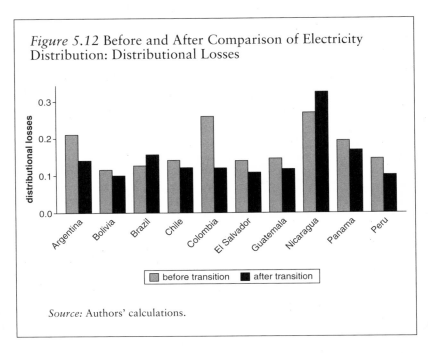

Figure 5.12 Before and After Comparison of Electricity Distribution: Distributional Losses

Source: Authors' calculations.

The mixed results are likely the result of a conflation of the two types of distributional losses: technical and commercial. To curb technical losses, new investments and upgrades are required that take time to implement. Hence, they would be expected to occur following the transition period. Commercial losses, on the other hand, can often be reduced quickly by shutting off the connections of nonpaying customers. Thus, drops in distributional losses during the transitional period could be attributed to commercial losses.

Connections per employee and energy sold per employee showed large gains in levels during both the transition and post-transition periods. When looking at growth rates, however, a temporary growth acceleration occurred during the transition followed by a deceleration after the transition. Distributional losses declined in both periods. Table 5.8 shows the econometric results, and a complete set of results can be found in appendix 3.

Impact on Prices

Electricity Distribution: Price Summary

Average prices in real local currency increased somewhat during transition and post-transition. Dollar prices appear to have fallen, but after excluding

Table 5.8 Electricity Distribution: Labor Productivity and Efficiency Results

	Connections per employee	Output per employee	Distributional losses
Percentage change in level			
Transition	55.6***	60.6***	–3.1**
Post-transition	44.5***	41.3***	–13.2***
Percentage change in level after controlling for time trend			
Transition	5.0***	9.0***	2.1
Post-transition	–3.6***	–7.7***	–3.9***
Percentage point change in annual growth rate			
Transition	4.8***	4.6**	–4.2***
Post-transition	–6.5***	–9.2***	1.5

Source: Author's calculations.

Note: The change for the post-transition period is with respect to the transition period values.

*Significant at 10 percent; **significant at 5 percent; ***significant at 1 percent.

Brazil (which experienced a currency devaluation in 1999), dollar prices seem to have increased slightly.

Average residential electricity prices in U.S. dollars and in real local currency are analyzed. The results seem somewhat peculiar—the tariffs in real local currency show a clearly increasing trend, but prices in dollars seem to be decreasing in the same period (figure 5.13). The econometric analysis showed statistically significant increases in real local currency prices of 11.1 percent during the transition and 7.4 percent after the transition (with respect to the transition level). In dollars, there was no significant change during the transition period and a –2.8 percent drop during the post-transition period.[13]

A plausible explanation for this is, in part, the 1999 currency devaluation in Brazil. To test this explanation, the analysis was repeated with Brazil excluded from the sample. With Brazil excluded, both series show increasing prices, but at a much lower rate. As a result of the smaller sample size and relatively small price changes, no significant differences were found between consecutive periods in the means and medians analysis. According to the same analysis, there were small but significant price increases in both local currency and dollars when comparing the pretransition and post-transition periods.[14]

While a natural trend in prices is not expected, it is nevertheless interesting to consider price growth patterns. There is some evidence that price growth was higher before the transition and that it then slowed, especially during the transition (see table 5.9, figure 5.13, and table A3.2).

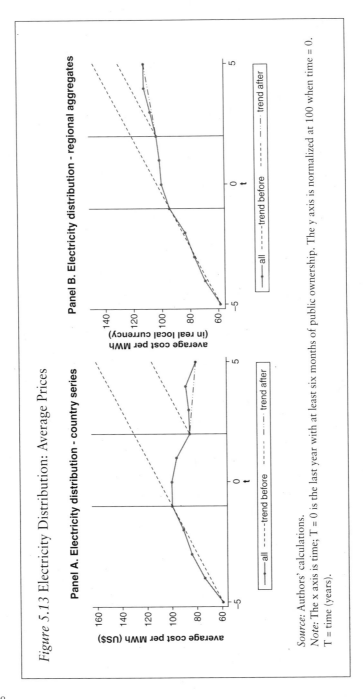

Figure 5.13 Electricity Distribution: Average Prices

Panel A. Electricity distribution - country series

Panel B. Electricity distribution - regional aggregates

Source: Authors' calculations.
Note: The x axis is time; T = 0 is the last year with at least six months of public ownership. The y axis is normalized at 100 when time = 0.
T = time (years).

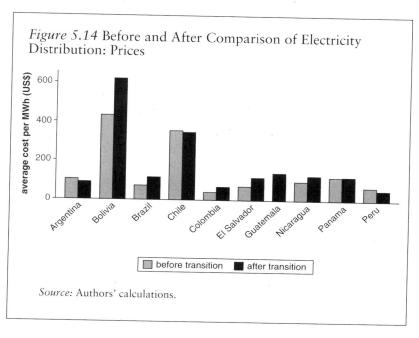

Figure 5.14 Before and After Comparison of Electricity Distribution: Prices

Source: Authors' calculations.

When absolute price levels are compared across countries, Bolivia and Chile stand out as having the highest prices. Specifically, the average price per MWh in Bolivia after the privatization transition was more than US$600, while prices in Chile exceeded US$300. In contrast, prices in all other countries hovered close to US$100 per MWh (figure 5.14).

Average prices in real local currency increased somewhat over both periods. Dollar prices appear to have fallen, but after excluding Brazil (which experienced a currency devaluation in 1999), dollar prices seem to have increased slightly. Table 5.9 summarizes the results of the econometric analysis (including price data from Brazil).

Impact on Quality

Electricity Distribution: Quality Summary

There is a relatively small amount of quality data from the pretransition period, but available data do indicate that both (i) the average duration of interruptions per consumer and (ii) the average frequency of interruptions per consumer fell during both the transition and post-transition periods. Combining these two indicators yields an overall quality measure that shows improvement in both periods.

Table 5.9 Electricity Distribution: Price Results

	Average prices in dollars	Average prices in real local currency
Percentage change		
Transition	−1.3	11.1***
Post-transition	−2.8***	7.4***
Percentage change after controlling for time trend		
Transition	8.1***	3.5***
Post-transition	3.7***	0.7
Percentage point change in annual growth rate		
Transition	−11.7***	−8.2***
Post-transition	2.3***	0.9

Source: Authors' calculations.
Note: The percentage change for the post-transition period is with respect to the transition period values.
*Significant at 10 percent; **significant at 5 percent; ***significant at 1 percent.

The quality of electricity distribution is measured by the frequency and duration of service interruptions per consumer. In general, these measures were defined at the time of reform, along with the creation of regulatory agencies, making it difficult to build long time series. Only Argentina and Brazil had some information for the years before the transition. Despite the lack of historical data, quality improvements on average have been substantial. Argentina stands out as having been particularly successful in reducing the average duration and frequency of interruptions per consumer, both in relative and absolute terms. Bolivia, on the other hand, has experienced some quality deteriorations since the privatization transition, even though absolute quality levels are second only to Argentina (figures 5.15 and 5.16). In countries where quantitative quality data before privatization are not available, strong anecdotal evidence suggests that quality was poor.

Both of the analysis methodologies found improvements in average frequency and duration of interruptions. According to the econometric analysis, the duration of interruptions fell 13.4 percent during the transition and an additional 29.1 percent after the transition. Similarly, the frequency of interruptions fell 10.1 percent during the transition and an additional 26.5 percent after it.[15] The means and medians analysis

Figure 5.15 Electricity Distribution: Quality

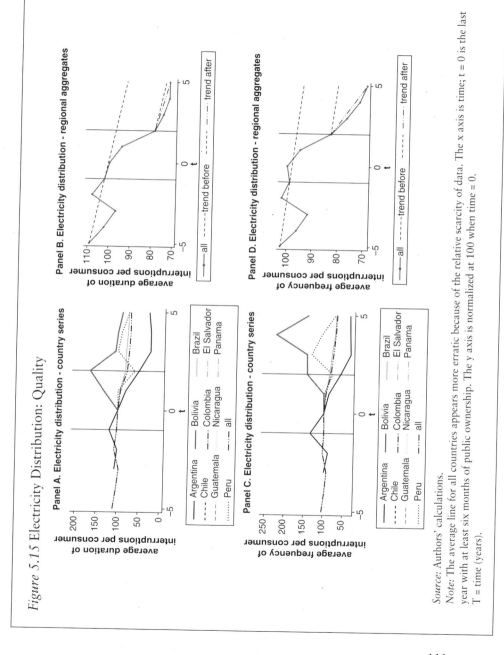

Source: Authors' calculations.

Note: The average line for all countries appears more erratic because of the relative scarcity of data. The x axis is time; t = 0 is the last year with at least six months of public ownership. The y axis is normalized at 100 when time = 0. T = time (years).

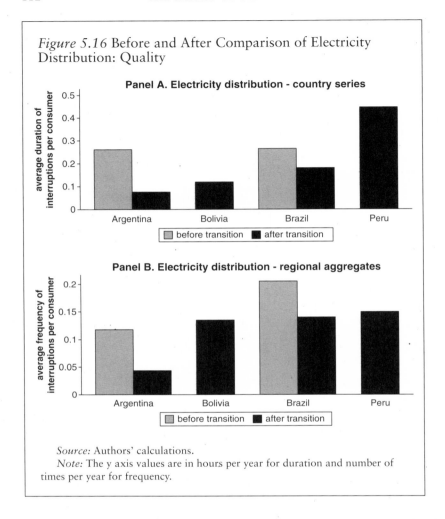

Figure 5.16 Before and After Comparison of Electricity Distribution: Quality

Source: Authors' calculations.
Note: The y axis values are in hours per year for duration and number of times per year for frequency.

found similar quality improvements, although the frequency of interruptions results were not statistically significant for the post-transition period.[16]

Available data suggest that both (i) the average duration of interruptions per consumer and (ii) the average frequency of interruptions per consumer fell during both the transition and post-transition periods. Combining these two indicators yields an overall quality measure that shows improvement in both periods. Table 5.10 summarizes the results of the econometric analysis.

Table 5.10 Electricity Distribution: Quality Results

	Duration of interruptions	Frequency of interruptions
Percentage change		
Transition	−13.4***	−10.1***
Post-transition	−29.1***	−26.5***
Percentage change after controlling for time trend		
Transition	7.0**	7.9***
Post-transition	−10.9***	−11.3***
Percentage point change in annual growth rate		
Transition	−6.3***	−5.0**
Post-transition	0.1	−4.8**

Source: Authors' calculations.

Note: The percentage change for the post-transition period is with respect to the transition period values.

*Significant at 10 percent; **significant at 5 percent; ***significant at 1 percent.

Table 5.11 Electricity Distribution Impact Summary

	Transition	Post-transition
Output and coverage		
Energy sold (MWh)[a]	=	↓
Number of connections[a]	=	=
Coverage[a]	=	=
Employment		
Number of employees	↓	↓
Labor productivity and efficiency		
Connections per employee[a]	↑	↓
Energy (MWh) per employee[a]	↑	↓
Distributional losses	↓	↓
Prices		
Average price per MWh (US$)	=/↑	=/↑
Average price per MWh (in real local currency)	↑	↑

(continued)

Table 5.11 Electricity Distribution Impact Summary *(continued)*

	Transition	Post-transition
Quality		
Average duration of interruptions per consumer (a)	↓	↓
Average frequency of interruptions per consumer (b)	↓	↓
Quality (a) + (b)	↑	↑

Source: Authors' calculations.

Note: Up and down arrows indicate that a positive or negative change occurred in addition to the natural change that would be expected in the absence of privatization. An equal sign indicates that the trend perceived during the previous period was sustained but not substantially exceeded or diminished. The arrow size represents the size of the change.

a. Impacts are shown after controlling for time trends.

Conclusion

The main results of this chapter are that the change in ownership did not change the growth trend for number of connections, energy sold, and coverage. Employment fell during both periods, but primarily during the transition. The labor productivity growth accelerated during the transition, followed by a deceleration during the post-transition period. Distributional losses and quality improved during both periods. Average prices in real local currency increased somewhat over both periods, although results for dollar price changes were less robust given Brazil's currency devaluation in 1999.

Table 5.11 summarizes the results of this chapter. The results for the output, coverage, and labor productivity indicators are reported after controlling for time trends. If time trends were not controlled for, each of these indicators would show significant increases. A natural increase is expected for each of these variables, regardless of whether ownership is public or private. For the other variables, a natural trend is not expected; hence, the results shown in table 5.11 do not incorporate the firm-specific time trend controls.

Notes

1. Empresa Eléctrica de Atacama (EMELAT, Sociedad Eléctrica de Melipilla, Colchagua y Maule S.A., Empresa Eléctrica de Coquimbo S.A. (EMEC), Empresa

Eléctrica de Arica S.A. (EMELARI), Empresa Eléctrica de Iquique S.A. (ELIQSA), and Empresa Eléctrica de Antofagasta S.A. (ELECDA).

2. ESEBA covered the rest of the province of Buenos Aires not covered by SEGBA.

3. These firms had around 7 million residential connections in 2003 (authors' calculation).

4. Of these 116 utilities, 18 were in Argentina, 7 in Bolivia, 45 in Brazil, 19 in Chile, 4 in Colombia, 5 in El Salvador, 4 in Guatemala, 2 in Nicaragua, 3 in Panama, and 9 in Peru.

5. For the rest of the chapter, we refer to "average" for a given variable as the simple average within the country.

6. According to the growth regressions in the econometric analysis, the annual growth rate in the amount of energy sold was 2.7 percentage points lower during the post-transition period than during the transition period (see table 5.6 and table A3.3).

7. These increases were found to be statistically significant by both the means and median analysis (table A3.1) and the econometric analysis (table A3.3).

8. Statistically significant drops were found by both the means and median analysis (tables A3.1 and A3.2) and the econometric analysis (table A3.3).

9. The means and medians analysis found complementary results: The mean number of employees during the transition was 38 percent lower than before the transition, and the mean number of employees after the transition was 14 percent lower than during the transition (see table A3.1).

10. Both of these changes were statistically significant.

11. Alternatively, when looking at the changes in the annual growth rate of employment between the pretransition and transition periods, a 5 percentage point drop occurred in the transition period. The annual growth rate of employment then increased by 6.4 percentage points after the transition.

12. The level increases were found to be statistically significant by both the means and median analysis (tables A3.1 and A3.2) and the econometric analysis (table A3.3).

13. The means and medians analysis shows similar trends, with significant increases in real local currency prices in both periods and significant decreases in dollar prices in both periods.

14. More detailed information on the price analysis excluding Brazil is available upon request from the authors.

15. These drops in interruptions were all statistically significant.

16. The means and medians analysis found a 23 percent drop in the duration of interruptions between the pretransition and transition periods and a 25 percent drop between the transition and post-transition periods. Both of these drops were significant. The frequency of interruptions fell 26 percent between the pretransition and post-transition periods and no statistically significant change occurred between the transition and post-transition periods (table A3.1).

6

The Impact on Fixed-Line
Telecommunications

Introduction

This chapter analyzes a data set built by the authors that covers 16 fixed telecommunications companies in Latin American countries for the years before and after their privatization. Similar to the electricity distribution chapter, two complementary methodologies were used to learn about the effects of changes in ownership: a means and medians analysis and an econometric analysis. In addition, the period under analysis is separated into three parts: preprivatization (pretransition), a three-year transition period, and postprivatization (post-transition). This separation yields information about short- versus long-term effects. For a description of the methodologies, see chapter 4. The full results of the means and medians analysis and econometric analysis, including statistical significance, are shown in appendix 3. This chapter synthesizes the results from the two methodologies, presenting summaries geared toward policy makers in the following areas: outputs and coverage, employment, labor productivity, efficiency, prices, and quality. The main results are summarized in each section as well as in the conclusion of the chapter.

The unique characteristics of the telecommunications sector make it possible to measure the effects of two additional phenomena: liberalization and competition. These measurements are included to counter the concern that either liberalization or competition—rather than privatization—was responsible for the performance changes discussed below. Hence, the section on Liberalization and Competition, above, adds the liberalization of the long-distance market as well as the development of the mobile telecommunications market as explanatory variables in the econometric analysis. Liberalization in long-distance services can be considered a proxy for second-generation reform of the local market.

The Privatization Process

The general privatization features in each of the countries in the region are quite similar (see table 6.1). During the 1980s and the 1990s, the state owned the fixed telecommunications company, which operated in a monopolistic market. After Chile's experience in the 1980s, most of the countries privatized their telecom companies.[1] The new owners generally had to comply with requirements such as network expansion and quality standards. In exchange, they were granted a monopoly period, after which new firms could enter the market.

In most countries, liberalization of the long-distance market took place within a few years after privatization (table 6.2). Hence, there is a possibility that the impacts of privatization perceived were actually instead

Table 6.1 Privatization Chronology of Fixed Telecommunications in LAC

Country	Year	Privatized firms
Argentina	1990	Telecom and Telefónica de Argentina
Bolivia	1995	Empresa Nacional de telecomunicaciones (ENTEL)
Brazil	1998	Tele Norte Leste, Tele Centro Sul, and Telesp Participacoes
Chile	1987	Compañía de Telecomunicaciones de Chile
El Salvador	1997	Telefónica de El Salvador
Guyana	1991	Guyana Telephone & Telegraph Co. (GT&T)
Jamaica	1989	Telecommunications of Jamaica Limited
Mexico	1990	Teléfonos de México
Nicaragua	2001	Empresa Nicaragüense de Telecomunicaciones
Panama	1997	Corporación Nacional de Telecomunicaciones
Peru	1994	Teléfonos del Perú
Trinidad and Tobago	1999	Telecommunications Services of Trinidad and Tobago
Venezuela, R. B. de	1991	Compañía Anónima Nacional Teléfonos de Venezuela (CANTV)

Source: Authors' elaboration.
Note: LAC = Latin America and the Caribbean.

Table 6.2 Privatization Chronology of Fixed Telecommunications in LAC: Liberalization and Competition

Country	Year of privatization	Year of the long-distance liberalization	Year first mobile company started	Year second mobile company started	Year third mobile company started
Argentina	1990	2000	1989	1994	1996
Bolivia	1995	2002	1991	1996	2000
Brazil	1998	1999	1990	1993	1994
Chile	1987	1994	1989	1989	1996
El Salvador	1997	1998	1993	1998	1999
Guyana	1991	n.a.	1995	1999	n.a.
Jamaica	1989	n.a.	1991	2001	2001
Mexico	1990	1996	1989	1990	1999
Nicaragua	2001	2004	1997	2000	2002
Panama	1997	1997	1996	1998	n.a.
Peru	1994	1998	1990	1993	2001
Trinidad and Tobago	1999	n.a.	1991	n.a.	n.a.
Venezuela, R. B. de	1991	2001	1991	1992	1999

Sources: Authors' elaboration based on Wallsten (2001) and International Telecommunication Union (2006).

Note: In some countries, the year of entrance of the second and the third operator corresponds to the year when a second (or a third operator) entered into the same market as the incumbent.

LAC = Latin America and the Caribbean; n.a. = not applicable.

caused by liberalization. Even though the indicators used above refer to local telephone service, liberalization of the long-distance market could be an indicator that liberalization of the local market was to come.

In 1971, the Chilean government intervened to take management control of CTC (Compañía de Teléfonos de Chile), and, in 1974, the Chilean Government's CORFO (Corporación de Fomento de la Producción) acquired 80 percent of CTC's shares. In August 1987, CORFO announced it would reduce its shareholdings and privatize CTC by selling approximately 30 percent of CORFO's CTC shares through an international open bidding process. In January 1988, the bidding process was completed. Following April 1988, they offered another additional purchase of common stocks. In April 1990, Telefónica Internacional de España S.A., indirectly acquired part of the stocks. In 1995, CTC completed the process of dividing its businesses into independent operating units.[2]

In Argentina, the State Reform Act of August 1989 and subsequent decrees set the stage for privatization, and in November 1990, the National Telecommunications Company (Empresa Nacional de Telecomunicaciones, ENTel) was privatized. The privatization was awarded to two companies: Telecom to operate in the north and Telefónica de Argentina to operate in the south. The contract specified a 99-year duration and the provision of public telecommunications services on an exclusive basis for a seven-year term, set to expire on November 8, 1997.[3] Since October 1999, the government has fully liberated the telecommunications market. Today, the companies provide fixed-line public telecommunications and basic telephone services, as well as international long-distance service, wireless telecommunications services, telephone directories publication, data transmission, and Internet services.

In Brazil, before the incorporation of Telebrás (Telecomunicações Brasileiras S.A) in 1972, more than 900 telecommunications companies were operating throughout Brazil. Between 1972 and 1975, Telebrás acquired almost all of these telephone companies and thus came to have a monopoly over the provision of public telecommunications services in almost all areas of the country. In 1998, Telebrás was restructured to form 12 new holding companies in addition to Telebrás itself. The 12 companies included eight cellular service providers (each operating in one of the regions into which Brazil was divided for cellular services); three regional fixed-line service providers (each providing local and intraregional long-distance service in one of the three regions into which Brazil was divided for purposes of fixed-line telecommunications); and Embratel (which provides domestic long-distance telephone service and international telephone service throughout Brazil) (TCS 2002). Later the same year, each of them was sold to private companies. In 1999, the telecommunications market began the process of liberalization.

Data

The authors built an unbalanced panel data of 168 year-firm observations of 16 privatized companies in this sector in Latin America and the Caribbean. The countries analyzed were Argentina, Bolivia, Brazil, Chile, El Salvador, Guatemala, Guyana, Jamaica, Mexico, Nicaragua, Panama, Peru, Trinidad and Tobago, and República Bolivariana de Venezuela. All of the firms in the sample have at least four years of preprivatization data.

Table 6.3 Description of Telecommunications Variables

Variable	Description
Output	
Number of connections	Total number of active connections as of December of each year
Number of minutes	Total number of local minutes consumed per year
Coverage	
	Number of active connections per 100 inhabitants (number of active connections divided by the number of inhabitants in the covered area)
Employment	
Number of employees	Number of employees
Labor Productivity	
Connections per employee	Number of active connections divided by the number of employees
Minutes per worker	Number of local minutes divided by the number of employees
Efficiency	
Incomplete calls	Percentage of total calls that are incomplete
Prices	
Three-minute local call (US$)	Average cost for a three-minute, nonpeak local call (in US$)[a]
Three-minute local call (real local currency)	Average cost for a local call of three minutes out of the peak time (in real local currency)[b]
Monthly residential service charge (US$)	Average monthly cost for a residential service (in US$)[a]
Monthly residential service charge (real local currency)	Average monthly cost for a residential service (in real local currency)[b]
Residential installation (US$)	Average cost for the installation of a residential line (in US$)[a]
Residential installation (real local currency)	Average cost for the installation of a residential line (in real local currency)[b]
Quality	
Digital percentage	Percentage of digital connections in the network

Source: Authors' elaboration.

a. Built with original nominal price data and converted using the exchange rate for each year.

b. Built with original nominal price data and converted using Consumer Price Index.

Impact on Output and Coverage

Telecommunications: Output and Coverage Summary

The number of connections increased during both periods, but after controlling for trends, only the transition period showed abnormally high growth rates. Again, after controlling for trends, the number of minutes increased in both periods, whereas the increases in coverage occurred mainly in the transition period.

Number of Connections

Two variables are used to measure output in the fixed telecommunications sector: the number of connections and the number of local minutes consumed each year. As seen in figure 6.1, the number of connections increased during all three periods for almost all countries. Both the means and medians analysis and the econometric analysis confirmed that there were statistically significant increases in the number of connections between the pretransition, transition, and post-transition periods (see table 6.9, as well as appendix 3, tables A3.4 and A3.6). In fact, the econometric analysis found a 29 percent increase in the number of connections during the transition period and an additional 64 percent increase during the post-transition period.

Turning to growth trends, figure 6.1 indicates that growth in the number of connections accelerated, possibly temporarily, in the first few years of private ownership. The means and medians analysis found that average annual growth in the number of connections increased from 6.9 percent in the pretransition period to 12.7 percent during the transition period, before falling back to 7.2 percent in the post-transition period. Similarly, the econometric analysis found that the average annual growth rate increased 2.7 percentage points during the transition, while there was no statistically significant change from that level after the transition.[4] After controlling for trends it seems that an increase occurred during the transition, but growth rates returned to normal levels after the transition.

One possible explanation for the surge in the number of connections during and shortly after the transition is that newly privatized companies took action to meet pent-up demand. According to the International Telecommunication Union (ITU), waiting lists for connections in the year before the reform numbered 780,000 in Argentina, 308,247 in Peru, and 175,000 in El Salvador. These numbers accounted for 26 percent, 46 percent, and 54 percent of the connections in operation at the time in Argentina, Peru, and El Salvador, respectively. Another contributing factor was the spread of mobile telecommunications, especially during the second half of the 1990s, which likely reduced the demand for new fixed connections.

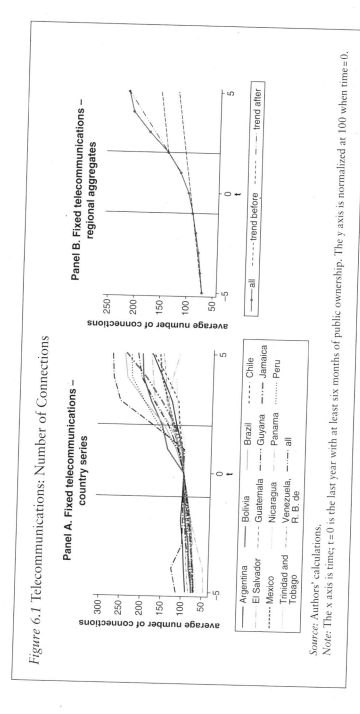

Figure 6.1 Telecommunications: Number of Connections

Source: Authors' calculations.

Note: The x axis is time; t = 0 is the last year with at least six months of public ownership. The y axis is normalized at 100 when time = 0.

As Ros (1999) pointed out, private ownership in fixed telecommunications could shift priorities away from network expansion. This shift occurs because, in a private company, shareholders may be reluctant to increase the network unless it is profitable or made mandatory in the contract. While this may be true, the analysis in this book finds that privatization led to greater network expansion.

Figure 6.2 shows the actual average number of connections (as opposed to the normalized values shown in figure 6.1). Brazil and Mexico stand out as having telecom companies that dwarf those in the rest of the countries in the sample, particularly after the transition.

Number of Minutes

The second output indicator is the number of minutes consumed per year. Figure 6.3 shows that, with the exception of Argentina, the average number of minutes consumed was generally increasing and growth was particularly strong after the transition. These results are not surprising given the increasing number of connections discussed above. The means and medians and econometric analyses generally confirm what can be seen in the figure, although results are not always robust because of the relatively small number of observations. For instance, the econometric analysis found

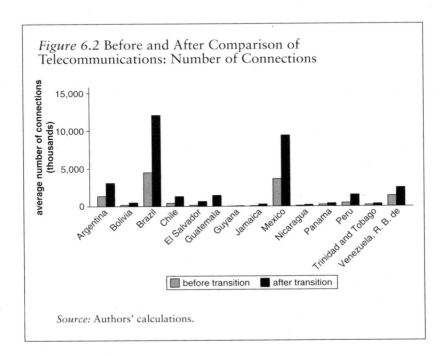

Figure 6.2 Before and After Comparison of Telecommunications: Number of Connections

Source: Authors' calculations.

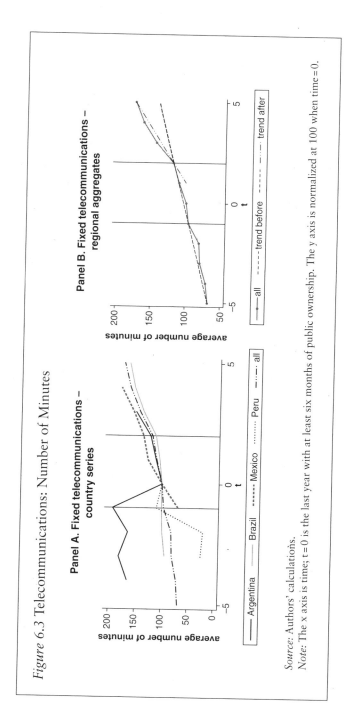

Figure 6.3 Telecommunications: Number of Minutes

Panel A. Fixed telecommunications –
country series

Panel B. Fixed telecommunications –
regional aggregates

Source: Authors' calculations.

Note: The x axis is time; t = 0 is the last year with at least six months of public ownership. The y axis is normalized at 100 when time = 0.

statistically significant increases of 8.2 percent and 37.6 percent during the transition and post-transition periods, respectively.[5]

When time trends are taken into account in the econometric analysis, there is no significant change during the transition period, whereas the post-transition period shows an increase of 14.2 percent over transition levels. The growth regressions, on the other hand, find statistically significant increases in the growth rates of 6.9 percentage points during the transition period and 5.3 percentage points during the post-transition period. Hence, the preponderance of evidence suggests that the number of minutes of fixed telecom services increased in both the transition and post-transition periods after controlling for the trend.

Figure 6.4 highlights the massive difference in actual minutes consumed per year for telecommunications firms in Brazil versus the other countries in the sample. The large difference in minutes is somewhat surprising given that the difference in number of connections seen in figure 6.2 is not nearly as large.

Coverage

Consistent with the output measures, coverage (or teledensity, defined as the number of connections per 100 inhabitants) increased substantially during the periods under study (figure 6.5). In fact, the econometric analysis found an increase of 18.3 percent during the transition period and an additional increase of 52.3 percent during the post-transition period.

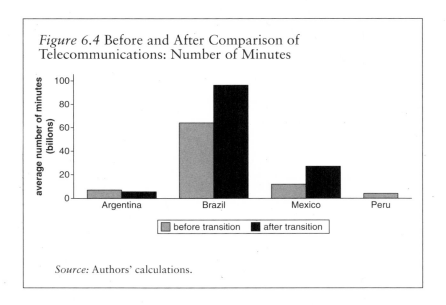

Figure 6.4 Before and After Comparison of Telecommunications: Number of Minutes

Source: Authors' calculations.

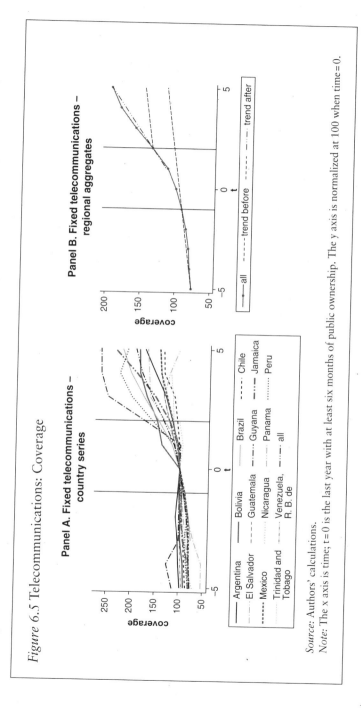

Figure 6.5 Telecommunications: Coverage

**Panel A. Fixed telecommunications –
country series**

Argentina
El Salvador
Mexico
Trinidad and
Tobago
Bolivia
Guatemala
Nicaragua
Venezuela,
R. B. de
Brazil
Guyana
Panama
all
Chile
Jamaica
Peru

**Panel B. Fixed telecommunications –
regional aggregates**

all   trend before   trend after

Source: Authors' calculations.
Note: The x axis is time; t = 0 is the last year with at least six months of public ownership. The y axis is normalized at 100 when time = 0.

127

Similarly, the means and medians analysis found substantial, statistically significant increases.

Looking at trends and growth rates indicates that coverage grew more rapidly during the transition period. The econometric analysis found that the annual growth rate increased by 3.7 percentage points during the transition period and registered no additional changes after the transition. The means and medians analysis found that the average annual growth rate increased by 6.1 percentage points during the transition period, but then fell by 5.9 percentage points (relative to transition rates) during the post-transition period.[6]

Figure 6.6 compares actual coverage levels across countries. While considerable heterogeneity exists, most countries in the sample have coverage levels of between 10 and 20 connections per 100 inhabitants.

The number of connections increased during both periods, but after controlling for trends, only the transition period showed abnormally high growth rates. Again, after controlling for trends, the number of minutes increased in both periods, whereas the increases in coverage occurred mainly in the transition period. Table 6.4 displays the changes in output and coverage levels and growth found by the econometric analysis.

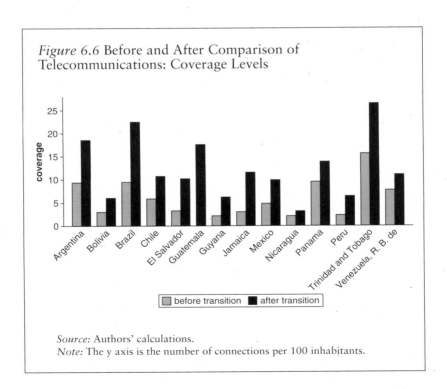

Figure 6.6 Before and After Comparison of Telecommunications: Coverage Levels

Source: Authors' calculations.
Note: The y axis is the number of connections per 100 inhabitants.

Table 6.4 Telecommunications: Output and Coverage Results

	Number of lines	Number of minutes	Coverage
Percentage change in level			
Transition	28.8***	8.2**	18.3***
Post-transition	63.9***	37.6***	52.3***
Percentage change in level after controlling for time trend			
Transition	–4.9**	0.2	–6.3***
Post-transition	12.0***	14.2***	9.5***
Percentage point change in annual growth rate			
Transition	2.7**	6.9***	3.7***
Post-transition	–0.2	5.3*	0.1

Source: Author's calculations.

Note: The percentage change for the post-transition period is with respect to the transition period values.

*Significant at 10 percent; **significant at 5 percent; ***significant at 1 percent.

Impact on Employment

Telecommunications: Employment Summary

The number of employees declined during the transition and post-transition periods, not accounting for time trends. On average, the number of employees in fixed telecommunications companies has been declining steadily since before the transition period. However, this average decline masks considerable differences across firms and countries (figure 6.7). The econometric analysis found that employment declined by 9.2 percent during the transition period and a further 23.2 percent after the transition period.[7] A natural trend in employment is not expected, but employment growth rates became increasingly negative during the transition and post-transition periods. The econometric analysis found that, during the transition, the annual growth rate of employment was 4.1 percentage points lower than during the previous period; annual growth fell an additional 2.6 percentage points after the transition.

One reason for the fall in employment during that transition period is that governments decided to trim the labor force reform before the ownership change, with the intention of increasing the value of the firm and bringing employment to a more sustainable equilibrium level. As mentioned in the electricity section, investors proved indifferent to these policies and, in the end, the value of the firm remained at the same level

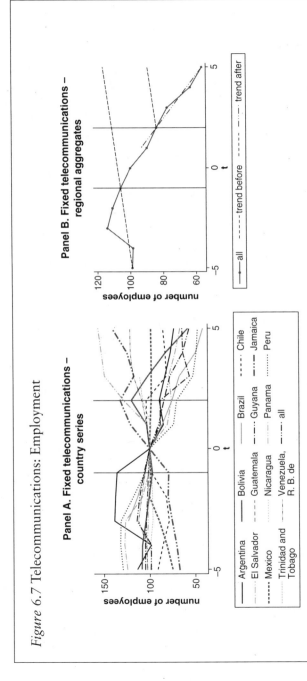

Figure 6.7 Telecommunications: Employment

Panel A. Fixed telecommunications – country series

Panel B. Fixed telecommunications – regional aggregates

Source: Authors' calculations.

Note: The x axis is time; t = 0 is the last year with at least six months of public ownership. The y axis is normalized at 100 when time = 0.

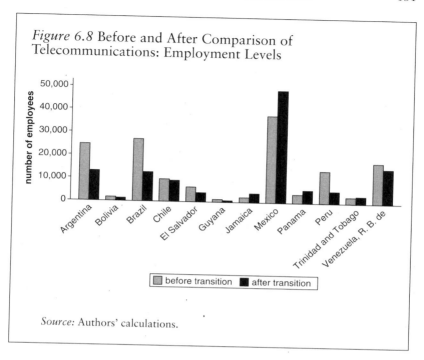

Figure 6.8 Before and After Comparison of Telecommunications: Employment Levels

Source: Authors' calculations.

or was even reduced when the government applied layoff programs in advance. One explanation is selection issues that provide incentives for good employees to leave while bad employees remain in the company (Chong and López-de-Silanes 2003a).

Figure 6.8 shows the average number of employees at telecom firms in each country. Mexico stands out as having by far the largest number of employees as well as for experiencing an increase in the number of employees between the pretransition and post-transition periods. In contrast, most of the other countries experienced a drop in employment.

The number of employees declined in both periods. Table 6.5 summarizes the changes in employment levels and growth found by the econometric analysis.

Impact on Labor Productivity and Efficiency

Telecommunications: Labor Productivity and Efficiency Summary

Labor productivity—measured by the number of connections per employee and minutes per employee—showed substantial increases, especially in the

Table 6.5 Telecommunications: Employment Results

	Number of employees
Percentage change in level	
Transition	−9.2***
Post-transition	−23.2***
Percentage change in level after controlling for time trend	
Transition	3.1
Post-transition	−6.7**
Percentage point change in annual growth rate	
Transition	−4.1***
Post-transition	−2.6*

Source: Author's calculations.
Note: The percentage change for the post-transition period is with respect to the transition period values.
*Significant at 10 percent; **significant at 5 percent; ***significant at 1 percent.

transition period. The percentage of incomplete calls experienced a significant fall only after the transition period.

Labor Productivity

Two indicators were used to measure labor productivity: connections per employee and minutes per employee. As a consequence of the increase in the output measures and the general negative trend in the number of employees, labor productivity improved substantially, especially after the transition (figures 6.9 and 6.10). Almost all of the countries in the data set at least doubled labor productivity in less than five years after the reform. The only exception was Panama, which already had a relatively high teledensity (that is, the number of active connections per 100 inhabitants). At the time of the reform, Panama's teledensity was 13 percent; neighboring Nicaragua, El Salvador, and Guatemala had teledensities of 3 percent, 6 percent, and 4 percent, respectively.[8]

According to the econometric analysis, the number of connections per employee increased 35.1 percent during the transition (compared with the pretransition period) and a whopping 106.9 percent after the transition. The results of the means and medians analysis were even greater: the increase during the transition was 65.6 percent, and the increase after the transition was 117.9 percent (see table A3.4). All changes were statistically significant.

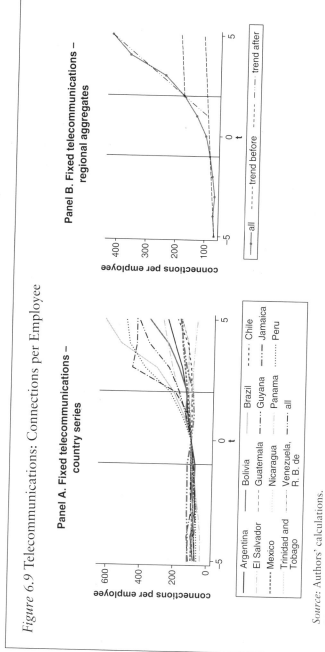

Figure 6.9 Telecommunications: Connections per Employee

Panel A. Fixed telecommunications – country series

connections per employee

t

Argentina — Bolivia — Brazil ..... Chile
El Salvador --- Guatemala -·-·- Guyana -·-·- Jamaica
Mexico ----- Nicaragua .... Panama .... Peru
Trinidad and ----- Venezuela, R. B. de
Tobago -·-·- all

Panel B. Fixed telecommunications – regional aggregates

connections per employee

t

— all ----- trend before ----- trend after

Source: Authors' calculations.
Note: The x axis is time; t = 0 is the last year with at least six months of public ownership. The y axis is normalized at 100 when time = 0.

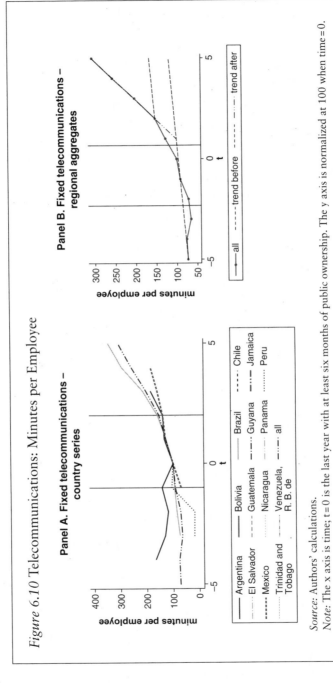

Figure 6.10 Telecommunications: Minutes per Employee

**Panel A. Fixed telecommunications –
country series**

minutes per employee

Argentina
El Salvador
Mexico
Trinidad and
Tobago

Bolivia
Guatemala
Nicaragua
Venezuela,
R. B. de

Brazil
Guyana
Panama
all

Chile
Jamaica
Peru

**Panel B. Fixed telecommunications –
regional aggregates**

minutes per employee

all   trend before   trend after

Source: Authors' calculations.
Note: The x axis is time; t = 0 is the last year with at least six months of public ownership. The y axis is normalized at 100 when time = 0.

Fewer data were available for minutes per employee, but the econometric analysis still found impressive statistically significant improvements: 32 percent during the transition and an additional 92.9 percent after the transition. Again, the means and medians analysis found even larger increases: 43.2 percent during the transition and 117.2 percent after the transition.

As was the case for the output indicators, controlling for trends dramatically reduces the impact of privatization on labor productivity (the results can be seen in table 6.6). Yet, it is more appropriate to look at the changes in trends given the underlying indicators: earlier in this chapter, it was argued that the output indicators follow natural trends, but the number of employees does not. One way to examine trend changes is through growth rates. In this case, the annual growth rate of number of connections per employee increased by 7 percentage points during the transition period and 3.3 percentage points after the transition. The annual growth rate of minutes per employee increased by 8.5 percentage points during the transition period, but did not register any additional statistically significant changes during the post-transition period.

Actual (that is, not normalized) labor productivity measures show a surprising amount of variance (figure 6.11). Brazil is by far the most productive with more than 1,000 connections per employee during the post-transition period. The next-closest country, Bolivia, had less than one-half that number. The number of minutes per employee in Brazil vastly exceeds that of other countries.

Table 6.6 Telecommunications: Labor Productivity and Efficiency Results

	Lines per employee	Minutes per employee	Incomplete calls
Percentage change in level			
Transition	35.1***	32.0***	−12.5
Post-transition	106.9***	92.9***	−29.7***
Percentage change in level after controlling for time trend			
Transition	−9.6***	−1.0	15.3***
Post-transition	20.3***	18.9***	0.6
Percentage point change in annual growth rate			
Transition	7.0***	8.5**	−6.2
Post-transition	3.3*	8.3	−3.5

Source: Author's calculations.

Note: The percentage change for the post-transition period is with respect to the transition period values.

*Significant at 10 percent; **significant at 5 percent; ***significant at 1 percent.

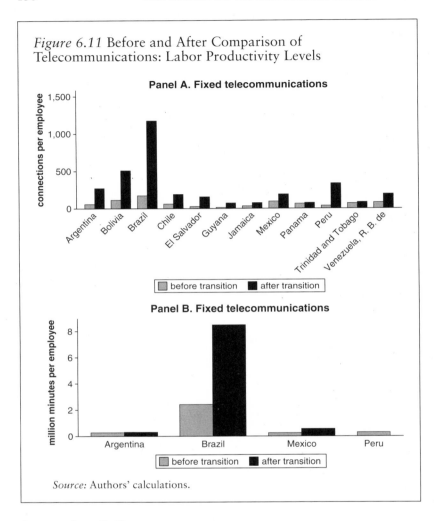

Figure 6.11 Before and After Comparison of Telecommunications: Labor Productivity Levels

Source: Authors' calculations.

Incomplete Calls

The percentage of incomplete calls was chosen as the most feasible measure of fixed telecommunications efficiency. While considerable heterogeneity exists across countries, figure 6.12 shows a substantial drop in the average percentage of incomplete calls. Despite a relatively small number of observations, the econometric analysis confirmed that there was indeed a statistically significant drop of 29.7 percent in the post-transition period. Neither the econometric results from the transition period nor the results of the means and medians analysis were statistically significant. Figure 6.13 shows that the actual percentage of incomplete calls in República Bolivariana de Venezuela and Mexico are far lower than in Brazil and Chile.

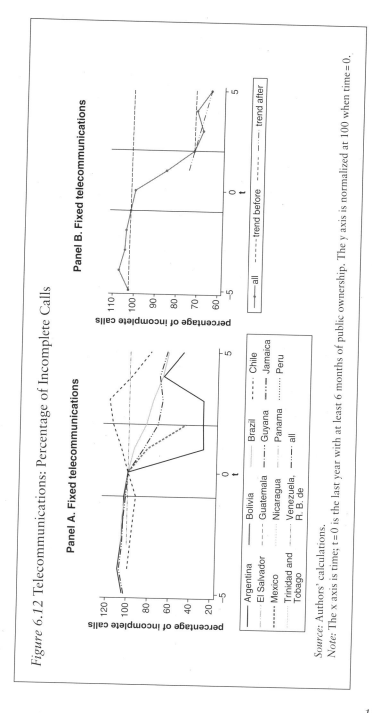

Figure 6.12 Telecommunications: Percentage of Incomplete Calls

Panel A. Fixed telecommunications

Panel B. Fixed telecommunications

Source: Authors' calculations.

Note: The x axis is time; t = 0 is the last year with at least 6 months of public ownership. The y axis is normalized at 100 when time = 0.

137

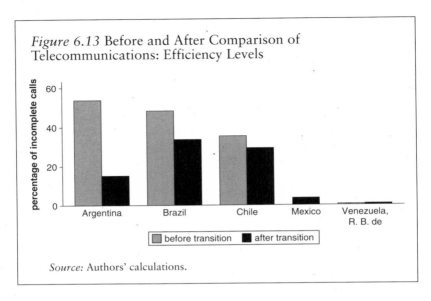

Figure 6.13 Before and After Comparison of Telecommunications: Efficiency Levels

Source: Authors' calculations.

Labor productivity—measured by number of connections per employee and minutes per employee—showed substantial increases, especially in the transition period. The percentage of calls that are incomplete experienced a significant fall only after the transition period. Table 6.6 shows the changes in labor productivity and efficiency levels and growth found by the econometric analysis.

Impact on Prices

Telecommunications: Price Summary

Prices for a three-minute local call increased during the transition, but did not significantly change after that. Residential monthly service charges increased during both periods, with the greatest increase coming during the transition. Residential line installation charges seem to have decreased during both periods. These results hold for prices in both dollars and real local currency.

Three measures of fixed telecommunications prices were analyzed in both dollars and real local currency: (i) the average price of a three-minute local call, (ii) the average monthly charge for residential service, and (iii) the average charge for the installation of a residential line. The average price of a three-minute local call was mainly increasing during public ownership. One exception was Chile, which experienced a tremendous fall in prices leading up to the ownership change. On average, however, prices increased during the first part of the transition, reaching a high point during the last year of public ownership. Prices then began to fall, but not as rapidly as the increases of previous years (figure 6.14). Trends in U.S. dollars and real local currency followed roughly similar patterns, although the 1999 devaluation in Brazil introduced some variation.

The econometric analysis found that average prices in both dollars and real local currency for a three-minute call increased by roughly 45 percent. There were no significant changes during the post-transition period, and the means and medians analysis did not find any statistically significant changes during either period. With respect to actual prices, figure 6.15 shows that most countries are comparable, with the exception of Chile. In fact, at more than US$0.50 for a three-minute local call, prices in Chile after the transition were more than three times higher than its closest competitor—Mexico.

Monthly charges for residential service increased significantly during and after the transition, both in dollars and in real local currency. The changes were largest during the transition: prices in dollars grew 75.9 percent and prices in real local currency grew 62.6 percent. After the transition, both dollar and real local currency prices were roughly 22 percent higher than transition levels. The means and medians analysis also found significant jumps (see table A3.4). Judging from figure 6.16 and the econometric trend analysis (table 6.7), it appears that residential monthly charges experienced an abnormal jump during the transition before returning to a slower rate of growth similar to the pretransition period. When looking at actual monthly service charges (figure 6.17), Chile again emerges as the most costly country.

The analysis of average installation charges for a residential line produced somewhat mixed results, although the preponderance of evidence suggests that prices declined during the transition and post-transition periods. Figure 6.18 shows a big drop in installation charges during the transition and more modest falls after that. The means and medians analysis found a large statistically significant drop during the transition period, but the drop during the post-transition period was not significant. The econometric analysis found the reverse: the drop during the transition was not significant, whereas the drop during the post-transition period was significant—roughly 25 percent in both dollars and real local currency. There were no significant changes in the growth rate. Figure 6.19 compares actual installation charges (in dollars) before and after the transition.

Prices for a three-minute local call increased during the transition, but did not significantly change after that. Residential monthly service charges increased during both periods, with the greatest increase coming during the transition. Residential line installation charges seem to have decreased during both periods. These results hold for prices in both dollars and real local currency. Table 6.7 summarizes the changes in price levels and growth found by the econometric analysis.

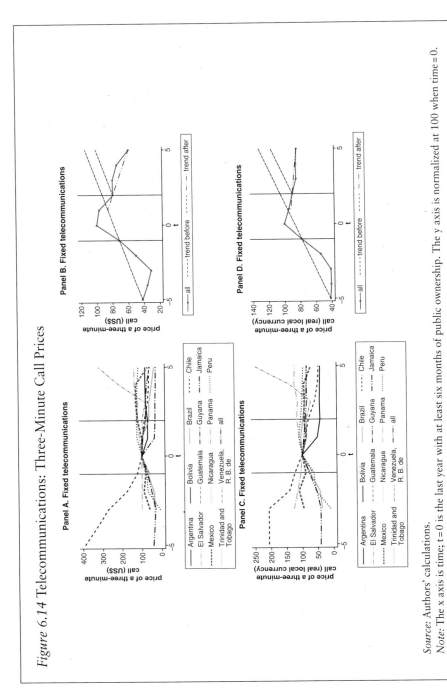

Figure 6.14 Telecommunications: Three-Minute Call Prices

Source: Authors' calculations.

Note: The x axis is time; t = 0 is the last year with at least six months of public ownership. The y axis is normalized at 100 when time = 0.

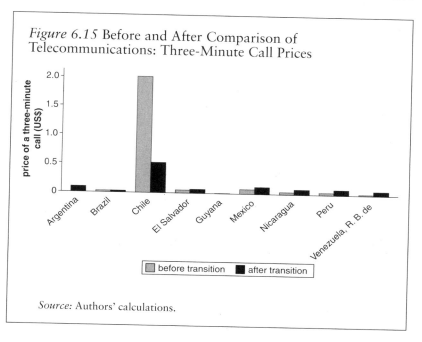

Figure 6.15 Before and After Comparison of Telecommunications: Three-Minute Call Prices

Source: Authors' calculations.

Impact on Quality

Telecommunications: Quality Summary

The network digitization percentage was selected as a proxy for quality in fixed telecommunications. Network digitization increased during the transition and post-transition periods, with the largest increase coming during the transition, not controlling for time trends. The econometric analysis found increases of 36.3 percent during the transition and 58.1 percent after the transition. Similarly, the means and medians analysis found increases of 75.4 percent and 69.5 percent in the two periods, respectively.

A natural trend is not assumed, but it is still interesting to control for trends and examine growth rate changes. The econometric analysis found that after controlling for firm-specific time trends, there was a statistically significant increase of 4.9 percent during the transition period; there was no significant change after the transition. On the other hand, the econometric growth analysis found a significant drop in the average annual growth rate of 5.6 percentage points after the transition but no significant change during the transition.

To provide a somewhat more robust measure of quality, a quality index was created that combines the percentage of completed calls and the share

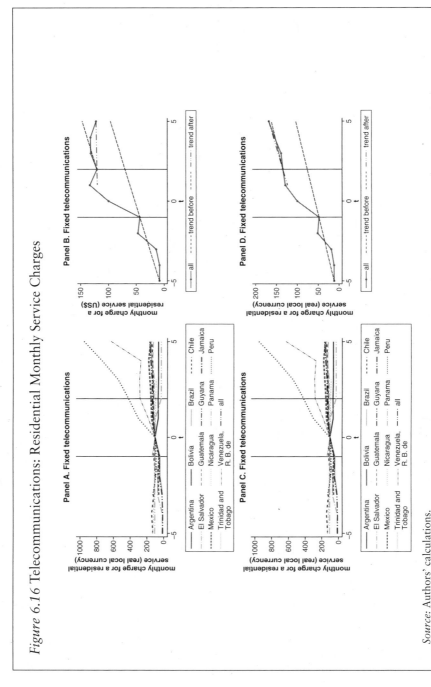

Figure 6.16 Telecommunications: Residential Monthly Service Charges

Source: Authors' calculations.

Note: The x axis is time; t = 0 is the last year with at least six months of public ownership. The y axis is normalized at 100 when time = 0.

Table 6.7 Telecommunications: Price Results

	Price of a three-minute local call (US$)	Price of a three-minute local call (real local currency)	Monthly residential service charge (US$)	Monthly residential service charge (real local currency)	Residential installation (US$)	Residential installation (real local currency)
Percentage change in level						
Transition	46.8 ***	44.9***	75.9***	62.6***	10.0	–16.3
Post-transition	–1.4	–8.6	23.2***	21.8**	–26.7***	–24.9*
Percentage change in level after controlling for time trend						
Transition	68.7***	43.0***	32.4***	6.9	35.0***	12.5
Post-transition	5.2	–15.5**	–6.5	–9.4	24.9***	27.6**
Percentage point change in annual growth rate						
Transition	–5.2	–5.6	–10.1	–4.7	–0.3	–14.0
Post-transition	1.9	–2.5	–3.4	0.1	–1.9	3.6

Source: Author's calculations.

Note: The percentage change for the post-transition period is with respect to the transition period values.

*Significant at 10 percent; **significant at 5 percent; ***significant at 1 percent

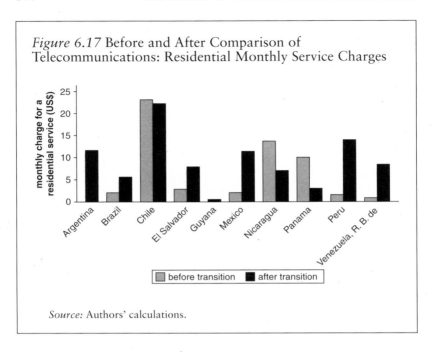

Figure 6.17 Before and After Comparison of
Telecommunications: Residential Monthly Service Charges

Source: Authors' calculations.

of the network that was digitized. The quality index steadily improved across all periods (figure 6.20) and actual quality levels after the transition were generally comparable across countries (figure 6.21). One exception was República Bolivariana de Venezuela, which experienced large gains but fell well short of actual levels in other countries.

Network digitization increased during both periods, with the largest increase coming during the transition. Table 6.8 displays the changes in quality levels and growth found by the econometric analysis.

Liberalization and Competition

Telecommunications: Liberalization and Competition Summary

Controlling for the liberalization of long-distance markets does not appreciably change the original results, although slight differences occur mainly in the price variables. Similarly, controlling for mobile subscribers yields few changes to the original results in terms of sign, value, and significance.

This section measures the impact of liberalization of long-distance markets and competition from mobile telecommunications on the performance

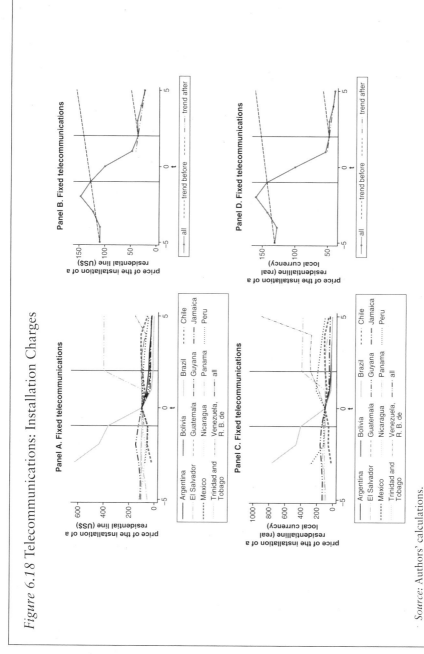

Figure 6.18 Telecommunications: Installation Charges

Source: Authors' calculations.

Note: The x axis is time; t = 0 is the last year with at least six months of public ownership. The y axis is normalized at 100 when time = 0.

Table 6.8 Telecommunications: Quality Results

	Percentage of network that is digital
Percentage change in level	
Transition	36.3***
Post-transition	58.1***
Percentage change in level after controlling for time trend	
Transition	4.9**
Post-transition	2.4
Percentage point change in annual growth rate	
Transition	−0.8
Post-transition	−5.6***

Source: Author's calculations.
Note: The percentage change for the post-transition period is with respect to the transition period values.
*Significant at 10 percent; **significant at 5 percent; ***significant at 1 percent.

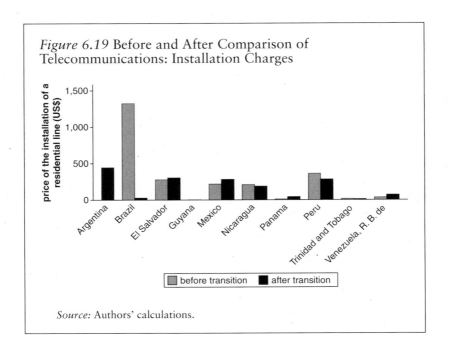

Figure 6.19 Before and After Comparison of Telecommunications: Installation Charges

Source: Authors' calculations.

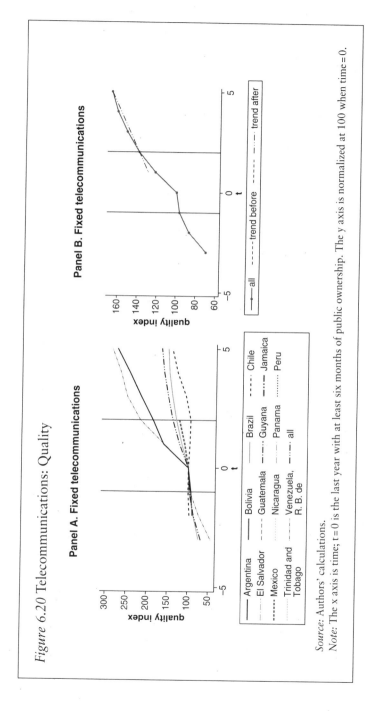

Figure 6.20 Telecommunications: Quality

Panel A. Fixed telecommunications

Panel B. Fixed telecommunications

Source: Authors' calculations.

Note: The x axis is time; t = 0 is the last year with at least six months of public ownership. The y axis is normalized at 100 when time = 0.

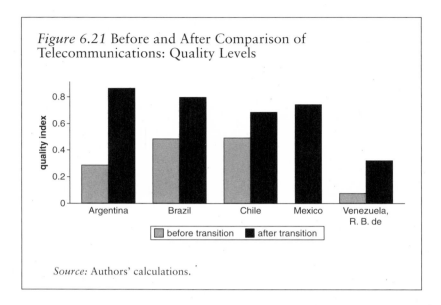

Figure 6.21 Before and After Comparison of Telecommunications: Quality Levels

Source: Authors' calculations.

indicators described above. These measurements were not possible in the electricity and water sectors because of a lack of comparable data. The aim is to separate the effects of liberalization and competition from privatization to avoid erroneously attributing performance changes to one or the other.[9]

Liberalization

To analyze the impact of long-distance liberalization, a dummy variable was added to the econometric analysis described in earlier in this chapter. The dummy is equal to one for those years that the market was liberalized (see table 6.2), and it is assumed that the liberalization process started the year of long-distance liberalization.[10] The results are qualitatively similar to the previous ones with some slight differences, mainly in the price variables (see table A3.7 compared with table A3.6).[11]

Adding the liberalization dummy variable to the model caused the impacts of privatization to change in roughly the following ways:

- Impacts on employment were less negative during both the transition and post-transition periods;
- The labor productivity increases were somewhat smaller, especially during the post-transition period;
- The drop in connection charges (in dollars) was smaller and the drop in the cost of a three-minute local call (in real local currency) was larger during the post-transition period; and

- The increase in the monthly charge (in real local currency) became insignificant.

Adding liberalization to the model provides estimates of the impact of liberalization, independent of its effects on privatization. For instance, liberalization had no significant effect on the number of connections or number of minutes consumed (after controlling for time trends). But it did further reduce the number of workers and increase the number of connections per worker, even after controlling for time trends for connections per worker. Liberalization increased coverage, the cost of a local call, and monthly charges (both in real local currency), while decreasing connection charges (in dollars).[12]

Competition from Mobile Service Providers

Tremendous growth in cellular phone use has been a phenomenon around the world. Hence, it would be reasonable to assume that competition from mobile service providers has had a substantial impact on fixed-line providers. To avoid conflating the impact of mobile competition and privatization on fixed-line providers, a new variable—the number of cellular lines in service—is added to the basic econometric specification used in preceding sections.[13] The results are then compared with those found above.

Table A3.8 expands on the privatization dates in table 6.1 to include the timing of the entrance of the mobile operators in each country. In some countries, the licenses were granted by geographic areas. The best example of this case is Brazil, where the Telebrás cellular operations were split into eight cellular service providers, each operating in one of eight regions.

Table A3.8 shows the results of controlling for the number of mobile subscribers. Perhaps surprisingly, the coefficients are quite close to the original results presented in table A3.6 in terms of sign, value, and significance. In other words, the significant impacts found in the previous sections are mostly valid after controlling for mobile subscribers. Again, for some variables—such as output and labor productivity—it makes more sense to compare results after controlling for time trends (see Models 2 and 3 of table A3.8).

Besides providing a more nuanced view of the impact of privatization, adding mobile subscribers to the model yields evidence about how fixed telecommunications markets behave when faced with competition. Perhaps surprisingly, the number of minutes consumed (of fixed telecom services) was found to be positively correlated with the number of mobile subscribers, even after controlling for time trends. Mobile subscribers were found to be negatively associated with the number of employees in fixed telecom, and adding mobile subscribers to the model reduced the impact of privatization on the number of employees during the post-transition period

Table 6.9 Fixed Telecommunications Impact Summary

	Transition	Post-transition
Output and coverage		
Number of connections[a]	↑	=
Number of minutes[a]	↑	↑
Coverage[a]	↑	=
Employment		
Number of employees	↓	↓
Labor productivity and efficiency		
Connections per employee[a]	↑	↑
Minutes per employee[a]	↑	=
Incomplete calls	=	↓
Prices		
Three-minute local call	↑	=
Monthly service charge	↑	↑
Installation charge	↓	↓
Quality		
Network digitization	↑	↑

Source: Authors' calculations.

Note: Up and down arrows indicate that a positive or negative change occurred in addition to the natural change that would be expected in the absence of privatization. An equal sign indicates that the trend perceived during the previous period was sustained but not substantially exceeded or diminished. The arrow size represents the size of the change.

a. Impacts are shown after controlling for time trends.

from –23.2 percent to –8.5 percent. Mobile subscribers did not have any significant effects on the percentage of incomplete calls, but it seems that a deceleration in the growth rate of network digitalization was associated with mobile subscribers.

Similar to the liberalization analysis findings, competition had important effects on prices. For instance, it seems that increasing numbers of cellular subscribers—rather than privatization effects—were responsible for the decrease in residential connection charges. Higher development in a country's cellular market was also associated with a drop in the cost of a three-minute local call (in dollars). Similarly, increased competition from mobile subscribers was associated with improvements in labor productivity and coverage in fixed telecommunications.[14]

Conclusion

The following is a brief summary of the chapter's main results. The change in ownership generally increased output and coverage, even after controlling for firm-specific time trends. Employment fell and labor productivity increased during the transition and post-transition periods, while efficiency (percentage of incomplete calls) improved during the post-transition period. Prices showed mixed results: the price of a local call increased during the transition; residential monthly charges increased in both periods; and installation charges decreased in both periods. Quality—as measured by network digitization—generally improved.

Controlling for the liberalization of long-distance markets does not appreciably change the original results, although there are slight differences, mainly in the price variables. Similarly, controlling for mobile subscribers yields few changes to the original results in terms of sign, value, and significance. In other words, the significant impacts found in the previous sections are still mostly valid after controlling for mobile subscribers.

Table 6.9 summarizes the results found in this chapter. The results for the output, coverage, and labor productivity indicators are reported after controlling for time trends.[15] If time trends were not controlled for, each of these indicators would show significant increases. The reasoning is that a natural increase is expected for each of these variables, regardless of whether ownership is public or private. For the other variables, a natural trend is not expected; hence, the results shown in table 6.9 do not incorporate the firm-specific time trend controls.

Notes

1. Currently, only six countries remain with public telecommunications firms: Colombia, Costa Rica, Ecuador, Honduras, Paraguay, and Uruguay.

2. The reorganization process started in 1991, when CTC transferred its concession for cellular telephone services to CTC-Celular S.A., which operated as a separate company since 1992. The reorganization process continued during 1992, when the operation of CTC's private telecommunications services, including data transmission and dedicated connections, along with the administration of CTC's large business and institutional customer accounts, were transferred to its subsidiary, CTC-Corp. In 1993, the marketing of telephone and terminal equipment, and the administration of public telephones, were transferred to CTC's subsidiary CTC-Equipos, previously CTC-Operaciones Telefónicas S.A.

3. The companies had the right, subject to regulatory approval and other conditions, to an extension of the exclusivity period. On March 13, 1998, the Argentine government issued Decree 264/98, whereby the exclusivity period for basic telephone services was extended until October 1999.

4. Results from the econometric analysis that controls for firm-specific time trends tell a somewhat different story. The number of connections fell by 4.9 percent during the transition, but then increased by 12 percent after the transition

(with respect to transition levels). This model specification is less useful in this particular case, however, given the fluctuating nature of the underlying data.

5. The means and medians analysis did not find a statistically significant difference between the pretransition and transition periods. Based on two observations, the analysis found that the average number of minutes was 40 percent higher during the post-transition period than during the transition period (see table A3.4).

6. The econometric analysis that controlled for firm-specific time trends found that coverage fell by 6.3 percent during the transition period and then increased by 9.5 percent during the post-transition period. This model specification may be less applicable, however, given the shape of the underlying data, (that is, the time trend analysis becomes less accurate when there is more than one shift in the presumed trend).

7. The means and medians analysis found that employment fell 14.5 percent during the transition and 18.2 percent more after the transition period. All of these changes were statistically significant.

8. Panama was a special case in that it actually had more connections in 1998 than in 2003. In 1998, 419,000 subscribers had fixed connections; at the end of 2003, only 380,000 had fixed connections. Not surprisingly, mobile telecommunications proliferated during the same years. In fact, mobile subscribers surpassed fixed-line subscribers, jumping from 49,000 in 1998 to 834,000 in 2003 (Ente Regulador de los Servicios Públicos 2004).

9. Other studies have taken similar concerns into account, including Ros (1999), Ros and Banerjee (2000), and Otken and Arin (2003).

10. This approach is analogous to the one used by Ros (1999). He found that competition did not affect network expansion, but had positive effects in labor productivity. He also found evidence of complementarity between privatization and competition. Ros pointed out that this dummy is a rules-based variable, given the fact that it does not quantify the degree of competition. Nevertheless, it denotes the starting point of the second-generation reforms that included, depending on the country, liberalization of the long-distance calls, changes in regulations, or competition with other services. See also Table 1 in Estache, Manacorda, and Valletti (2002) for a summary of key reforms in Latin America's telecommunications sector.

11. As described earlier in this chapter, the output and labor productivity variables are likely driven by trends, so Models 2 and 3 in table A3.7 are more relevant.

12. The results found here for coverage and labor productivity, after controlling for time trends, were consistent with those found by Ros (1999).

13. A similar approach with additional features was used by Wallsten (2001) who analyzed privatization and competition in LAC and Africa focusing on indicators of coverage, labor productivity, and prices.

14. Note that while the prices results presented here are qualitatively consistent with Wallsten (2001), those related to coverage and labor productivity are not. Both results show positive effects of competition on coverage, but this analysis still finds an important effect caused by privatization. Contrary to Wallsten's results, this analysis also finds significant effects on labor productivity of both privatization and competition.

15. Time trends (or lack thereof) can be found through two complementary methods: Model 2 in the econometric analysis, which controls for firm-specific time trends; and Model 3 of the econometric analysis, which looks at growth rate changes (see appendix 3 for the complete results from each model).

7

The Impact on Water
and Sewerage

Introduction

Historically, the water and sewerage sectors have not been well analyzed in Latin America. In contrast to electricity and telecommunications, firms tend to be based at the local or regional government level, making the private participation process slower and more fragmented. Despite the slow process, currently, at least 11 percent of the water in Latin American households is supplied by private firms. For the analysis in this chapter, data were collected for 49 firms with a change in ownership in the last 15 years.

Similar to the electricity distribution and telecommunications chapters, two complementary methodologies were used to learn about the effects of changes in ownership: a means and medians analysis and an econometric analysis. For a description of these methodologies, see chapter 4. The full results of the means and medians analysis and econometric analysis, including statistical significance, are shown in appendix 3. This chapter synthesizes the results from the two methodologies, presenting summaries geared toward policy makers in the following areas: outputs and coverage, employment, labor productivity, efficiency, prices, and quality.

As described in chapter 4, the period under analysis is separated into three parts: preprivatization (pretransition), a three-year transition period, and postprivatization (post-transition), allowing for the separation of short- versus long-term effects. The main results of the analysis are summarized in each section as well as in the conclusion of the chapter.

The Privatization Process

During the 1990s, most countries in Latin America undertook major reforms to their water supply industries. Chile was the first to attempt to modernize its water sector, with new legislation passed as early as 1988. By 1991, both Argentina and Mexico were beginning to conduct a series of experiments with private sector participation. In a second wave, Peru, Colombia, and Bolivia enacted ambitious new legislation in the mid-1990s. During the second half of the decade, reform began to take root in Brazil and Central America. By the end of the 1990s, few countries remained that had not either completed reforms, had major reforms in process, or were actively considering reforms.

In general, the water sector reforms were composed of three components: decentralization, regulation, and private sector participation.

Before 1990, many Latin American countries (for example, Argentina, Chile, Colombia, Panama, and Peru) had organized their water industry as national monopolies under the direct control of the central government. Growing dissatisfaction with the performance of the national monopolies, combined with wider political pressure for devolution across all areas of government, created the conditions for a move toward decentralized control in the 1980s and 1990s. In countries such as Argentina, Colombia, and Peru, this entailed a sudden fragmentation of the industry into literally hundreds of small municipal providers.

As part of the reform process, many countries created national regulatory agencies for water, similar to the Water Services Regulation Authority (OfWAT) model developed in the United Kingdom. The responsibilities of these agencies typically included the determination of tariffs, approval of investment plans, oversight on quality of service, and consumer protection. In some cases (for example, Peru), the agencies did not have final authority to determine tariffs. In the larger federal countries (Argentina, Brazil, and Mexico), regulatory functions were often organized at the state or provincial level.

The regulatory agencies were seen as a precursor to private participation in the sector, although the ultimate scope of private participation was modest relative to initial expectations. Indeed, in some countries—for example, Panama, Peru, and until recently Chile—regulation has been introduced without privatization. In others—such as Bolivia and Colombia—regulatory reform has been nationwide, but privatization has been confined to metropolitan areas or a handful of major provincial centers. Overall, it is estimated that although 41 percent of urban water consumers now enjoy regulatory protection, only 15 percent are serviced by private sector operators (see table 7.1).

Some of the most important private participation experiences are listed in table 7.2, and these results will form the central focus of this study. Although the bulk of these experiences relate to the concession modality, the list also includes important examples of divestiture (the Chilean cases), mixed enterprise ownership (some of the Colombian cases), and management contracts (such as in Honduras). A significant number of the concession contracts were

Table 7.1 Overview of Water Sector Reform[a]

	Decentralization	Percentage of population covered by regulation	Percentage of population covered by PSP
Argentina	To provincial level	88	62
Bolivia	To municipal level	100	28
Brazil	To municipal level	24	1
Chile	To regional level	100	86
Colombia	To municipal level	100	13
Costa Rica	None	100	0
Ecuador	To municipal level	25	25
El Salvador	None	0	0
Guatemala	None	0	0
Honduras	To municipal level	16	16
Mexico	To municipal level	19	19
Nicaragua	None	100	0
Panama	None	100	0
Paraguay	None	100	0
Peru	To municipal level	100	0
Uruguay	None	17	17
Venezuela, R. B. de	To municipal level	3	3

Source: Foster 2005.

Note: PSP = private sector participation.

a. The percentage numbers refer to the percentage of the urban population that enjoys regulatory protection and receives its service directly from a private sector operator (excluding BOT projects).

distressed as a result of currency devaluations (Argentina) or social backlash (Bolivia) and subsequently have been canceled.

Data

Data were collected for companies in Argentina, Bolivia, Brazil, Chile, Colombia, Mexico, and Trinidad and Tobago. The sample consists of unbalanced panel data that includes 49 firms and 515 firm-year observations. Each of the firms included in the sample contains at least one year of preprivatization data, and 35 of the 49 firms have information for at

Table 7.2 Privatization Chronology of Water and Sewerage in LAC

Country	Year	Privatized firms
Argentina	1991	Aguas de Corrientes
	1992	Sudamericana de Aguas (Pilar)
	1993	Aguas Argentinas S.A.
	1994	Aguas de Balcarse S.A.
	1995	Aguas de Formosa S.A. and Aguas de Santa Fe
	1996	Aguas de Tucumán S.A. and Aguas de Laprida
	1997	Aguas Cordobesas and Aguas de Santiago S.A.
	1998	Aguas de Campana S.A., Aguas de Salta, and Obras Sanitarias Mendoza S.A.
	1999	Aguas de Misiones S.A., Empresa Provincial de Obras Sanitaria de la Rioja and Azurix Buenos Aires S.A.
	2000	Aguas del Valle (Catamarca)
Bolivia	1997	Aguas de Illimani (former Servicio Autónomo Municipal de Agua Potable y Alcantarillado [SAMAPA])
	1999	Cochabamba
Brazil	1994	Pereiras
	1995	Limeira
	1996	Aguas do DO Paraiba (RJ), Mineiros do Tiete, and Tuiuti
	1997	Mairinque (SP), Paranagua (PR), and Prolagos (RJ)
	1998	Cachoeiro do Itapemirim (ES), Cajamar (SP), Juturnaiba, Noteroi (RJ), and Petropolis (RJ)
	1999	Nobres and Nova Friburgo (RJ)
	2000	Manaus (AM)
	1999	Jundai
Chile	1990	Aguas Andinas SA (former Empresa Metropolitana de Obras Sanitarias S.A. [EMOS]) and EAP Los Dominicos S.A.
	1995	Aguas Decima S.A.
	1998	Aguas Quinta S.A. and Empresa de Servicios Sanitarios de Valparaíso S.A. (ESVAL)
	1999	Empresa de Servicios Sanitarios de Los Lagos S.A. (ESSAL)

(continued)

Table 7.2 Privatization Chronology of Water and Sewerage in LAC *(continued)*

Country	Year	Privatized firms
	2000	Empresa de Servicios Sanitarios del Bio-Bío S.A. (ESSBIO) and Empresa de Servicios Sanitarios del Libertados S.A. (ESSEL)
	2001	Aguas Nuevo Sur Maule (former Empresa de Servicios Sanitarios del Maule S.A. [ESSAM])
Colombia	1992	Barranquilla
	1995	Cartagena
	1996	Tunja
	1998	Palmira and Santa Marta
	1999	Girardot
	2000	Monteria
	2002	CONHYDRA (Buenaventura) and Empresa de Servicios Varios de Florencia (SERVAF)
Ecuador	2001	Interaguas
Honduras	2001	Aguas de San Pedro
Mexico	1992	Chihuahua, Chihuahua
	1993	Aguascalientes
	1994	Cancún, Quintana Roo
	1996	Bahias de Huatulco and Navojoa
Trinidad and Tobago	1996	Severn Trent (management contractor)

Source: Authors' elaboration.
Note: LAC = Latin America and the Caribbean.

least the previous two years. Table 7.3 contains a description of the water and sewerage variables used in the analysis.

Impact on Output and Coverage

Water and Sewerage: Output and Coverage Summary

The number of water and sewage connections increased during the transition and post-transition periods, but these improvements were consistent with existing trends. Similar results were found for both water and sewerage coverage. Water production increased somewhat in both periods, but after controlling for trends, a small growth deceleration occurred in the post-transition period.

Table 7.3 Description of Water and Sewerage Variables

Variable	Description
Output	
Water connections	Total number of residential water subscribers
Sewerage connections	Total number of residential sewerage subscribers
Water production	Total water production in cubic meters per year
Coverage	
Water coverage	Number of residential water subscribers per 100 households
Sewerage coverage	Number of residential sewerage subscribers per 100 households
Employment	
Number of employees	Total number of employees
Labor productivity and efficiency	
Connections per employee	Number of connections divided by the number of employees
Distributional losses	Percentage of total water produced not charged to consumers
Prices	
Water price (US$)	Average price per cubic meter of supplied water (in US$)[a]
Water price (real local currency)	Average price per cubic meter of supplied water (in real local currency)[b]
Sewerage price (US$)	Average price per cubic meter of sewerage collected (in US$)[a]
Sewerage price (real local currency)	Average price per cubic meter of sewerage collected (in real local currency)[b]
Quality	
Continuity	Average number of hours per day with water service
Potability	Percentage of the samples that passed a potability test

Source: Authors' elaboration.

a. Built with original nominal price data and converted using the exchange rate for each year.

b. Built with original nominal price data and converted using Consumer Price Index.

Number of Connections

Two variables are used to measure output in the water and sewerage sector: the number of residential connections (for both water and sewerage) and the amount of water produced (in cubic meters) each year. The number of connections for both water and sewerage increased substantially during both the transition and post-transition periods (figure 7.1). In fact, the econometric analysis found significant increases of between 15 and 20 percent for each period (see table 7.4 and table A3.12). The means and medians analysis found similar results, which can be found in table A3.10.

A closer look at the results shows the increases can be accounted for by the existence of a trend. After controlling for firm-specific time trends, the econometric analysis found no significant changes in the number of water or sewerage connections. When considering growth rates, the econometric analysis found no significant changes during the transition, while the average annual growth rate fell by 1 percent after the transition for both water and sewerage (see table 7.4 and table A3.12).

When actual (as opposed to normalized) water connection numbers are considered (figure 7.2), Argentina and Chile stand out as having the largest water distribution companies. For sewerage, Argentina, Chile, and Colombia have companies of roughly the same size. In contrast to the results found in other sectors, water and sewerage companies in Brazil and Mexico fall at the small end of the spectrum.

Water Production

The second output indicator is the number of cubic meters of water produced per year (figure 7.3). The econometric analysis found that water production increased by 4.1 percent during the transition period and an additional 1.5 percent after the transition period. However, taking trends into account—by controlling for firm-specific time trends or looking at changes in growth rates—erases those gains. In fact, the econometric analysis found no significant change in water production during the transition and a small drop after the transition.[1] As will be seen later, a possible justification for this deceleration is the improvement in efficiency caused by the reduction of distributional losses.

Figure 7.4 indicates that the actual levels of water production in Argentina are far higher than those in other countries. This result is somewhat surprising given that the gap between the average number of connections in Argentina and the average number in Chile was quite a bit smaller.

The number of connections increased during both periods for water and sewerage, but these improvements were consistent with existing trends. Water production increased somewhat in both periods, but after

Figure 7.1 Water and Sewerage: Number of Connections

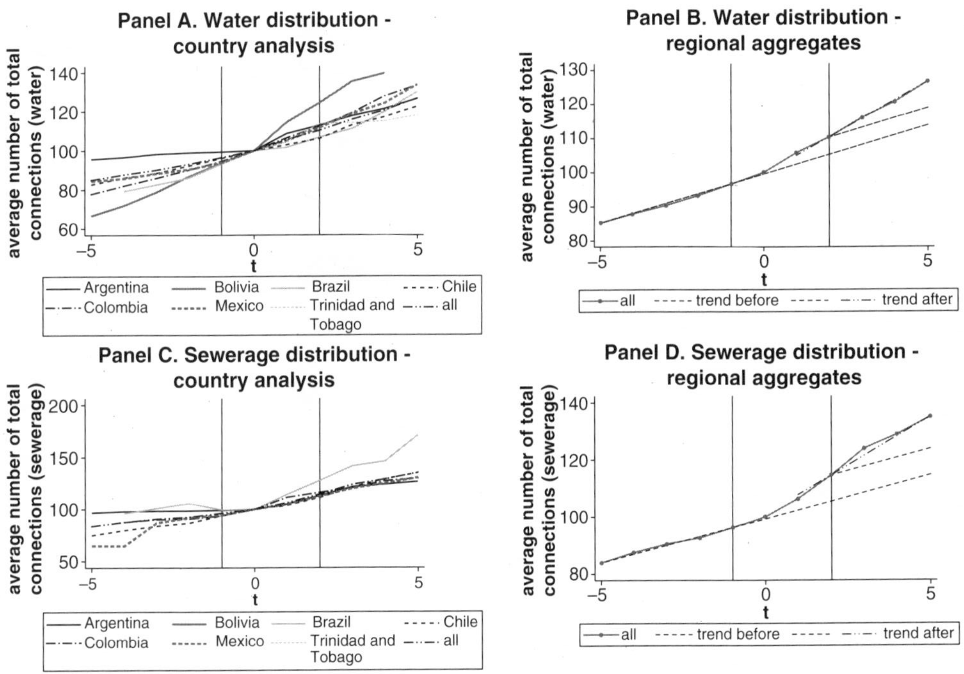
Panel A. Water distribution - country analysis
average number of total connections (water)
140
120
100
80
60
–5
0
5
t
Argentina
Bolivia
Brazil
Chile
Colombia
Mexico
Trinidad and Tobago
all
Panel B. Water distribution - regional aggregates
average number of total connections (water)
130
120
110
100
90
80
–5
0
5
t
all
trend before
trend after
Panel C. Sewerage distribution - country analysis
average number of total connections (sewerage)
200
150
100
50
–5
0
5
t
Argentina
Bolivia
Brazil
Chile
Colombia
Mexico
Trinidad and Tobago
all
Panel D. Sewerage distribution - regional aggregates
average number of total connections (sewerage)
140
120
100
80
–5
0
5
t
all
trend before
trend after

Source: Authors' calculations.

Note: The x axis is time; t = 0 is the last year with at least six months of public ownership. The y axis is normalized at 100 when time = 0.

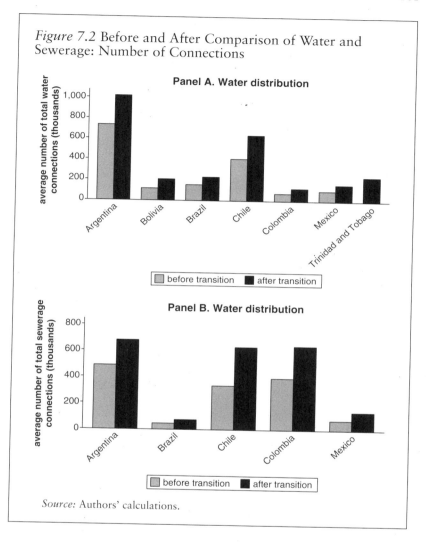

Figure 7.2 Before and After Comparison of Water and Sewerage: Number of Connections

Panel A. Water distribution

average number of total water connections (thousands)

before transition   after transition

Panel B. Water distribution

average number of total sewerage connections (thousands)

before transition   after transition

Source: Authors' calculations.

controlling for trends, there was a small growth deceleration in the post-transition period. Table 7.4 summarizes the changes in output levels and growth found by the econometric analysis.

Coverage

Coverage in both water and sewerage improved during the transition and post-transition periods (figure 7.5). According to the econometric analysis, these improvements were statistically significant and ranged

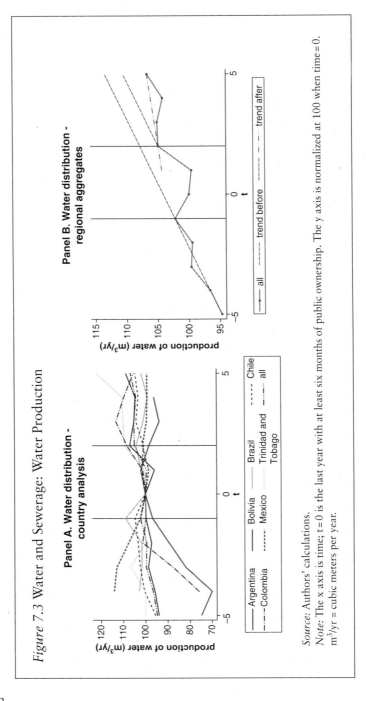

Figure 7.3 Water and Sewerage: Water Production

Panel A. Water distribution - country analysis

production of water (m³/yr)

Panel B. Water distribution - regional aggregates

production of water (m³/yr)

Source: Authors' calculations.
Note: The x axis is time; t = 0 is the last year with at least six months of public ownership. The y axis is normalized at 100 when time = 0. m³/yr = cubic meters per year.

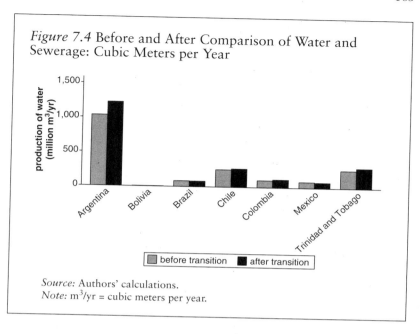

Figure 7.4 Before and After Comparison of Water and Sewerage: Cubic Meters per Year

Source: Authors' calculations.
Note: m³/yr = cubic meters per year.

Table 7.4 Water and Sewerage: Output Results

	Number of water connections	Number of sewerage connections	Cubic meters per year
Percentage change in level			
Transition	15.1***	19.0***	4.1***
Post-transition	14.9***	18.9***	1.5***
Percentage change in level after controlling for time trend			
Transition	0.6	−0.6	−0.7
Post-transition	−0.2	−0.5	−1.3*
Percentage point change in annual growth rate			
Transition	0.1	0.6	−0.8
Post-transition	−1.0***	−1.1***	−2.5***

Source: Author's calculations.
Note: The percentage change for the post-transition period is with respect to the transition period values.
*Significant at 10 percent; ***significant at 1 percent.

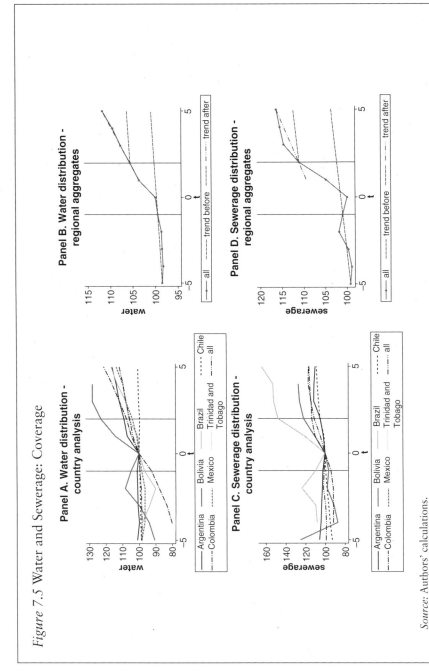

Figure 7.5 Water and Sewerage: Coverage

Panel A. Water distribution - country analysis

water

Argentina —— Bolivia —— Brazil ------ Chile
- · - Colombia ········ Mexico —— Trinidad and ········ all
Tobago

Panel B. Water distribution - regional aggregates

water

—— all —————— trend before ------ trend after

Panel C. Sewerage distribution - country analysis

sewerage

Argentina —— Bolivia —— Brazil ------ Chile
- · - Colombia ········ Mexico —— Trinidad and ········ all
Tobago

Panel D. Sewerage distribution - regional aggregates

sewerage

—— all —————— trend before ------ trend after

Source: Authors' calculations.
Note: The x axis is time; t = 0 is the last year with at least six months of public ownership. The y axis is normalized at 100 when time = 0.

from 2.5 percent to 6.7 percent (table 7.5). The means and medians analysis found similar increases of between 6.9 and 11.1 percent (table A3.10). These improvements apparently were driven by trends, however, and they likely would have occurred in the absence of privatization. After controlling for firm-specific time trends, the econometric analysis found no significant changes. And looking at growth rates yielded no significant changes during the transition period, combined with a small drop in the average annual growth rate of 0.4 percentage points for water and 0.8 percentage points for sewerage after the transition. Not surprisingly, these results are quantitatively similar to those found for the number of connections above.

When actual (not normalized) water coverage levels are considered, levels for most countries are relatively high—more than 90 percent (figure 7.6). Mexico stands out as an exception with less than 80 percent coverage. For sewerage, actual coverage levels are lower—closer to 60 percent for some countries. Chile is the outlier, with close to 100 percent sewerage coverage.

Coverage increased during both periods for water and sewerage, but these improvements were consistent with existing trends. Table 7.5 summarizes the changes in coverage levels and growth found by the econometric analysis.

Impact on Employment

Water and Sewerage: Employment Summary

The number of employees declined during transition and post-transition, not accounting for time trends. All of the analyses found significant drops in employment during both of these periods, although the drop during the transition seems to have been the greatest (figure 7.7). Specifically, the means and medians analysis found a 26.3 percent drop during the transition and a 11.7 percent drop after the transition. The econometric analysis found a 16.5 percent drop during the transition and a 17.6 percent drop after the transition.[2]

Given that most state-owned enterprises had excess numbers of personnel, the drops seen during the transition period should not be surprising. Many governments opted to trim the labor force before the ownership change in an attempt to increase the value of the firm. Figure 7.8 shows the average actual number of employees per water and sewerage firm in each country. Argentina stands out as having by far the most employees as well as experiencing the largest absolute reduction in employee numbers between the pretransition and post-transition periods.

The number of employees declined in both periods, with larger drops seen during the transition period. Table 7.6 presents the changes in employment levels and growth found by the econometric analysis.

Table 7.5 Water and Sewerage: Coverage Results

	Water coverage	Sewerage coverage
Percentage change in level		
Transition	2.5***	5.4***
Post-transition	5.0***	6.7***
Percentage change in level after controlling for time trend		
Transition	0.0	−0.5
Post-transition	−0.1	−0.8
Percentage point change in annual growth rate		
Transition	0.1	0.3
Post-transition	−0.4***	−0.8**

Source: Author's calculations.
Note: The percentage change for the post-transition period is with respect to the transition period values.
**Significant at 5 percent; ***significant at 1 percent.

Impact on Labor Productivity and Efficiency

Water and Sewerage: Labor Productivity and Efficiency Summary

Labor productivity—measured by the number of water connections per employee—showed substantial increases. When looking at growth rates changes, however, one notices that a significant increase occurred during the transition followed by a growth deceleration during the post-transition period. Distributional losses fell during both periods, with the greatest improvements coming in the post-transition period.

Labor Productivity

Labor productivity—measured by the number of water connections per employee—clearly increased greatly during both the transition and post-transition periods (figure 7.9). This was a result of changes in the underlying indicators: the number of connections increased while the number of employees fell. The econometric analysis found that water connections per employee increased 30.7 percent during the transition and another 42.5 percent after the transition. The means and medians analysis found similar large jumps.

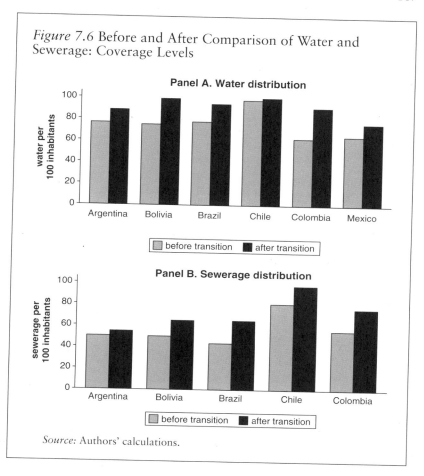

Figure 7.6 Before and After Comparison of Water and Sewerage: Coverage Levels

Controlling for trends tells a somewhat different story. According to the econometric growth rate analysis, the average annual growth rate of connections per employee increased by 4.7 percentage points during the transition. This was followed by a drop of 3.7 percentage points after the transition (relative to the transition levels). In other words, there was a temporary acceleration in labor productivity growth (largely because of employment changes) during the transition, and then the annual growth rate returned to roughly 1 percentage point above the pretransition level. The means and medians analysis identified similar changes: a 11.6 percentage point increase during the transition followed by a 9.6 percentage point decrease after the transition. There was no statistically significant

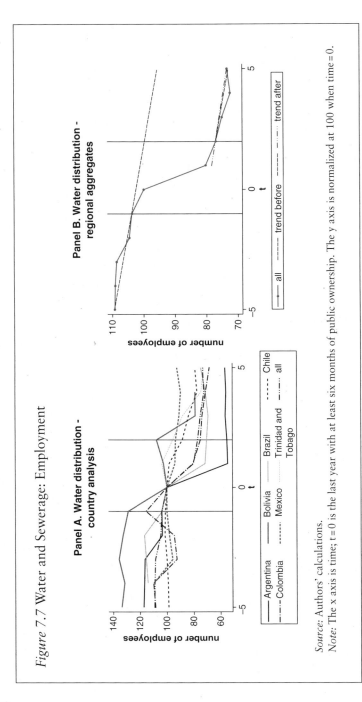

Figure 7.7 Water and Sewerage: Employment

**Panel A. Water distribution -
country analysis**

**Panel B. Water distribution -
regional aggregates**

Source: Authors' calculations.
Note: The x axis is time; t = 0 is the last year with at least six months of public ownership. The y axis is normalized at 100 when time = 0.

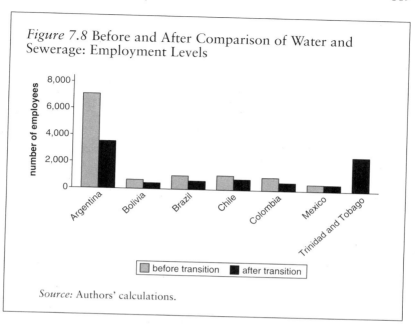

Figure 7.8 Before and After Comparison of Water and Sewerage: Employment Levels

Source: Authors' calculations.

Table 7.6 Water and Sewerage: Employment Results

	Number of employees
Percentage change in level	
Transition	−16.5***
Post-transition	−17.6***
Percentage change in level after controlling for time trend	
Transition	8.7***
Post-transition	7.1***
Percentage point change in annual growth rate	
Transition	−4.8***
Post-transition	4.8***

Source: Author's calculations.

Note: The percentage change for the post-transition period is with respect to the transition period values.

***Significant at 1 percent.

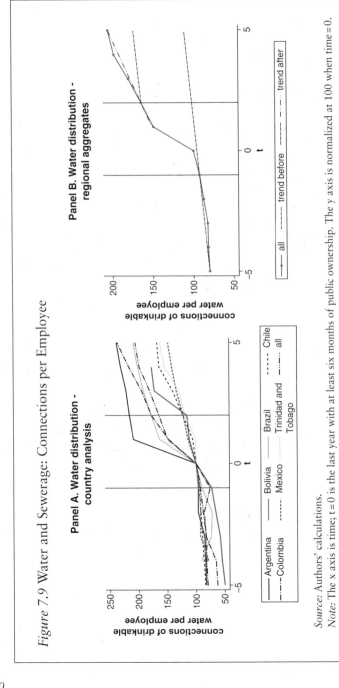

Figure 7.9 Water and Sewerage: Connections per Employee

Panel A. Water distribution - country analysis

Panel B. Water distribution - regional aggregates

Source: Authors' calculations.
Note: The x axis is time; t = 0 is the last year with at least six months of public ownership. The y axis is normalized at 100 when time = 0.

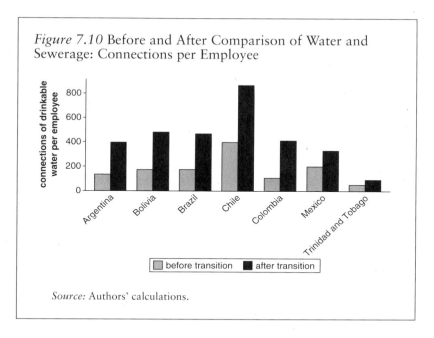

Figure 7.10 Before and After Comparison of Water and Sewerage: Connections per Employee

Source: Authors' calculations.

difference between the pretransition and post-transition growth rates in the means and medians analysis.

Labor productivity is fairly similar across countries, hovering close to 400 connections of drinkable water per employee (figure 7.10). The exceptions are Chile, which vastly outperforms the others, and Trinidad and Tobago, which is an underperformer.

Distributional Losses

Distributional losses clearly fell substantially during both the transition and post-transition periods (figure 7.11). Indeed, the econometric analysis found a 3.8 percent drop in the percentage of water lost during the transition period followed by a 14.4 percent drop during the post-transition period. The means and medians analysis found results of a slightly larger magnitude (8.1 percent and 18.3 percent, respectively). Trends are not controlled for because a natural trend is not expected, and figure 7.11 does not signal a trend in the preprivatization period.

Actual levels of lost water are somewhat consistent across countries, especially after the transition (figure 7.12). Specifically, firms in the countries studied lost close to 40 percent of their water on average during the post-transition period.

Labor productivity—measured by number of water connections per employee—showed substantial increases. When looking at growth rate

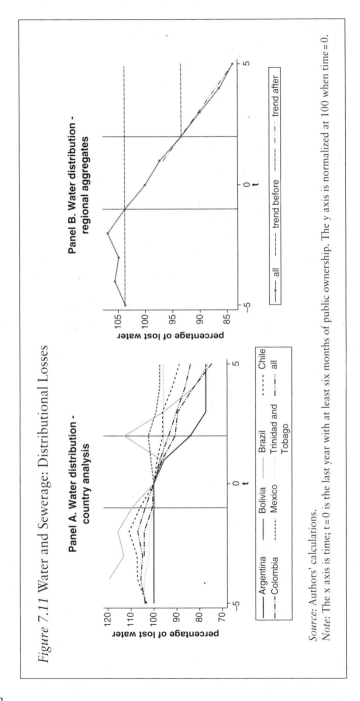

Figure 7.11 Water and Sewerage: Distributional Losses

Panel A. Water distribution - country analysis

Panel B. Water distribution - regional aggregates

Source: Authors' calculations.

Note: The x axis is time; t = 0 is the last year with at least six months of public ownership. The y axis is normalized at 100 when time = 0.

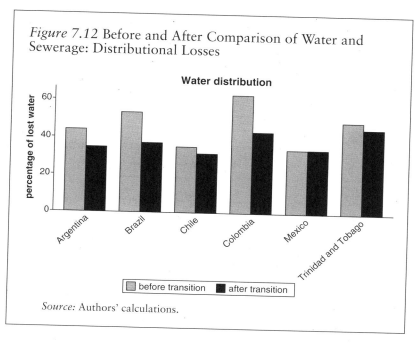

Figure 7.12 Before and After Comparison of Water and Sewerage: Distributional Losses

Source: Authors' calculations.

changes, one notes there was a significant increase during the transition followed by a growth deceleration during the post-transition period. Distributional losses fell during both periods, with the greatest improvements coming in the post-transition period. Table 7.7 presents the changes in labor productivity and efficiency levels and growth found by the econometric analysis.

Impact on Prices

Water and Sewerage: Price Summary

Water prices in dollars showed little change during the transition (thanks to Brazil's devaluation) and rose after the transition. Water prices in real local currency increased fairly substantially in both the transition and post-transition periods. Because of the small sample size, not much can be said about sewerage prices; however, a significant sewerage price increase in real local currency occurred during the post-transition period.

Four measures of prices were analyzed: (i) water prices in dollars, (ii) water prices in real local currency, (iii) sewerage prices in dollars, and (iv) sewerage prices in real local currency. Water prices seem to have increased in both periods in dollars and in real local currency (figure 7.13). Brazil's currency devaluation in 1999 accounted for the main difference between

Table 7.7 Water and Sewerage: Labor Productivity
and Efficiency Results

	Water connections per employee	Distributional losses
Percentage change in level		
Transition	30.7***	−3.8**
Post-transition	42.5***	−14.4***
Percentage change in level after controlling for time trend		
Transition	−7.3***	−1.4
Post-transition	−2.7	0.0
Percentage point change in annual growth rate		
Transition	4.7***	0.0
Post-transition	−3.7***	−1.2*

Source: Author's calculations.
Note: The percentage change for the post-transition period is with respect to the transition period values.
*Significant at 10 percent; **significant at 5 percent; ***significant at 1 percent.

the two types of currencies. As a result of the devaluation, Brazil's water prices in dollars fell, while they mainly rose in real local currency. Given that the Brazil devaluation skewed the dollar price's results so that they appeared artificially low, it is preferable to look at the changes in real local currency.

According to the econometric analysis, water prices in dollars did not change significantly during the transition, but increased by 10.2 percent after the transition. In contrast, water prices showed statistically significant increases in real local currency of 15.7 percent during the transition and 23.7 percent after transition. In the means and medians analysis, there were no significant changes between adjacent periods in dollars, but there was a statistically significant increase between the pre- and post-transition periods. In real local currency, the means and medians analysis found significant price increases in each period. When Brazil was excluded from the sample, the means and medians analysis found statistically significant increases of 32.6 percent during the transition and 16.9 percent after the transition.

When comparing actual price levels in dollars, there is a fairly wide dispersion between Brazil, Chile, and Colombia (figure 7.14). After the transition, Brazil had the cheapest prices and water in Chile was the most expensive.

Figure 7.13 Water and Sewerage: Water Prices

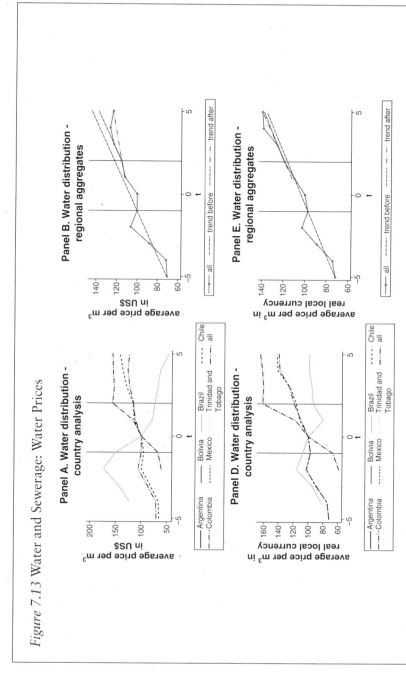

Source: Authors' calculations.

Note: The x axis is time; t = 0 is the last year with at least six months of public ownership. The y axis is normalized at 100 when time = 0.

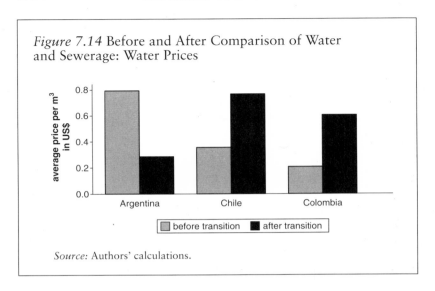

Figure 7.14 Before and After Comparison of Water and Sewerage: Water Prices

Source: Authors' calculations.

Sewerage prices seem to have behaved in a similar fashion as water prices (figure 7.15). Because of the small number of observations, those results were not statistically significant for the most part. In fact, according to both the econometric and means and medians analyses, the only significant change was an increase in real local currency prices after the transition period (this increase was 24.9 percent in the econometric analysis).

Water prices in dollars showed little change during the transition (thanks to Brazil's devaluation) and rose after the transition. Water prices in real local currency increased fairly substantially in both periods. Not much can be said about sewerage prices because of the small sample size. However, a significant sewerage price increase in real local currency in the post-transition period was found. Table 7.8 summarizes the changes in price levels and growth found by the econometric analysis.

Impact on Quality

Water and Sewerage: Quality Summary

Water distribution quality is measured by service continuity (the average number of hours per day with water service) and potability (the percentage of the water samples that passed a potability test). Service continuity improved during transition and post-transition. Potability also improved during both periods, but the bulk of the changes occurred during the transition.

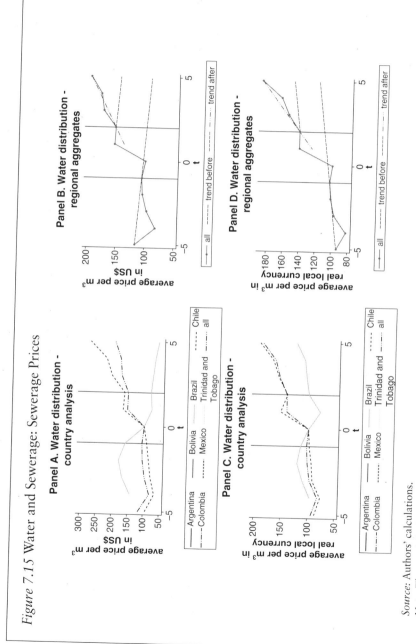

Figure 7.15 Water and Sewerage: Sewerage Prices

Panel A. Water distribution - country analysis

average price per m³ in US$

Argentina — Bolivia — Brazil ····· Chile
Colombia -·-·- Mexico ········ Trinidad and —··— all
Tobago

Panel B. Water distribution - regional aggregates

average price per m³ in US$

all ——— trend before ——— trend after

Panel C. Water distribution - country analysis

average price per m³ in real local currency

Argentina — Bolivia — Brazil ····· Chile
Colombia -·-·- Mexico ········ Trinidad and —··— all
Tobago

Panel D. Water distribution - regional aggregates

average price per m³ in real local currency

all ——— trend before ——— trend after

Source: Authors' calculations.
Note: The x axis is time; t = 0 is the last year with at least six months of public ownership. The y axis is normalized at 100 when time = 0.

177

Table 7.8 Water and Sewerage: Price Results

	Water prices (US$)	Water prices (real local currency)	Sewerage prices (US$)	Sewerage prices (real local currency)
Percentage change in level				
Transition	5.7	15.7***	−1.4	11.0
Post-transition	10.2**	23.7***	−9.2	24.9***
Percentage change in level after controlling for time trend				
Transition	0.3	−4.7	2.6	1.7
Post-transition	−4.6	−2.4	1.3	4.6
Percentage point change in annual growth rate				
Transition	−20.3***	−9.9***	−5.4	0.7
Post-transition	−1.8	−1.1	−0.5	0.6

Source: Author's calculations.

Note: The percentage change for the post-transition period is with respect to the transition period values.

**Significant at 5 percent; ***significant at 1 percent.

Service Continuity

Improvements in service continuity appear to have occurred during both the transition and post-transition periods, although no improvements occurred during the pretransition period (figure 7.16). The means and medians analysis found that on average continuity improved by 27.8 percent during the transition period and 14.8 percent after the transition, presumably because of a relatively small sample size; the econometric analysis found a statistically significant improvement (of 7.7 percent) only in the post-transition period.

When actual service continuity numbers are considered, the preprivatization data from Colombia are striking: water was available for less than 10 hours per day on average. With the exception of Trinidad and Tobago, the other countries in the sample enjoyed more than 20 hours per day of water after the transition (figure 7.17).

Potability

Despite a relatively small number of observations, it seems evident that water potability improved (figure 7.18). Most of the changes occurred during the transition: according to the econometric analysis, potability improved by 6.1 percent during the transition and 1.2 percent in the

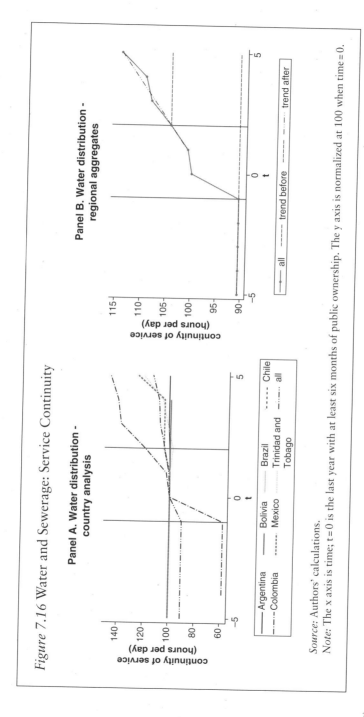

Figure 7.16 Water and Sewerage: Service Continuity

Panel A. Water distribution - country analysis

Panel B. Water distribution - regional aggregates

Source: Authors' calculations.

Note: The x axis is time; t = 0 is the last year with at least six months of public ownership. The y axis is normalized at 100 when time = 0.

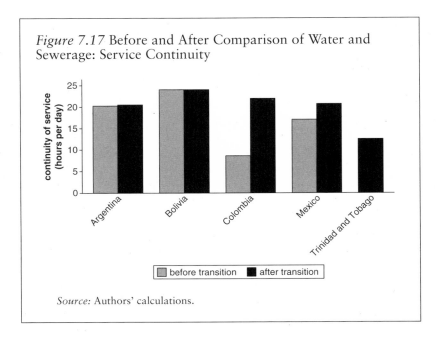

Figure 7.17 Before and After Comparison of Water and Sewerage: Service Continuity

Source: Authors' calculations.

post-transition period. Given that potability numbers were already close to 100 percent for many countries (with the exception of Colombia), it is not surprising that the improvements seen in the post-transition period were quite modest (figure 7.19).

Service continuity improved during both periods. Potability also improved during both periods, but the bulk of the changes occurred during the transition. Table 7.9 presents the changes in quality levels and growth found by the econometric analysis.

Conclusion

The following is a brief summary of the water and sewerage results. Output and coverage measures improved, but the improvements were consistent with the existing trend. Meanwhile, the number of employees dropped substantially during the last years under public management. These changes significantly increased labor productivity, especially during the transition period, but when looking at growth rates, labor productivity rates accelerated during the transition and decelerated in the post-transition period. Efficiency—measured by distributional losses—improved mainly after the transition. Price increases were seen in both water and sewerage, although the increases for sewerage were generally not robust

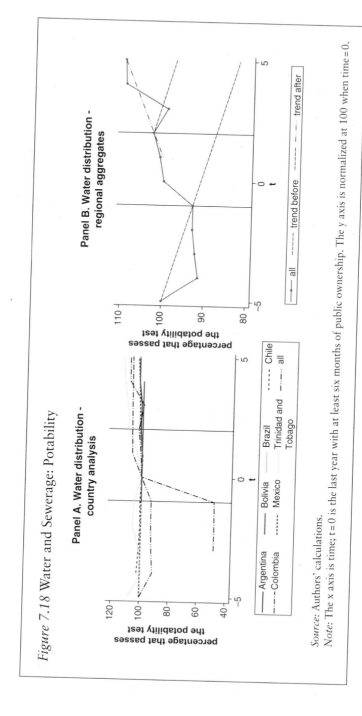

Figure 7.18 Water and Sewerage: Potability

Panel A. Water distribution - country analysis

percentage that passes the potability test

t

Argentina
Colombia
Bolivia
Mexico
Brazil
Trinidad and Tobago
Chile
all

Panel B. Water distribution - regional aggregates

percentage that passes the potability test

t

all
trend before
trend after

Source: Authors' calculations.
Note: The x axis is time; $t = 0$ is the last year with at least six months of public ownership. The y axis is normalized at 100 when time $= 0$.

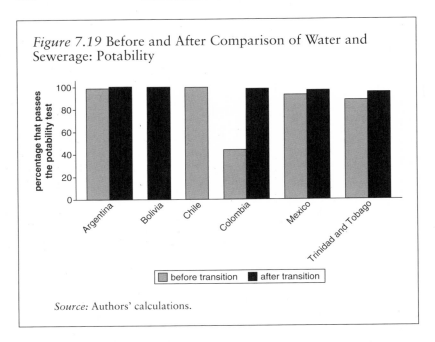

Figure 7.19 Before and After Comparison of Water and Sewerage: Potability

Source: Authors' calculations.

Table 7.9 Water and Sewerage: Quality Results

	Service continuity	Potability
Percentage change in level		
Transition	3.9	6.1*
Post-transition	7.7***	1.2**
Percentage change in level after controlling for time trend		
Transition	0.0	−0.2
Post-transition	0.0	−0.2
Percentage point change in annual growth rate		
Transition	0.2	0.9
Post-transition	−0.1	−0.5

Source: Authors' calculations.
Note: The percentage change for the post-transition period is with respect to the transition period values.
*Significant at 10 percent; **significant at 5 percent; ***significant at 1 percent.

Table 7.10 Water and Sewerage Impact Summary

	Transition	Post-transition
Output and coverage		
Number of water connections[a]	=	=
Number of sewerage [a]	=	=
Water production[a]	=	↓
Water coverage[a]	=	=
Sewerage coverage[a]	=	=
Employment		
Number of employees	↓	↓
Labor productivity and efficiency		
Water connections per employee[a]	↑	↓
Distributional losses	↓	↓
Prices		
Water price (US$)	=	↑
Water price (real local currency)	↑	↑
Sewerage price (US$)	?	?
Sewerage price (real local currency)	?	↑
Quality		
Service continuity	↑	↑
Potability	↑	↑

Source: Authors' calculations.

Note: Up and down arrows indicate that a positive or negative change occurred in addition to the natural change that would be expected in the absence of privatization. An equal sign indicates that the trend perceived during the previous period was sustained but not substantially exceeded or diminished. A question mark indicates that insufficient observations were available to reach a conclusion. The arrow size represents the size of the change.

a. Impacts are shown after controlling for time trends.

because of a small sample size. Two measures were used for quality: the continuity of the water service and the number of water samples that passed a potability test. Both measures improved in both periods, but potability improvements occurred mainly during the transition.

Table 7.10 summarizes the results found in this chapter. The results for the output, coverage, and labor productivity indicators are reported after controlling for time trends.[3] If time trends were not controlled for, each of these indicators would show significant increases. The reasoning is that a natural increase is expected for each of these variables, regardless of whether ownership is public or private. For the other variables, a natural trend is not expected; hence, the results shown in the table do not incorporate the firm-specific time trend controls.

Notes

1. The only significant result of the means and medians analysis was a drop of roughly 3 percent in the mean amount of water produced between the transition and post-transition periods.

2. While a natural trend in employment is not expected, the numbers after controlling for trends are reported in table 7.6.

3. Time trends (or lack thereof) can be found through two complementary methods: Model 2 in the econometric analysis, which controls for firm-specific time trends; and Model 3 of the econometric analysis, which looks at growth rate changes (see appendix 3 for complete results for each model).

8

An Assessment of the Electricity Distribution Performance of Private and Public Utilities

Introduction

Previous chapters looked at the performance of infrastructure firms before, during, and after privatization. This chapter compares the performance of public versus private utilities over the period 1995–2005, providing an alternative lens through which to measure the impacts of privatization. Ideally, the contrast between public and private utilities would be made for all three sectors examined in previous chapters. Regrettably, because of data limitations, public versus private performance is compared here only for the electricity distribution sector.[1]

The results in this chapter are based on calculating simple averages for 26 indicators across 250 public and private utilities. The utilities presented in this chapter fall into the following three categories: (i) public utilities throughout the period of 1995–2005 (38 percent of the utilities in the database); (ii) utilities that privatized before 1995 and remained private throughout 2005 (25 percent); and (iii) utilities that privatized after 1995 and remained private throughout 2005 (36 percent). To most accurately assess and compare the performance of public and private distribution utilities, we considered the initial conditions in 1995 as well as the overall trend of the past 10 years. The chapter splits both the public and private utilities into three groups according to their performance. The first group contains the top 10 percent of firms; the second group contains the bottom 10 percent of firms; and the third group contains the middle 80 percent. The average performance of each of these groups—reported separately for public and private utilities—is then charted over time.

Main Findings

The main findings of this chapter attest to the considerable improvement in the performance of the electricity sector. The main findings can be summarized as follows:

- *When comparing private and public utilities, the main differences in performance are marked by labor productivity, distribution losses, quality of service, and tariffs.* In contrast, other indicators such as coverage and operation expenditures exhibit similar trends or do not present significant changes between the groups.
- *On average, private utilities performed better than public utilities with clear differences after the change in ownership.* Significant improvements in labor productivity are a distinguishing factor when assessing the performance of the sector. In 1995, the labor productivity of utilities privatized post-1995 was only 12.1 percent greater when measuring connections per employee, but by the end of the decade, the labor productivity of post-1995 privatizations increased threefold and doubled the amount of public utilities. Another indicator exhibiting significant improvement after the change in ownership is distribution losses. In 1995, public utilities and utilities privatized post-1995 had 17.3 and 15.9 distributional losses on average, respectively. By 2005, the utilities that were privatized post-1995 had reduced distribution losses by 12.6 percent, while loss had increased by 4.9 percent for public utilities.
- *More remarkable are the cases in which public utilities and utilities privatized post-1995 experienced similar initial conditions in 1995, yet after the change in ownership, diverged in their performance.* One such instance is quality of service. In 1995, public utilities experienced on average 23 interruptions per connection—two interruptions less than that of private utilities. By the end of the decade, however, public utilities reduced the average frequency of interruptions by four, a modest improvement considering that private utilities cut their average frequency of interruptions by half. This distinction is more evident when comparing the average duration of interruptions for public and private utilities (where private utilities refers to the combination of utilities privatized both before and after 1995). In 1995, the average duration of interruptions per connection was roughly similar—between 21 and 23 hours—for both public and private utilities. By the end of 2005, interruption durations had increased (meaning worsened) by 49 percent for public utilities, whereas durations had fallen (improved) by 28 percent for private utilities.
- *There are good public and private utilities and underperforming private and public utilities.* For several indicators, the top 10 percent

of public utilities performed better than the average private utilities, and the bottom 10 percent of the private utilities performed worse than the average public utilities.

Coverage

Significant progress has been made in the last 10 years by both public and private utilities to expand electricity coverage. Starting with 69 percent coverage in 1995, *public utilities* increased at an annual rate of 1.7 percent to reach 81 percent coverage by 2005 (see figure 8.1). Similarly, *utilities that privatized after 1995* started around the same range with 71 percent coverage in 1995 and increased at an annul rate of 2 percent to reach 87 percent coverage by the end of 2005. While *utilities that privatized before 1995* experienced a smaller annual growth rate of 0.9 percent, these utilities experienced an 8.2 percentage point increase during the last 10 years, covering 92.3 of electricity connections by 2005. Despite the fact that public utilities and post-1995 privatized utilities started in the same range, with only a 2.7 percentage point difference, post-1995 privatized utilities ended with 6.1 percentage points higher coverage than public utilities by the end of 2005 and 4.9 percentage points lower than utilities privatized before 1995.

Output

Assessing output in terms of the amount of energy sold per connection per year is a multifaceted measurement dependent on demand. On average, consumption per connection for public utilities was 3.7 MWh per year; for private utilities, consumption was 4.2 MWh, 12.5 percent higher. Pre-1995 privatized utilities experienced a 16.5 percent increase in consumption over the time period, and post-1995 privatizations experienced an increase of 10.3 percent. Perhaps the most striking improvement is the increase in consumption of privatized utilities when compared with that of public utilities. In 1995, both public and pre-1995 privatized utilities sold similar amounts of energy—roughly 3.8 MWhs per connection. Throughout the decade, the gap widened considerably, with pre-1995 privatizations selling 0.63 MWh more per connection than public utilities by the end of 2005 (see figure 8.2).

Labor Productivity

When measuring the number of residential connections per employee, the major increase in the labor productivity of private utilities creates a stark contrast with the productivity levels of public utilities. In 1995, the

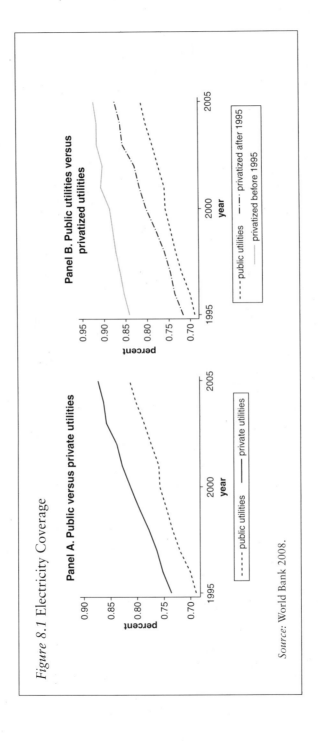

Figure 8.1 Electricity Coverage

Panel A. Public versus private utilities

percent

year

- - - - - public utilities   ——— private utilities

Panel B. Public utilities versus privatized utilities

percent

year

- - - - - public utilities   —·—·— privatized after 1995
——— privatized before 1995

Source: World Bank 2008.

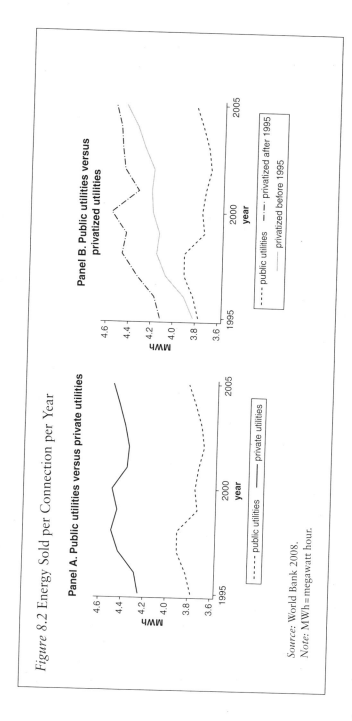

Figure 8.2 Energy Sold per Connection per Year

Panel A. Public utilities versus private utilities

Panel B. Public utilities versus privatized utilities

Source: World Bank 2008.
Note: MWh = megawatt hour.

labor productivity of public utilities was 223 residential connections per employee, while that of post-1995 privatizations was only 27 connections higher. By the end of the decade, however, the labor productivity of post-1995 privatizations had increased threefold, doubling that of public utilities. Not only did post-1995 privatizations exceed public utilities by 357 connections per employee, but post-1995 privatizations overtook pre-1995 privatizations by 193 connections, growing steadily to 684 residential connections per employee in 2005 (see figure 8.3).

Labor productivity measured as the energy (MWh) sold per employee exhibits a significant increase for private utilities in contrast to the slight change in public utilities. A closer look at the evolution of labor productivity shows an increase of 112 percent in pre-1995 privatizations between 1995 and 2005 (a 7.8 percent annual growth rate), and an increase of 192 percent in post-1995 privatizations (see figure 8.4). Energy sold per employee grew at a much lower annual rate—4.2 percent—in public utilities. Both public utilities and post-1995 privatizations displayed approximately the same level of labor productivity in 1995: 961 MWhs for public utilities and 1061 MWhs for post-1995 privatizations. Post-1995 privatized utilities tripled their labor productivity to 3,099 MWhs of energy sold per employee; public utilities increased by only 50.5 percent, resulting in 1,447 MWhs in 2005. The labor productivity of post-1995 privatizations more than doubled that of public utilities during the past 10 years.

Operating Performance

When measuring distribution losses, private utilities have visibly improved. In 1995, private utilities (including both pre- and post-1995 privatizations) experienced 16 percent distribution losses, which decreased to 14 percent by 2005 (see figure 8.5). Post-1995 privatized utilities followed a similar pattern, reducing distribution losses by 0.8 percentage points, from 16.5 percent in 1995 to 15.7 percent in 2005. Pre-1995 privatized utilities experienced a 2.7 percentage point drop from 13.8 percent in 1995 to 11.1 percent in 2005. Conversely, public utilities increased their distributional losses by 0.9 percentage points from 17.3 in 1995 to 18.2 in 2005. Despite the fact that public and private utilities started in the same range of 17.3 percent and 16.5 percent (a 0.8 percentage point difference), respectively, in 1995, the difference between the two utility types grew to 2.7 percentage points by the end of 2005. Based on these results, private utilities have significantly exceeded public utilities in decreasing and maintaining low levels of distribution losses.

Tariffs

Except for a brief period in 2002, average residential tariffs for public utilities have consistently been lower than those for private utilities (see figure 8.6).

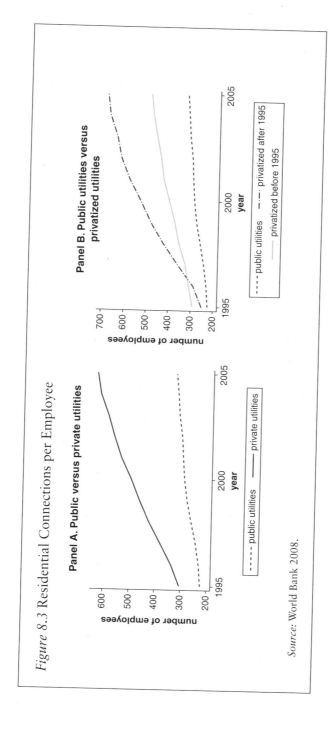

Figure 8.3 Residential Connections per Employee

Source: World Bank 2008.

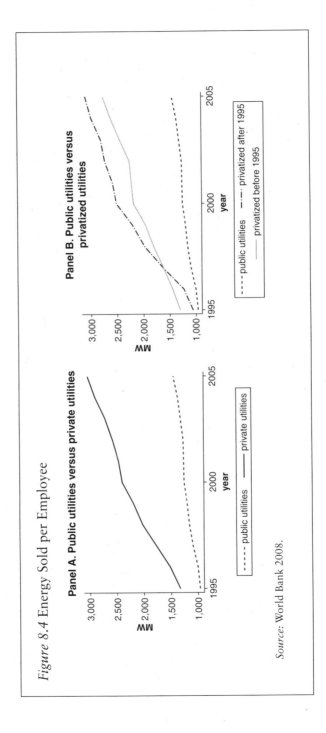

Figure 8.4 Energy Sold per Employee

Panel A. Public utilities versus private utilities

MW

3,000

2,500

2,000

1,500

1,000

1995   2000   2005

year

----- public utilities   ——— private utilities

Panel B. Public utilities versus privatized utilities

MW

3,000

2,500

2,000

1,500

1,000

1995   2000   2005

year

----- public utilities   —·—· privatized after 1995   ——— privatized before 1995

Source: World Bank 2008.

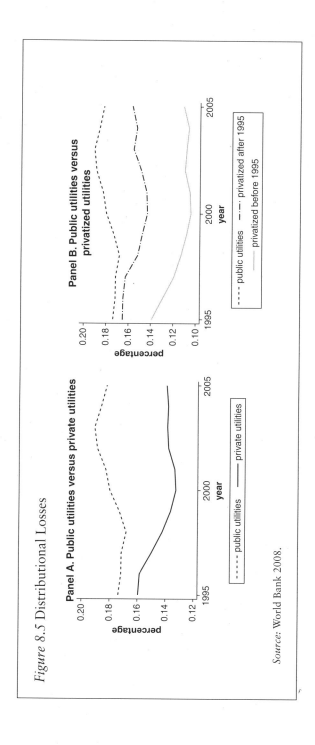

Figure 8.5 Distributional Losses

Source: World Bank 2008.

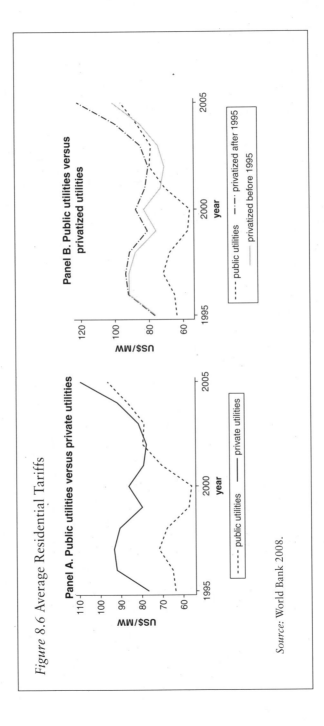

Figure 8.6 Average Residential Tariffs

Source: World Bank 2008.

In both 1995 and 2005, this gap was roughly US$12–14 per MWh, despite large price increases over the time period for both types of utilities.[2] Utilities privatized post-1995 exhibited the greatest increase in residential tariffs and charged the highest prices in 2005, averaging US$122 per MWh. This amount is US$45 greater than the group's 1995 tariffs, US$25 more than public utility tariffs in 2005, and US$20 more than 2005 tariffs charged by utilities privatized pre-1995.

Industrial tariffs charged by public utilities in 1995 averaged US$77.3 per MWh, US$5.1 less than the price charged by private utilities (see figure 8.7). By 2005, however, average public industrial tariffs reached US$90.6, a 17.2 percent increase compared with the modest 4.5 percent increase exhibited by private utilities. When considering the industrial charges administered by pre-1995 utilities, the first part of the decade experienced a significant drop. This drop was driven by the Brazilian utilities that underwent a devaluation, followed by a gradual increase in the last five years. Utilities that privatized after 1995 increased tariffs by 19.2 percent. By the end of 2005, post-1995 utilities charged US$1.1 more than public utilities.

Quality of Service

Most public and private utilities have only recently started to collect and disclose data on the frequency and duration of interruptions. Thus, the following information is partial and indicative. Based on the data collected in our sample, the average frequency of interruptions per connection per year dropped from 12.9 times per connection in 1995 to 8.9 times in 2005 for pre-1995 privatized utilities (see figure 8.8). Interruptions increased from 15.2 to 20 in post-1995 privatized utilities. Public utilities, which in 1995 averaged 23.2 interruptions per connection, reduced the frequency of interruptions to 18.9 interruptions in 2005. These results indicate that both pre-1995 privatized utilities and public utilities managed to reduce the average frequency of interruptions by four interruptions per connection.

Regarding the average duration of interruptions per connection, the results exhibit a slight decrease for private utilities and a significant increase for public utilities. In 1995, the average duration for public utilities was 21 hours per connection compared with 31 hours in 2005. Unlike the increase in duration for public utilities, the aggregated results for private utilities demonstrate a gradual decrease throughout most of the decade with the exception of the last year. Utilities that privatized after 1995 show a 35 percent total increase in average interruption duration, resulting in average interruptions of 24 hours in 2005. The best performers when measuring the quality of service are the utilities privatized before 1995, with a 34 percent reduction between 1995 and 2005 and 12 hour average interruption durations by 2005 (see figure 8.9).

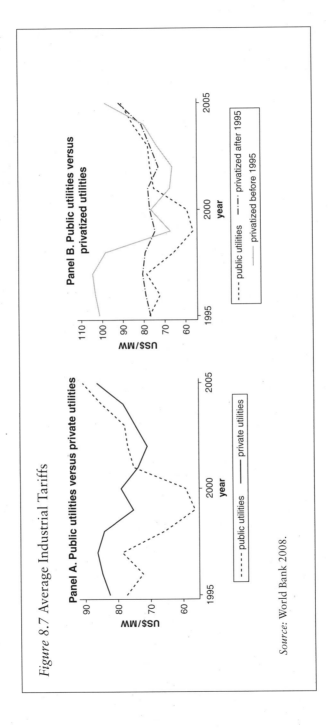

Figure 8.7 Average Industrial Tariffs

Source: World Bank 2008.

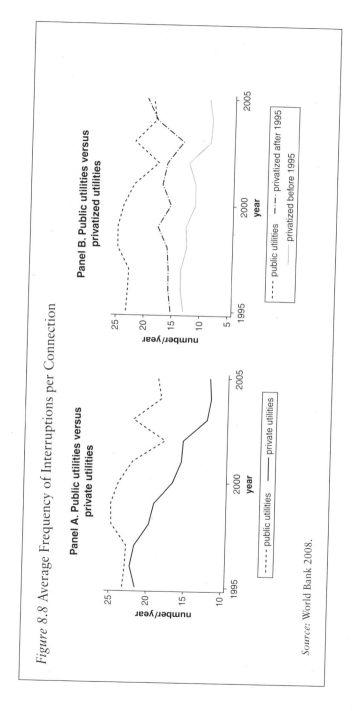

Figure 8.8 Average Frequency of Interruptions per Connection

Source: World Bank 2008.

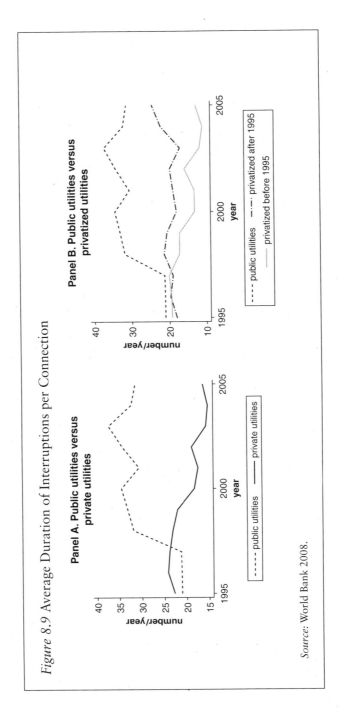

Figure 8.9 Average Duration of Interruptions per Connection

Panel A. Public utilities versus private utilities

number/year

year

----- public utilities ——— private utilities

Panel B. Public utilities versus privatized utilities

number/year

year

----- public utilities ——·— privatized after 1995
——— privatized before 1995

Source: World Bank 2008.

Top 10 Percent and Bottom 10 Percent Performers

The following section adds an additional level of detail to the above analysis, breaking both public and private utilities into three groups on the basis of their performance. The first group contains the top 10 percent of firms; the second group contains the bottom 10 percent of firms; and the third group contains the middle 80 percent. Although private utilities performed better than public utilities with clear differences after the change in ownership, in some cases, the top 10 percent of public utilities outperformed the average private utilities, and the bottom 10 percent of private utilities performed poorer than the average public utilities. In other words, there is a great deal of variability in the performance of the two groups of companies. The following indicators were selected because they exhibit significant changes that may not be evident in the previous comparisons.

Output

An in-depth perspective on the energy sold per connection is gained when comparing the top and bottom 10 percent of public and private performers. In the case of output, by 2005, the top 10 percent of public utilities sold twice as much energy as the average private utilities. The same proportion is applicable when comparing the average public utilities with the bottom 10 percent of private utilities. By 2005, the bottom 10 percent sold less than half of the energy (MW) sold by the average public utilities (see figure 8.10).

Labor Productivity

When considering the exceptional improvement in the labor productivity of private utilities, we witness that, despite initial conditions in 1995, the private utilities in the mean and top 10 percent experienced double the improvement of the public utilities in the same categories. Nevertheless, it is worth considering that the top 10 percent of public utilities outperformed the private utilities found in the mean. In addition, the public utilities in the mean had double the labor productivity of private utilities in the bottom decile (see figure 8.11).

Figure 8.12 uses energy sold per employee to provide an additional perspective on labor productivity. Whereas private utilities are on average more efficient than public utilities, public utilities in the top 10 percentile surpass the efficiency of the private utilities in the mean. Additionally, the top 10 percent of both public and private utilities exhibit a significant increasing trend. Conversely, the bottom 10 percentile of both public and private utilities fell in the same range and maintained their initial level of performance.

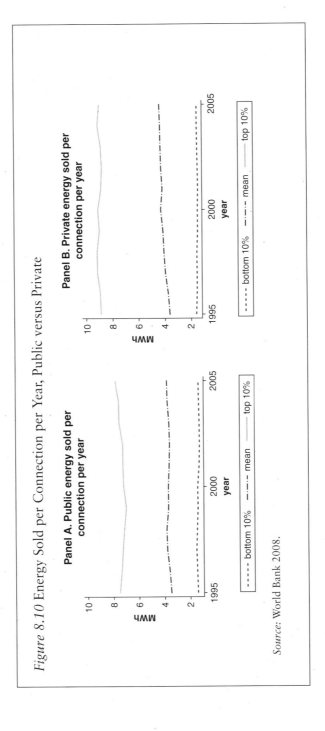

Figure 8.10 Energy Sold per Connection per Year, Public versus Private

Panel A. Public energy sold per connection per year

Panel B. Private energy sold per connection per year

Source: World Bank 2008.

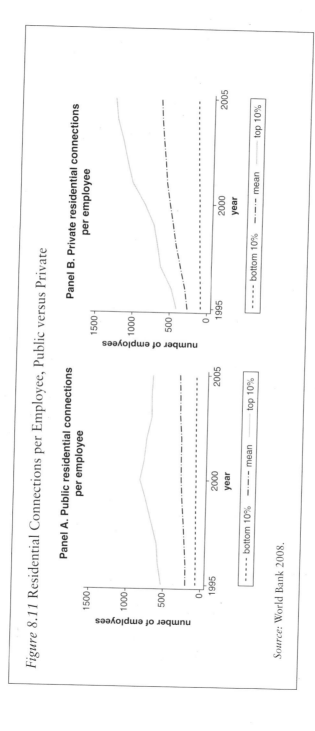

Figure 8.11 Residential Connections per Employee, Public versus Private

Panel A. Public residential connections per employee

Panel B. Private residential connections per employee

Source: World Bank 2008.

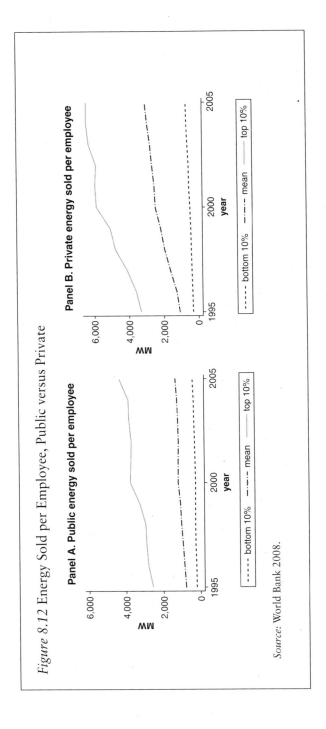

Figure 8.12 Energy Sold per Employee, Public versus Private

Panel A. Public energy sold per employee

Panel B. Private energy sold per employee

Source: World Bank 2008.

Operating Performance

The breakdown of performance according to distributional losses is similar to previous variables. Public utilities in the bottom 10 percent perform better than the average private utilities. (In this case, the bottom decile is the best). Likewise, the private utilities forming the top (or worst) decile experience more distributional losses than the average public utilities (see figure 8.13).

Quality of Service

The mean frequency of interruptions for both public and private utilities is roughly similar and did not change much over the period 1995–2005. However, there was a drastic reduction in the frequency of interruptions for the worst performing decile (in this case denoted top 10 percent) for both public and private utilities. A similar trend is noticeable when measuring the average duration of interruptions per connection (see figure 8.14).

Conclusion

The results presented in this chapter indicate that, on average, private utilities performed better than public utilities, with clear differences after the change in ownership. While there have been modest improvements by public utilities, on average, private utilities surpassed the performance (improvement) of public utilities. These improvements are evident by indicators measuring labor productivity, distribution losses, quality of service, and tariffs.

Despite the fact that private and public utilities experienced similar initial conditions in 1995, by the end of the decade the two groups diverged in performance. For instance, when measuring distributional losses, private and public utilities were separated by a 2 percentage point gap in 1995, yet by the end of 2005, there was a 4 percentage point difference between the two utility types. With respect to labor productivity, in 1995, public utilities had 10.7 percent fewer residential connections per employee than post-1995 privatized utilities. Yet by the end of 2005, the labor productivity of post-1995 privatized utilities had almost tripled, yielding productivity values that were twice those of public utilities.

For the indicators measuring output, labor productivity, and operating performance, the top 10 percent public utilities outperformed the average private utilities and the bottom 10 percent private utilities performed poorer than the average public utilities.

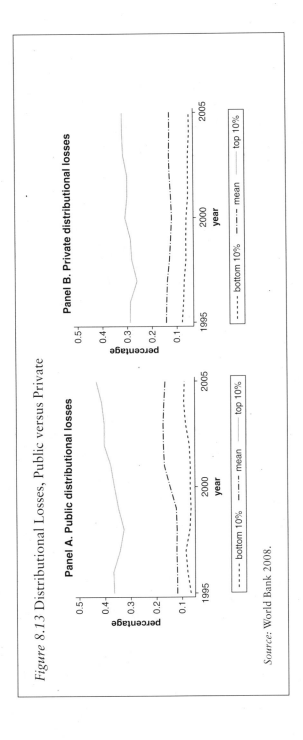

Figure 8.13 Distributional Losses, Public versus Private

Source: World Bank 2008.

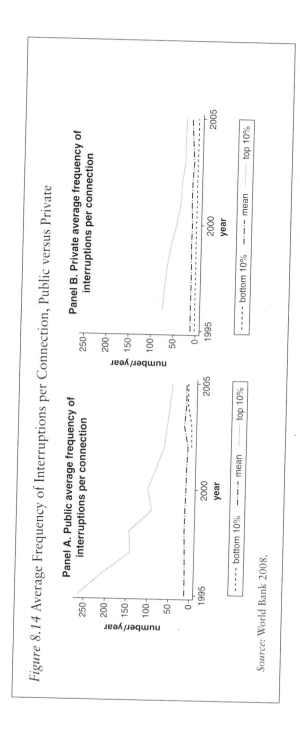

Figure 8.14 Average Frequency of Interruptions per Connection, Public versus Private

Panel A. Public average frequency of interruptions per connection

number/year

1995   year   2000   2005

- - - - - bottom 10%   — · — · — mean   ——— top 10%

Panel B. Private average frequency of interruptions per connection

number/year

1995   year   2000   2005

- - - - - bottom 10%   — · — · — mean   ——— top 10%

Source: World Bank 2008.

Notes

1. Similar to the electricity sector analysis in chapter 4, only electricity distribution companies are considered here. Generation and transmission companies are not included, because they largely rely on a different set of performance variables.

2. In this case, private utilities refers to those privatized before 1995 as well as those privatized after 1995.

9

Determinants of Impact: Regulatory and Contract Variables

Introduction

This chapter deepens the analysis in chapters 5–7 by introducing a number of regulatory and privatization contract and process variables. The variables come from a separate World Bank data set containing the characteristics of nearly 1,000 infrastructure transactions in Latin America and the Caribbean between 1989 and 2002 (see Guasch 2004). This separate regulatory and contract characteristics data set was merged with the data set containing firm performance data used in chapters 5–7. Merging the two databases makes it possible to identify whether privatization characteristics like the sale method (for example, auction), degree of autonomy of the regulatory body, tenure of regulatory body appointees, investor nationality, award criterion, and tariff regulation affect the performance variables discussed in previous chapters. The match between the two databases was quite high—88 percent of the utilities covered in the previous chapters were matched to the regulatory and contract data set.[1]

There are many reasons to suspect that characteristics of the privatization process and regulatory environment would affect firm performance both during and after the transition to private ownership. First, large unexplained differences in performance across firms were found in the analyses in chapters 5–7. For example, large drops in employment occurred on average during both the transition and post-transition periods in the electricity sector. However, some firms experienced much larger drops than others. These large performance differences suggest that differences in privatization procedures or the regulatory environment may have played a significant role.

Further evidence comes from studies of privatizations in Mexico and Central Europe. López-de-Silanes (1997) showed that the prices of Mexican privatizations could be influenced by the type of auction mechanism as well as by the implementation and timing. Analyzing transition economies in Central Europe, Frydman, Gray, Hessel, and Rapaczynski (1999) found that ownership changes had significant beneficial effects in those cases in which the buyer was an outsider, but the effect was not significant when the buyers were insiders. This result suggested that the effects of transferring ownership to insiders and outsiders may have important implications in the design and effectiveness of privatization programs in transition economies.

The main aim of this chapter is not to advocate a certain type of regulatory or contract design. Rather it is to emphasize that privatization is not simply a yes-no decision. Indeed, many privatization design variables can influence performance outcomes. The results in this chapter show that, depending on the priorities of a country, certain privatization contract or regulatory characteristics might be more important than others. For example, if reducing prices is of central importance to a country, then a partially or fully autonomous regulatory body would be preferable to a nonautonomous one.

The findings of the chapter can be summarized in three main points. First, regulatory and contract characteristics matter: the way privatizations are undertaken can generate significant performance differences. Second, each regulatory and contract characteristic affects each performance variable differently. In other words, a certain contract characteristic could have a positive influence on one performance variable while having a negative or insignificant impact on another. Third, some regulatory and contract variables have bigger impacts than others. For instance, in some cases, the changes attributed to a fully autonomous regulatory body are much larger than changes attributed to other regulatory variables.

The three sectors—water distribution, electricity distribution, and telecommunications—were pooled to maximize the amount of variation in the data set.[2] For more details on the data and methodology, see chapter 4. See also appendix 2 for more details on the econometric analysis. The econometric analysis included several different regression specifications using different combinations of independent variables. In other words, for each performance variable (for example, output, employment, and so on), the impact of each regulatory or contract variable was tested while controlling for different combinations of other regulatory and contract variables. Controlling for other regulatory and contract variables addresses collinearity issues, while tending to reduce the number of statistically significant results. Multiple regression specifications also can produce a range of results. For this reason, the following sections mention either a range of impacts (for example, a drop in employees of between 9 and 18 percent for auctioned firms) or mixed results. Table A3.13 reports

Table 9.1 Base Case for Regulatory and Contract Variables

Category	Base case	Variables
Sale method	No auction	Auction
Autonomy of regulatory body	No autonomy	Partial autonomy; full autonomy
Duration of regulatory body appointments	Less than five years	Five or more years
Investor nationality	Local only	Foreign only; foreign and local
Award criteria	Other criteria	Highest price; best investment plan
Tariff regulation	Other regulation	Rate of return; price cap

Source: Authors' elaboration.

the minimum and maximum percentage changes in each performance variable disaggregated by the regulatory and contract variables.

Similar to the preceding chapters, results from two time periods are analyzed: (i) changes between the period before the transition to private ownership and the transition period; and (ii) changes between the transition and post-transition periods. Also in line with the analysis in previous chapters, results for the number of subscribers (or connections), output, coverage, and labor productivity are reported after controlling for time trends.

Overall changes are not reported in this section. Rather, the changes shown are relative to the base case for each variable (see table 9.1 for a list of the base cases). For instance, when it is reported that the number of connections decreased by 5.8 to 6.8 percent when an auction process was used, this change is relative to cases in which auctions were *not* used—"no auction" being the base case.

Sale Method

Privatizations and concessions that were sold via an auction process experienced a reduction of 5.8 to 6.8 percent in connection numbers (depending on the regression specification) below the firm-specific time trend during the transition. In contrast, no significant changes were encountered during the post-transition period. Whether or not privatizations or concessions were auctioned did not have a significant effect on output. When privatizations or concessions were auctioned, a relative decrease in coverage of about 3 percent occurred during the transition, but no significant changes occurred after the transition (see table 9.2).

Privatizations and concessions that followed an auction process experienced a drop in employment of about 18 to 20 percent during the transition. After the transition, an additional drop of 9 to 17 percent occurred, depending on the econometric specification. To measure labor productivity, both output per employee and connections per employee were analyzed. In both cases, whether or not a utility was auctioned made little difference. Some evidence was found of a decrease in labor productivity after the transition, but this decrease was accompanied by several nonsignificant results, depending on the regression specification.

Regardless of whether privatization processes took place through an auction, distributional losses were not affected during the transition period. After the transition, however, cases that were auctioned displayed distributional loss reductions between 10 and 31 percent.

Finally, when companies were privatized via auctions, average prices in U.S. dollars rose during the transition and then fell after the transition. Prices in real local currency followed a similar trajectory.

Table 9.2 Impact of Sale Method

	Sale method	
	Auction	
	Transition	*Post-transition*
Number of connections (or Subscribers)[a]	↓	NS
Output[a]	NS	NS
Coverage[a]	↓	NS
Number of employees	↓	↓
Labor productivity: connections per employee[a]	NS	Mixed
Labor productivity: output per employee[a]	NS	Mixed
Distributional losses	NS	↓
Average prices in U.S. dollars	↑	↓
Average prices in real local currency	↑	↓
Quality	↑	↑

Source: Authors' calculations.

Note: NS = the results were not significant. Up and down arrows indicate that a positive or negative change occurred in addition to the natural change that would be expected in the absence of privatization. The arrow size represents the size of the change.

a. Results are shown after controlling for time trends.

Autonomy of Regulatory Body

When the regulatory body was partially autonomous, the number of connections decreased between 3.1 and 6.9 percent during the transition, but no significant changes occurred after the transition. When the regulatory body was fully autonomous, no significant changes occurred during either period. With respect to output, when the regulatory body was partially autonomous, output decreased between 5.9 and 8.2 percent during the transition; however, no significant changes occurred after the transition. When the regulatory body was fully autonomous, output fell by 5.3 to 8.6 percent during the transition and by about 4.5 percent after the transition.

Coverage appeared to decrease slightly during the transition, when the regulatory body was partially autonomous, while no significant changes were encountered after the transition. When the regulatory body was fully autonomous, output fell between 1.6 and 3.5 percent during the transition; no substantial changes occurred after the transition.

Privatizations that had a partially autonomous regulatory body experienced employee reductions during the transition that were between 10 and 48 percent greater than reductions experienced without an autonomous body. The analysis found some evidence of relative increases in employee numbers after the transition when the regulator was partially autonomous, but the results were not always significant. When the regulatory body was fully autonomous, employee reductions were greater than those observed under partial autonomy. During the transition, privatization processes with a fully autonomous regulator experienced employment reductions that were between 27 and 54 percent greater than cases in which the regulator was not autonomous. Changes in employment after the transition were not significant.

When the regulatory body was partially autonomous, connections per employee increased between 14 and 21 percent during the transition and then fell by 15 and 26 percent after the transition. Labor productivity defined as output per employee followed a similar pattern, although the drop experienced after the transition was even greater, between 14 and 42 percent. When the regulatory body was fully autonomous, large increases in labor productivity were experienced during the transition: connections per employee increased between 27 and 60 percent and output per employee increased between 15 and 48 percent. After the transition, the full autonomy cases experienced decreases of 10 to 35 percent in labor productivity.

No significant effects on distributional losses were detected during the transition when the regulatory body was partially autonomous. Mixed results were found during the post-transition period, but the majority of the specifications pointed toward reductions in distributional losses when regulators were partially autonomous. Results were quite different when the regulatory body had total autonomy: distributional losses increased between 11 and 29 percent during the transition, followed by significant losses (between 22 and 38 percent) after the transition.

When regulatory bodies were partially autonomous, prices in dollars fell during the transition by 45 to 52 percent. After the transition, the analysis exhibits mixed results for prices in dollars. Diverse results were found for partial autonomy in real local currency in both periods. In cases in which the regulatory body was completely autonomous, significant price reductions in dollars—that is, 26 to 68 percent—were visible during the transition. Similar to the partial autonomy cases, various results (in dollars) were found after the transition for full autonomy, although most of the regression specifications indicated a drop in prices. In real local currency, mixed results were found for the full autonomy cases during the transition, and price increases of about 10 to 14 percent were found after the transition.

In cases in which the regulatory body was partially autonomous, the quality index fell by approximately 24 percent during the transition period and an additional 14 to 50 percent during the post-transition period. When the regulator was fully autonomous, most results pointed to large increases in quality during the transition. After the transition, the results for full autonomy varied (see table 9.3).

Duration of Regulatory Body Appointments

Regarding the number of connections, no significant changes were observed during either period. However, privatizations and concessions that were regulated by bodies appointed for terms of five or more years experienced decreases in output between 9.7 and 11.6 percent during the transition. However, no significant changes occurred after the transition. Privatizations and concessions that were regulated by similar bodies appeared to experience small drops in coverage both during and after the transition. These results are dependent on the regression specification, and some specifications had no significant results.

When the duration of regulatory board appointments lasted five or more years, the number of employees decreased by roughly 25 to 30 percent during the transition. After the transition, the results were less robust, but employment appeared to fall by an additional 14 percent. Additionally, connections per employee increased between 27 and 31 percent during the transition. Results after the transition were less clear-cut, but connections per employee again seem to have increased. Changes in output per employee were not robust, but there was some evidence of a decrease during the transition followed by an increase after the transition. These results became insignificant when additional controls were added to the regression specifications.

Table 9.3 Impact of Autonomy of Regulatory Body

	Autonomy			
	Partial		Full	
	Transition	Post-transition	Transition	Post-transition
Number of connections (or subscribers)[a]	↓	NS	NS	NS
Output[a]	↓	NS	↓/?	↓/?
Coverage[a]	↓/?	NS	↓	NS
Number of employees	↓	↑/?	↓	NS
Labor productivity: connections per employee[a]	↑/?	↓	↑	↓/?
Labor productivity: output per employee[a]	Mixed	↓	↑	↓
Distributional losses	NS	↓/?	↑	↓
Average prices in U.S. dollars	↓	Mixed	↓	↓/?
Average prices in real local currency	Mixed	Mixed	Mixed	↑/?
Quality	↓	↓	↑	Mixed

Source: Authors' calculations.

Note: NS = the results were not significant. Up and down arrows indicate that a positive or negative change occurred in addition to the natural change that would be expected in the absence of privatization. A question mark indicates that insufficient observations were available to reach a conclusion. The arrow size represents the size of the change.

a. Results are shown after controlling for time trends.

When regulatory boards were appointed for a longer duration, the results suggest that there were increases in losses between 12 and 16 percent during the transition. In the post-transition period, relatively large reductions in losses—roughly 40 percent—were observed, more than offsetting the increases seen during the transition period (see table 9.4).

When considering the impact of the longer-duration regulatory body appointments on dollar prices during the transition, mixed results were found. Dollar prices rose during the post-transition period, whereas prices in real local currency fell between 9 and 16 percent during both the transition and post-transition periods.

There was some evidence that quality increased when appointments to the regulatory body were of a longer duration, although not all results were significant. Changes after the transition were not significant.

Table 9.4 Impact of Duration of Regulatory Body Appointments

| | Duration of regulatory body | |
| | More than five years | |
	Transition	Post-transition
Number of connections (or subscribers)[a]	NS	NS
Output[a]	↓	NS
Coverage[a]	↓/?	↓/?
Number of employees	↓	↓/?
Labor productivity: connections per employee[a]	↑	↑/?
Labor productivity: output per employee[a]	Mixed	Mixed
Distributional losses	↑	↓
Average prices in U.S. dollars	Mixed	↑
Average prices in real local currency	↓	↓
Quality	↑/?	NS

Source: Authors' calculations.

Note: NS = the results were not significant. Up and down arrows indicate that a positive or negative change occurred in addition to the natural change that would be expected in the absence of privatization. A question mark indicates that insufficient observations were available to reach a conclusion. The arrow size represents the size of the change.

a. Results are shown after controlling for time trends.

Investor Nationality

When only foreign investors were considered, the analysis yielded mixed results during the transition and yielded nonsignificant results after the transition. When foreign and local investors were mixed, the number of connections fell by 1 to 2.2 percent during the transition. After the transition, the basic regression specification showed an increase of 1.4 percent in the number of connections. After other controls were added to the regression, however, the results were no longer significant, suggesting that covariance exists with some of the other variables. Additionally, output decreased between 4.4 and 10.9 percent during the transition and between 2.1 and 4 percent after the transition. When both foreign and local investors were involved, slight increases in output were observed before controlling for other regulatory characteristics. After adding other controls to the regression specification, the changes became insignificant.

Coverage decreased by roughly 3 to 4 percent during the transition (relative to coverage levels with only local investors), when only foreign investors were present, while no significant changes were observed after the transition. Similar results were found when foreign and local investors were mixed.

Employee reductions were about 12 to 31 percent higher during the transition for companies with foreign investors in relation to companies with no foreign investors. After the transition, no additional changes were observed. Companies with both foreign and local investors had smaller changes during the transition than those with only foreign investors; after the transition, however, they experienced additional employee reductions. Furthermore, when contracts were awarded to firms with only foreign investors, the changes in labor productivity were either unclear or insignificant. When both local and foreign investors were involved, labor productivity appeared to decrease during the transition, followed by an increase after the transition. Changes in both directions were generally between 6 and 10 percent.

For firms with only foreign ownership, no significant changes were observed during the transition (see table 9.5). In the post-transition period, distributional losses fell by roughly 12 to 26 percent. A similar pattern emerged for firms with both foreign and domestic ownership: no significant changes occurred during the transition and a reduction in losses between 15 and 19 percent occurred after the transition.

When only foreign investors were involved, mixed results were found in prices in dollars during the transition, while prices increased by between 14 and 26 percent after the transition. In the case of only foreign investors and real local currency, prices fell during the transition and increased after the transition. When both foreign and local investors were involved, prices in dollars fell substantially (by roughly 23 percent) during the transition, only to recover after that. In contrast, prices in real local currency did not experience significant changes during the transition; after the transition, however, there is some evidence that prices fell, but several of the regression specifications produced insignificant results.

Results for firms with foreign investors were not robust, but some specifications exhibit decreases in quality both during and after the transition. For firms with both foreign and local ownership, quality increased by about 29 percent during the transition. Some specifications also found increases after the transition.

Award Criteria

The impact of two types of award criteria was analyzed: highest price and best investment plan. Concessions awarded based on the highest-price criterion experienced drops in the number of connections of between 1.3

Table 9.5 Impact of Investor Nationality

	Investor nationality			
	Only foreign		Foreign and local	
	Transition	Post-transition	Transition	Post-transition
Number of connections (or subscribers)[a]	Mixed	NS	↓/?	NS
Output[a]	↓	↓	NS	NS
Coverage[a]	↓	NS	↓	NS
Number of employees	↓	NS	↓	↓
Labor productivity: connections per employee[a]	NS	Mixed	↓	Mixed
Labor productivity: output per employee[a]	Mixed	NS	↓/?	Mixed
Distributional losses	NS	↓	NS	↓
Average prices in U.S. dollars	Mixed	↑/?	↓	↑
Average prices in real local currency	↓	↑	NS	↓/?
Quality	NS	NS	↑	↑/?

Source: Authors' calculations.
Note: NS = the results were not significant. Up and down arrows indicate that a positive or negative change occurred in addition to the natural change that would be expected in the absence of privatization. A question mark indicates that insufficient observations were available to reach a conclusion. The arrow size represents the size of the change.
a. Results are shown after controlling for time trends.

and 2.6 percent during the transition. No significant changes occurred after the transition. On the contrary, concessions that were awarded to the bidder with the best investment plan experienced a small increase (roughly 2.5 percent) in the number of connections during the transition. No significant impacts on the number of connections were found after the transition for either type of award criteria. When privatizations and concessions were awarded based on the highest-price criterion, no significant results were found on output. When the award criterion was based on the best investment plan, no significant impacts on output were found during the transition, but an increase in output of about 2 percent was noticed after the transition. These results reflect controlling for time trends.

When privatizations and concessions were awarded based on a highest-price criterion, coverage appeared to decrease slightly during the transition, but then increase faintly after the transition. When the award criterion was the best investment plan, the opposite occurred: coverage increased slightly during the transition but then decreased mildly after the transition. These results were obtained after controlling for time trends.

Privatizations and concessions awarded according to the highest price reported some reduction during the transition, but after controlling for other factors, these changes were not significant. Employment reductions were encountered during the post-transition period. Privatizations and concessions awarded according to the best investment plan had some relative increases in employee numbers both during and after the transition, but after controlling for other factors, these changes were less significant. Moreover, when contracts were awarded according to the best investment plan, no significant changes in labor productivity were observed. When contracts were awarded based on the highest price offer, output per employee appears to have fallen by roughly 20 percent during the transition, followed by an increase of about the same amount after the transition. Connections per employee for highest price cases seem to have increased by about 50 percent after the transition.

Whether or not a contract was awarded according to the highest bid did not significantly affect performance during the transition. After the transition, distributional losses seem to have increased slightly in highest-bid cases. In cases in which the winner was determined by the best investment plan, no significant results were observed (see table 9.6).

When contracts were awarded according to the highest-price criteria, prices in dollars appeared to drop during the transition but then increase after the transition. However, different regression specifications produced somewhat mixed results. In real local currency, various results were found during the transition, followed by a drop after the transition. When contracts were awarded based on the best investment plan, no significant results were found in dollars during the transition, whereas an increase of 14 percent was observed after the transition. When the case of the best investment plan is considered in real local currency, prices appear to have fallen during the transition. However, no clear results in local currency were found after the transition.

When contracts were awarded based on a highest-price criterion, various results (some positive, some negative) on quality were found during the transition. After the transition, some results pointed to a decrease in quality, whereas others were not significant. No significant results in quality were exposed after the transition. When contracts were awarded based on a best investment plan, quality seems to have decreased by about 18 percent during the transition. No significant changes were found for the post-transition period.

Table 9.6 Impact of Award Criteria

| | Award criterion | | | |
| | Best invest. plan | | Highest price | |
	Transition	Post-transition	Transition	Post-transition
Number of connections (or subscribers)[a]	↑	NS	↓/?	NS
Output[a]	NS	↑	NS	NS
Coverage[a]	↑	↓	↓/?	/?
Number of employees	↑	↑	↓/?	↓/?
Labor productivity: connections per employee[a]	NS	NS	NS	↑
Labor productivity: output per employee[a]	NS	NS	↓	↑/?
Distributional losses	↓/?	NS	NS	Mixed
Average prices in U.S. dollars	NS	↑	↓/?	↑/?
Average prices in real local currency	↓/?	NS	Mixed	↓
Quality	↓	NS	Mixed	↓/?

Source: Authors' calculations.

Note: NS = the results were not significant. Up and down arrows indicate that a positive or negative change occurred in addition to the natural change that would be expected in the absence of privatization. A question mark indicates that insufficient observations were available to reach a conclusion. The arrow size represents the size of the change.

a. Results are shown after controlling for time trends.

Tariff Regulation

To identify the effect of the type of tariff regulation on network expansion, both rate-of-return and price-cap regulation were analyzed. Concessions regulated according to rate of return experienced an increase in the number of connections between 2.4 and 6.3 percent during the transition. After the transition, the number of connections increased an additional 2 percent. Concessions subject to price-cap tariff regulation do not appear to have experienced significant changes, although a parallel analysis of changes in growth rates indicated a decrease in the number of connections during the transition. When analyzing output, no significant changes were found when tariffs where regulated according to rate of return. Price-cap regulation yielded an increase in output of about 5 percent during the transition yet no significant changes after the transition.

Small increases in coverage were seen under rate-of-return tariff regulation during the transition, but no significant changes were observed for price-cap tariff regulation schemes.

Utilities subject to rate-of-return regulation showed large relative employee reductions—roughly 60 percent—during the transition in some (but not all) of the econometric specifications. Relative employment increases were identified in some specifications after the transition, but one of the specifications showed a slight decrease. Firms regulated under price-cap systems experienced some employee reductions during the transition; however, these changes were not significant after controlling for other factors. When tariffs for privatizations and concessions were regulated according to a rate-of-return system, there is some evidence that labor productivity increased during the transition. Nevertheless, no significant results were encountered in labor productivity after the transition. Under price-cap regulation, labor productivity appears to have increased during the transition, but no significant changes were observed after the transition.

When tariffs were regulated according to rate of return, no significant changes occurred during the transition, and distributional losses fell somewhat following the transition. Under price-cap tariff regulation, distributional losses seem to have increased after the transition.

When tariffs were regulated according to a price-cap methodology, no significant results were found in dollars (see table 9.7). In real local currency, however, prices increased during both periods. When rate-of-return tariff regulation was implemented, prices in dollars first increased during the transition but then decreased after the transition. Prices in real local currency showed mixed results.

When tariffs were regulated according to a rate-of-return method, mixed results were found during the transition. After the transition, one regression specification showed quality reductions, but these reductions became insignificant after more controls were added to the regression.

Conclusion

The findings in this chapter illustrate the three main points. First, regulatory and contract characteristics matter: the way privatizations are undertaken can generate significant performance differences. Second, each regulatory and contract characteristic affects each performance variable differently. Third, some regulatory and contract variables have bigger

Table 9.7 Impact of Tariff Regulation

| | Tariff regulation | | | |
| | Price cap | | Rate of return | |
	Transition	Post-transition	Transition	Post-transition
Number of connections (or subscribers)[a]	↓/?	NS	↑	↑
Output[a]	↑/?	NS	NS	NS
Coverage[a]	NS	NS	↑	NS
Number of employees	Mixed	NS	↓	Mixed
Labor productivity: connections per employee[a]	↓	NS	↑	NS
Labor productivity: output per employee[a]	↓	NS	NS	NS
Distributional losses	NS	↑	NS	↓
Average prices in U.S. dollars	NS	NS	↑	↓
Average prices in real local currency	↑	↑	Mixed	Mixed
Quality	↑	NS	Mixed	NS

Source: Authors' calculations.

Note: NS = the results were not significant. Up and down arrows indicate that a positive or negative change occurred in addition to the natural change that would be expected in the absence of privatization. A question mark indicates that insufficient observations were available to reach a conclusion. The arrow size represents the size of the change.

a. Results are shown after controlling for time trends.

impacts than others. The following summary of the econometric results further illustrates these points (see also table A3.13 for a summary of the minimum and maximum changes observed for each variable):

- *Sale method*: Auctions tended to decrease employee numbers and increase quality by fairly large amounts. Auctions also resulted in price increases during the transition and price decreases after the transition, as well as distributional loss reductions after the transition.
- *Autonomy of regulatory body*: Full autonomy resulted in moderate drops in output during both periods, as well as large drops in employment during the transition. Large increases in labor productivity, distributional losses, and quality were all observed during the

transition. After the transition, labor productivity and distributional losses reversed direction and plummeted. Results for partial autonomy were often similar but less robust.

- *Duration of regulatory body*: When the duration of regulatory body appointments was five years or more, output fell during the transition, and the number of employees fell substantially during both periods; similarly, connections per employee fell substantially during both periods. Distributional losses first increased during the transition, then decreased by a much greater margin after the transition, and prices in real local currency fell during both periods.

- *Investor nationality*: The presence of only foreign investors caused output to fall somewhat during both periods, coverage to fall during the transition, the number of employees to fall substantially during the transition, and distributional losses to fall after the transition. Average dollar prices seem to have increased during both periods, while prices in real local currency first decreased, then increased. When both foreign and local investors were involved, employment fell during both periods, distributional losses fell after the transition, prices in dollars first fell then rose, and quality improved.

- *Award criterion*: When concessions were awarded according to the best investment plan, employment fell substantially during both periods, prices in dollars appear to have risen after the transition, and prices in real local currency appear to have fallen during the transition. When concessions were awarded based on the highest price, the number of connections fell slightly during the transition, coverage first fell slightly then increased, the number of employees fell substantially, and prices in real local currency fell moderately during both periods.

- *Tariff regulation*: Price-cap tariff regulation caused output and quality to increase slightly and number of employees and labor productivity to decrease slightly, all during the transition. Distributional losses increased after the transition, and prices in real local currency increased during both periods. Rate-of-return regulation caused the number of connections to increase moderately, coverage to increase slightly during the transition, and employment to drop dramatically during both periods. Distributional losses fell after the transition, and prices in dollars first increased, then decreased.

Overall, the theory predicts that regulation matters for sector performance on three aspects: (i) the existence of a regulatory agency matters, (ii) the experience of the regulatory agency matters, and (iii) regulatory governance matters as well. The results are consistent with the literature on the impact of private sector participation. They show the relevance of the existence of a regulatory agency and its governance, defined as the agency's institutional design and structure that allows it to carry its functions as an independent regulator. Our results indicate a significant improvement in utility performance through the involvement of a regulatory agency even in the case of state-owned enterprises. The results strongly support the notion that the highest achievements are reached with a combination of private sector participation and a regulatory agency that exhibits good governance.

Notes

1. The match was better for telecommunications and electricity distribution. In the case of the water sector, the regulatory database contains information on only 38 utilities, which is 77 percent of the total number of utilities covered in chapter 6.

2. The models were run for each sector separately (these tables are available upon request). Results were qualitatively similar to the ones presented in this chapter. The book presents the results from the pooled sectors to simplify the explanation of the results.

10

Conclusion

This book has provided the most comprehensive analysis to date of the impacts of private participation—as well as the determinants of those impacts—in the electricity, telecommunications, and water sectors in Latin America. This concluding chapter begins by stressing the two important methodological contributions of this study, both of which are designed to avoid any overstatement of the benefits of private sector participation in infrastructure. The chapter recaps the main findings and suggests key corrections to move forward in new and ongoing private sector participation programs in infrastructure.

Key Methodological Contributions

The *first* key methodological contribution is the distinction between transition period effects and longer-term changes in performance. Often the most dramatic effects of private sector participation are found in the transition period, when the enterprise is overhauled as part of the transaction process, and often while it is still under public control. These transactions constitute a one-time adjustment and present a pace of improvement that is not necessarily sustained in the longer term. Hence, studies that take place too soon after private participation begins or that fail to distinguish between these two periods of time in the analysis are likely to overstate the benefits of the reform. This is not to say that the transition benefits cannot be attributed as benefits of private participation, but rather that they represent a one-time gain from reform, rather than an improved steady-state situation. For example, in the case of water prices, this study finds that a large and significant negative change occurred in the time trend during the transition period. After the transition period, the price trend is not significantly different from zero (see table 7.8).

The *second* key methodological contribution is the comparison of pre- and postprivate participation trends rather than levels. By accounting for the fact that improvement trends may well have existed under the earlier state-owned regime, this framework provides an internal counterfactual and thereby avoids overstating the benefits of private participation by focusing not simply on whether performance has improved but on whether the rate of performance has improved. For example, in the case of the electricity distribution sector, a simple analysis of levels suggests that coverage continues to rise in the transition and post-transition period. When trends are taken into account, however, it becomes evident that the positive impact disappears (see table 5.6). Such results imply that studies of private participation impacts must obtain an adequate length of data series before and after the privatization event to support the calculation of longer-term trends.

Main Findings

The main cross-cutting findings of the study—which are relevant across the infrastructure sectors—are highlighted below. First and foremost it shows that overall significant improvements in sector performance were associated with private sector participation. The highlights are the consistent improvements in efficiency and quality, and reductions in the workforce. There do not appear to be significant impacts on output and coverage. Prices tended to increase somewhat, although the picture is highly variable across sectors.

The impact on *employment* is clear-cut. Reductions in the workforce are unambiguous, particularly during the transition period. Employment reductions were on average roughly 15 to 25 percent of the workforce during the transition period and a further 15 to 25 percent during the post-transition period. Nevertheless, the total number of jobs eliminated across all countries and all sectors considered in this study amounted to no more than 70,000. At least half of these redundancies took place in Brazil and in Argentina (where the preprivatization workforce was particularly large). When historic trends are taken into account and the changes are expressed in average annual growth rates, the impact is on the order of –4 to –5 percent of the workforce per year during the transition period, reverting to a positive trend of roughly 5 percent per year during the post-transition period. And when the indicator is overall sector employment, the trend in the medium and long term is significant employment gains.

Given the magnitude of workforce reductions, it is not surprising that *labor productivity* also increased substantially. In the electricity sector, the number of connections per employee rose from less than 500 before the privatization to around 750 after privatization. In the water sector, the increase in the same labor productivity indicator was from less than 200 connections per employee to around 400 after privatization. In telecommunications, preprivatization ratios stood at around 100 connections per employee, which nearly tripled to 300 after privatization. The econometric analysis shows that the significant improvements in the labor productivity trend were largely confined to the transition period. Thereafter, the change in the labor productivity trend was insignificant or even negative in some cases.

The other enterprise efficiency measure that was used in the study was *distributional losses*, which capture the percentage of production that does not reach the final consumer. The study finds consistent improvements in this efficiency indicator following privatization. To give an idea of the magnitude of the change, distributional losses in power utilities dropped from around 20 percent to around 10 percent following privatization, whereas those in water utilities fell from the 40 to 60 percent range down to the 30 to 40 percent range. In the case of power, the substantial improvements in the trend for distributional losses took place during the transition period, with no significant changes thereafter. In the case of water, no significant change in trend occurred during the transition period, but a small but significant improvement occurred in the trend thereafter. This may reflect the fact that improvements in unaccounted for water cannot be made rapidly over time, unlike reductions in the workforce.

Although the availability of data on *service quality* is comparatively limited, the findings for those quality variables that could be captured show an unambiguous improvement in quality trends across the three sectors. In the case of water, continuity of service increased from 10 to 15 hours per day to more than 20 hours per day, while the percentage of samples passing potability tests converged around the 98 percent level. By far the largest improvements in water service quality were found in the case of Colombia. In electricity, substantial reductions in the frequency and duration of supply interruptions can be observed. In telecommunications, firms typically doubled their scores on standard quality-of-service indexes. Notwithstanding these substantial improvements in levels, the econometric analysis does not find evidence of significant improvements in trends, except in the case of frequency of power interruptions, which continued to improve at a rate of around 5 percent per year after the transition.

Coverage rates increased substantially across the privatization period, but no significant change could be found in the long-term coverage trends. Thus, in power, coverage increased by at least 5 percentage points and by as much as 30 percentage points in Central America. In telecommunications, coverage increased from typically less than 10 percent of the population to somewhere between 10 and 20 percent of the population. Coverage of water rose from the 60 to 80 percent range to the 80 to 100 percent range, and for sewerage from the 40 to 60 percent range to the 60 to 80 percent range. Nevertheless, across all sectors, the rate of growth of coverage did not change significantly before and after privatization, although telecommunications showed some improvement during the transition. In the case of telecommunications, intense competition from rapidly expanding mobile telephony likely explains the lack of a major expansion in fixed-line service. In the case of electricity, many of the markets considered already had close to universal coverage, limiting the possibility or need for growth. In the case of water, the result is harder to understand given the significant unmet needs and the essential nature of the service. One possible explanation is the commercially unattractive nature of expanding services to relatively low-income groups under tariff regimes characterized by substantial cross-subsidies.

The same lack of a significant change in trend was found for the *volume of output produced*. Because output volumes are closely related to the number of customers, this finding is closely linked to that for coverage. Moreover, the scope for average consumption per customer of essential services to increase is likely limited in the short term. The exceptions are water and electricity, for which output fell after the transition period. This result likely reflects the improvements in distribution losses reported above, such that a lower volume of output is needed to serve a given level of demand.

The results on *prices* are much harder to generalize, partly because the initial conditions varied substantially. Many initial prices, particularly in the water sector, were highly subsidized and did not reflect cost recovery. Private participation tended to bring back cost recovery, which generated an upward pressure on prices. For the water sector, substantial price increases occurred in Chile and Colombia and a major price reduction occurred in Brazil. Overall, the changes were not found to be statistically significant. In electricity, prices increased significantly, toward a level of US$100 per MWh in most cases, although considerably higher in Bolivia and Chile. The analysis of price trends was richest for the telecommunications sector and indicated the presence of tariff rebalancing, with monthly fixed and variable charges rising by 45 percent and 65 percent, respectively. Changes in installation charges were generally quite modest, except in Brazil, where a significant reduction took place. Interestingly, controlling for market liberalization and growing cellular competition did not materially affect the results that were obtained for privatization of fixed-line telephony.

Most of the analysis in this book is based on the construction of an internal counterfactual based on the projection of preprivatization performance trends to draw more rigorous conclusions about the extent of any real changes in firm behavior as a result of privatization. It is also interesting to look at external counterfactuals, that is to say, enterprises that have remained in public control. In the case of electricity, it was possible to assemble such a control sample of Latin American distribution utilities that had remained in public hands throughout the study period.

The differences between publicly and privately operated distribution utilities showed up primarily with regard to labor productivity, distribution losses, quality of service, and tariffs. In contrast, other indicators such as coverage and operation expenditures exhibited similar trends or did not present significant changes between the groups. Nevertheless, the distribution of performance overlaps, with the top decile of performers in the public utility group outperforming the average private utility, and the bottom decile of performers in the private utility group outperformed by the average public utility.

In the case of labor productivity and distributional losses, both groups of utilities displayed similar starting values. Following privatization, the performance of the privatized group improved substantially. For example, labor productivity ended up being twice as high as that of the public utilities. In the case of distribution losses, private utilities improved their performance by 12 percent, while public utilities saw their performance deteriorate by 5 percent. With regard to continuity of service, both groups started at around 24 interruptions per year. The private utilities reduced this to around 12 compared with a reduction to around 19 for the public utilities. Similarly, public utilities saw the average duration of their outages increase by almost 50 percent, compared with a reduction of almost 30 percent from the private utilities, from a similar starting value.

Determinants of impact. Most of the analysis in the book treats private sector participation as a homogenous event, but the reality is that specific transactions differ enormously with respect to the way that they are designed. Key dimensions of the design include sale method, award criteria, nationality of the firm, and details of the subsequent regulatory framework, including degree of autonomy of any regulatory body and principles used to determine tariff. According to economic theory, each of these aspects can significantly affect the incentives faced by the private party and, hence, could be expected to influence the different aspects of enterprise behavior reviewed above. By pooling all the cases available across sectors, and adding a new set of variables to capture the transactional and regulatory environment, it was possible to measure the impact of each of these factors.

The main findings can be summarized by the following points. First, regulatory and contract characteristics matter: the way privatizations are undertaken can generate significant performance differences. Second, each regulatory and contract characteristic affects each performance variable differently. In other words, a certain contract characteristic could have a positive influence on one performance variable and a negative or insignificant impact on another. Third, some regulatory and contract characteristics have bigger impacts than others. For instance, in some cases, the changes attributed to having a fully autonomous regulatory body are much larger than changes attributed to other regulatory variables.

Finally, some commentators have talked about a "privatization paradox," referring to the broadly positive impacts found in technical studies as opposed to the strong negative feeling that has characterized the recent social backlash against privatization in Latin America. To what extent can the findings of this study contribute to the resolution of the paradox? The clue may lie in the recent opinion research in Peru (described in chapter 2) that tries to pin down the key sources of public discontent. Among the top four most negative consequences of privatization identified by the public were "rise in unemployment" and "services are more expensive." The findings of this study broadly suggest that private sector participation was very successful in improving efficiency and quality and mildly successful in improving coverage. Additionally, findings suggest that employment in the short term did decrease, although in the medium term and sectorwide, the trend tended to reverse and the impact on prices was mixed. The effect on prices has to be taken with caution, because the starting prices were often highly distorted and did not represent cost recovery. When this is the case, the negative impacts precisely coincide with the areas that seem to matter the most to the general public. Efficiency (although important to analysts) evidently is not a concern to the general public, except in so far as it feeds into lower prices, which—in sectors characterized by historic underpricing—it was not able to do. Quality did improve as a result of privatizations, and although it is likely to be a high concern to the public, it was not highlighted in the opinion studies. Perhaps the quality impacts were not clearly perceived or were outweighed by countervailing movements in prices.

Moving Forward

What insights do these results yield in terms of future policy options? First, it is clear that private sector participation is a complex undertaking that encompasses a variety of performance variables. Impacts on each of these variables is not necessarily straightforward, with differences determined by sector, time (in terms of proximity to the privatization event), and regulatory and contract characteristics.

Policy makers considering future private sector participation should first prioritize their performance objectives. Once the most important objectives are identified, the detailed results presented in this book can be mined to determine the circumstances in which those objectives are likely to be achieved. For instance, if increasing quality and efficiency are much more important objectives than retaining workers, then privatization would be a highly attractive option. Similarly, if reducing distributional losses is a key objective, then privatization using an auction process and encouraging the involvement of foreign investors should be considered.

The results presented in this book are instructive to policy makers in terms of highlighting potential private sector participation pitfalls. Many of the pitfalls were due to poor design and faulty implementation. If such pitfalls are known in advance, then proactive countermeasures can be employed. Consider the case of an electricity distribution policy maker who has prioritized improving quality and reducing distributional losses—and hence decided to move ahead with privatization. Drawing on the impacts detailed in this book, the policy maker could design a public relations campaign about expected benefits as well as potential price increases and reductions in sector employment. As a whole, this book can help policy makers make more informed and nuanced decisions, allowing them to maximize both technical and political objectives.

As mentioned, the program and reforms could have been implemented better. The overall results are quite positive, but the perception appears quite negative. Although it seems a paradox, valid reasons explain the divergence between perceptions and facts. To solve this paradox, it is important to understand the reasons that generate the discontent of the citizens and their point of view. The process of private sector participation could have been better in communication and content, and could have obtained greater benefits and higher popular approval. The context in which the programs of private participation were developed was one of excessive optimism and belief in quick positive profits, many promises, a lack of realism, poor handling of the expectations, and a breach in contractual agreements by both parties. The social criticism of privatization is ample and varied, including concerns about (i) corruption within privatization transactions (transparency of the process and handling of the resources, before and after, and the regulatory deficiencies and regulatory capture); (ii) excessive profits of the operators; (iii) social policy in relation to the increased tariffs, access, and benefits to the poor; (iv) the often lack of social tariffs for those who cannot afford the costs of the service; (v) treatment and dismissals of the affected workers; (vi) design of the concessions and privatizations; and (vii) abuses of renegotiation. The common denominator of these complaints seems to be the social distribution and the lack of transparency within the process. It is certain that most of the discontent, and the source of the opposition, is legitimate because of the deficiencies in the design and implementation of the programs that need to be better understood and corrected in future programs.

Again, while the benefits of the private sector participation programs in infrastructure were significant overall, the benefits could have been even larger if the process and its implementation were better. Maximizing benefits and securing a broad consensus must be the objectives of future programs. Now that we know best practices and understand how to apply them correctly, there is no excuse to commit past mistakes. As countries move forward—including those just starting the private participation process and those going for a second or third phase by reengaging the private sector—it is essential that the lessons from the past are accounted for and properly addressed. The corrections fall into four areas: strategy, design, incentives, and evaluations. It is useful to recall the main deficiencies of past programs to address those shortcomings moving forward.

The main deficiencies of the private participation in infrastructure (PPI) programs were as follows:

- *Lack of motivation and communication programs.* Rarely did countries develop a proactive strategy of communication, during or after the reform, to inform the public of the following: (i) the necessity of the programs; (ii) the cost of maintaining the status quo; or (iii) the real benefits of the programs. Governments were especially remiss for not communicating the improvements obtained in the process, such as the halving of electricity tariffs after the reform of the sector, the dramatic decrease in long-distance phone calls, and, on average, the improvement that the poor greatly benefited from in the coverage made by private operators.
- *Absence of social programs in the affected sectors and lack of attention to adversely affected workers.* Rarely were social tariffs implemented, including universal coverage obligations, assistance programs for the poor to obtain access to the services, or unemployment. A particular emphasis was placed on consumption in spite of the low correlation between consumption and income and in spite of the fact that the poorest usually were not connected. This is, perhaps, the most important and genuine causal deficiency of such great opposition.
- *Extremely poor targeting of subsidies.* Most countries had tariff structures that did not recover costs for most of the population. The so-called leakage factor—users receiving the subsidy when, because of their level of income, they should not be—was more than 80 percent in many countries.
- *Prioritization of fiscal consideration.* Fiscal considerations were prioritized in the design of the reforms, as opposed to prioritizing greater efficiency in overall sector performance. Thus, the concessions were designed with an element of exclusivity, minimal risks to the operator, no universal service obligation, and so on to maximize the price paid to the government for the sale or concession of infrastructure services.
- *Substantial problems in transparency and participation.* First, what happened to funds collected from the transaction was rarely explained, and how they were allocated in the process was rarely monitored, and these conditions often appeared highly favorable to the operators. Second, a number of accusations of corruption were validated. Finally, affected communities were rarely involved or consulted. The decisions and processes went from top to bottom, by decree, and almost never by consensus.
- *Weak framework.* Only a feeble effort was made to develop an appropriate regulatory framework and a capable regulatory agency with sufficient capacity to avoid a public monopoly from becoming a private monopoly. Although many countries passed laws to create this

regulatory framework and a regulatory agency, the resources assigned and the political commitment made to that effort left much to be desired. A number of problems resulted from the limited regulatory efficiency, insufficient regulatory capacity, and slow development of regulatory instruments, which mainly were seen in tariff adjustment, investment fulfillment, and coverage expansion.

- *Poor design of concession agreements and privatization programs.* This problem ended up costing the governments enormous sums of money, led to unending conflicts, and discredited the program, feeding the backlash malaise. For example, the Mexican freeway system cost the government US$12 billion. Many concessions were granted rapidly in series, motivated by a desire to amortize investments or eliminate inappropriate subsidies, leading to a substantial increase in tariffs, instead of distributing the increases across several years. The concessions lacked considerable and usable sanctions as guarantees in the event of a contract breach.
- *Poorly stated clauses on financial equilibrium.* While the principle of financial equilibrium is valid and appropriate, it cannot be open ended, as it has been in many contracts. This principle has been abused and manipulated, leading to a large number of inappropriate renegotiations.
- *Lack of regulatory accounting and information obligations on the operators.* Adequate accounting is essential to facilitate effective regulation, properly assess costs and the assets base, and make forward-looking tariff adjustments.
- *Excessive disposition by governments to consider demands for renegotiation of the original contracts.* This disposition is reflected by the excessively large number of renegotiated contracts. Overall, more than 50 percent of the contracts were renegotiated. The most affected sectors were water and transport, with 88 percent and 71 percent of contracts renegotiated, respectively.
- *Contract violations.* The violation of the contract by both parties—operators and governments—often rendered competitive contracts irrelevant, as reflected in the excessively high numbers of individual contracts renegotiated almost immediately after privatization. These renegotiated contracts often transferred significant benefits that were not present in the original contract to the operators. The continuing conflicts between operator, regulator, and the government all fed the perception that some actors in the process, especially multinationals and the government, benefited unjustly, and often at the cost of excluded clients, workers, and poor people.
- *Timid, ineffective, and unpredictable conflict resolution mechanisms.* The lack of a conflict resolution framework led to contentious and acrimonious accusations and, not surprisingly, to heated arguments and to a costly and difficult process.

In moving forward, the above issues and lessons from the past need to be accounted for and corrected. The ultimate objective is to secure improved sector performance and long-term efficiency, reduce poverty through better concession design and regulation, and foster compliance with the terms agreed to by both the government and the operator. To establish such an environment, concession laws and contracts should (i) focus on securing long-term sector efficiency and proper risk assignments and mitigation, as well as discourage opportunistic bidding and renegotiation; (ii) be embedded in regulations that foster transparency and predictability, support incentives for efficient behavior, and impede opportunistic renegotiation and force contract compliance; and (iii) address social concerns and focus on poverty.

Governments remain at the heart of infrastructure service delivery. Private participation complements the need for public involvement, rather than reducing that need. Governments need to regulate infrastructure provision as well as contribute a good share of the investment. They must leverage their resources to attract as much complementary financing as possible. And they are still responsible for setting distributional objectives and ensuring that resources and policies are available to permit access for the poor.

The private sector is needed for its know-how and financing to complement scarce public funds. But bringing it back in a substantive manner requires addressing past problems and building on the lessons of the last decade. By the beginning of the century, private transactions had collapsed to less than a quarter of their peak level, and only in 2006 did they begin to show some tepid signs of recovering, particularly given investors' disaffection with emerging markets. Bringing back the private sector will require increasing transparency and improving the risk-return ratio for projects. This process entails decreasing regulatory risks and improving the framework for PPI as well as developing risk mitigation mechanisms. It also means improving public perceptions of PPI, which are so overwhelmingly negative in some countries as to be a serious constraint on further participation. This, in turn, requires greater transparency, improved transaction design and oversight to reduce renegotiations and poor performance, and better management of those who stand to lose out.

To make new public-private partnerships sustainable, not only do the technical and financial aspects need to be addressed, but also the social aspects most responsible for the backlash. Better communication is critical to create popular support. It is essential to promote the program's infrastructure improvements, advertise the initiative, explain the impact of not improving (but rather maintaining) the status quo, and realistically argue the program's cost-benefit tradeoff. The communication must not only justify the programs, but also periodically inform on the progress of the program, as well as of any changes or problems. The reforms must not only be successful, but that success must also be communicated. Greater transparency is necessary to provide a safeguard against corruption at all the levels and to obtain greater popular support. Also needed is greater fairness and support to those adversely affected in the design of the transaction. This goal can be achieved through the incorporation of social policies, such as social tariffs and financial assistance to those adversely affected by the programs, such as those losing their jobs. Programs or policies should be implemented to support users and workers. Affected communities must be part of the strategy of a successful program, and these communities must be involved from the start. Initiatives should be launched and supported from the bottom up in areas and locations where the benefits and costs will be incurred.

Critical Elements to Be Introduced in Moving Forward to Secure Success and Maximum Benefit of Private Participation Programs

The preceding sections on performance impact evaluations and the detrimental effects of renegotiation highlight the importance of proper regulatory and contract design and implementation. Although the results of the process of private participation were generally positive, they could have been better. The accumulated experience of roughly 20 years of PPI programs indicates that PPI can and must be better. These experiences show that the key elements of a successful program must include the following:

Improved Institutionality

Four stages and institutions should guide the life of the projects:

- Projects generally should be selected by the sectoral ministry, as a consequence of the country's strategic planning program and objectives.
- An interministerial group should be led by the finance minister to evaluate and approve the projects (accompanied by the appropriate economic and financial analysis) identified by the sectors.
- An implementing agency should receive the projects approved by the interministerial committee and prepare them for adjudication and bidding. The role of that agency ends once the transaction is completed.
- Once the project is adjudicated, the fiscalization, contract compliance, monitoring, and regulation should be handled by a separate and autonomous agency.

Improved Contract and Concession Design

- Concession contracts should be awarded competitively and designed to avoid ambiguities as much as possible—rather than direct adjudication or bilateral negotiation—and only after contracts have been carefully designed and reviewed and the qualifications of bidders have been screened.

- The implementing agency should compile a library of model contracts (which are broadly available) that incorporates best practices in practically all settings and for most typologies of projects. Their use would shorten preparation times and reduce a large percentage of past problems.
- To ensure consistency, lock-in effects, and adequate tariffs, contracts generally should be awarded on the basis of the highest proposed transfer fee (or minimum subsidy) rather than the lowest proposed tariff.[1]
- Outcome targets (regulation by objectives or service levels) should be the norm in contracts rather than investment obligations (regulation by means).
- Contracts should clearly define the treatment of assets, evaluation of investments, outcome indicators, procedures and guidelines to adjust and review tariffs, criteria and penalties for early termination of concessions, and procedures for resolution of conflicts.
- The sanctity of the bid is essential. For private sector participation to be successful and achieve the desired objectives, contracts and regulations need to be designed and enforced appropriately. The key objective should be to ensure that the contracting parties—private sector and government—comply with the agreed conditions. Thus, barring major unforeseen events and contingencies (which can be spelled out in the contract), the key issue is to increase the likelihood that the signatory parties to a concession contract, the private sector operator and the government, comply with the terms of the contract and that opportunistic renegotiation by either party is dissuaded. A key starting point is the design of better contracts that, while seeking long-term sector efficiency, does not facilitate renegotiation and penalize noncompliance.
- Concession contracts should contain clauses committing governments to a policy of no renegotiation except in the case of well-defined triggers. They should stipulate the process for and level of adjustments. The contract should specify that the operators will be held to their submitted bids. This approach forces operators to bear the costs of aggressive bids and of normal commercial risks—even if doing so results in the abandonment of concessions. In addition, the first tariff review should not be entertained for a significantly long period (at least five years) unless contract contingencies are triggered.
- Concession contracts should provide for significant compensation, including penalties, to operators in the event of unilateral changes to the contract by the government.

- Consideration should be given to making operators pay a significant fee for any renegotiation request. If the renegotiation is decided in the operator's favor, the fee would be reimbursed.
- Detailed analysis of seemingly aggressive bids—or at least of the top two bids, particularly if they differ significantly—should be required before a concession is awarded. And if the financial viability of aggressive bids appears highly dubious, a mechanism should be in place to allow those bids to be disqualified or to increase the performance bond significantly in relation to the difference between the bids. In either case, operators should be required to post performance bonds of significant value. Claims for renegotiation should be reviewed as transparently as possible, possibly through external, professional panels to assist regulators and governments in their analysis and decisionmaking. Any adjustments granted should be explained to the public as quickly as possible.
- Hurried, quickly organized concession programs should be avoided. Such an approach might secure more transactions, but it also leads to less satisfactory outcomes.

Regulatory Framework

- An appropriate regulatory framework and agency should be in place before the award of concessions, with sufficient autonomy and implementation capacity to ensure high-quality enforcement and to deter political opportunism. In addition, the tradeoffs between types of regulation—price cap and rate of return—should be well understood, including their different allocations of risk and implications for renegotiation. Technical regulation should fit information requirements and existing risks, and regulation should be by objectives and not by means. Thus, performance objectives should be used instead of investment obligations.

Regulatory Instruments

- Proper regulatory accounting of all assets and liabilities should be in place to avoid any ambiguity about the valuation of assets and liabilities and about the regulatory treatment and allocation of cost, investments, asset base, revenues, transactions with related parties, management fees, and operational and financial variables. Cost and financial models of the regulated utility should be standard regulatory instruments to assess performance, with particular emphasis on the evaluation of the cost of capital.
- Extensive use of benchmarking should be a common best practice of regulatory agencies and is critical to assess the efficiency of operations and to assist in the ordinary five-year tariff reviews.

- Improved capacity and experience should be a critical factor to produce effective regulation that leads to inducing efficient production of the service and the alignment of costs and prices.

Conflict Resolution Mechanism

- Effective conflict resolution mechanisms should be used. The most effective method is binding arbitration through a panel of experts (not chosen by any of the parties) and one that is based on the contract and not on principles and fairness (as used in Chile).

Addressing Social Issues

- Social tariffs, such as support for those adversely affected, should be a standard component of all projects. In particular, adoption and use of social tariffs and programs to subsidize access for the poor should be a part of all the relevant projects. In addition, programs or policies should be implemented to support adversely affected workers.
- Involvement of the affected communities from the start, at least in a consultative process, should be an integral part of any project. Initiatives should be launched and supported from the bottom up in areas and locations where the benefits and costs will be incurred.

Transparency and Communications

- Better communication is essential to create popular support, promote the program's infrastructure improvements, advertise the initiative, explain the likely impact and the consequences of maintaining the status quo, and realistically argue the program's cost-benefit tradeoff of the program. The communication must not only justify the programs, but also periodically inform on the program's progress, as well as any changes or problems. The reforms must be successful, and that success must be communicated.
- Greater transparency in the overall process, financing, use of funds, and adjudication is critical to provide a safeguard against corruption at all levels and to obtain greater popular support.

Evaluation and Monitoring

- It is essential to periodically evaluate the accomplishments to improve efficiency, achieve the expected results, and broadly communicate advances and pitfalls.

Private sector participation can and should play a major role in the improvement of infrastructure sectors in developing countries. The newer modalities of private participation—beyond strict privatization—offer significant potential. But to bring the private sector back, to generate the potential significant benefits of their participation, and to capture (for the users) a larger share of those benefits, will require correcting the mistakes of the past and improving concession and contract design. In particular, chances of success will be highly enhanced for programs that comply with the above-listed elements. Improvements in infrastructure for growth and poverty cannot be delayed. There are significant threats and opportunities. Most countries, including those in Latin America, are at a crossroads on PPI. Investment must urgently modernize infrastructure, and most governments have serious fiscal limitations. Success will require some form of private sector involvement and financing. If problems such as poor perception of private participation are not corrected, the significant gains and necessary modernization of the sector might collapse, and the private financing will prove costly if not difficult. Conversely, opportunity exists to refine the model by attacking the problems and deficiencies of the past, through second-generation reforms that are constructive and broadly participatory, and to design new processes that incorporate lessons learned.

Note

1. The least present value of revenues criteria developed by Engel, Fischer, and Galetovic (2001) should be strongly considered for road concessions, given its built-in incentives deterring renegotiation.

Appendix 1

Existing Literature

While many studies have been conducted to date, the literature on infrastructure privatization analysis has gaps. Most studies take an extremely wide-angle approach, are country case studies, or relate to the privatization of fixed telecommunications. For instance, Chong and López-de-Silanes (2005) looked at all types of privatization, not just infrastructure, as did Birdsall and Nellis (2003). Ros and Baneerjee (2000) analyzed 23 countries in Latin America to evaluate the relationship between privatization, network expansion, and efficiency in telecommunications. Ramamurti (1996) examined the privatization of telecommunications and transport in Mexico, Argentina, Jamaica, and República Bolivariana de Venezuela. And La Porta and López-de-Silanes (1999) evaluated privatized nonfinancial firms in Mexico. In addition, much of the literature has focused on the performance of financial indicators, rather than broader measures of importance to citizens (Megginson, Nash, and van Randenborgh 1994; D'Souza and Megginson 1999). Hence, there is a distinct lack of cross-sectoral studies that fully and accurately measure the impact of private participation in infrastructure in Latin America. Table A1.1 summarizes selected studies of infrastructure privatization related to Latin America.

Most of the literature related to ownership change refers to transportation (for example, Ramamurti 1996; Laurin and Bozec 2001), telecommunications (for example, Ramamurti 1996; Ros 1999) and manufacturing (for example, Boardman and Vining 1989; Frydman, Gray, Hessel, and Rapaczynski 1999). In the case of privatization of the distribution of electricity and water, in particular for countries in Latin America and the Caribbean (LAC), there is no comprehensive reference. Most of the articles that analyze this issue respond to case studies or a country analysis (for example, Galal, Jones, Tandon, and Vogelsang 1994; La Porta and López-de-Silanes 1999), and only the telecommunications sector has been more deeply analyzed in the region (see, for example, Ros and Banerjee 2000). Some exceptions in these sectors include Estache and

Rossi (2004) for the case of electricity distribution and Galiani, Gertler, and Schargrodsky (2005) for water.

Ehrlich, Gallais-Hamonno, Liu, and Lutter (1994) provided good evidence on productivity differences between state-owned and privately owned firms. They used a sample of 23 comparable international air connections of different (and in some cases changing) ownership categories over the period 1973–83 for which they obtained good and comparable cost, output, and ownership data. The researchers developed a model of endogenous, firm-specific productivity growth as a function of firm-specific capital, and used the model as a basis for their fixed-effects regressions, estimating a cost function in a simultaneous framework with input-demand equations. They used ownership,[1] output,[2] capital quantity and price indexes, labor quality and price indexes, fuel indexes, total factor productivity (TFP) indexes and productivity trend, technical factors, regulatory measures,[3] and firm- and country-specific variables. The study found a significant relationship between ownership and firm-specific rates of productivity growth. The results suggest that private ownership leads to higher rates of productivity growth and declining costs in the long run, and that these differences are not affected by the degree of market competition or regulation.

Boardman and Vining (1989) used data from the 500 largest manufacturing and mining corporations in the world outside the United States, as compiled by *Fortune* magazine in 1983. They classified these firms as state-owned enterprises (SOEs), mixed enterprises, and private companies, and used four profitability and two efficiency measures. Their results provide evidence that, after controlling for a wide variety of factors, large industrial mixed and public enterprises perform substantially worse than private ones. They concluded that partial privatizations may be not be the best strategy, because, according to their indicators, they perform quite similarly to SOEs.

Frydman, Gray, Hessel, and Rapaczynski (1999) compared the performance of privatized and state firms in the transition economies of Central Europe, and explicitly tried to control for selection bias. Their study was based on a panel of more than 200 privatized and state firms in the Czech Republic, Hungary, and Poland. In particular, their findings show that, in the context of Central Europe, privatization has no beneficial effect on any performance measure in the case of firms controlled by insider owners (managers or employees) and that it has a pronounced effect on firms with outsider owners. In any case, the effects of transferring ownership to insiders and outsiders may have important implications for the design and effectiveness of privatization programs in the transition economies. Also, their study indicates that, in those cases in which privatization is effective, its effects vary considerably, depending on the performance measure under examination. In particular, their findings show that while the effect of privatization on revenue is pronounced for certain types of owners, there is no significant effect of ownership change in cost reduction.

Finally, by obtaining firm fixed-effect estimates of the various effects of privatization and using different types of control groups, as well as by controlling for changes in the macroeconomic environment, the study attempts to deal with most kinds of selection bias that could potentially affect the results.

Galal, Jones, Tandon, and Vogelsang (1994) compared the actual postprivatization performance of 12 large firms, mostly air connections and regulated utilities in Britain, Chile, Malaysia, and Mexico, with the predicted performance of firms that had not been divested. Using this counterfactual approach, the authors documented net welfare gains in 11 of the 12 cases considered, gains which equal, on average, 26 percent of the firm's predivestiture sales. They found no case in which workers were significantly worse off, and in three cases, workers significantly benefited.

La Porta and López-de-Silanes (1999) found that the former Mexican SOEs they studied rapidly closed a large performance gap with industry-matched private firms that existed before divestment. These firms, which were highly unprofitable before privatization, became very profitable thereafter. Output increased by 54.3 percent, in spite of a reduced level of investment spending, and sales per employee roughly doubled. The privatized firms reduced (blue- and white-collar) employment by half, but those workers who remained were paid significantly more. The authors attributed most of the performance improvement to productivity gains resulting from better incentives, with at most one-third of the improvement being attributable to lower employment costs.

The LAC electrical sector has broad descriptions of the reforms but without an empirical analysis (see, for example, Dussan 1996; Estache and Rodriguez-Pardina 1998; Millan, Lora, and Micco 2001). Other studies focused on developing countries, where some information about the region concerned in this paper can be found (see, for example, Bacon and Besant-Jones 2001). Finally, Joskow's (2003) review summarized the lessons learned across countries in the electricity market, and Jamasb, Mota, Newbery, and Pollitt (2005) provided a survey of electricity market reforms in developing countries.

The reason underlying the lack of empirical analysis in electricity was the nonexistence of available systematic data. Still, there is some country analysis for this sector. For example, Chisari, Estache, and Romero (1999) built a general equilibrium model to analyze the impact of privatizations in Argentina between 1993 and 1995. Among the regional empirical research that can be mentioned is Estache and Rossi (2004). The authors analyzed the impact of change in ownership on labor productivity and prices. They also evaluated how the different regulatory environments affected these outcomes in the region. They found that private firms use significantly less labor force to produce a given bundle of output than public firms. Using similar data, Rossi (2004) also analyzed the firms' operating and maintenance expenses. He found that this cost did not change significantly after the reform and argued that outsourcing, in part, may be biasing the results in the decrease in labor usage and their productivity.

The case of water and sewerage sectors is less developed in the literature. Again, most of the references are descriptions of the reforms or country analysis, but little empirical research has been made for water in the region. The explanation for this is that little information is available. One exception is the study by Galiani, Gertler, and Schargrodsky (2005), which used household surveys and other sources to evaluate the impact of the water privatizations on child mortality. Although trends before the reforms in cities that would privatize this service compared with those reforms that did not change ownership during the period under analysis were not significantly different, the authors found that after the change in ownership, the cities with private water operators presented an important reduction in child mortality.

In contrast to the previous sectors, telecommunications was the most studied sector in the region. Nevertheless, most of the references for the region focus on country studies (Galal, Jones, Tandon, and Vogelsang 1994; Ramamurti 1996). A few exceptions, including Ros (1999) and Ros and Banerjee (2000), analyzed the region or included these countries in their study.

Ramamurti (1996) studied the privatization of telecommunications in Mexico, Argentina, Jamaica, and República Bolivariana de Venezuela. He reported important network growths during the first years after the change in ownership. He also found important improvements in labor productivity in these countries.

Ros (1999) examined the number of connections per 100 inhabitants, as well as the number of connections per employee. He found that privatization led to higher growth in coverage in countries with a gross domestic product (GDP) per capita lower than $10,000. He also found positive effects on labor productivity. Finally, he concluded that while competition seemed to have no effect on network expansion, he found positive effects on labor productivity.

Ros and Banerjee (2000) used the same data as Ros (1999) but focused on 23 countries in LAC. The authors found positive relationships in the region between privatization and network expansion, and in terms of efficiency. They also investigated the effects of tariff rebalancing. They found that abandoning the policy of below-cost pricing of residential basic service may relieve the supply bottleneck, and that, after controlling for rebalancing, privatization had positive effects on efficiency.

With respect to competition in this sector, Wallsten (2001) analyzed a sample of countries in Latin America and Africa and found no significant effects of privatizations on coverage, labor efficiency, and prices when the models were controlled by competition. Nevertheless, competition, measured by mobile operators not owned by the incumbent, had a positive correlation with coverage and a negative one with prices, whereas no significant effects were found for labor productivity.

Table A1.1 Infrastructure Privatization in Selected Cross-Country and Latin American Country Studies

Country	Sector	Summary	Source
Argentina	Multi	Access increased, relative prices of services decreased, and employment fell but has since recovered.	Ennis and Pinto 2003
Argentina	Multi	Significant gains from improvements in quality, access, and productivity, especially among the poor. But gains are not enough to offset credit shocks. Fiscal gains are larger under bad regulatory environment.	Benitez, Chisari, and Estache 2003
Argentina	Multi	General increase in employment; gains (price decrease or improvement in quality) from privatization accrue mainly to the rich; while gains from regulation of privatized firms accrue to low-income classes.	Chisari, Estache, and Romero 1999
Argentina	Water	Society as a whole benefits. The government is the big winner, whereas consumers, particularly the poor, stand to lose from the proposed reform. The projected outcome for investors is mixed.	van den Berg and Katakura 2004
Argentina	Multi	Social policy measures adopted at time of sector reform are poorly targeted toward low-income households. Targeting performance can be substantially improved by subsidizing connection rather than consumption.	Foster and Araujo 2004
Argentina	Water	After the change in ownership, the cities with private water operators demonstrated an important reduction in child mortality.	Galiani, Gertler, and Schargrodsky 2005

(continued)

Table A1.1 Infrastructure Privatization in Selected Cross-Country and Latin American Country Studies *(continued)*

Country	Sector	Summary	Source
Chile	Electricity	Overall welfare gain, but the government and previously nonpaying customers are worse off. Large gains for both domestic and foreign shareholders as well as employees in their capacity as shareholders.	Galal, Jones, Tandon, and Vogelsang 1994
Chile	Telecom	Overall welfare gain, with consumers gaining the most mainly through expanded services and unchanged tariffs, although with some deterioration in quality.	Galal, Jones, Tandon, and Vogelsang 1994
Chile	Multi	Significant increases in coverage, especially among the poor. No clear trend in prices.	Paredes 2003
Guatemala	Multi	New connections to water, electricity, and sanitation services increased significantly. Most dramatic change in the telecommunications sector. The poor, rural, and indigenous households have doubled their probability of receiving services but in absolute terms are still least likely to receive services.	Foster and Tré 2003; Foster and Araujo 2004
Mexico	Water	Mixed effect on quality. With the introduction of metering, the number of low-income consumers receiving a water bill rose, while water bills for high-income consumers fell or stayed the same. Mixed outcome for middle-income consumers.	Haggarty, Brook, and Zuluaga 2002
Mexico	Telecom	Overall welfare gains, but consumers lose from rising prices. High proportion of foreign ownership also suggests that benefits have leaked abroad.	Galal, Jones, Tandon, and Vogelsang 1994

(continued)

Table A1.1 Infrastructure Privatization in Selected Cross-Country and Latin American Country Studies (*continued*)

Country	Sector	Summary	Source
Mexico	Multi	Former SOEs rapidly closed a large performance gap with industry-matched private firms that existed before divestment. The privatized firms reduced employment by half, but those workers who remained were paid significantly more.	La Porta and López-de-Silanes 1999
Nicaragua	Electricity	The increase in the price of electricity reduced welfare at all expenditure deciles, with larger losses at the top of the distribution. Households that obtained access during the reform period experienced substantial gains in welfare, with larger gains among poorer households.	Freije and Rivas 2002
Panama	Water	Simulation of alternative subsidy designs to mitigate tariff impacts of proposed concession on the poor.	Foster, Gómez-Lobo, and Halpern 2000
Peru	Telecom	Privatization brought dramatic improvements in coverage, quality, and technology. Privatization improved total consumer welfare, mainly by increasing access to the service. But price increases negatively affected low- and, especially, very-low-income households.	Torero, Schroth, and Pascó-Font 2003
Peru (Lima)	Water	Overall welfare gains, but workers lose from forced early retirements. Consumers gain from expanded connections net of higher prices. Welfare gains would have been higher with full reform, analyzed as a counterfactual to actual partial reform.	Alcázar, Xu, and Zuluaga 2002

(*continued*)

Table A1.1 Infrastructure Privatization in Selected Cross-Country and Latin American Country Studies *(continued)*

Country	Sector	Summary	Source
Peru	Multi	Improvement in access for all sectors. But water is still of low quality, electricity reform has led to tariff increase (and consumer surplus has decreased), and prices of phone calls have increased (and consumer surplus has fallen).	Torero and Pascó-Font 2001
23 OECD countries	Telecom	Insignificant reduction in employment.	Boylaud and Nicoletti 2000
21 developing and transition countries	Multi	Privatization and competition lead to significant improvements in mainline penetration. But a comprehensive reform program, involving both policies and the support of an independent regulator, produced the largest gains. The sequence of reform matters: mainline penetration is lower if competition is introduced after privatization, rather than at the same time.	Clarke and Wallsten 2002
17 countries	Telecom	Expanded retail access is likely to lower the industrial price and increase the price differential between industrial customers and household customers. The unbundling of generation and the introduction of a wholesale spot market did not necessarily lower the price and possibly may have resulted in a higher price.	D'Souza and Megginson 1999

(continued)

Table A1.1 Infrastructure Privatization in Selected Cross-Country and Latin American Country Studies *(continued)*

Country	Sector	Summary	Source
21 industrial and developing countries	Telecom	Sound regulatory governance has a positive impact on network expansion and efficiency. Openness of markets to competition and divestment of former state-owned operators also contributed positively to better performance. Competition and privatization have greater impact for lower-income countries than for higher-income ones, but regulatory reforms have a smaller impact on lower-income countries.	D'Souza, Bortolotti, Fantini, and Megginson 2000
Latin America	Electricity	Private firms use significantly less labor force to produce a given bundle of output than public firms.	Estache and Rossi 2004
Latin America	Electricity	Firms' operating and maintenance expenses did not change significantly after the reform. Outsourcing, in part, may be biasing the results in the decrease in labor usage and the firms' productivity.	Rossi 2004
86 developing countries	Telecom	Both reforms improve access, but there is no consistent impact on quality. Deregulation associated with lower prices and employment increases; privatization with higher prices and employment decreases.	Fink, Mattoo, and Rathindran 2003
22 Latin American countries	Telecom	Sound regulatory governance has a positive impact on network expansion and efficiency. Openness of markets to competition and divestment of former state-owned operators also contributed positively to better performance. Competition and privatization have greater impact for lower-income countries than for higher-income ones, but regulatory reforms have a smaller impact on lower-income countries.	Gutiérrez 2003

(continued)

Table A1.1 Infrastructure Privatization in Selected Cross-Country and Latin American Country Studies *(continued)*

Country	Sector	Summary	Source
Latin American survey	Multi	Recent studies conclude that privatization has contributed only slightly to rising unemployment and inequality, and either reduces poverty or has no effect on it. However, the benefits of privatization are spread widely in the medium term, while the costs are large and immediate.	Nellis 2003
26 developing countries	Telecom	Both reforms improve access, but there is no consistent impact on quality. Deregulation associated with lower prices and employment increases; privatization with higher prices and employment decreases.	Petrazzini and Clark 1996
4 Latin American countries	Telecom and Transport	Important network growth during the first years after the change in ownership. Important improvements in labor productivity.	Ramamurti 1996
130 countries	Telecom	Privatization associated with network expansion (except in lower-income countries) and efficiency. Competition associated with greater efficiency but not network expansion. No discernible impact on quality.	Ros 1999
23 Latin American countries	Telecom	Positive relationships between privatization and network expansion, and efficiency. Regarding tariff rebalancing, abandoning the policy of below-cost pricing of residential basic service may relieve the supply bottleneck. After controlling for rebalancing, privatization still had positive effects on efficiency.	Ros and Banerjee 2000

(continued)

Table A1.1 Infrastructure Privatization in Selected Cross-Country and Latin American Country Studies *(continued)*

Country	Sector	Summary	Source
30 African and Latin American countries	Telecom	Increased competition associated with increase in access and decrease in cost. Privatization not helpful unless coupled with effective regulation.	Wallsten 2001
51 developing countries	Electricity	Competition associated with higher service penetration and lower prices for industrial users (no significant effect on residential users), among others. On their own, privatization and regulation have insignificant effects. Together, they lead to greater electricity availability, generation capacity, and labor productivity.	Zhang, Parker, and Kirkpatrick 2002
Latin America	Multi	Increased productivity and profitability, accelerating restructuring and output growth, mounting tax revenues, and improving product quality following privatization.	Chong and López-de-Silanes 2005
Global survey	Multi	Most privatization programs appear to have worsened the distribution of assets and income in the short run. This is more evident in transition economies than in Latin America, and less clear for utilities (such as electricity and telecom), where the poor have benefited from greater access, than for banks, oil companies, and other natural resource producers.	Birdsall and Nellis 2003

(continued)

Table A1.1 Infrastructure Privatization in Selected Cross-Country and Latin American Country Studies *(continued)*

Country	Sector	Summary	Source
11 cases from Latin American, transition, and Asian economies	Multi	In Latin America, major infrastructure privatizations have generally increased access to power, telephone services, and water, particularly for the poor. Although some privatized firms have raised prices, a move that has burdened lower-income households, the bottom line is still one of absolute gains in welfare for the poor. On the other hand, privatization was generally carried out without thought to its potential to reduce the region's high inequality.	Nellis and Birdsall 2005

Source: Foster, Tiongson, and Ruggeri Laderchi 2005; authors' elaboration.

Note: While the above studies all analyze privatizations, in many cases privatizations were combined with regulatory reform, restructuring, and tariff reform.

OECD = Organisation for Economic Co-operation and Development; SOE = state-owned enterprise.

Notes

1. Percentage of equity owned by the state.

2. An index of four types of output: (i) scheduled passenger kilometers, (ii) scheduled freight, (iii) scheduled mail, and (iv) nonscheduled service in tons per kilometer actually flown, with all of these types of output weighted by corresponding revenues shares.

3. Dummies for the regulatory change in the United States in 1976 and in the North Atlantic market in 1978.

Appendix 2

Details of Econometric Approach

For the treatment or regression approach, a simple version of the model is used as a starting point, as specified below:

$$\ln\left(y_{ijt}\right) = \beta_0 PRIV_{ijt} + \sum_{ij} \phi_{ij} D_{ij} + v_{ijt} \tag{A2.1}$$

where y_{ijt} are the variables of interest (outputs, inputs, labor productivity, efficiency, quality, coverage, and prices). The main coefficient in this model is the dummy, $PRIV_{ijt}$, that is equal to one if the firm i of country j had private owners at time t. Given the fact that several variables are not observable to the econometrician, fixed effects are included to capture the characteristics of the firm, such as management, initial conditions, size, density of the network, and so on, which are assumed to be constant for each firm across time. Hence, β_0 captures the effect on the outcome of interest, given by the privatization or the concession. As was pointed out by Frydman, Gray, Hessel, and Rapaczynski (1999), adding the firm fixed effects may reduce the selection bias of the firms in the sample.

A second version of equation (A2.1) is also estimated, introducing a firm-specific time trend:

$$\ln\left(y_{ijt}\right) = \beta_0 PRIV_{ijt} + \sum_{ij} \phi_{ij} D_{ij} + \sum_{ij} \phi_{ij} t_{ij} + v_{ijt} \tag{A2.2}$$

Equation (A2.2) uses the same dependent variables and the dummy used in the static model, $PRIV_{ijt}$. The third coefficient captures the time trend of the variable of interest. Several factors may affect this, like the initial conditions. Hence, it is important to control for the firm's specific value. Finally, as in the previous model, firm fixed effects are included to capture the characteristics of the firm not observed by the econometrician. Again, the relevant coefficient is β_0, which captures the effect on the outcome of interest caused by the privatization or the concession.

Most of the literature that was reviewed focused on basic approaches like equation (A2.1), and in some cases used specifications like equation (A2.2). In other words, they evaluated the change exactly before and after the change in ownership. In this case, to identify the outcomes during the transitional years, specific dummies are defined for the transition and the after-transition period, so that equations (A2.1) and (A2.2) become:

$$\ln(y_{ijt}) = \delta^T DUMMY\_TRAN_{ijt} + \delta^P DUMMY\_POST_{ijt}$$
$$+ \sum_{ij} \phi_{ij} D_{ij} + v_{ijt} \tag{A2.1a}$$

$$\ln(y_{ijt}) = \delta^T DUMMY\_TRAN_{ijt} + \delta^P DUMMY\_POST_{ijt}$$
$$+ \sum_{ij} \phi_{ij} D_{ij} + \sum_{ij} \theta_{ij} t_{ij} + v_{ijt} \tag{A2.2a}$$

where

$$DUMMY\_TRAN_{ijt} \begin{cases} 1 & \text{if } s_{ijt} \geq -1 \\ 0 & \text{otherwise} \end{cases}$$

and

$$DUMMY\_POST_{ijt} \begin{cases} 1 & \text{if } s_{ijt} \geq 2 \\ 0 & \text{otherwise} \end{cases}$$

where S_{ijt} is a time trend that has a value equal to zero for the year when the privatization was awarded. In this sense, the first dummy identifies the average change in the dependent variable during the transition with respect to the average level previous to these years. The second dummy identifies the average change of the dependent variable after the transition with respect to the transition itself.

The first basic specification is equations (A2.1a) and (A2.2a) using the log level of the indicators. In particular, this helps to identify most of the conclusions. For those variables that present trends (for example, number of connections), equation (A2.2a) is more enlightening. However, it relies on the assumption that trends between the three periods of analysis are the same. To relax this assumption, a third set of equations (A2.1a) and (A2.2a) was run, but the annual growth in each indicator was used. In this case, the first equation identifies average changes in growth between the periods.

Given the fact that a semilogarithmic functional form of these models is used for each of the indicators, when interpreting the coefficient estimates of the dummy, the percentage impact in each indicator is given by $e^{\delta} - 1$ (Halvorsen and Palmquist 1980).

To correct for potential nonspherical errors, a Generalized Least Square (GLS) approach will be more adequate. However, the GLS estimation requires the knowledge of the unconditional variance matrix of v_{ijt}, Ω, up to scale. Hence, one must be able to write $\Omega = \sigma^2 C$, where C is a known GxG positive definite matrix. But, in this case, as this matrix is not known, a Feasible GLS (FGLS) approach is followed that replaces the unknown matrix Ω with a consistent estimator.

Adding Contract and Regulatory Characteristics

A second part of the econometric analysis incorporates the contract and regulatory characteristics described in chapter 4. Specifically, dummies were built for each of the variables described in table 4.3 and then interacted with the transition and post-transition dummies described above. To identify the effects of the characteristics, (A2.1a) and (A2.2a) were modified as follows:

$$\ln\left(y_{ijt}\right) = \delta^T DUM\_TRAN_{ijt} \times X_{ijt} + \delta^P DUM\_POST_{ijt} \times X_{ijt}$$
$$+ \sum_{ij} \phi_{ij} D_{ij} + v_{ijt} \tag{A2.1b}$$

$$\ln\left(y_{ijt}\right) = \delta^T DUM\_TRAN_{ijt} \times X_{ijt} + \delta^P DUM\_POST_{ijt} \times X_{ijt}$$
$$+ \sum_{ij} \phi_{ij} D_{ij} + \sum_{ij} \theta_i t_{ij} + v_{ijt} \tag{A2.2b}$$

where

$$DUM\_TRAN_{ijt} \begin{cases} 1 & \text{if } s_{ijt} \geq -1 \\ 0 & \text{otherwise} \end{cases}$$

and

$$DUM\_POST_{ijt} \begin{cases} 1 & \text{if } s_{ijt} \geq 2 \\ 0 & \text{otherwise} \end{cases}$$

where S_{ijt} is a time trend that has a value equals to zero for the last year when the company had a public owner. In the previous specifications, δ^T was a scalar number; in this specification, it is a vector with the coefficients for each characteristic of the vector X_{ijt} that is of the form $\left(1, x_{ijt}^1, ..., x_{ijt}^N\right)$, where N is the total number of characteristics evaluated. The previous specifications—(A2.1a) and (A2.2a)—were a particular case in which the vector X_{ijt} was equal to $(1, 0, ..., 0)$. For those specifications, the first coefficient identifies the average effect of change in ownership during the transitional period on a given indicator. For this specification—(A2.1b) and (A2.2b)—the first coefficient of the vector δ^T becomes the average effect of change in ownership during the transitional period on a given indicator for a firm without the characteristics evaluated in the other elements of the vector X_{ijt}. Equivalently, the vector δ^p contains the coefficients for the different characteristics of vector X_{ijt}, but for the post-transitional years.

Firm-specific time trends are taken into account in equation (A2.2b). Again, this relies on the assumption that trends between the three periods of analysis are the same. To relax this assumption, a second set of equation (A2.1b) is run using the (log) annual growth in each indicator. In this case, it will identify average changes in growth between the periods.

Estimation

To make the estimations, an Ordinary Least Square (OLS) analysis is run first. To get consistent estimators, the orthogonality condition assumption should be stated:

Assumption A2.1: $E\left[X'_{ijt} v_{ijt} \right] = 0$

Additionally, the rank condition assumption should be stated:

Assumption A2.2: $rank\left[\sum_{t=1}^{T} E\left(X'_{ijt} X_{ijt} \right) \right] = K$

In particular, the first set of estimations is called Pooled Ordinary Least Square (POLS) estimators, because they correspond to running OLS on the observations pooled across i, j, and t (see Wooldridge 2002). To apply the usual OLS statistics, homoskedasticity and no serial correlation assumptions should be added:

Assumption A2.3:   (a) $E\left(v_{ijt}^2 x'_{ijt} x_{ijt} \right) = \sigma^2 E\left(x'_{ijt} x_{ijt} \right), \quad t = 1, ..., T,$

where $\sigma^2 = E\left(v_{ijt}^2 \right)$ for all t;

(b) $E\left(v_{ijt} v_{ijs} x'_{ijt} x_{ijs} \right) = 0$ for $t \neq s$, t, s = 1, ..., T

These assumptions guarantee consistency, but not necessary unbiasedness. To get an unbiased estimator, a much stronger condition than assumption A2.1 should be stated. The condition·will be the zero conditional mean assumption:

Assumption A2.4: $E\left[v_{ijt} \middle| X'_{ijt} \right] = 0$

If there are nonspherical errors, there will be unbiased estimators. However, as a consequence, the Gauss-Markov theorem breaks down, and the conditional variance of the OLS estimator is different. Hence, the confidence intervals and tests must be modified to account for this. To correct for potential nonspherical errors, a GLS approach is more appropriate. The assumptions for the GLS model will be slightly different[1] than OLS, but under the fixed effect model, the estimators will be the same.

The GLS estimation requires knowledge of the unconditional variance matrix of v_{ijt}, Ω, up to scale. Hence, one must be able to write $\Omega = \sigma^2 C$, where C is a known GxG positive definite matrix. But, in this case, because this matrix is not known, the second set of estimators will be an FGLS that replaces the unknown matrix Ω with a consistent estimator.

Endogeneity

For some applications, the first assumption is violated. In this case, instrumental variables (IV) procedures are indispensable. For this empirical analysis, several arguments are in favor of the presumption that the ownership dummies are endogenous. As was described by Ros (1999), the decision to privatize may not be viewed as an exogenous event that can be considered fixed in repeated sampling. Besides, there is the possibility of selection bias, though it is argued that this is not the case here.[2] However, several hypotheses can be used to argue endogeneity, such as that the government privatizes those firms that are more likely to be sold. Second, countries with worsening financial performances may have higher incentives to privatize to acquire much-needed revenue. Third, private investors may be more interested in firms with higher expected rates of return.

Hence, the following approach is used:

$$\ln\left(y_{ijt}\right) = \delta^T DUMMY\_TRAN_{ijt} + \delta^P DUMMY\_POST_{ijt}$$
$$+ \sum_{ij} \phi_{ij} D_{ij} + v_{ijt} \tag{A2.3}$$

$$DUMMY\_TRAN_{ijt} = \xi' Z_{ijt} + u_{ijt} \tag{A2.4}$$

$$\Pr ob\left(DUMMY\_TRAN_{ijt} = 1\right) = \Pr ob\left(u_{ijt} > -\xi' Z_{ij}\right)$$
$$= 1 - F\left(-\xi' Z_{ijt}\right) \tag{A2.5}$$

Using a logistic model yields:

$$1 - F\left(-\xi' Z_{ijt}\right) = \frac{\exp\left(\hat{\xi}' Z_{ijt}\right)}{1 + \exp\left(\hat{\xi}' Z_{ijt}\right)} = \hat{p} \tag{A2.6}$$

Finally, substituting (A2.6) into (A2.3) yields the following expression:

$$\ln\left(y_{ijt}\right) = \delta^T DUMMY\_TRAN_{ijt}\left(\hat{p}\right) + \delta^P DUMMY\_POST_{ijt}$$
$$+ \sum_{ij} \phi_{ij} D_{ij} + \upsilon_{ijt} \qquad (A2.7)$$

When endogeneity is tested using the Durbin-Wu-Hausman Chi-squared test,[3] in most of the specifications, the hypothesis that the dummy is exogenous can be rejected.

To summarize the econometric analysis, three sets of estimators are calculated: OLS, FGLS, and an IV approach. Because of their limited relevance, the OLS estimates are not shown and the IV estimates are shown only for telecommunications (see table A3.9).

Notes

1. Assumption A2.1a: $E\left[X'_{ijt} \otimes \upsilon_{ijt}\right] = 0$

Assumption A2.2a: Ω is positive definite and $E\left[X'_{ijt}\Omega^{-1}X_{ijt}\right]$ is nonsingular.

Where Ω is the unconditional variance matrix of υ_{ijt}.

Assumption A2.3a: $E\left[\upsilon_{ijt}\middle|X'_{ijt}\right] = 0$.

2. See Ros (1999, 79) for a detailed explanation of this argument.

3. The test was first proposed by Durbin (1954) and separately by Wu (1973) (his T4 statistic), and Hausman (1978).

Appendix 3

Detailed Results of Empirical Analysis

Table A3.1 Means and Medians Analysis in Levels—Electricity Distribution

Variable	Stats	Mean			Difference in levels			T-stat (Z-stat) for difference in means (medians) in levels		
		Preprivat (1)	Transition (2)	Postprivat (3)	(2)–(1) (4)	(3)–(2) (5)	(3)–(1) (6)	(2)–(1) (7)	(3)–(2) (8)	(3)–(1) (9)
Outputs										
Residential connections	mean	85.83	102.26	120.48	17.32	17.11	35.16	-16.209***	-17.493***	-16.809***
	p50	85.94	102.00	119.59	17.11	16.55	34.33	-7.843***	-7.306***	-7.459***
	sd	9.20	2.53	10.04	9.68	8.76	16.94			
	N	82	116	74	82	74	71			
MWh sold per year	mean	82.29	102.67	119.22	20.82	15.60	36.74	-13.119***	-11.882***	-7.554***
	p50	82.59	101.20	117.13	19.88	15.17	34.60	-7.399***	-6.945***	-6.128***
	sd	14.11	6.44	21.12	14.28	17.77	25.69			
	N	81	116	74	81	74	69			
Inputs										
Number of employees	mean	162.71	100.65	86.59	-61.37	-14.27	-78.19	8.949***	8.678***	5.432***
	p50	147.46	100.00	86.17	-48.38	-14.76	-63.63	6.252***	5.903***	5.057***
	sd	54.42	6.76	23.63	52.22	20.18	63.71			
	N	58	116	59	58	59	50			

(continued)

Table A3.1 Means and Medians Analysis in Levels—Electricity Distribution (continued)

Variable	Stats	Mean			Difference in levels			T-stat (Z-stat) for difference in means (medians) in levels		
		Preprivat (1)	Transition (2)	Postprivat (3)	(2)–(1) (4)	(3)–(2) (5)	(3)–(1) (6)	(2)–(1) (7)	(3)–(2) (8)	(3)–(1) (9)
Efficiency										
Connections per employee	mean	60.24	103.33	147.42	45.38	40.83	88.62	−14.738***	−13.344***	−9.334***
	p50	59.90	100.00	135.26	44.65	32.10	88.86	−6.543***	−6.093***	−6.438***
	sd	18.65	9.86	42.10	23.25	33.31	46.49			
	N	57	116	58	57	58	49			
GW per employee	mean	58.56	103.97	145.09	47.50	37.64	86.27	−17.097***	−11.362***	−6.901***
	p50	59.68	100.00	129.76	46.04	26.76	71.15	−6.567***	−6.093***	−6.182***
	sd	18.58	11.98	53.86	20.98	41.54	53.15			
	N	57	116	58	57	58	49			
Distributional losses	mean	112.19	98.73	87.78	−12.92	−9.75	−25.14	3.658***	4.657***	3.515***
	p50	104.37	100.00	85.34	−6.13	−11.06	−19.93	3.268***	4.272***	3.341***
	sd	26.96	7.33	26.03	27.14	21.12	37.79			
	N	59	116	58	59	58	49			

(continued)

Table A3.1 Means and Medians Analysis in Levels—Electricity Distribution *(continued)*

Variable	Stats	Mean			Difference in levels			T-stat (Z-stat) for difference in means (medians) in levels		
		Preprivat (1)	*Transition* (2)	*Postprivat* (3)	(2)–(1) (4)	(3)–(2) (5)	(3)–(1) (6)	(2)–(1) (7)	(3)–(2) (8)	(3)–(1) (9)
Quality										
Duration of interruptions per year per consumer	mean	134.49	100.34	72.42	−30.61	−25.32	−41.34	3.250***	2.687***	3.782***
	p50	123.37	100.00	65.42	−24.11	−30.41	−34.37	3.477***	3.143***	4.019***
	sd	67.57	20.00	42.58	57.28	41.80	75.35			
	N	37	116	39	37	39	24			
Frequency of interruptions per year per consumer	mean	132.59	98.63	82.71	−34.90	−13.65	−31.66	4.256***	1.300	1.078
	p50	119.54	100.00	67.96	−21.20	−29.20	−32.86	3.809***	3.571***	4.326***
	sd	57.83	13.77	93.00	49.88	79.05	119.29			
	N	37	116	39	37	39	24			
Coverage										
Residential connections per 100 HHs	mean	94.93	101.17	110.66	6.93	8.67	16.46	−6.886***	−8.162***	−8.333***
	p50	95.35	100.00	108.92	5.60	7.62	14.16	−6.016***	−6.110***	−6.323***
	sd	7.91	2.22	10.09	8.42	8.26	15.09			
	N	70	116	63	70	63	56			

(continued)

Table A3.1 Means and Medians Analysis in Levels—Electricity Distribution (continued)

Variable	Stats	Mean			Difference in levels			T-stat (Z-stat) for difference in means (medians) in levels		
		Preprivat (1)	Transition (2)	Postprivat (3)	(2)–(1) (4)	(3)–(2) (5)	(3)–(1) (6)	(2)–(1) (7)	(3)–(2) (8)	(3)–(1) (9)
Prices										
Avg tariff per residential GW (in dollars)	mean	106.24	98.48	94.87	-9.49	-2.88	-9.91	3.305***	2.808***	1.313*
	p50	97.85	100.00	95.61	-0.09	-1.38	-16.37	2.437**	2.690***	1.702*
	sd	23.68	7.52	24.63	23.85	18.73	26.18			
	N	69	116	73	69	73	55			
Avg tariff per residential GW (in real local currency)	mean	91.77	100.81	109.61	9.21	8.46	17.90	-5.164***	-5.143***	-5.067***
	p50	88.27	100.00	107.07	15.25	4.64	24.26	-4.774***	-4.181***	-4.643***
	sd	12.83	4.97	18.59	14.81	14.27	25.81			
	N	69	116	73	69	73	55			

Source: Authors' calculations.

Note: GW = gigawatt hours; HH = household. MWh = megawatt hour.

*Significant at 10 percent; **significant at 5 percent; ***significant at 1 percent.

Table A3.2 Means and Medians Analysis in Growth—Electricity Distribution

Variable	Stats	Average annual growth			Annual difference in growth			T-stat (Z-stat) for difference in means (medians) in growth		
		Preprivat (1)	Transition (2)	Postprivat (3)	(2)–(1) (4)	(3)–(2) (5)	(3)–(1) (6)	(2)–(1) (7)	(3)–(2) (8)	(3)–(1) (9)
Outputs										
Residential connections	mean	4.3%	5.5%	3.4%	1.3%	-2.8%	-0.8%	-1.787**	3.590***	1.976**
	p50	4.4%	4.7%	3.2%	0.4%	-1.7%	-1.0%	-1.456	5.116***	2.366**
	sd	2.6%	5.5%	2.0%						
	N	79	84	60	79	60	56			
MW sold per year	mean	6.7%	6.7%	3.2%	-0.5%	-5.0%	-3.2%	0.616	3.085***	3.362***
	p50	6.6%	5.9%	2.8%	-0.7%	-2.9%	-2.7%	0.708	4.096***	3.159***
	sd	4.5%	8.7%	4.7%						
	N	74	85	57	74	57	51			
Inputs										
Number of employees	mean	-6.6%	-9.9%	-2.1%	-3.2%	9.7%	2.1%	2.056*	-5.398***	-1.519*
	p50	-6.1%	-9.0%	-1.8%	-3.8%	8.7%	4.0%	2.306**	-4.505***	-1.776*
	sd	8.1%	10.0%	4.8%						
	N	53	69	44	53	44	32			

(continued)

Table A3.2 Means and Medians Analysis in Growth—Electricity Distribution (continued)

| Variable | Stats | Average annual growth | | | Annual difference in growth | | | T-stat (Z-stat) for difference in means (medians) in growth | | |
		Preprivat (1)	Transition (2)	Postprivat (3)	(2)–(1) (4)	(3)–(2) (5)	(3)–(1) (6)	(2)–(1) (7)	(3)–(2) (8)	(3)–(1) (9)
Efficiency										
Connections per employee	mean	13.4%	18.4%	5.5%	4.2%	−16.4%	−4.2%	−1.813**	5.691***	2.183**
	p50	11.1%	14.0%	5.6%	4.5%	−10.6%	−3.5%	2.333**	4.975***	2.300**
	sd	12.6%	16.8%	5.1%						
	N	53	66	43	53	43	32			
GW per employee	mean	15.1%	20.3%	5.5%	3.7%	−19.9%	−6.7%	1.426*	6.539***	2.826***
	p50	12.8%	15.0%	4.0%	3.0%	−16.4%	−6.3%	−1.624	5.084***	3.011***
	sd	13.5%	16.9%	7.6%						
	N	53	66	43	53	43	32			
Distributional losses	mean	0.6%	−5.5%	−1.3%	−4.7%	6.4%	−2.0%	3.301***	−3.474***	0.960
	p50	0.1%	−4.9%	−0.1%	−4.5%	6.5%	−1.5%	3.317***	−2.944***	0.786
	sd	7.8%	10.2%	9.6%						
	N	57	73	46	57	46	36			

(continued)

Table A3.2 Means and Medians Analysis in Growth—Electricity Distribution (continued)

Variable	Stats	Average annual growth			Annual difference in growth			T-stat (Z-stat) for difference in means (medians) in growth		
		Preprivat (1)	Transition (2)	Postprivat (3)	(2)–(1) (4)	(3)–(2) (5)	(3)–(1) (6)	(2)–(1) (7)	(3)–(2) (8)	(3)–(1) (9)
Quality										
Duration of interruptions per year per consumer	mean	4.1%	-9.8%	-3.8%	-11.2%	3.4%	-10.5%	1.788*	4.476***	5.122***
	p50	-5.2%	-12.9%	-3.2%	-7.0%	8.5%	-5.1%	2.132**	-0.749	0.711
	sd	31.6%	25.7%	24.8%						
	N	32	51	26	32	26	11			
Frequency of interruptions per year per consumer	mean	2.7%	-10.6%	-11.4%	-11.1%	-2.9%	-17.8%	1.653*	0.378	3.093***
	p50	-5.0%	-10.8%	-6.6%	-2.8%	-2.4%	-14.4%	1.664*	-0.165	2.490**
	sd	29.0%	20.3%	20.5%						
	N	32	51	26	32	26	11			
Coverage										
Residential connections per 100 HHs	mean	2.0%	2.2%	1.9%	0.4%	-1.0%	-0.6%	-0.903	1.702**	0.780
	p50	1.5%	1.9%	1.3%	0.4%	-0.9%	-0.3%	-1.408	3.186***	0.619
	sd	3.9%	3.0%	3.6%						
	N	65	76	50	65	50	42			

(continued)

Table A3.2 Means and Medians Analysis in Growth—Electricity Distribution (continued)

Variable	Stats	Average annual growth			Annual difference in growth			T-stat (Z-stat) for difference in means (medians) in growth		
		Preprivat (1)	Transition (2)	Postprivat (3)	(2)–(1) (4)	(3)–(2) (5)	(3)–(1) (6)	(2)–(1) (7)	(3)–(2) (8)	(3)–(1) (9)
Prices										
Average tariff per residential GW (in dollars)	mean	9.3%	–3.3%	2.0%	–15.2%	4.3%	–11.4%	6.251***	–1.821**	3.172***
	p50	9.7%	–6.3%	0.1%	–15.1%	1.3%	–13.1%	5.329***	–1.442	2.785***
	sd	16.0%	9.0%	14.1%						
	N	59	86	57	59	57	35			
Average tariff per residential GW (in real local currency)	mean	10.2%	2.0%	0.6%	–7.8%	0.2%	–12.3%	4.744***	–0.172	4.899***
	p50	5.9%	2.3%	1.8%	–5.3%	0.9%	–9.7%	4.454***	–0.734	4.063***
	sd	12.6%	7.3%	7.9%						
	N	59	86	56	59	56	35			

Source: Authors' calculations.
*Significant at 10 percent; **significant at 5 percent; ***significant at 1 percent.

Table A3.3 Econometric Analysis—Electricity Distribution

	(1) Number of connections	(2) Energy sold per year	(3) Number of employees	(4) Connections per employee	(5) Energy per employee
Model 1: Log levels without firm-specific time trend					
Transition	0.150***	0.201***	−0.307***	0.442***	0.474***
(t>=−1)	(0.005)	(0.007)	(0.016)	(0.019)	(0.021)
Post-transition	0.176***	0.169***	−0.193***	0.368***	0.346***
(t>=2)	(0.005)	(0.007)	(0.016)	(0.019)	(0.021)
Observations	823	808	586	575	570
Model 2: Log levels with firm-specific time trend					
Transition	−0.002	0.040***	−0.054***	0.049***	0.086***
(t>=−1)	(0.002)	(0.005)	(0.013)	(0.012)	(0.017)
Post-transition	0.009***	−0.014***	0.047***	−0.037***	−0.080***
(t>=2)	(0.002)	(0.005)	(0.013)	(0.013)	(0.017)
Observations	823	808	586	575	570
Model 3: Growth					
Transition	0.001	−0.002	−0.050***	0.048***	0.046***
(t>=−1)	(0.001)	(0.003)	(0.008)	(0.008)	(0.010)
Post-transition	−0.003***	−0.027***	0.064***	−0.065***	−0.092***
(t>=2)	(0.001)	(0.003)	(0.008)	(0.008)	(0.010)
Observations	803	783	566	557	554

Source: Authors' calculations.

Note: Standard errors are in parentheses. The *Transition* and *Post-transition* variables are dummy independent variables in regressions where the dependent variable is given by the column heading (Number of Connections). *Transition* = 1 starting two years before the privatization or concession was awarded and continuing for all years after. *Post-transition* = 1 for all years after the transition period, that is, starting one year after the privatization was awarded.

*Significant at 10 percent; **significant at 5 percent; ***significant at 1 percent.

(6) Distributional losses	(7) Duration of interruptions	(8) Frequency of interruptions	(9) Coverage	(10) Average price per MW (US$)	(11) Average price per MW (in real local currency)
−0.031**	−0.144***	−0.107***	0.053***	−0.013	0.105***
(0.013)	(0.028)	(0.025)	(0.004)	(0.018)	(0.008)
−0.141***	−0.344***	−0.308***	0.077***	−0.028***	0.071***
(0.013)	(0.026)	(0.022)	(0.004)	(0.010)	(0.007)
614	376	377	698	687	685
0.021	0.068**	0.076***	−0.007***	0.078***	0.034***
(0.013)	(0.033)	(0.029)	(0.002)	(0.012)	(0.008)
−0.040***	−0.115***	−0.120***	0.009***	0.036***	0.007
(0.013)	(0.031)	(0.027)	(0.002)	(0.009)	(0.007)
614	376	377	698	687	685
−0.042***	−0.063***	−0.050**	−0.000	−0.117***	−0.082***
(0.010)	(0.023)	(0.024)	(0.001)	(0.011)	(0.007)
0.015	0.001	−0.048**	−0.000	0.023***	0.009
(0.010)	(0.021)	(0.021)	(0.000)	(0.008)	(0.006)
592	339	341	669	633	631

Table A3.4 Means and Medians Analysis In Levels—Fixed Telecommunications

		Mean			Difference in levels			T-stat (Z-stat) for difference in means (medians) in levels		
Variable	Stats	Preprivat (1)	Transition (2)	Postprivat (3)	(2)–(1) (4)	(3)–(2) (5)	(3)–(1) (6)	(2)–(1) (7)	(3)–(2) (8)	(3)–(1) (9)
Outputs										
Total number of lines	mean	78.98	115.39	181.31	36.41	65.70	102.77	−10.022***	−8.627***	−6.742***
	p50	76.93	112.16	178.47	33.90	67.92	93.40	−3.516***	−3.408***	−3.408***
	sd	12.55	13.76	48.91	14.53	37.74	46.14			
	N	16	16	15	16	15	15			
Total number of minutes	mean	107.32	103.05	146.89	0.82	41.13	69.57	−0.049	−3.973*	−19.420**
	p50	97.39	100.00	146.89	9.05	41.13	69.57	0.105	−1.342	−1.342
	sd	41.60	5.04	8.32	40.84	3.00	24.76			
	N	6	16	2	6	2	2			
Inputs										
Number of employees	mean	117.88	100.72	82.02	−17.12	−18.37	−37.18	2.213**	2.671***	2.675***
	p50	111.71	100.28	81.31	−22.64	−20.05	−50.94	1.761*	2.166**	2.291**
	sd	30.44	7.88	29.61	29.96	25.70	52.09			
	N	15	16	14	15	14	14			

(continued)

Table A3.4 Means and Medians Analysis In Levels—Fixed Telecommunications *(continued)*

Variable	Stats	Mean			Difference in levels			T-stat (Z-stat) for difference in means (medians) in levels		
		Preprivat (1)	Transition (2)	Postprivat (3)	(2)–(1) (4)	(3)–(2) (5)	(3)–(1) (6)	(2)–(1) (7)	(3)–(2) (8)	(3)–(1) (9)
Efficiency										
Total number of lines per employee	mean	72.98	119.54	262.84	47.86	140.97	191.73	–4.972***	–5.262***	–4.957***
	p50	70.13	110.66	217.38	38.93	102.05	154.59	–3.237***	–3.233***	–3.233***
	sd	24.63	26.54	126.18	37.28	106.41	136.35			
	N	15	16	14	15	14	14			
Total number of minutes per employee	mean	79.81	105.38	238.94	34.53	123.54	172.50	–2.879**	–2.059	–1.486
	p50	76.03	100.00	238.94	44.60	123.54	172.50	–1.782*	–1.342	–1.342
	sd	22.83	12.63	135.73	29.38	117.59	118.47			
	N	6	16	2	6	2	2			
Percentage of incomplete calls	mean	580.77	141.09	101.20	–368.95	–93.78	–472.93	1.050	1.098	1.378
	p50	111.56	100.00	74.51	–17.23	–27.47	–37.37	1.782*	2.201**	2.366**
	sd	1133.58	167.34	74.92	860.92	180.06	1055.53			
	N	6	16	7	6	7	6			

(continued)

Table A3.4 Means and Medians Analysis In Levels—Fixed Telecommunications *(continued)*

Variable	Stats	Mean			Difference in levels			T-stat (Z-stat) for difference in means (medians) in levels		
		Preprivat (1)	Transition (2)	Postprivat (3)	(2)–(1) (4)	(3)–(2) (5)	(3)–(1) (6)	(2)–(1) (7)	(3)–(2) (8)	(3)–(1) (9)
Quality										
Percentage of digitalized network	mean	68.64	116.56	199.92	51.75	81.00	138.97	−4.407***	−2.964***	−2.339**
	p50	70.82	107.27	136.01	41.82	29.26	78.72	−3.180***	−3.180***	−3.129***
	sd	22.80	31.58	161.58	42.33	129.55	169.03			
	N	13	16	14	13	14	13			
Coverage										
Number of lines per 100 HHs	mean	83.65	113.47	167.28	29.82	53.25	84.53	−7.573***	−7.708***	−6.025***
	p50	80.18	109.18	169.15	28.25	56.28	68.99	−3.516***	−3.408***	−3.351***
	sd	12.73	13.75	45.46	15.75	34.23	42.48			
	N	16	16	15	16	15	15			
Prices										
Average price for a three minute call (US$)	mean	144.83	100.45	99.89	−46.64	−1.03	−58.79	0.718	0.710	0.058
	p50	57.48	99.98	91.72	34.44	−11.25	1.74	−0.866	−0.178	1.255
	sd	219.85	15.00	63.61	205.46	61.29	248.59			
	N	10	16	12	10	12	9			

(continued)

Table A3.4 Means and Medians Analysis In Levels—Fixed Telecommunications (continued)

Variable	Stats	Mean			Difference in levels			T-stat (Z-stat) for difference in means (medians) in levels		
		Preprivat (1)	Transition (2)	Postprivat (3)	(2)–(1) (4)	(3)–(2) (5)	(3)–(1) (6)	(2)–(1) (7)	(3)–(2) (8)	(3)–(1) (9)
Average monthly charge for residential service (US$)	mean	55.46	101.25	143.43	39.02	41.60	105.49	−2.983***	−2.083**	−1.295
	p50	41.00	100.00	120.51	53.32	15.16	43.43	−2.293**	−2.073**	−0.804
	sd	36.35	19.28	124.99	41.36	115.87	151.92			
	N	10	16	13	10	13	9			
Average charge for the installation of a residential line (US$)	mean	634.94	123.11	100.51	−502.46	−25.83	−256.72	1.814*	0.777	1.122
	p50	95.78	101.06	77.29	11.18	−39.79	8.92	0.051	−0.314	1.376
	sd	887.73	40.50	108.31	875.99	72.80	808.89			
	N	10	16	10	10	10	6			
Average price for a three minute call (in real local currency)	mean	84.40	100.65	97.58	12.63	−3.46	16.28	−0.711	−0.599	0.250
	p50	64.40	100.00	87.14	30.96	−14.01	25.78	−0.980	−1.120	1.478
	sd	50.71	7.71	44.03	50.24	43.72	76.87			
	N	8	16	10	8	10	8			

(continued)

273

Table A3.4 Means and Medians Analysis In Levels—Fixed Telecommunications *(continued)*

Variable	Stats	Mean			Difference in levels			T-stat (Z-stat) for difference in means (medians) in levels		
		Preprivat (1)	Transition (2)	Postprivat (3)	(2)–(1) (4)	(3)–(2) (5)	(3)–(1) (6)	(2)–(1) (7)	(3)–(2) (8)	(3)–(1) (9)
Average monthly charge for residential service (in real local currency)	mean	60.42	100.26	135.11	36.59	34.54	88.96	−2.782**	−2.750**	−1.654*
	p50	49.78	100.00	115.76	49.77	16.83	79.48	−2.191**	−2.310**	−1.334
	sd	35.69	12.69	77.55	41.60	69.27	97.05			
	N	10	16	11	10	11	9			
Average charge for the installation of a residential line (in real local currency)	mean	842.23	122.99	132.07	−699.77	1.25	−252.68	1.915**	0.692	−0.028
	p50	108.37	100.00	58.62	−6.06	−31.83	1.91	0.700	−0.105	0.420
	sd	1045.40	41.81	152.59	1033.62	126.57	894.37			
	N	8	16	8	8	8	6			

Source: Author's calculations.
*Significant at 10 percent; **significant at 5 percent; ***significant at 1 percent.

Table A3.5 Means and Medians Analysis in Growth—Fixed Telecommunications

| Variable | Stats | Average annual growth | | | Annual difference in growth | | | T-stat (Z-stat) for difference in means (medians) in growth | | |
		Preprivat (1)	Transition (2)	Postprivat (3)	(2)–(1) (4)	(3)–(2) (5)	(3)–(1) (6)	(2)–(1) (7)	(3)–(2) (8)	(3)–(1) (9)
Outputs										
Total number of	mean	6.9%	12.7%	7.2%	5.8%	−6.5%	0.4%	−2.546**	1.917**	−0.152
lines	p50	7.2%	11.7%	6.6%	3.8%	−12.0%	−2.1%	−2.223**	1.852*	−0.157
	sd	6.2%	6.3%	8.2%	9.1%	12.8%	10.7%			
	N	16	16	14	16	14	14			
Total number of	mean	4.1%	2.1%	3.8%	−6.7%	3.2%	−0.8%	1.158	—	—
minutes	p50	4.6%	1.7%	3.8%	−4.1%	3.2%	−0.8%	1.219	—	—
	sd	1.9%	15.3%		12.9%	3.2%				
	N	5	6	1	5	1	1			
Inputs										
Number of	mean	−0.5%	−3.1%	−6.9%	−2.6%	−3.4%	−6.5%	0.916	1.258	2.861***
employees	p50	−0.8%	−4.5%	−7.7%	−1.5%	−1.3%	−3.9%	0.909	0.785	2.291**
	sd	6.9%	9.8%	9.0%	11.1%	10.0%	8.4%			
	N	15	15	14	15	14	14			

(continued)

275

Table A3.5 Means and Medians Analysis in Growth—Fixed Telecommunications *(continued)*

| Variable | Stats | Average annual growth | | | Annual difference in growth | | | T-stat (Z-stat) for difference in means (medians) in growth | | |
		Preprivat (1)	Transition (2)	Postprivat (3)	(2)–(1) (4)	(3)–(2) (5)	(3)–(1) (6)	(2)–(1) (7)	(3)–(2) (8)	(3)–(1) (9)
Efficiency										
Total number of lines per employee	mean	7.8%	17.6%	16.0%	9.8%	-3.1%	8.0%	-2.452**	0.610	-1.791**
	p50	6.6%	21.3%	15.7%	10.9%	-9.9%	9.4%	-2.101**	0.659	-1.726*
	sd	11.6%	15.3%	11.5%	15.5%	18.9%	16.7%			
	N	15	15	14	15	14	14			
Total number of minutes per employee	mean	5.2%	13.2%	28.6%	5.5%	11.9%	19.1%	-3.000**	—	—
	p50	9.5%	16.3%	28.6%	4.4%	11.9%	19.1%	-2.023**	—	—
	sd	9.6%	11.7%		4.1%					
	N	5	6	1	5	1	1			
Percentage of incomplete calls	mean	-1.5%	-16.4%	-14.3%	-13.9%	-0.2%	-13.7%	1.293	0.046	2.145**
	p50	-1.5%	-7.8%	-9.3%	-5.1%	0.0%	-8.8%	1.363	0.000	2.201**
	sd	1.0%	23.4%	14.7%	26.4%	14.0%	15.6%			
	N	6	8	7	6	7	6			

(continued)

Table A3.5 Means and Medians Analysis in Growth—Fixed Telecommunications (continued)

Variable	Stats	Average annual growth			Annual difference in growth			T-stat (Z-stat) for difference in means (medians) in growth		
		Preprivat (1)	Transition (2)	Postprivat (3)	(2)–(1) (4)	(3)–(2) (5)	(3)–(1) (6)	(2)–(1) (7)	(3)–(2) (8)	(3)–(1) (9)
Quality										
Percentage of digitalized network	mean	51.5%	17.1%	4.9%	–33.1%	–13.5%	–50.1%	1.085	3.602***	1.434*
	p50	22.1%	14.2%	0.9%	–4.4%	–12.0%	–11.9%	1.293	2.734***	2.824***
	sd	116.3%	15.9%	6.8%	110.1%	13.5%	121.1%			
	N	13	14	13	13	13	12			
Coverage										
Number of lines per 100 HHs	mean	4.9%	11.0%	6.0%	6.1%	–5.9%	1.2%	–3.001***	2.040**	–0.438
	p50	4.4%	9.4%	4.9%	4.5%	–8.0%	–0.1%	–2.637***	1.852*	–0.471
	sd	5.9%	6.2%	7.8%	8.1%	10.8%	10.0%			
	N	16	16	14	16	14	14			
Prices										
Average price for a three minute call (US$)	mean	46.7%	–3.1%	–5.7%	–44.4%	–2.3%	–60.8%	1.981**	0.295	1.788*
	p50	40.9%	–1.3%	–0.4%	–41.4%	–7.9%	–52.5%	1.820*	0.459	1.572
	sd	69.0%	16.8%	12.4%	63.5%	25.1%	83.3%			
	N	8	13	10	8	10	6			

(continued)

Table A3.5 Means and Medians Analysis in Growth—Fixed Telecommunications (continued)

Variable	Stats	Average annual growth			Annual difference in growth			T-stat (Z-stat) for difference in means (medians) in growth		
		Preprivat (1)	Transition (2)	Postprivat (3)	(2)–(1) (4)	(3)–(2) (5)	(3)–(1) (6)	(2)–(1) (7)	(3)–(2) (8)	(3)–(1) (9)
Average monthly charge for residential service (US$)	mean	42.8%	13.9%	5.2%	−21.9%	−10.5%	−45.8%	1.088	0.830	1.785*
	p50	15.7%	6.0%	0.0%	−33.1%	−3.3%	−28.4%	1.007	0.978	1.272
	sd	54.6%	31.0%	28.1%	60.4%	41.9%	67.9%			
	N	9	14	11	9	11	7			
Average charge for the installation of a residential line (US$)	mean	−1.9%	−14.7%	−13.7%	−9.6%	−5.7%	−32.6%	0.785	0.381	1.626
	p50	−1.8%	−2.3%	−29.3%	−5.2%	−2.6%	−18.2%	1.008	0.533	1.826*
	sd	25.8%	38.7%	33.7%	36.5%	44.6%	40.1%			
	N	9	14	9	9	9	4			
Average price for a three minute call (in real local currency)	mean	35.7%	−2.5%	−0.6%	−30.5%	2.7%	−36.7%	1.696*	−0.389	1.549*
	p50	44.3%	4.3%	0.6%	−32.1%	−5.2%	−21.2%	1.352	0.178	1.153
	sd	55.4%	19.1%	4.9%	47.6%	21.1%	58.0%			
	N	7	10	9	7	9	6			

(continued)

Table A3.5 Means and Medians Analysis in Growth—Fixed Telecommunications *(continued)*

Variable	Stats	Average annual growth			Annual difference in growth			T-stat (Z-stat) for difference in means (medians) in growth		
		Preprivat (1)	Transition (2)	Postprivat (3)	(2)–(1) (4)	(3)–(2) (5)	(3)–(1) (6)	(2)–(1) (7)	(3)–(2) (8)	(3)–(1) (9)
Average monthly charge for residential service (in real local currency)	mean	35.6%	16.5%	7.1%	−12.7%	−9.4%	−29.4%	0.721	0.959	1.426
	p50	−0.9%	15.6%	3.2%	−32.9%	−1.9%	0.6%	0.770	0.866	0.676
	sd	50.1%	32.1%	13.1%	52.9%	30.9%	54.6%			
	N	9	12	10	9	10	7			
Average charge for the installation of a residential line (in real local currency)	mean	−8.6%	−16.1%	−11.6%	−4.7%	−6.7%	−19.1%	0.289	0.370	0.789
	p50	−26.3%	−20.0%	−30.5%	−35.0%	−2.0%	1.4%	0.000	0.845	−0.365
	sd	32.3%	46.4%	40.4%	43.5%	48.0%	48.4%			
	N	7	10	7	7	7	4			

Source: Author's calculations.

*Significant at 10 percent; **significant at 5 percent; ***significant at 1 percent.

Table A3.6 Econometric Analysis—Fixed Telecommunications

	(1) Number of connections	(2) Number of minutes	(3) Number of employees	(4) Connections per worker	(5) Minutes per worker	(6) Incomplete calls
Model 1: Log levels without firm-specific time trend						
Transition	0.253***	0.079**	−0.097***	0.301***	0.278***	−0.133
(t >=−1)	(0.030)	(0.035)	(0.033)	(0.054)	(0.059)	(0.083)
Post-transition	0.494***	0.319***	−0.264***	0.727***	0.657***	−0.353***
(t >=2)	(0.028)	(0.032)	(0.033)	(0.054)	(0.084)	(0.057)
Observations	168	71	161	162	69	70
Model 2: Log levels with firm-specific time trend						
Transition	−0.050**	0.002	0.031	−0.101***	−0.010	0.142***
(t >=−1)	(0.024)	(0.038)	(0.026)	(0.038)	(0.044)	(0.042)
Post-transition	0.113***	0.133***	−0.069**	0.185***	0.173***	0.006
(t >=2)	(0.025)	(0.041)	(0.027)	(0.041)	(0.060)	(0.044)
Observations	168	71	161	162	69	70
Model 3: Growth						
Transition	0.027**	0.069***	−0.041***	0.070***	0.085**	−0.062
(t >=−1)	(0.011)	(0.012)	(0.015)	(0.021)	(0.042)	(0.041)
Post-transition	−0.002	0.053*	−0.026*	0.033*	0.083	−0.035
(t >=2)	(0.010)	(0.031)	(0.015)	(0.020)	(0.052)	(0.028)
Observations	165	60	158	158	59	64

Source: Author's calculations.

Note: Standard errors are in parentheses. The *Transition* and *Post-transition* variables are dummy independent variables in regressions where the dependent variable is given by the column heading (Number of connections). *Transition* = 1 starting two years before the privatization or concession was awarded and continuing for all years after. *Post-transition* = 1 for all years after the transition period, that is, starting one year after the privatization was awarded.

r.l.c. = real local currency.

*Significant at 10 percent; **significant at 5 percent; ***significant at 1 percent.

(7) Network digitization	*(8)* Coverage	*(9)* Cost of three-minute local call *(US$)*	*(10)* Monthly charge *(US$)*	*(11)* Connection charge *(US$)*	*(12)* Cost of three-minute local call *(r.l.c)*	*(13)* Monthly charge *(r.l.c)*	*(14)* Connection charge *(r.l.c)*
0.310***	0.168***	0.384***	0.565***	0.095	0.371***	0.486***	−0.178
(0.053)	(0.025)	(0.080)	(0.118)	(0.114)	(0.081)	(0.113)	(0.171)
0.458***	0.421***	−0.014	0.209***	−0.310**	−0.090	0.197**	−0.286*
(0.046)	(0.026)	(0.053)	(0.049)	(0.108)	(0.063)	(0.086)	(0.153)
131	165	104	114	107	91	110	87
0.048**	−0.065***	0.523***	0.281***	0.300**	0.358***	0.067	0.118
(0.024)	(0.019)	(0.104)	(0.100)	(0.063)	(0.082)	(0.092)	(0.154)
0.024	0.091***	0.051	−0.067	0.222**	−0.168**	−0.099	0. 244**
(0.026)	(0.021)	(0.091)	(0.087)	(0.082)	(0.082)	(0.080)	(0.097)
131	165	104	114	107	91	110	87
−0.008	0.037***	−0.052	−0.101	−0.003	−0.056	−0.047	−0.140
(0.026)	(0.010)	(0.077)	(0.097)	(0.048)	(0.065)	(0.067)	(0.107)
−0.056***	0.001	0.019	−0.034	−0.019	−0.025	−0.001	−0.036
(0.022)	(0.010)	(0.048)	(0.056)	(0.056)	(0.046)	(0.059)	(0.073)
122	162	93	105	98	82	102	79

Table A3.7 Econometric Analysis—Fixed Telecommunications, Liberalization

	(1) Number of connections	(2) Number of minutes	(3) Number of employees	(4) Connections per worker	(5) Minutes per worker	(6) Incomplete calls
Model 1: Log levels without firm-specific time trend						
Transition	0.232***	0.064*	−0.046	0.272***	0.232***	−0.140*
(t >=−1)	(0.027)	(0.036)	(0.030)	(0.049)	(0.050)	(0.081)
Post–transition	0.432***	0.279***	−0.151***	0.602***	0.432***	−0.335***
(t >=2)	(0.028)	(0.043)	(0.031)	(0.051)	(0.078)	(0.076)
Liberalization	0.275***	0.065	−0.361***	0.673***	0.487***	−0.027
Dummy	(0.037)	(0.046)	(0.047)	(0.083)	(0.082)	(0.088)
Observations	168	71	161	162	69	70
Model 2: Log levels with firm-specific time trend						
Transition	−0.050**	0.001	0.026	−0.089**	−0.006	0.133***
(t >=−1)	(0.024)	(0.043)	(0.026)	(0.038)	(0.049)	(0.043)
Post–transition	0.116***	0.127***	−0.066**	0.192***	0.164***	0.009
(t >=2)	(0.025)	(0.041)	(0.027)	(0.041)	(0.060)	(0.043)
Liberalization	0.002	0.037	−0.046	0.117**	0.108	−0.041
Dummy	(0.032)	(0.063)	(0.042)	(0.049)	(0.090)	(0.053)
Observations	168	71	161	162	69	70
Model 3: Growth						
Transition	0.028**	0.066***	−0.041***	0.075***	0.073*	−0.059
(t >=−1)	(0.011)	(0.013)	(0.015)	(0.020)	(0.040)	(0.040)
Post–transition	0.010	0.030	−0.027*	0.047**	−0.006	−0.011
(t >=2)	(0.011)	(0.041)	(0.016)	(0.021)	(0.058)	(0.033)
Liberalization	−0.053***	0.037	0.007	−0.075**	0.183***	−0.037
Dummy	(0.019)	(0.039)	(0.029)	(0.034)	(0.067)	(0.039)
Observations	165	60	158	158	59	64

Source: Author's calculations.

Note: Standard errors are in parentheses. The *Transition* and *Post-transition* variables are dummy independent variables in regressions where the dependent variable is given by the column heading (Number of connections). *Transition* = 1 starting two years before the privatization or concession was awarded and continuing for all years after. *Post-transition* = 1 for all years after the transition period, that is, starting one year after the privatization was awarded. The *Liberalization dummy* = for those years that the long-distance telecommunications market was liberalzed.

*Significant at 10 percent; **significant at 5 percent; ***significant at 1 percent.

(7) Network digitization	(8) Coverage	(9) Cost of three-minute local call (US$)	(10) Monthly charge (US$)	(11) Connection charge (US$)	(12) Cost of three-minute local call (r.l.c.)	(13) Monthly charge (r.l.c.)	(14) Connection charge (r.l.c.)
0.307***	0.166***	0.422***	0.558***	0.033	0.359***	0.398***	−0.107
(0.057)	(0.025)	(0.088)	(0.131)	(0.073)	(0.085)	(0.112)	(0.191)
0.446***	0.364***	0.011	0.220***	−0.151*	−0.162**	0.102	−0.131
(0.055)	(0.025)	(0.057)	(0.058)	(0.083)	(0.073)	(0.086)	(0.163)
0.023	0.230***	−0.097	0.001	−0.491***	0.150*	0.443***	−0.529**
(0.069)	(0.035)	(0.088)	(0.144)	(0.171)	(0.091)	(0.155)	(0.221)
131	165	104	114	107	91	110	87
0.044*	−0.066***	0.441***	0.192	0.245***	0.296***	−0.007	0.130
(0.025)	(0.020)	(0.109)	(0.136)	(0.083)	(0.082)	(0.087)	(0.165)
0.023	0.091***	−0.011	−0.111	0.197**	−0.193**	−0.135*	0.246**
(0.026)	(0.021)	(0.091)	(0.093)	(0.081)	(0.078)	(0.076)	(0.097)
−0.016	−0.007	−0.356***	−0.410***	−0.030	−0.240***	−0.500***	0.035
(0.028)	(0.025)	(0.116)	(0.147)	(0.092)	(0.090)	(0.136)	(0.169)
131	165	104	114	107	91	110	87
0.006	0.036***	0.006	0.072	−0.021	−0.038	−0.004	−0.253*
(0.028)	(0.011)	(0.077)	(0.095)	(0.066)	(0.065)	(0.047)	(0.138)
−0.046*	0.008	0.142***	0.038	−0.022	0.012	0.053	0.003
(0.025)	(0.010)	(0.053)	(0.059)	(0.067)	(0.053)	(0.049)	(0.085)
−0.044	−0.027	−0.451***	−0.428***	0.002	−0.161**	−0.387***	0.251*
(0.031)	(0.017)	(0.080)	(0.111)	(0.098)	(0.070)	(0.108)	(0.132)
122	162	93	105	98	82	102	79

Table A3.8 Econometric Analysis—Fixed Telecommunications, Mobile Competition

	(1) Number of connections	(2) Number of minutes	(3) Number of employees	(4) Connections per worker	(5) Minutes per worker	(6) Incomplete calls
Model 1: Log levels without firm-specific time trend						
Transition	0.247***	0.047	−0.059**	0.291***	0.178***	−0.143*
(t >= −1)	(0.027)	(0.037)	(0.027)	(0.043)	(0.050)	(0.077)
Post-transition	0.413***	0.221***	−0.089***	0.500***	0.269***	−0.337***
(t >= 2)	(0.027)	(0.050)	(0.030)	(0.046)	(0.085)	(0.089)
Mobile subs.	0.013***	0.005**	−0.025***	0.037***	0.030***-	0.000
	(0.002)	(0.002)	(0.001)	(0.002)	(0.004)	(0.004)
Observations	168	71	161	162	69	70
Model 2: Log levels with firm-specific time trend						
Transition	−0.064***	0.019	0.008	−0.070*	0.029	0.111**
(t >= −1)	(0.025)	(0.051)	(0.025)	(0.039)	(0.063)	(0.045)
Post-transition	0.120***	0.112***	−0.044*	0.176***	0.061	0.022
(t >= 2)	(0.025)	(0.034)	(0.026)	(0.041)	(0.048)	(0.046)
Mobile subs.	−0.006*	0.010**	−0.017***	0.010**	0.032***	−0.004
	(0.003)	(0.005)	(0.003)	(0.005)	(0.006)	(0.005)
Observations	168	71	161	162	69	70
Model 3: Growth						
Transition	0.023**	0.068***	−0.043***	0.068***	0.075*	−0.062
(t >= −1)	(0.011)	(0.014)	(0.015)	(0.021)	(0.040)	(0.042)
Post-transition	0.011	0.068	−0.017	0.039*	−0.004	−0.033
(t >= 2)	(0.011)	(0.053)	(0.016)	(0.022)	(0.064)	(0.040)
Mobile subs.	−0.002**	−0.001	−0.002	−0.001	0.006*	−0.000
	(0.001)	(0.002)	(0.002)	(0.002)	(0.003)	(0.002)
Observations	165	60	158	158	59	64
Number of firms	16	11	16	16	11	8

Source: Author's calculations.

Note: Standard errors are in parentheses. The *Transition* and *Post-transition* variables are dummy independent variables in regressions where the dependent variable is given by the column heading, e.g. (Number of connections). *Transition* = 1 starting two years before the privatization or concession was awarded and continuing for all years after. *Post-transition* = 1 for all years after the transition period, i.e. starting one year after the privatization was awarded. "*Mobile subs.*" is an independent variable measuring millions of mobile subscribers.

*Significant at 10 percent; **significant at 5 percent; ***significant at 1 percent.

(7) Network digitization	(8) Coverage	(9) Cost of three-minute local call (US$)	(10) Monthly charge (US$)	(11) Connection charge (US$)	(12) Cost of three-minute local call (r.l.c.)	(13) Monthly charge (r.l.c.)	(14) Connection charge (r.l.c.)
0.313***	0.171***	0.432***	0.506***	−0.030	0.311***	0.365***	−0.165
(0.053)	(0.022)	(0.079)	(0.120)	(0.021)	(0.075)	(0.102)	(0.106)
0.442***	0.342***	0.038	0.189***	0.032	−0.221***	0.003	0.031
(0.053)	(0.025)	(0.053)	(0.046)	(0.030)	(0.067)	(0.077)	(0.110)
0.001	0.014***	−0.015***	0.013	−0.151***	0.017***	0.042***	−0.132***
(0.003)	(0.002)	(0.006)	(0.010)	(0.017)	(0.004)	(0.009)	(0.017)
131	165	104	114	107	91	110	87
0.017	−0.068***	0.166***	−0.056	0.327***	0.201***	−0.043	0.349**
(0.022)	(0.021)	(0.063)	(0.105)	(0.073)	(0.047)	(0.044)	(0.161)
0.042*	0.099***	0.293***	0.055	0.195**	0.083*	−0.005	0.225**
(0.023)	(0.022)	(0.060)	(0.061)	(0.088)	(0.049)	(0.041)	(0.090)
−0.021***	−0.003	−0.117***	−0.148***	0.039*	−0.063***	−0.105***	0.076***
(0.003)	(0.003)	(0.007)	(0.015)	(0.024)	(0.005)	(0.011)	(0.025)
131	165	104	114	107	91	110	87
0.006	0.035***	−0.005	−0.076	−0.031	−0.023	−0.043	−0.175*
(0.025)	(0.011)	(0.063)	(0.090)	(0.054)	(0.059)	(0.059)	(0.093)
−0.030	0.004	0.117***	0.051	−0.063	0.051	0.071	−0.039
(0.024)	(0.011)	(0.042)	(0.062)	(0.060)	(0.047)	(0.056)	(0.076)
−0.005***	−0.001	−0.026***	−0.032***	0.018*	−0.014***	−0.025***	0.028***
(0.001)	(0.001)	(0.004)	(0.008)	(0.011)	(0.004)	(0.007)	(0.011)
122	162	93	105	98	82	102	79
14	16	12	13	13	11	13	11

Table A3.9 Econometric Analysis—Fixed Telecommunications, Instrumental Variables

	(1) Number of connections	(2) Number of minutes	(3) Number of employees	(4) Connections per worker	(5) Minutes per worker	(6) Incomplete calls
Model 1: Log levels without firm-specific time trend						
Transition	0.462***	0.326***	−0.198***	0.646***	0.717***	−0.086
(t >=−1)	(0.052)	(0.109)	(0.070)	(0.111)	(0.135)	(0.079)
Post-transition	0.436***	0.364***	−0.222***	0.674***	0.724***	−0.262***
(t >=2)	(0.043)	(0.097)	(0.059)	(0.094)	(0.120)	(0.060)
Observations	121	54	114	115	52	42
Model 2: Log levels with firm-specific time trend						
Transition	0.003	0.229*	0.160*	−0.126	0.204	0.109**
(t >=−1)	(0.063)	(0.134)	(0.087)	(0.103)	(0.153)	(0.042)
Post-transition	0.115**	0.114	0.057	0.095	0.173	−0.018
(t >=2)	(0.046)	(0.138)	(0.064)	(0.077)	(0.151)	(0.042)
Observations	121	54	114	115	52	42
Model 3: Growth						
Transition	0.035	0.056	−0.024	0.062	0.084	−0.049
(t >=−1)	(0.024)	(0.141)	(0.031)	(0.038)	(0.152)	(0.046)
Post-transition	−0.028	−0.049	−0.054**	0.023	−0.037	−0.036
(t >=2)	(0.019)	(0.113)	(0.025)	(0.030)	(0.123)	(0.028)
Observations	118	45	111	112	44	37

Source: Author's calculations.

Note: Standard errors are in parentheses. The *Transition* and *Post-transition* variables are dummy independent variables in regressions where the dependent variable is given by the column heading (Number of connections). *Transition* = 1 starting two years before the privatization or concession was awarded and continuing for all years after. *Post-transition* = 1 for all years after the transition period, that is, starting one year after the privatization was awarded.

*Significant at 10 percent; **significant at 5 percent; ***significant at 1 percent.

(7) Network digitization	(8) Coverage	(9) Cost of three-minute local call (US $)	(10) Monthly charge (US $)	(11) Connection charge (US $)	(12) Cost of three-minute local call (r.l.c.)	(13) Monthly charge (r.l.c.)	(14) Connection charge (r.l.c.)
0.490***	0.377***	0.877***	1.041***	−0.692**	0.754***	0.910***	−1.060***
(0.105)	(0.046)	(0.147)	(0.221)	(0.300)	(0.136)	(0.209)	(0.355)
0.363***	0.371***	−0.069	0.331*	−0.204	0.012	0.332**	0.035
(0.084)	(0.039)	(0.111)	(0.174)	(0.260)	(0.097)	(0.163)	(0.283)
107	120	79	90	93	71	90	77
0.129	0.027	1.370***	0.982***	0.912***	0.837***	0.507	0.862**
(0.199)	(0.060)	(0.278)	(0.350)	(0.309)	(0.213)	(0.304)	(0.375)
0.014	0.108**	0.099	−0.147	0.593***	−0.022	−0.209	0.723**
(0.150)	(0.045)	(0.226)	(0.264)	(0.220)	(0.176)	(0.213)	(0.271)
107	120	79	90	93	71	90	77
0.243*	0.050**	−0.559***	−0.477***	−0.197	−0.470***	−0.313**	−0.095
(0.124)	(0.022)	(0.170)	(0.173)	(0.144)	(0.151)	(0.150)	(0.202)
−0.146*	−0.038**	−0.147	−0.116	0.043	−0.088	−0.088	0.046
(0.087)	(0.018)	(0.107)	(0.118)	(0.111)	(0.085)	(0.103)	(0.140)
101	117	72	84	87	64	84	71

Table A3.10 Means and Medians Analysis in Levels—Water and Sewerage

Variable	Stats	Mean			Difference in levels			T-stat (Z-stat) for difference in means (medians) in levels		
		Preprivat (1)	Transition (2)	Postprivat (3)	(2)–(1) (4)	(3)–(2) (5)	(3)–(1) (6)	(2)–(1) (7)	(3)–(2) (8)	(3)–(1) (9)
Outputs										
Residential water connections	mean	85.85	103.15	119.74	16.20	16.31	29.43	−10.988***	−8.762***	−12.059***
	p50	87.37	102.61	117.09	15.18	13.88	28.10	−4.197***	−5.086***	−3.724***
	sd	6.32	3.72	13.17	7.07	10.85	10.35			
	N	23	49	34	23	34	18			
Residential sewerage connections	mean	84.88	102.75	122.59	18.83	19.43	32.90	−7.932***	−8.950***	−9.735***
	p50	85.48	101.89	119.62	18.62	17.46	29.38	−3.883***	−4.937***	−3.408***
	sd	11.21	5.02	15.08	10.62	12.28	13.09			
	N	20	49	32	20	32	15			
Cubic meter of produced water	mean	99.98	103.62	97.27	2.21	−2.91	−1.33	−0.745	1.416*	0.299
	p50	100.99	100.00	99.04	1.95	−0.72	3.15	−0.879	1.078	−0.973
	sd	8.89	22.20	14.80	11.88	11.45	16.60			
	N	16	49	31	16	31	14			

(continued)

Table A3.10 Means and Medians Analysis in Levels—Water and Sewerage (continued)

Variable	Stats	Mean			Difference in levels			T-stat (Z-stat) for difference in means (medians) in levels		
		Preprivat (1)	Transition (2)	Postprivat (3)	(2)–(1) (4)	(3)–(2) (5)	(3)–(1) (6)	(2)–(1) (7)	(3)–(2) (8)	(3)–(1) (9)
Inputs										
Number of employees	mean	141.43	103.97	92.35	-37.20	-12.18	-57.36	3.961***	3.668***	4.766***
	p50	125.11	100.00	97.04	-21.34	-8.36	-52.01	3.527***	3.339***	3.237***
	sd	49.22	14.22	23.85	38.72	17.26	46.62			
	N	17	49	27	17	27	15			
Efficiency										
Water connections per employee	mean	70.50	103.34	144.11	36.53	38.73	83.86	-9.979***	-4.201***	-5.177***
	p50	68.46	100.00	125.05	36.39	20.71	69.30	-3.621***	-4.532***	-3.408***
	sd	18.93	12.65	59.84	15.09	48.79	62.73			
	N	17	49	28	17	28	15			
Distributional losses	mean	107.22	100.02	82.08	-8.70	-18.26	-23.18	2.577**	3.755***	3.110***
	p50	106.01	100.00	81.64	-8.33	-16.63	-20.12	2.327**	3.254***	2.605**
	sd	16.43	7.42	21.22	13.51	23.33	27.88			
	N	16	49	23	16	23	14			

(continued)

289

Table A3.10 Means and Medians Analysis in Levels—Water and Sewerage (continued)

Variable	Stats	Mean			Difference in levels			T-stat (Z-stat) for difference in means (medians) in levels		
		Preprivat (1)	Transition (2)	Postprivat (3)	(2)–(1) (4)	(3)–(2) (5)	(3)–(1) (6)	(2)–(1) (7)	(3)–(2) (8)	(3)–(1) (9)
Quality										
Continuity (hours per day)	mean	78.34	101.01	116.79	21.81	14.94	21.66	-1.781*	-2.748***	-1.330
	p50	97.11	100.00	104.35	2.48	2.17	4.05	-2.192**	-2.774***	-1.971**
	sd	37.52	4.68	24.68	36.74	21.06	46.07			
	N	9	49	15	9	15	8			
Percentage of the samples that passed the potability test	mean	88.35	100.30	103.89	11.55	2.58	4.94	-1.250	-2.088**	-1.682*
	p50	99.50	100.00	100.51	0.58	0.46	1.08	-1.630	-2.603***	-1.941*
	sd	27.92	1.53	6.87	26.14	4.62	7.20			
	N	8	49	14	8	14	6			
Coverage										
Residential water connections per 100 HHs	mean	94.25	101.84	111.12	6.52	8.71	10.37	-4.498***	-4.379***	-4.478***
	p50	95.13	100.00	106.88	4.86	5.26	8.76	-4.107***	-4.584***	-3.823***
	sd	5.70	3.96	14.11	6.80	10.71	10.10			
	N	22	49	29	22	29	19			

(continued)

Table A3.10 Means and Medians Analysis in Levels—Water and Sewerage (continued)

| Variable | Stats | Mean | | | Difference in levels | | | T-stat (Z-stat) for difference in means (medians) in levels | | |
		Preprivat (1)	Transition (2)	Postprivat (3)	(2)–(1) (4)	(3)–(2) (5)	(3)–(1) (6)	(2)–(1) (7)	(3)–(2) (8)	(3)–(1) (9)
Residential sewerage connections per 100 HHs	mean	91.47	101.77	110.03	10.23	8.67	13.59	−4.539***	−3.981***	−5.277***
	p50	91.72	100.00	106.87	8.02	5.76	8.98	−3.479***	−3.920***	−3.180***
	sd	8.76	6.88	11.55	9.29	9.74	9.29			
	N	17	49	20	17	20	13			
Prices										
Average price per m³ of water (US$)	mean	93.62	101.39	106.70	10.43	1.46	40.24	−0.635	−0.173	−2.261**
	p50	87.95	100.00	98.60	11.81	3.27	32.70	−1.274	−0.314	−2.240**
	sd	43.54	9.53	37.16	51.89	30.57	50.34			
	N	10	49	13	10	13	8			
Average price per m³ of water (real local currency)	mean	84.00	103.53	130.09	25.70	17.68	57.87	−2.478**	−2.903***	−4.150***
	p50	82.76	100.00	121.21	22.22	19.65	44.80	−1.988**	−0.411**	−2.521**
	sd	23.18	11.71	32.81	32.80	21.96	39.44			
	N	10	49	13	10	13	8			

(continued)

Table A3.10 Means and Medians Analysis in Levels—Water and Sewerage *(continued)*

		Mean			Difference in levels			T-stat (Z-stat) for difference in means (medians) in levels		
		Preprivat	Transition	Postprivat	(2)–(1)	(3)–(2)	(3)–(1)	(2)–(1)	(3)–(2)	(3)–(1)
Variable	*Stats*	*(1)*	*(2)*	*(3)*	*(4)*	*(5)*	*(6)*	*(7)*	*(8)*	*(9)*
Average price per m^3 of sewerage (US$)	mean	114.61	100.53	107.79	–19.43	0.03	44.29	0.375	0.001	–0.835
	p50	79.43	100.00	107.68	16.46	–12.60	44.29	0.000	0.365	–0.447
	sd	89.74	6.94	32.73	89.77	35.56	75.05			
	N	3	49	4	3	4	2			
Average price per m^3 of sewerage (real local currency)	mean	93.06	101.80	152.44	13.26	32.25	53.34	–0.512	–3.012**	–37.266***
	p50	74.75	100.00	135.93	30.91	33.12	53.34	–0.535	–1.826*	–1.342
	sd	45.93	10.88	51.26	44.86	21.42	2.02			
	N	3	49	4	3	4	2			

Source: Author's calculations.
Note: HH = household.
*Significant at 10 percent; **significant at 5 percent; ***significant at 1 percent.

Table A3.11 Means and Medians Analysis in Growth—Water and Sewerage

Variable	Stats	Average annual growth			Annual difference in growth			T-stat (Z-stat) for difference in means (medians) in growth		
		Preprivat (1)	Transition (2)	Postprivat (3)	(2)–(1) (4)	(3)–(2) (5)	(3)–(1) (6)	(2)–(1) (7)	(3)–(2) (8)	(3)–(1) (9)
Outputs										
Residential water connections	mean	4.4%	6.5%	4.7%	0.9%	-1.9%	1.5%	-1.095	1.649*	-1.113
	p50	4.1%	5.2%	3.8%	-0.1%	-1.8%	1.2%	-0.923	2.229**	-0.943
	sd	3.0%	4.4%	4.6%	3.5%	5.6%	3.2%			
	N	17	43	24	17	24	6			
Residential sewerage connections	mean	3.8%	6.7%	7.4%	3.1%	1.5%	0.0%	-1.222	-0.569	0.009
	p50	4.3%	5.5%	3.6%	2.1%	-1.4%	0.1%	-0.966	0.693	-0.135
	sd	5.9%	6.8%	10.7%	9.8%	12.3%	3.2%			
	N	15	40	23	15	23	5			
Cubic meter of produced water	mean	2.1%	7.5%	0.5%	-0.9%	-1.8%	1.6%	0.741	1.117	-0.718
	p50	1.6%	1.0%	0.9%	0.0%	0.0%	1.5%	0.000	0.817	-0.674
	sd	4.6%	38.6%	5.0%	4.1%	7.3%	5.0%			
	N	12	38	21	12	21	5			

(continued)

Table A3.11 Means and Medians Analysis in Growth—Water and Sewerage (continued)

| Variable | Stats | Average annual growth | | | Annual difference in growth | | | T-stat (Z-stat) for difference in means (medians) in growth | | |
		Preprivat (1)	Transition (2)	Postprivat (3)	(2)–(1) (4)	(3)–(2) (5)	(3)–(1) (6)	(2)–(1) (7)	(3)–(2) (8)	(3)–(1) (9)
Inputs										
Number of	mean	−0.4%	−10.0%	−1.5%	−9.6%	7.5%	−1.0%	3.425***	−3.460***	0.309
employees	p50	0.1%	−8.3%	−1.0%	−9.8%	7.8%	−1.4%	2.432***	−2.765***	0.135
	sd	4.2%	10.2%	7.2%	9.7%	9.2%	7.4%			
	N	12	32	18	12	18	5			
Efficiency										
Water	mean	5.5%	17.5%	7.3%	11.6%	−9.6%	1.2%	−3.068***	2.939***	−0.348
connections	p50	4.9%	15.8%	4.5%	9.9%	−7.8%	0.1%	2.551**	2.656	0.105
per employee	sd	5.4%	13.5%	10.1%	13.7%	14.3%	8.3%			
	N	13	32	19	13	19	6			
Distributional	mean	−3.1%	−0.6%	−5.5%	0.5%	0.5%	0.6%	−0.297	−0.310	−0.363
losses	p50	−2.6%	−2.0%	−5.1%	−0.1%	0.3%	0.8%	−0.267	−0.450	−0.843
	sd	3.8%	21.5%	9.1%	5.3%	6.2%	4.0%			
	N	11	26	17	11	17	6			

(continued)

Table A3.11 Means and Medians Analysis in Growth—Water and Sewerage *(continued)*

Variable	Stats	Average annual growth			Annual difference in growth			T-stat (Z-stat) for difference in means (medians) in growth		
		Preprivat	Transition	Postprivat	(2)–(1)	(3)–(2)	(3)–(1)	(2)–(1)	(3)–(2)	(3)–(1)
		(1)	(2)	(3)	(4)	(5)	(6)	(7)	(8)	(9)
Quality										
Continuity	mean	0.0%	7.2%	4.6%	22.4%	−0.1%	0.0%	−1.000	0.057	–
(hours per day)	p50	0.0%	0.0%	0.9%	0.0%	0.0%	0.0%	−1.000	0.075	–
	sd	0.0%	16.0%	8.7%	38.7%	6.0%	.			
	N	3	18	11	3	11	1			
Percentage of	mean	0.8%	5.2%	0.4%	18.6%	−0.5%	−1.0%	−1.074	1.273	1.000
the samples	p50	0.6%	0.2%	0.0%	2.2%	0.0%	−1.0%	−0.928	1.315	1.000
that passed the	sd	1.0%	16.4%	0.7%	34.6%	1.2%	1.4%			
potability test	N	4	18	9	4	9	2			
Coverage										
Residential	mean	1.0%	4.1%	3.3%	1.1%	−1.3%	0.4%	−2.050**	0.914	−0.570
water	p50	0.3%	2.8%	1.6%	0.2%	−1.3%	0.1%	−1.448	1.690*	−0.944
connections	sd	1.7%	5.0%	4.4%	2.1%	6.1%	1.7%			
per 100 HHs	N	16	34	19	16	19	5			

(continued)

295

Table A3.11 Means and Medians Analysis in Growth—Water and Sewerage (continued)

Variable	Stats	Average annual growth			Annual difference in growth			T-stat (Z-stat) for difference in means (medians) in growth		
		Preprivat (1)	Transition (2)	Postprivat (3)	(2)–(1) (4)	(3)–(2) (5)	(3)–(1) (6)	(2)–(1) (7)	(3)–(2) (8)	(3)–(1) (9)
Residential sewerage connections per 100 HHs	mean	1.6%	8.0%	2.8%	2.9%	-0.9%	-1.6%	-1.815	0.529	2.735**
	p50	1.4%	2.9%	0.6%	0.1%	-1.6%	-0.9%	-1.036	1.601	2.023**
	sd	17.9%	17.9%	6.1%	6.0%	6.2%	1.3%			
	N	14	25	14	14	14	5			
Prices										
Average price per m^3 of water (US $)	mean	12.2%	1.9%	-3.4%	-12.1%	-7.2%	-3.9%	2.493**	0.835	0.666
	p50	10.9%	-2.2%	-1.1%	-13.8%	-3.3%	-2.1%	1.820*	0.889	0.535
	sd	10.4%	22.2%	20.0%	13.8%	26.0%	10.1%			
	N	8	17	9	8	9	3			
Average price per m^3 of water (real local currency)	mean	10.1%	9.4%	4.5%	-6.0%	-8.9%	-0.8%	2.078**	1.060	0.346
	p50	10.1%	5.4%	2.6%	-4.3%	-6.5%	-2.5%	1.540	1.007	0.000
	sd	6.7%	18.4%	10.0%	8.1%	25.1%	4.0%			
	N	8	17	9	8	9	3			

(continued)

Table A3.11 Means and Medians Analysis in Growth—Water and Sewerage *(continued)*

Variable	Stats	Average annual growth			Annual difference in growth			T-stat (Z-stat) for difference in means (medians) in growth		
		Preprivat (1)	Transition (2)	Postprivat (3)	(2)–(1) (4)	(3)–(2) (5)	(3)–(1) (6)	(2)–(1) (7)	(3)–(2) (8)	(3)–(1) (9)
Average price per m³ of sewerage (US$)	mean	-0.6%	-5.1%	-7.9%	2.3%	-6.4%	-7.7%	-0.298	0.799	—
	p50	-0.6%	-8.7%	-7.9%	2.3%	-10.8%	-7.7%	-0.447	1.069	—
	sd	17.1%	16.1%	11.6%	10.8%	13.9%	.			
	N	2	5	3	2	3	1			
Average price per m³ of sewerage (real local currency)	mean	-1.1%	7.0%	9.7%	5.0%	-4.3%	-15.1%	3.881*	0.302	—
	p50	-1.1%	1.4%	9.8%	5.0%	-18.4%	-15.1%	-1.342	0.000	—
	sd	13.9%	13.5%	16.0%	1.8%	24.7%				
	N	2	5	3	2	3	1			

Source: Author's calculations.
Note: HH = household.
*Significant at 10 percent; **significant at 5 percent; ***significant at 1 percent.

Table A3.12 Econometric Analysis—Water Distribution and Sewerage

	(1) Number of water connections	(2) Number of sewerage connections	(3) Cubic meters per year	(4) Number of employees	(5) Water connections per employee	(6) Distributional losses
Model 1: Log levels without firm-specific time trend						
Transition	0.141***	0.174***	0.040***	−0.180***	0.268***	−0.039**
(t >= −1)	(0.010)	(0.016)	(0.009)	(0.030)	(0.034)	(0.017)
Post-transition	0.139***	0.173***	0.015***	−0.194***	0.354***	−0.155***
(t >= 2)	(0.008)	(0.011)	(0.006)	(0.024)	(0.027)	(0.015)
Observations	259	239	195	201	199	179
Model 2: Log levels with firm-specific time trend						
Transition	0.006	−0.006	−0.007	0.083***	−0.076***	−0.014
(t >= −1)	(0.004)	(0.009)	(0.010)	(0.026)	(0.023)	(0.012)
Post-transition	−0.002	−0.005	−0.013*	0.069***	−0.027	0.000
(t >= 2)	(0.003)	(0.005)	(0.007)	(0.017)	(0.019)	(0.001)
Observations	259	239	195	201	199	179
Model 3: Growth						
Transition	0.001	0.006	−0.008	−0.048***	0.047***	−0.000
(t >= −1)	(0.004)	(0.006)	(0.009)	(0.018)	(0.018)	(0.012)
Post-transition	−0.010***	−0.011***	−0.025***	0.048***	−0.037***	−0.012*
(t >= 2)	(0.002)	(0.002)	(0.007)	(0.012)	(0.012)	(0.007)
Observations	235	216	172	176	178	160

Source: Author's calculations.

Note: Standard errors are in parentheses. The *Transition* and *Post-transition* variables are dummy independent variables in regressions where the dependent variable is given by the column heading (Number of connections). *Transition* = 1 starting two years before the privatization or concession was awarded and continuing for all years after. *Post-transition* = 1 for all years after the transition period, that is, starting one year after the privatization was awarded.

*Significant at 10 percent; **significant at 5 percent; ***significant at 1 percent.

(7) Continuity of the service	(8) Potability	(9) Water coverage	(10) Sewerage coverage	(11) Avg price per m^3 of water (US$)	(12) Avg price per m^3 of water (in r.l.c.)	(13) Avg price per m^3 for sewerage (US$)	(14) Avg price per m^3 for sewerage (in r.l.c.)
0.038	0.059*	0.025***	0.053***	0.055	0.146***	−0.014	0.104
(0.064)	(0.034)	(0.007)	(0.009)	(0.041)	(0.026)	(0.142)	(0.083)
0.074***	0.012**	0.049***	0.065***	0.097**	0.213***	−0.096	0.222***
(0.015)	(0.005)	(0.005)	(0.007)	(0.038)	(0.027)	(0.110)	(0.077)
97	90	243	198	112	112	37	37
0.000	−0.002	−0.000	−0.005	0.003	−0.048	0.026	0.017
(0.006)	(0.005)	(0.001)	(0.006)	(0.050)	(0.034)	(0.093)	(0.082)
0.000	−0.002	−0.001	−0.008	−0.047	−0.024	0.013	0.045
(0.002)	(0.009)	(0.001)	(0.005)	(0.031)	(0.020)	(0.088)	(0.078)
97	90	243	198	112	112	37	37
0.002	0.009	0.001	0.003	−0.203***	−0.099***	−0.054	0.007
(0.020)	(0.013)	(0.002)	(0.004)	(0.034)	(0.027)	(0.080)	(0.059)
−0.001	−0.005	−0.004***	−0.008**	−0.018	−0.011	−0.005	0.006
(0.005)	(0.005)	(0.002)	(0.004)	(0.021)	(0.019)	(0.076)	(0.065)
81	77	217	180	101	101	31	31

Table A3.13 Summary of Minimum and Maximum Changes Disaggregated by Regulatory and Contract Variables

		Number of subscribers[a]		Output[a]		Coverage[a]		Number of employees	
		Min. %	Max. %	Min. %	Max. %	Min. %	Max. %	Min. %	Max. %
Auction	Transition	−5.8	−6.8	NS	NS	NS	−3.1	−17.8	−19.9
	Post-transition	NS	NS	NS	NS	NS	NS	−9.1	−16.6
Partial autonomy	Transition	−3.1	−6.9	−5.9	−8.2	NS	−1.9	−9.5	−47.8
	Post-transition	NS	NS	NS	NS	NS	NS	8.9	16.6
Full autonomy	Transition	NS	NS	−5.3	−8.6	−1.6	−3.5	−27.0	−53.7
	Post-transition	NS	NS	−4.4	−4.5	NS	NS	NS	NS
Duration of regulatory board	Transition	NS	NS	−9.7	−11.6	NS	−2.6	−25.5	−30.6
	Post-transition	NS	NS	NS	NS	NS	−2.8	NS	−13.9
Only foreign investors	Transition	1.7	−1.8	−4.4	−10.9	−3.3	−3.9	−11.5	−31.3
	Post-transition	NS	NS	−2.1	−4.0	NS	NS	NS	NS
Foreign and local investors	Transition	−1.0	−2.2	NS	NS	−2.2	−3.5	−13.0	−14.0
	Post-transition	NS	1.4	NS	NS	NS	NS	−8.1	−13.7
Award: best investment plan	Transition	2.5	—	NS	NS	2.1	—	30.1	—
	Post-transition	NS	NS	2.2	—	−1.3	—	14.1	—
Award: highest price	Transition	−1.3	−2.6	NS	NS	NS	−1.2	−21.0	NS
	Post-transition	NS	NS	NS	NS	1.2	1.5	−17.9	−25.5
Price-cap tariff regulation	Transition	NS	NS	4.8	—	NS	NS	−8.4	—
	Post-transition	NS	NS	NS	NS	NS	NS	NS	NS
Rate-of-return tariff regulation	Transition	2.4	6.3	NS	NS	1.2	1.6	−60.1	−60.3
	Post-transition	1.9	2.0	NS	NS	NS	NS	−8.3	42.5

Source: Author's calculations.
Note: NS = Not significant.
a. Results are obtained after controlling for time trends.

Connections per employee[a]		Output per employee[a]		Distributional losses		Average prices (US$)		Average prices (real local currency)		Quality	
Min. %	Max. %	Min. %	Max. %	Min. %	Max. %	Min. %	Max. %	Min. %	Max. %	Min. %	Max. %
NS	NS	NS	NS	NS	NS	21.0	196.2	15.5	66.7	NS	26.0
NS	−10.1	NS	−13.1	−9.7	−30.7	−5.8	−28.8	−11.3	−18.9	22.9	94.3
14.0	21.4	NS	19.2	NS	NS	−45.2	−52.2	−36.6	645.6	—	−24.0
−15.0	−26.0	−14.1	−41.8	−13.2	34.3	−10.2	37.2	−13.8	30.5	−14.4	−50.5
27.6	60.2	15.3	48.0	11.1	29.2	−26.0	−68.1	−31.8	1160.4	87.8	196.5
NS	−34.9	−9.8	−26.3	−22.0	−37.5	−21.3	27.5	10.3	14.2	−44.2	13.2
26.6	30.7	NS	−8.3	11.6	15.6	NS	−8.0	−9.2	−16.6	NS	188.6
NS	14.8	NS	26.2	−38.3	−43.3	13.4	35.8	−10.6	−16.1	NS	NS
NS	NS	NS	−14.4	NS	NS	—	7.6	−5.7	−17.1	NS	−23.3
NS	−15.0	NS	NS	−11.9	−26.0	13.9	25.5	4.7	7.3	NS	−9.7
NS	−10.5	NS	−6.9	NS	NS	−22.5	−24.0	NS	NS	28.4	29.4
NS	5.9	NS	6.1	−15.2	−19.0	19.2	27.0	NS	−2.7	NS	15.0
NS	NS	NS	NS	NS	—	NS	NS	—	−11.5	−18.3	—
NS	NS	NS	NS	NS	NS	14.2	—	NS	NS	NS	NS
NS	NS	NS	−19.1	NS	NS	NS	−15.9	−17.1	−90.6	−27.2	14.5
5.4	50.5	NS	19.6	NS	14.9	−6.9	9.4	−10.6	−11.8	NS	−12.3
−5.7	—	—	−8.1	NS	NS	NS	—	—	18.9	7.9	—
NS	NS	NS	NS	21.9	—	NS	NS	—	13.0	NS	NS
NS	19.5	NS	NS	NS	NS	NS	32.4	−6.6	22.5	−6.3	19.2
NS	NS	NS	NS	NS	−11.8	NS	−15.4	NS	−8.5	NS	−4.7

Appendix 4

Summary of Power Market Reforms in Latin America and the Caribbean

Table A4.1 Latin America and the Caribbean Region Summary of Power Market Reforms

	Argentina	Brazil	Chile	Colombia	El Salvador	Peru
Variables						
Installed generation capacity 2004 (MW)	28,185	90,733	10,737	13,398	1,105	6,016
Electricity demand 2004 (GW)	84,744	346,745	43,829	38,556	4,915	21,270
Reform timing						
Law enacted	1991	1995–1998 (new market model in 2004)	1982	1994	1996	1992
Restructuring	1992–93	1995	1981	1995–99	1997–99	1994
Privatization		1995–2001	1986–89			1994–97
Industry structure						
Unbundling	Separate G, T, D	Separate G, T, D (affiliated companies allowed)	Separation of accounts G, T, D	Separate G, T, D for new companies	Separate G, T, D	Separate G, T, D
Market model	Wholesale competition	Wholesale competition	Wholesale competition	Wholesale competition	Retail competition	Wholesale competition
Market participants						
Gencos	41	25	12	66	4	18
Self-gen. & IPPs		89	6		10	6
Transcos	57	54	4	11	1	33
Distcos	62	43	31	32	5 (2 groups)	0
Marketers	46	42	0	67	5	
Large consumers	1496 (21% of demand)	577 (21% of demand)	30% of demand	4206 (31% of demand)	5 (10% of demand)	46% of demand

(continued)

Table A4.1 Latin America and the Caribbean Region Summary of Power Market Reforms (continued)

	Argentina	Brazil	Chile	Colombia	El Salvador	Peru
Private participation						
Generation	80%	26%	100%	57%	64%	66%
Transmission	100%	10%	100%	3%	0%	100%
Distribution	60%	64%	~100%	46%	~100%	71%
Wholesale market arrangements						
Economic dispatch	Cost-based bids	Centralized, cost based	Centralized, cost based	Cost-based bids	Price bids	Centralized, cost based
Spot transactions	Nodal prices, generators, LC	Nodal prices G, D, LC	Nodal prices, generators	Single node, G, D, LC	Single node, G, D, LC	Nodal prices, generators
Capacity charges	Yes		Yes	Yes	Yes	Yes
Large consumers	5 MW, reduced to 30 kW	10 MW, reduced to 500 kW	2 MW, reduced to 500 kW	2 MW, reduced to 100 kW	Full retail competition	1 MW
Long-term contracts	Negotiated	Competitive tender by central agency for 100% demand regulated market; negotiated for market of large consumers	Negotiated	Negotiated	Negotiated	Negotiated

(continued)

Table A4.1 Latin America and the Caribbean Region Summary of Power Market Reforms (*continued*)

	Argentina	Brazil	Chile	Colombia	El Salvador	Peru
Transmission expansion	Negotiated third-party access	Central planning	Negotiated third-party access	Central planning	Central planning	Negotiated third-party access
Prices to regulated consumers	Average of seasonal spot prices	Weighted average of spot and contract prices	Average of 48-month expected marginal costs	Moving average of spot and contract prices	Average of spot prices	Average of 48-month expected marginal costs
Institutional arrangements						
Policy making	Ministry of Energy	Ministry	Ministry	Ministry of Energy	Ministry	Ministry of Energy
Expansion planning		Special agency (EPE)	CNE, gov. participation	Agency of ME	None	
Regulation	ENRE, independent	ANEEL, independent		CREG, gov. participation	SIGET, independent	OSINERG, independent
Market administration	ISO, CAMMESA	ISO, ONS. CCEE	ISO, CDEC	Business unit of T	ISO, UT	ISO, COES
Major market changes	Intervention of market prices in 2002	After energy crisis of 2001, a new market model was adopted in 2004 to strengthen central planning, long-term contracts and energy security.	Ley Corta I, II of 2004 and 2005, introduced incentives for generation and transmission expansion.		Changed to cost-based bids in 2006	

(*continued*)

Table A4.1 Latin America and the Caribbean Region Summary of Power Market Reforms *(continued)*

Variables	Bolivia	Dominican Republic	Guatemala	Nicaragua	Panama
Installed generation capacity 2004 (MWh)	1,450	3,290	2,016	756	1,583
Electricity demand 2004 (GWh)	3,779	12,163	6,216	1,719	4,656
Reform timing					
Law enacted	1994	2001	1996	1998	1997
Restructuring	1994–95	1997	1996–98	1999	1998
Privatization		1999		2000–02	1998
Industry structure					
Unbundling	Separate G, T, D	Separate G, T, D (T & G (hydro) are bundled)	Separate G, T, D (T & G (hydro) are bundled)	Separate G, T, D	Separate G, T, D
Market model	Wholesale competition	Wholesale competition	Wholesale competition	Wholesale competition	Wholesale competition
Market Participants					
Gencos	8	11	10	9	8
Self-gen. & IPPs		2	12	1	10
Transcos	2	1	1	1	1
Distcos	6	3	3+13 (small municipal)	1	3
Marketers	0	0	7	0	0
Large consumers	2		32% of demand	9 (8% of demand)	5 (2% of demand)

(continued)

Table A4.1 Latin America and the Caribbean Region Summary of Power Market Reforms (*continued*)

	Bolivia	Dominican Republic	Guatemala	Nicaragua	Panama
Private participation					
Generation	100%	83% (G (hydro) reserved to SOE)	68%	69% (G (hydro) reserved to SOE)	89%
Transmission	100%	0% (T reserved to SOE)	0%	0% (T reserved to SOE)	0% (T reserved to SOE)
Distribution	93%	32%	91%	~100%	100%
Wholesale market arrangements					
Economic dispatch	Centralized, cost based	Centralized, cost based	Centralized, cost based	Centralized, cost based	Centralized, cost based
Spot transactions	Nodal prices, generators	Single node, G, D	Single node, G, D	Single node, G, D	Single node, G, D
Capacity charges	Yes	Yes	Yes	Yes	Yes
Large consumers	1 MW	2 MW reduced to 200 kW	100 kW	2 MW	100 kW
Long-term contracts	Distcos must tender for up to 80% of demand	Distcos must tender for up to 80% of demand	Competitive bidding	Distcos must tender for up to 80% of demand	Distcos must tender for up to 100% of demand
Transmission expansion	Negotiated third-party access	Central planning	Central planning	Central planning	Central planning

(*continued*)

Table A4.1 Latin America and the Caribbean Region Summary of Power Market Reforms *(continued)*

	Bolivia	Dominican Republic	Guatemala	Nicaragua	Panama
Prices to regulated consumers	Average of expected marginal costs	Weighted average of spot and contract prices	12-month weighted average of spot and contract prices	12-month weighted average of spot and contract prices	Weighted average of spot and contract prices
Institutional arrangements					
Policy making	Ministry of Energy	CNE, gov. participation	Ministry of Energy	CNE, gov. participation	CNPE, gov. participation
Expansion planning					
Regulation	SIRESE, independent	SIE, independent	CNEE, attached to ministry	INE, independent	ERSP, independent
Market administration	ISO, CNDC	ISO, OC	ISO, AMM	Business unit of T	Business unit of T
Major market changes			Private investor with 68% participation in distcos pull out in 2003		Private investor with 100% of distcos in serious difficulties

(continued)

Table A4.1 Latin America and the Caribbean Region Summary of Power Market Reforms *(continued)*

	Costa Rica	Ecuador	Honduras	Mexico	Uruguay	Venezuela, R. B. de
Variables						
Installed generation capacity 2004 (MW)	1,961	3,541	1,041	52,979	2,169	22,124
Electricity demand 2004 (GWh)	6,824	10,735	4,110	158,094	6,260	68,097
Reform timing						
Law enacted	1990	1996	1994	1992 amendment to 1975 electricity law	1997	2001
Restructuring	No	1997–?	None	No	2002–?	No
Privatization	Small renewable IPPs (1994–?)	No	IPPs (1994–?)	IPPs (1994–?)	Small renewable IPPs (2006–?)	
Industry structure						
Unbundling	Vertically integrated monopoly & small municipal and cooperatives	Separate G, T, D	Vertically integrated monopoly & IPPs	Vertically integrated monopoly	Vertically integrated company, separation of accounts	Vertically integrated monopolies
Market model	Monopoly G, T, D, licensed small IPPs are permitted	Wholesale competition	Single buyer	Monopoly G, T, D, licensed IPPs and cogenerators are permitted	Wholesale competition	Power pool

(continued)

Table A4.1 Latin America and the Caribbean Region Summary of Power Market Reforms (*continued*)

		Costa Rica	Ecuador	Honduras	Mexico	Uruguay	Venezuela, R. B. de
Market participants	Gencos	1	13	1	1	2	7 vertically integrated monopolies, 2 D, 4 G
	Self-gen. & IPPs	4 small cooperatives and municipalities and 30 small renewable IPPs	16	22	403 power stations (362 self-generators, 18 IPP, 36 cogen)	1	
	Transcos	1	1	1	1	1	
	Distcos	1 + 6 small municipal and cooperatives	20	1	1	1	
	Marketers	0	0	0	0	0	
	Large consumers	0	11% of demand	1 (2%)	0	0	0
Private participation							
	Generation	12% (small renewables)		65%	19% (only IPPs)	0%	14%
	Transmission	0%	0%	0%	0%	0%	
	Distribution	0%	0%	0%	0%	0%	

(*continued*)

Table A4.1 Latin America and the Caribbean Region Summary of Power Market Reforms (*continued*)

	Costa Rica	Ecuador	Honduras	Mexico	Uruguay	Venezuela, R. B. de
Wholesale market arrangements						
Economic dispatch	—	Centralized, cost based	Centralized, cost based	—	Centralized, cost based	Centralized
Spot transactions	—	Nodal prices, G, D, LC	No	Vertically integrated market. Laws allow IPPs, cogens and self-generators under license. CFE purchase energy from licensed IPPs under long-term contracts and excess power from cogenerators and self-generators.	Law of 1997 established wholesale power market, with spot transactions and long-term contracts, and large consumers >250 kW, similar to Argentina, to facilitate integration with that much larger market.	A regulated power pool of vertically integrated companies is in operation, until a 2001 law that creates a wholesale market is implemented.
Capacity charges	Vertically integrated market and small municipal companies and cooperatives. ICE purchases energy from IPPs at avoided cost under long-term contracts.	Yes	No			
Large consumers		1 MW	1 MW			
Long-term contracts		Negotiated, initial contracts with hydros for 100% generation	With single buyer, competitive tender			
Transmission expansion		Central planning	Central planning			
Prices to regulated consumers		4-year average of expected marginal costs	Expected marginal costs			

(*continued*)

Table A4.1 Latin America and the Caribbean Region Summary of Power Market Reforms *(continued)*

	Costa Rica	Ecuador	Honduras	Mexico	Uruguay	Venezuela, R. B. de
Institutional arrangements						
Policy making	Ministry	Ministry	Dispersed	Ministry	Ministry	Ministry
Expansion planning			SOE			
Regulation	SOE ARESEP, independent	CONELEC, independent	CNE, independent	CRE, independent, does not approve tariffs	URSEA, independent, does not approve tariffs	Government office, FUNDELEC, provisional
Market administration	SOE	ISO, CENACE	No market	SOE	ISO, ADME, has not assumed functions	OPSIS, power pool

(continued)

Table A4.1 Latin America and the Caribbean Region Summary of Power Market Reforms *(continued)*

	Costa Rica	Ecuador	Honduras	Mexico	Uruguay	Venezuela, R. B. de
Major market changes		Initiatives to privatize gencos and distcos failed. Tariffs do not reflect costs and wholesale market of SOE is besieged by nonpayment in the supply chain.	1994 law established unbundling, but law was not applied.		Wholesale market model is being revised. Priority given to security of energy supply and developing renewable generation with private participation. Operating as a single buyer model.	Law of 2001 (LOSE) established a wholesale market, unbundling, large consumers, independent regulator and market administrator. It has not been implemented.

Source: Authors' elaboration.

Note: Gencos = generation companies; Self-gen. & IPPs = self-generation and independent power producers; Transcos = transmission companies; Distcos = distribution companies; AMM = Administrador del Mercado Mayorista; ANEEL = Agencia Nacional de Energia Eléctrica; CAMMESA = Compañía Administradora del Mercado Mayorista Eléctrico; CCEE = Câmara de Comercialização de Energia Elétrica; CDEC = Centre de Despacho Económico de Carga; CNDC = Comité Nacional de Despacho de Carga; CNE (Chile, Dominican Republic, Honduras, and Nicaragua) = Comisión Nacional de Energía; CNEE = Comisión Nacional de Energía Eléctrica; CNPE = Comisión Nacional de Política Energética; COES = Comité de Operación Económica del Sistema Interconectado Nacional; CREG = Comisión de Regulación de Energía y Gas; ENRE = Ente Nacional Regulador de la Electricidad; EPE = Empresa de Pesquisa Energética; ERSP = Ente Regulador de Los Servicios Públicos; G (hydro) = hydroelectric generation; G, T, D = generation, transmission, distribution; INE = Instituto Nicaraguense de Energía; ISO = independent system operator; KW = kilowatt; LC = long-term contracts; MW = megawatt; OC = Organismo Coordinador del Sistema Eléctrico Nacional Interconectado; ONS = Operador do Nacional do Sistema Eletrico; OSINERG = Organismo Supervisor de Inversion en Energia; SIE = Superintendencia de Electricidad; SIGET = Superintendencia General de Electricidad y Telecomunicaciones; SIRESE = Sistema de Regulatión Sectorial; SOE = State-owned enterprise; UT = Unidad de Transacciones. — = not available.

Appendix 5

Utility Companies

Country	Acronym	Name
Argentina	EDEA	Empresa Distribuidora de Energía Atlántica
Argentina	EDECAT	Empresa Distribuidora de Energía de Catamarca S.A.
Argentina	EDEERSA	Energía de Entre Ríos S.A.
Argentina	EDEFOR	Empresa Distribuidora de Energía de Formosa S.A.
Argentina	EDELAP	Empresa Distribuidora de Energía La Plata S.A.
Argentina	EDELAR	Empresa Distribuidora de Electricidad de la Rioja S.A.
Argentina	EDEMSA	Empresa Distribuidora de Electricidad de Mendoza S.A.
Argentina	EDEN	Empresa Distribuidora de Energía Norte S.A.
Argentina	EDENOR	Empresa Distribuidora y Comercializadora Norte S.A.
Argentina	EDERSA	Empresa de Energía Rió Negro
Argentina	EDES	Empresa Distribuidora de Energía Sur S.A.
Argentina	EDESA	Empresas Distribuidora de Electricidad de Salta S.A.
Argentina	EDESAL	Empresa Distribuidora San Luis S.A.

(continued)

Country	Acronym	Name
Argentina	EDESUR	Empresa Distribuidora Sur S.A.
Argentina	EDET	Empresa de Distribución Eléctrica de Tucumán S.A.
Argentina	EJESA	Empresa Jujeña de Energía S.A.
Argentina	ESJSA	Energía San Juan S.A.
Bolivia	CESSA	Compañía Eléctrica de Sucre S.A.
Bolivia	CRE	Cooperativa Rural de Electrificación— ÁREA INTERGRADA
Bolivia	ELECTROPAZ	Electricidad De La Paz S.A.
Bolivia	ELFEC	Empresa de Luz y Fuerza Eléctrica Cochabamba S.A.
Bolivia	ELFEO	Empresa de Luz y Fuerza Eléctrica Oruro S.A.
Bolivia	SEPSA	Servicios Eléctricos Potosí
Bolivia	SETAR— CENTRAL	Servicios Eléctricos Tarija S.A.
Brazil	AES SUL	AES SUL Distribuidora Gaúcha de Energia S/A
Brazil	BANDEIRANTE	Bandeirante Energia S/A.
Brazil	CAIUA	Caiuá Serviços de Eletricidade S/A
Brazil	CEAL	Companhia Energética de Alagoas
Brazil	CEB	Companhia Energética de Brasília
Brazil	CELB	Companhia Energética da Borborema
Brazil	CELESC	Centrais Elétricas Santa Catarina S/A
Brazil	CELG	Companhia Energética de Goiás
Brazil	CELPA	Centrais Elétricas do Pará S/A
Brazil	CELPE	Companhia Energética de Pernambuco
Brazil	CELTINS	Companhia de Energia Elétrica do Estado do Tocantins
Brazil	CEMAR	Companhia Energética do Maranhão
Brazil	CEMAT	Centrais Elétricas Matogrossenses S/A
Brazil	CEMIG	Companhia Energética de Minas Gerais
Brazil	CENF	Companhia de Eletricidade Nova Friburgo

(continued)

Country	Acronym	Name
Brazil	CEPISA	Companhia Energética do Piauí
Brazil	CERJ	Companhia de Eletricidade do Rio de Janeiro
Brazil	CERON	Centrais Elétricas de Rondônia S/A
Brazil	CFLO	Companhia Força e Luz do Oeste
Brazil	COCEL	Companhia Campolarguense de Energia
Brazil	COELBA	Companhia de Eletricidade do Estado da Bahia
Brazil	COELCE	Companhia Energética do Ceará
Brazil	COPEL	Companhia Paranaense de Energia
Brazil	COSERN	Companhia Energética do Rio Grande do Norte
Brazil	CPEE	Companhia Paulista de Energia Elétrica
Brazil	CPFL	Companhia Paulista de Força e Luz
Brazil	DEMEI	Departamento Municipal de Energia de Ijuí
Brazil	ELEKTRO	Elektro Eletricidade e Serviços S/A.
Brazil	ELETROCAR	Centrais Elétricas de Carazinho S/A.
Brazil	ELETROPAULO	Eletropaulo Metropolitana— Eletricidade de São Paulo S/A
Brazil	ENERGIPE	Empresa Energética de Sergipe
Brazil	ENERSUL	Empresa Energética de Mato Grosso do Sul S/A
Brazil	ESCELSA	Espírito Santo Centrais Elétricas S/A
Brazil	FORCEL	Força e Luz Coronel Vivida Ltda
Brazil	LIGHT	Light Serviços de Eletricidade S/A
Brazil	MANAUS	Manaus Energia S/A
Brazil	MUXFELDT	Muxfeldt Marin & Cia. Ltda
Brazil	NOVAPALMA	Usina Hidroelétrica de Nova Palma
Brazil	PANAMBI	Hidroelétrica Panambi S/A (HIDROPAN)
Brazil	RGE	Rio Grande Energia S/A
Brazil	SAELPA	Saelpa S/A de Eletrificação da Paraíba
Brazil	SULGIPE	Companhia Sul Sergipana de Eletricidade

(continued)

Country	Acronym	Name
Chile	CGE	Compañía General de Electricidad S.A.
Chile	CHILECTRA	Chilectra S.A.
Chile	CHILGENER	
Chile	CHILMETRO	
Chile	CHILQUINTA	Enerquinta (Chilquinta Energies S.A.)
Chile	CONAFE	Compañía Nacional de Fuerza Eléctrica S.A.
Chile	COOPREL	Cooperativa Rural Eléctrica de Rió Bueno Ltda
Chile	COPELEC	Cooperativa de Consumo de Energía Eléctrica de Chillán
Chile	CURICO	Cooperativa Eléctrica de Curicó S.A.
Chile	EDELAYSEN	Empresa Eléctrica de Aysen S.A.
Chile	EDELMAG	Empresa Eléctrica de Magallanes S.A.
Chile	EEC	Empresa Eléctrica de Colina S.A.
Chile	ELECDA	Empresa Eléctrica de Antofagasta S.A.
Chile	ELIQSA	Empresa Eléctrica de Iquique S.A.
Chile	EMEC	Empresa Eléctrica EMEC S.A.
Chile	EMELARI	Empresa Eléctrica de Arica S.A.
Chile	EMELAT	Empresa Eléctrica de Atacama S.A.
Chile	FRONTEL	Empresa Eléctrica de la Frontera S.A.
Chile	SAESA	Sociedad Austral de Electricidad S.A.
Chile	TIL TIL	Empresa Eléctrica Municipal de Til-Til
Colombia	CODENSA	CODENSA S.A. ESP
Colombia	ElectriCaribe	Electrificadora del Caribe S.A. E.S.P.
Colombia	ElectroCosta	Electrificadora de La Costa Atlántica S.A.
Colombia	EPSA	Empresa de Energía del Pacifico
El Salvador	CAESS	Compañía de Alumbrado Eléctrico de San Salvador, S.A.
El Salvador	CLESA	AES CLESA y Compañía, S. en C. de C.V.
El Salvador	DEL SUR	Distribuidora de Electricidad del Sur

(continued)

Country	Acronym	Name
El Salvador	DEUSEM	Distribuidora Eléctrica de Usulatan, S.A.
El Salvador	EEO	Empresa Eléctrica de Oriente, S.A.
Guatemala	DEOCSA	Distribuidora de Electricidad de Occidente
Guatemala	DEORSA	Distribuidora de Electricidad de Oriente
Guatemala	EEGSA	Empresas Eléctricas de Guatemala S.A.
Nicaragua	DISNORTE	Distribuidora de Electricidad del Norte
Nicaragua	DISSUR	Distribuidora de Electricidad del Sur
Panama	EDECHI	Empresa de Distribución Eléctrica Chiriquí, S.A
Panama	EDEMET	Empresa de Distribución Eléctrica Metro Oeste, S.A.
Panama	ELEKTRA NORESTE	Empresa de Distribución Eléctrica Noreste
Peru	CHANGAY	Edelnor—Zonal Chancay
Peru	EDECAÑETE	Empresa de Distribución Eléctrica Canete S.A.
Peru	EDELNOR	Edelnor
Peru	ELC	Electro Centro S.A.
Peru	ELECTRO NORTE MEDIO	Electronorte Medio S.A.-Hidradina S.A.
Peru	ELSM	Electro Sur Medio S.A.
Peru	ENOSA	Electro Nor Oeste S.A.
Peru	ENSA	Electro Norte S.A.
Peru	LUZ del Sur	Luz del Sur

Bibliography

Alcázar, L., L. C. Xu, and A. M. Zuluaga. 2002. "Institutions, Politics, and Con-tracts: The Privatization Attempt of the Water and Sanitation Utility of Lima, Peru." In M. M. Shirley, ed., *Thirsting for Efficiency: The Economics and Politics of Urban Water System Reform*, 103–38. Amsterdam: Pergamon.

Anas A., K. Lee, and M. Murray. 1996. "Infrastructure Bottlenecks, Private Provision, and Industrial Productivity." World Bank Policy Research Working Paper No. 1603. World Bank, Washington, DC.

Andrés, L., M. Diop, and J. L. Guasch. 2008. "Achievements and Challenges of Private Participation in Infrastructure in Latin America: Evaluation and Future Prospects." In Henry Davis, ed., *Euromoney Infrastructure Financing*, Oxford, U.K.: Oxford University Press.

Apoyo. 2002. "Encuesta: Actitudes sobre la Privatización." Lima, Peru.

Bacon, R. W., and J. E. Besant-Jones. 2001. "Global Electric Power Reform, Privatization and Liberalization of the Electric Power Industry in Developing Countries." *Annual Reviews of Energy and the Environment* 26: 331–59.

Bain, R., and A. Wilkinson. 2002. "Road Risk." *Project Finance* (September Supplement): 2–5.

Benitez, D., O. Chisari, and A. Estache. 2003. "Can the Gains from Argentina's Utilities Reform Offset Credit Shocks?" In C. Ugaz and C. Waddams Price, eds., *Utility Privatization and Regulation: A Fair Deal for Consumers?* Cheltenham, U.K.: Edward Elgar.

Birdsall, N., and J. Nellis. 2003. "Winners and Losers: Assessing the Distributional Impact of Privatization." *World Development* 31 (10): 1617–33.

Boardman, A., and A. R. Vining. 1989. "Ownership and Performance in Com-petitive Environments: A Comparison of the Performance of Private, Mixed, and State-Owned Enterprises." *Journal of Law and Economics* 32 (1): 1–33.

Boix, C. 2005. "Privatization and Public Discontent in Latin America." Background paper commissioned for *Infrastructure in Latin America and the Caribbean: Recent Developments and Key Challenges*. Inter-American Development Bank, Washington, DC.

Boubakri, N., and J. C. Cosset. 1998. "The Financial and Operating Performance of Newly Privatized Firms: Evidence from Developing Countries." *Journal of Finance* 53 (3): 1081–110.

———. 2002. "Does Privatization Meet the Expectations? Evidence from African Countries." *Journal of African Economies* 11 (Suppl. 1): 111–40.

Boylaud, O., and G. Nicoletti. 2000. "Regulation, Market Structure and Perfor-mance in Telecommunications." Economics Department Working Paper No. 237, Organisation for Economic Co-operation and Development, Paris.

Briceño-Garmendia, C., A. Estache, and N. Shafik. 2004. "Infrastructure Services in Developing Countries: Access, Quality, Costs and Policy Reform." World Bank Policy Research Working Paper No. 3468, World Bank, Washington, DC.

Brook, P. J., and T. C. Irwin. 2003. *Infrastructure for Poor People: Public Policy for Private Provision.* Washington, DC: World Bank.

Calderón, C., W. Easterly, and L. Servén. 2003. "Latin America's Infrastructure in the Era of Macroeconomic Crises." In W. Easterly and L. Servén, eds., *The Limits of Stabilization: Infrastructure, Public Deficits and Growth in Latin America,* 21–94. Washington, DC: Stanford University Press and World Bank.

Calderón, C., and L. Servén. 2004a. "The Effects of Infrastructure Development on Growth and Income Distribution." Policy Research Working Paper No. 3400, World Bank, Washington, DC.

Calderón, C., and L. Servén. 2004b. "Trends in Infrastructure in Latin America, 1980-2001." World Bank Policy Research Working Paper No. 3401, World Bank, Washington, DC.

Cárdenas, C. 2003. "Diagóstico del Sector Eléctrico: 1990-2002." Unidad de Análisis de Políticas Sociales y Económicas, Gobierno de Bolivia.

Chisari, O., A. Estache, and C. Romero. 1999. "Winners and Losers from the Privatization and Regulation of Utilities: Lessons from a General Equilibrium Model of Argentina." *World Bank Economic Review* 13 (2): 357–78.

Chong, A., and F. López-de-Silanes. 2003a. "Privatization and Labor Restructuring around the World." Yale University, New Haven, CT.

Chong, A., and F. López-de-Silanes. 2003b. "The Truth about Privatization in Latin America." Latin American Research Network, Research Network Working Paper No. R-486, Inter-American Development Bank, Washington, DC.

Chong, A., and F. López-de-Silanes, eds. 2005. *Privatization in Latin America: Myths and Reality.* Palo Alto, CA; Washington, DC: Stanford University Press and the World Bank.

Clarke, G. R. G., and S. J. Wallsten. 2002. "Universal(ly Bad) Service: Providing Infrastructure Services to Rural and Poor Urban Consumers." Policy Research Paper No. 2868, World Bank, Washington, DC.

De Ferranti, D., G. E. Perry, F. H. G. Ferreira, and M. Walton. 2004. *Inequality in Latin America: Breaking with History?* Washington, DC: World Bank.

D'Souza, J., B. Bortolotti, M. Fantini, and W. Megginson. 2000. "Sources of Performance Improvement in Privatized Firms: A Clinical Study of the Global Telecommunications Industry." University of Oklahoma, Norman, OK.

D'Souza, J., and W. L. Megginson. 1999. "The Financial and Operating Performance of Newly Privatized Firms in the 1990s." *Journal of Finance* 54 (4): 1397–438.

Durbin, J. 1954. "Errors in Variables." *Review of the International Statistical Institute* 22 (1): 23–32.

Dussan, M. 1996. "Electric Power Sector Reform in Latin America and the Caribbean." Working Paper IFM-104, Inter-American Development Bank, Washington, DC.

Ehrlich, I., G. Gallais-Hamonno, Z. Liu, and R. Lutter. 1994. "Productivity Growth and Firm Ownership: An Empirical Investigation." *Journal of Political Economy* 102 (5): 1006–38.

El Cronista. 2005, April 18. "La mayoría cree que los servicios públicos deben volver al Estado, Bueros Aires."

Engel, E. M. R. A., R. D. Fischer, and A. Galetovic. 2001. "Least-Present-Value-of-Revenue Auctions and Highway Franchising." *Journal of Political Economy* 109: 993–1020.

Ennis, H. M., and S. M. Pinto. 2003. "Privatization and Income Distribution in Argentina." http://www.depeco.econo.unlp.edu.ar/semi/semi300503.pdf.

Ente Regulador de los Servicios Públicos. 2004. República de Panamá Web site. http://www.enteregulador.gob.pa/

Escobal, J., and M. Torero. 2004. "Análisis de los Servicios de Infraestructura Rural y las Condiciones de Vida en las Zonas Rurales de Perú." Grupo de Análisis para el Desarrollo (GRADE), Peru.

ESRI (Public Data). 2006. World Country Boundaries MAP, California: ESRI.

Escribano, A., J. L. Guasch, and J. Pena. 2007. "A Robust Assessment of the Impact of Infrastructures on African Firm's Productivity: Analysis Based on Firm Level Data from 1999 to 2005." Africa Infrastructure Country Diagnostic Study, World Bank, Washington, DC.

Escribano, A., J. L. Guasch, J. Pena, and M. de Orte. 2007a. "Investment Climate Assessment on Economic Performance using Firm Level Data: Brazil and Chile." Working Paper, Universidad Carlos III de Madrid.

Escribano, A., J. L. Guasch, J. Pena, and M. de Orte. 2007b. "Investment Climate Assessment on Economic Performance using Firm Level Data: Pooling Manufacturing Firms from Indonesia, Malaysia, Philippines and Thailand from 2001 to 2002." Working Paper, Universidad Carlos III de Madrid.

Estache, A., V. Foster, and Q. Woodon. 2002. *Accounting for Poverty in Infrastructure Reform: Learning from Latin America's Experience*. Studies in Development Series. Washington, DC: World Bank Institute.

Estache, A., M. Manacorda, and T. M. Valletti. 2002. "Telecommunications Reforms, Access Regulation, and Internet Adoption in Latin America." Working Paper No. 2802, World Bank, Washington, DC.

Estache, A., and M. E. Pinglo. 2004. *Are Returns to Private Infrastructure Projects in Developing Countries Commensurate with Risks Since the Asian Crisis?* Policy Research Working Paper No. 3373, World Bank, Washington, DC.

Estache, A., and M. Rodriguez-Pardina. 1998. "Light and Lightening at the End of the Public Tunnel: The Reform of the Electricity Sector in the Southern Cone." Policy Research Working Paper No. 2074, World Bank, Washington, DC.

Estache, A., and M. Rossi. 2004. "Have Consumers Benefited from the Reforms in the Electricity Distribution Sector in Latin America?" World Bank, Washington, DC.

Ettinger, S., M. Schur, S. von Klaudy, G. Dellacha, and S. Hahn. 2005. "Developing Country Investors and Operators in Infrastructure." Public-Private Infrastructure Advisory Facility, Trends and Policy Options Report No. 3, PPIAF, Washington, DC.

Fan, S., D. Nyange, and N. Rao. 2005. "Public Investment and Poverty Reduction in Tanzania: Evidence from Household Survey Data." DSGD Discussion Paper No. 18, International Food Policy Research Institute (IFPRI), Washington, DC.

Fay, M. 2001. "Financing the Future: Infrastructure Needs in Latin America 2000–05." Policy Research Working Paper No. 2545, World Bank, Washington, DC.

Fay, M., and M. Morrison. 2006. *Infrastructure in Latin America and the Caribbean: Recent Developments and Key Challenges.* Washington, DC: World Bank.

Fink, C., A. Mattoo, and R. Rathindran. 2003. "An Assessment of Telecommunications Reform in Developing Countries." *Information Economics and Policy* 15 (September): 443–66.

Foster, V. 2005. "Ten Years of Water Service Reform in Latin America: Toward an Anglo-French Model." Water Supply and Sanitation Sector Board Discussion Paper No. 3, World Bank, Washington, DC.

Foster, V., and C. Araujo. 2004. "Does Infrastructure Reform Work for the Poor? A Case Study from Guatemala." Policy Research Working Paper No. 3185, World Bank, Washington, DC.

Foster, V., A. Gómez-Lobo, and J. Halpern. 2000. "Designing Direct Subsidies for Water and Sanitation Services. Panama: A Case Study." Policy Research Working Paper No. 2344, World Bank, Washington, DC.

Foster, V., E. Tiongson, and C. Ruggeri Laderchi. 2005. "Utility Reforms." In A. Coudouel and S. Paternostro, eds., *Analyzing the Distributional Impacts of Reforms,* 73–144. Washington, DC: World Bank.

Foster, V., and J. P. Tré. 2003. "Measuring the Impact of Energy Interventions on the Poor—An Illustration from Guatemala." In P. J. Brook and T. C. Irwin, eds., *Infrastructure for Poor People,* 125–78. Washington, DC: World Bank.

Freije, S., and L. A. Rivas. 2002. "Privatization, Inequality and Welfare: Evidence from Nicaragua." http://www.cgdev.org/doc/event%20docs/ 2.24.03-Privatization/Rivas_Nicaragua_paper.pdf.

Frydman, R., C. W. Gray, M. Hessel, and A. Rapaczynski. 1999. "When Does Privatization Work? The Impact of Private Ownership on Corporate Performance in Transition Economies." *Quarterly Journal of Economics* 114 (4): 1153–91.

Galal, A. 1999. "Welfare Impact of Telecom Reform in Egypt: An Ex Ante Analysis." Partners for Development: New Roles for Government and Private Sector in the Middle East and North Africa, World Bank, Washington, DC.

Galal, A., L. Jones, P. Tandon, and I. Vogelsang. 1994. *Welfare Consequences of Selling Public Enterprises.* Oxford, U.K.: Oxford University Press.

Galiani, S., P. Gertler, and E. Schargrodsky. 2005. "Water for Life: The Impact of the Privatization of Water Services on Child Mortality." *Journal of Political Economy* 113 (February): 83–120.

Gannon, C., and Z. Liu. 1997. "Poverty and Transport." Transport, Water, and Urban Development (TWU) Discussion Paper No. 30, World Bank, Washington, DC.

Gibson, J., and S. Rozelle. 2003. "Poverty and Access to Roads in Papua New Guinea." *Economic Development and Cultural Change* 52 (1): 159–85.

Guasch, J. L. 2001. "Concessions and Regulatory Design: Determinants of Performance: Fifteen Years of Evidence." World Bank, Washington, DC.

———. 2004. *Granting and Renegotiating Infrastructure Concessions: Doing It Right.* Washington, DC: World Bank Institute Development Studies.

Guasch, J.L., and R. Hahn. 1999. "The Costs and Benefits of Regulation: Implications for Developing Countries." *World Bank Research Observer* 14 (1): 137–58.

Guasch, J. L., and J. Kogan. 2001. "Inventories in Developing Countries: Levels and Determinants—A Red Flag for Competitiveness and Growth." Working Paper No. 2552, World Bank, Washington, DC.

———. 2003. "Just-in-Case Inventories." Working Paper No. 3012, World Bank, Washington, DC.

————. 2005. "Inventories and Logistic Costs in Developing Countries: Levels and Determinants, a Red Flag on Competitiveness and Growth." *Revista de la Competencia y la Propiedad Intelectual* 1 (1). http://www.indecopi.gob.pe/ArchivosPortal/boletines/recompi/castellano/numAnteriores.jsp.

Gutiérrez, L. H. 2003. "The Effect of Endogenous Regulation on Telecommunications Expansion and Efficiency in Latin America." *Journal of Regulatory Economics* 23 (3): 257–86.

Haggarty, L., P. Brook, and A. M. Zuluaga. 2002. "Water Sector Service Contracts in Mexico City, Mexico." In M. M. Shirley, ed., *Thirsting for Efficiency: The Economics and Politics of Urban Water System Reform*, 139–88. Amsterdam: Pergamon.

Halvorsen, R., and R. Palmquist. 1980. "The Interpretation of Dummy Variables in Semilogarithmic Equations." *American Economic Review* 70 (3): 474–75.

Harris, C. 2003. "Private Participation in Infrastructure in Developing Countries: Trends, Impacts and Policy Lessons." Working Paper No. 5, World Bank, Washington, DC.

Hausman, J. 1978. "Specification Tests in Econometrics." *Econometrica* 46 (3): 262–80.

Heckman, J., and R. Robb. 1985. "Alternative Methods of Evaluating the Impact of Interventions." In J. Heckman and B. Singer, eds., *Longitudinal Analysis of Labor Market Data*, 156–245. New York: Cambridge University Press.

INEI (*Instituto Nacional de Estadística e Informática*). 2006. "Encuesta Nacional de Hogares Annual 2004-2006." Lima, Peru.

International Telecommunications Union. 2006. "World Telecommunication/ICT Indicators Database." CD-Rom, 10th edition., Geneva: ITU.

Izaguirre A. K., and G. Rao. 2000. "Private Infrastructure: Private Activity Fell by 30 Percent in 1999." *Private Sector* (September): 5–8.

Jamasb, T., R. Mota, D. Newbery, and M. Pollitt. 2005. "Electricity Sector Reform in Developing Countries: A Survey of Empirical Evidence on Determinants and Performance." Policy Research Working Paper No. 3549, World Bank, Washington, DC.

Joskow, P. 2003. "Electricity Sector Restructuring and Competition: Lessons Learned." *Cuadernos de Economía* 40 (121): 548–58.

Kumbhakar, S., and L. Hjalmarsson. 1998. "Relative Performance of Public and Private Ownership under Yardstick Competition: Electricity Retail Distribution." *European Economic Review* 42 (1): 97–122.

La Porta, R., and F. López-de-Silanes. 1999. "Benefits of Privatization—Evidence from Mexico." *Quarterly Journal of Economics* 114 (4): 1193–242.

Latinobarómetro. 1998. Latinobarómetro Survey Data. Corporación Latinobarómetro: Santiago, Chile.

————. 2004. Latinobarómetro Survey Data. Corporación Latinobarómetro: Santiago, Chile.

Laurin, C., and Y. Bozec. 2001. "Privatization and Productivity Improvement: The Case of Canadian National (CN)." *Transportation Research: Part E: Logistics and Transportation Review* 37 (5): 355–74.

Lee, K. S., A. Anas, and G.-T. Oh. 1996. "Cost of Infrastructure Deficiencies in Manufacturing in Indonesia, Nigeria, and Thailand." Policy Research Working Paper No. 1604, World Bank, Washington, DC.

López-de-Silanes, F. 1997. "Determinants of Privatization Prices." *Quarterly Journal of Economics* 112 (4): 965–1025.

Lora, E., and U. Panizza. 2002. "Structural Reform in Latin America under Scrutiny." Research Department Working Paper No. 470, Inter-American Development Bank, Washington, DC.

Manzetti, L., ed. 2000. *Regulatory Policy in Latin America: Post-Privatization Realities.* Miami, FL: University of Miami, North-South Press Center.

Martimort, D., and S. Straub. 2005. "The Political Economy of Private Participation, Social Discontent and Regulatory Governance." Background paper commissioned for *Infrastructure in Latin America and the Caribbean: Recent Developments and Key Challenges.* Inter-American Development Bank, Washington, DC.

McKenzie, D., and D. Mookherjee. 2003. "The Distributive Impact of Privatization in Latin America: Evidence from Four Countries." *Economia* 3 (2): 161–233.

Megginson, W., R. Nash, and M. van Randenborgh. 1994. "The Financial and Operating Performance of Newly Privatized Firms: An International Empirical Analysis." *Journal of Finance* 49 (2): 403–52.

Megginson, W., and J. Netter. 2001. "From State to Market: A Survey of Empirical Studies on Privatization." *Journal of Economic Literature* 39 (2): 321–89.

Ménard, C., and G. Clarke. 2000. "A Transitory Regime Water Supply in Conakry, Guinea." Policy Research Paper No. 2362, World Bank, Washington, DC.

Millan, J., E. Lora, and A. Micco. 2001. "Sustainability of the Electricity Sector Reforms in Latin America." Research Department IDB-IIC 42nd Annual Meeting, "Towards Competitiveness: The Institutional Path." Inter-American Development Bank, Washington, DC.

Moguillansky, G. 1997. "La Gestión Privada y la Inversión en el Sector Eléctrico Chileno." *Serie Reformas Económicas.* Vol. 1. United Nations Economic Commission for Latin America.

Mueller, B. 2001. "Institutions for Commitment in the Brazilian Regulatory System." *Quarterly Review of Economics and Finance* 41 (5): 621–43.

Nellis, J. 2003. "Privatization in Latin America." Working Paper No. 31, Center for Global Development, Washington, DC.

Nellis, J., and N. Birdsall, eds. 2005. *Reality Check: The Distributional Impact of Privatization in Developing Countries.* Washington, DC: Center for Global Development.

Newbery, D. M., and M. G. Pollitt. 1997. "The Restructuring and Privatisation of Britain's CEGB: Was It Worth It?" *Journal of Industrial Economics* 45 (3): 269–303.

Okten, C., and P. Arin. 2003. "How Does Privatization Affect Efficiency, Productivity and Technological Choice? Evidence from Turkey." Louisiana State University, Baton Rouge.

OLADE (Organización Latinoamericana de Energía). 1996. "Energía y Desarrollo en América Latina y el Caribe: Síntesis del Estudio de caso sobre Chile." Quito, Ecuador: OLADE.

Paredes, R. M. 2003. "Redistributive Impact of Privatization and Regulation of Utilities in Chile." In C. Ugaz and C. Waddams Price, eds., *Utility Privatization and Regulation: A Fair Deal for Consumers?* 234–56. Cheltenham, U.K.: Edward Elgar.

Petrazzini, B. A., and T. H. Clark. 1996. "Costs and Benefits of Telecommunications Liberalization in Developing Countries." Paper presented at the conference "Liberalizing Telecommunications, Institute for International Economics," Washington, DC, January 29.

Plane, P. 1999. "Privatization, Technical Efficiency and Welfare Consequences: The Case of the Côte d'Ivoire Electricity Company (CIE)." *World Development* 27 (2): 343–60.

Public Works Financing. 1995, 1998, 2003. "International Major Projects Survey."

Ramamurti, R. 1996. *Privatizing Monopolies: Lessons from the Telecommunications and Transport Sector in Latin America.* Baltimore, MD: Johns Hopkins University Press.

Reinikka, E., and J. Svensson. 2002. "Coping with Poor Public Capital." *Journal of Development Economics* 69 (1): 51–69.

Ros, A. 1999. "Does Ownership or Competition Matter? The Effects of Telecommunications Reform on the Network Expansion and Efficiency." *Journal of Regulatory Economics* 15 (1): 65–92.

Ros, A., and A. Banerjee. 2000. "Telecommunications Privatization and Tariff Rebalancing: Evidence from Latin America." *Telecommunications Policy* 24 (3): 233–52.

Rossi, M. 2004. "Ownership and Efficiency: Evidence from Latin American Electric Utilities." University of Oxford, Oxford, U.K.

Saal, D. S., and D. Parker. 2001. "Productivity and Price Performance in the Privatized Water and Sewerage Companies of England and Wales." *Journal of Regulatory Economics* 20 (1): 61–90.

Shirley, M. 2004. "Why Is Sector Reform So Unpopular in Latin America." Ronald Coase Institute Working Paper No. 4, St. Louis, MO.

Sirtaine, S., M. E. Pinglo, J. L. Guasch, and V. Foster. 2005. "How Profitable Are Private Infrastructure Concessions in Latin America? Empirical Evidence and Regulatory Implications." *Quarterly Review of Economics and Finance* 45 (2–3): 380–402.

Spiller, P. T. 1993. "Institutions and Regulatory Commitment in Utilities' Privatization." *Industrial and Corporate Change* 2 (3): 387–450.

Straub, S. 2008a. "Infrastructure and Growth in Developing Countries: Recent Advances and Research Challenges." Policy Research Working Paper No. 4460, World Bank, Washington, DC.

———. 2008b. "Infrastructure and Development: A Critical Appraisal of the Macro Level Literature Policy Research Working Paper No. 4590, World Bank, Washington, DC.

TCS (*Tele Centro Sul*). 2002. Securities and Exchange Commission Form 20-F filed by Tele Centro Sul of Brazil for Fiscal Year Ending December 31, 2002. Brasilia, Brazil.

Thomas, D., and J. Strauss. 1992. "Prices, Infrastructure, Household Characteristics and Child Height." *Journal of Development Economics* 39 (2): 301–31.

Torero, M., and A. Pascó-Font. 2001. "The Social Impact of Privatization and Regulation of Utilities in Peru." WIDER Discussion Paper 20001/17, United Nations University, World Institute for Development Economics Research, Helsinki. In C. Ugaz and C. Waddams Price, eds., *Utility Privatization and Regulation: A Fair Deal for Consumers?* Cheltenham, U.K. Edward Elgar.

Torero, M., E. Schroth, and A. Pascó-Font. 2003. "The Impact of Telecommunications Privatization in Peru on the Welfare of Urban Consumers." *Economia: Journal of the Latin American and Caribbean Economic Association* 4 (1): 99–128.

van den Berg, C., and Y. Katakura. 2004. "Winners and Losers in Argentina's Water Utility Reform: An Analytic and Economic Financial Framework." Finance, Private Sector and Infrastructure Department, Latin America and Caribbean Region, World Bank, Washington, DC.

Wallsten, S. 2001. "An Econometric Analysis of Telecom Competition, Privatization, and Regulation in Africa and Latin America." *Journal of Industrial Economics* 49 (1): 1–19.

Wooldridge, J. 2002. *Econometric Analysis of Cross Section and Panel Data.* Cambridge, MA: MIT Press.

World Bank. 1994. *World Development Report 1994: Infrastructure for Development.* New York: Oxford University Press.

————. 2003. *Private Participation in Infrastructure: Trends in Developing Countries in 1990/01.* Washington, DC: Public Private Infrastructure Advisory Facility and World Bank.

————. 2004a. *Global Development Finance.* Washington, DC: World Bank.

————. 2004b. *World Development Report 2005: A Better Investment Climate for Everyone.* Washington, DC: World Bank and Oxford University Press.

————. 2004c. *Colombia: Recent Economic Developments in Infrastructure (REDI).* Washington, DC: World Bank.

————. 2006. "Peru: Rethinking Private Sector Participation in Infrastructure: Towards Effective Public Private Partnerships/Concessions in the Provision of Infrastructure Services." Report No. 32674/PE, World Bank, Washington, DC.

————. 2007a. "Private Participation in Infrastructure Project (PPI) Database." World Bank, Washington, DC. http://ppi.worldbank.org/.

————. 2007b. Public-Private Infrastructure Advisory Facility (PPIAF) Working Database. Derived from the PPI Database. World Bank, Washington, DC. http://ppiaf.org.

————. 2007c. "Energy Sector—Retrospective Review and Challenges." ESMAP Study, Latin America and the Caribbean Region. World Bank, Washington, DC.

————. 2007d. World Development Indicators Database. Washington, DC: World Bank.

————. 2008. "Benchmarking Analysis of the Electricity Distribution Sector in the Latin American and Caribbean Region." World Bank, Washington, DC.

Wu, D. M. 1973. "Alternative Tests of Independence between Stochastic Regressors and Disturbance." *Econometrica* 42 (3): 529–46.

Zhang, Y., D. Parker, and C. Kirkpatrick. 2002. "Electricity Sector Reform in Developing Countries: An Econometric Assessment of the Effects of Privatisation, Competition and Regulation." Working Paper RP0216, Aston Business School, Birmingham, U.K.

Index

Boxes, figures, and tables are indicated by "b," "f," and "t," following the page numbers.

A

access to services, 46, 50–54
accounting, 231
Agencia Nacional de Energia
    Eléctrica (ANEEL), 88
airports, 19, 42n8
ANEEL. *See* Agencia Nacional de
    Energia Eléctrica (ANEEL)
Argentina
    electricity sector, 86t5.4, 87,
        115n3
    literature review of studies,
        243tA1.1
    summary of power reforms in,
        304–06tA4.1
    utility companies in, 315–16tA5
Asociación Iberoamericana de
    Entidades Reguladores de
    Energía (ARIAE), 66
asset ownership, impact of reforms
    on, 46–47, 53t3.1

B

benchmarking study, for electricity,
    60, 65–67
Bolivia
    electricity sector, 86t5.4, 87–88
    summary of power market
        reforms in, 307–09tA4.1
    utility companies in, 316tA5

Bolivian Company of Electrical
    Energy (COBEE), 87–88
BOO. *See* build-own-operate
    (BOO) contracts
BOT. *See* build-operate-transfer
    (BOT) contracts
Brazil
    electricity sector, 88
    private sector investment in,
        13, 15
    summary of power reforms in,
        304–06tA4.1
    Telebras, 120, 149
    telecommunications sector,
        135–36
    utility companies in,
        316–17tA5
    water sector, 173–74
build-operate-transfer (BOT)
    contracts, 22,
    41–42n6, 44
build-own-operate (BOO)
    contracts, 22f2.10,
    41–42n6

C

Caribbean Community
    (CARICOM), 80–81
cellular telephone services, 149–50,
    151n2, 284–85tA3.8

Central Europe, 208, 240–41
child mortality, 10
Chile
  literature review of studies,
    244*t*A1.1
  private investment in, 15
  privatization of electricity sector,
    85, 86*t*5.4, 114–15*n*1
  summary of power reforms in,
    304–6*t*A4.1
  telecommunications sector,
    138–39
  utility companies in, 318*t*A5
CHILECTRA, 85
CIER. *See* Comisión de Integración
    Energética Regional
    (CIER)
COBEE. *See* Bolivian Company of
    Electrical Energy (COBEE)
coefficients, 73, 77*n*16, 149,
    280*t*A3.6
Colombia
  summary of power reforms in,
    304–6*t*A4.1
  utility companies in, 318*t*A5
Comisión de Integración Energética
    Regional (CIER), 66
communications, 230, 236
  See also telecommunications
    sector
Compañia de Teléfonos de Chile
    (CTC), 119–20, 151*n*2
competition
  and concession contracts,
    24–25
  electricity sector, 80–85
  telecommunications sector,
    118–20, 144, 149–50,
    152*n*14, 282–83*t*A3.7,
    284–85*t*A3.8
concession contracts, 22–25, 48, 154
  design of, 223–35, 237*n*1
  electricity sector, 85
  public perception of, 39*b*2.2
  renegotiation of, 30–32
  See also contracts
conflict resolution, 231, 236

connections
  for electricity sector, 90, 91*t*5.5,
    93–95, 113*t*5.11, 115*n*79,
    187, 189*f*8.2, 191*f*8.3,
    201*f*8.11
  labor productivity and
    efficiency summary,
    91*t*5.5, 101–06, 113*t*5.11,
    187, 190, 199, 211
  PSP study findings, 224
  literature review of, 242
  and regulatory and contract
    variables
    autonomy of regulatory body,
      211, 213*t*9.3
    contract award criteria, 216,
      218*t*9.6
    duration of regulatory body
      appointments, 212,
      214*t*9.4
    tariff regulations, 218–19,
      220*t*9.7, 221
  for telecommunications,
    121*t*6.3, 122–24,
    128–29, 131–36, 150*t*6.9,
    151–52*n*4, 152*n*8
  for water and sewerage sectors,
    158*t*7.3, 159–61, 163*f*7.4,
    163*t*7.4, 170*f*7.9,
    171*f*7.10, 174*t*7.7,
    183*t*7.10, 298*t*A3.12
consumer welfare, impact of reform
    on, 50–54
contracts
  design of, 233–35, 237*n*1
  econometric analysis of, 65*t*4.3,
    73–74, 255–57,
    300–301*t*A3.13
  and regulatory and contract
    variables
    autonomy of regulatory body,
      211–12, 213*t*9.3, 220–21
    award criteria, 215–18, 221
    changes disaggregated by,
      300–01*t*A3.13
    data sets, 60, 65*t*4.3,
      76–77*nn*4–9

duration of regulatory body
appointments, 212–14, 221
impact of sale method on
output, 209–11, 220
and tariff regulations,
218–19, 220*t*9.7, 221
renegotiation and violations
of, 231
See also concession contracts
Corporación de Fomento de la
Producción (CORFO), 85,
119–20, 151*n*2
corporate crises, and capital
flows, 11
corruption, 36–37*b*2.1, 38–39*b*2.2
Costa Rica, 7, 8*f*2.1, 310–14*t*A4.1
costs
cost recovery, 226
and inventories, 7–8
coverage
electricity sector, 90–98,
113*t*5.11, 115*nn*6–7, 187,
188*f*8.1, 268*t*A3.3
growth analysis of,
264–67*t*A3.2
levels analysis of, 260–
63*t*A3.1
impact of reforms on, 46,
53*f*3.6, 54*t*3.1
PSP study findings concerning,
225–26
and regulatory and contract
variables
autonomy of regulatory body,
211, 213*t*9.3
contract award criteria, 217,
218*t*9.6
duration of regulatory body
appointments, 212,
214*t*9.4
nationality of investors,
214–15, 216*t*9.5, 221
tariff regulations, 219,
220*t*9.7
telecommunications sector,
121*t*6.3, 122–29, 150*t*6.9,
151–52*nn*4–6

growth analysis of,
275–79*t*A3.5
levels analysis of,
270–74*t*A3.4
water and sewerage sectors,
157–65, 166*t*7.5,
167*f*7.6, 183*t*7.10,
298*t*A3.12
growth analysis of,
293–97*t*A3.11
levels analysis of,
288–92*t*A3.10
CTC. *See* Compañía de Teléfonos
de Chile (CTC)
currency devaluations, 30, 107

D

data and data sets, 3
contract and regulatory
characteristics, 60, 65*t*4.3,
76–77*nn*4–9
electricity sector, 60, 65–67, 90,
115*n*4
overview, 58, 76*n*1
performance indicators, 58–60,
61–62*t*4.1, 63–64*t*4.2,
76*nn*2–3
PPIAF, 42*n*13
PPI database, 17*f*2.8
regulatory and contract data
matched with performance
data, 207, 222*n*1
sources of, 66
telecommunications sector,
58–60, 61–62*t*4.1,
63–64*t*4.2, 76*nn*2–3,
120–21
water and sewerage sectors, 3,
155, 157, 158*t*7.3
World Bank's PPI, 17*f*2.8, 41*n*4,
41–42*n*6
World Wide Web as source, 66
developing countries
impact of infrastructure on, 1–2
literature review of privatization
in, 246–49*t*A1.1

PPI in, 10–11, 41*n*4
distributional losses, 210
   in electricity sector, 91*t*5.5,
      102, 104–06, 115*t*5.1,
      260–63*t*A3.1
      operating performance, 190,
         193*f*8.5, 203, 204*n*8.13
      PSP study findings, 225,
         226, 227
      and regulatory and contract
         variables
         autonomy of regulatory body,
            211–12, 213*t*9.3
         contract award criteria, 217,
            218*t*9.6
         duration of regulatory board
            appointments, 213,
            214*t*9.4
         nationality of investors,
            214–15, 216*t*9.5
         tariff regulations, 219,
            220*t*9.7
   in water and sewerage sectors,
      158*t*7.3, 171–73, 174*t*7.7,
      183*t*7.10
distribution of services, impact of
   reform on, 50–54
divestitures, 23, 25–26, 40
Dominican Republic, 307–9*t*A4.1

E

East Asia and Pacific (EAP)
      countries, 12–13, 20,
      21*t*2.1
ECA. *See* Europe and Central Asia
   (ECA)
ECLAC. *See* Economic Commission
   for Latin America and the
   Caribbean (ECLAC)
econometric analysis, 208–09
   electricity sector, 90–98
      electricity distribution,
         268–69*t*A3.3
      employment summary,
         91*t*5.5, 98–101, 113*t*5.11,
         115*nn*8–11

labor productivity and
      efficiency summary,
      91*t*5.5, 101–06, 107*t*5.8,
      111*n*12, 113*t*5.11
   price summary, 91*t*5.5,
      106–09, 110*t*5.9,
      113*t*5.11, 115*nn*13–14
   quality summary, 91*t*5.5,
      109–14, 115*nn*15–16
endogeneity, 74–76, 257–58
equations used in, 253–58,
      258*n*1
estimations, 256–57
overview, 71, 73–76, 77*n*16
regulatory and contract
      variables, 255–57
telecommunications sector,
      121*t*6.3, 122–29,
      151–52*nn*4–6,
      280–81*t*A3.6
   employment summary,
      121*t*6.3, 129–31, 132*t*6.5,
      150*t*6.9, 152*n*7
   and instrumental variables,
      286–87*f*A3.9
   labor productivity and
      efficiency summary,
      121*t*6.3, 131–38, 150*t*6.9,
      152*n*8
   liberalization and competition
      summary, 119*t*6.2, 144,
      148–50, 151, 152*nn*10–12,
      152*n*14, 282–83*t*A3.7
   mobile competition, 284–
      85*t*A3.8
   price summary, 121*t*6.3,
      138–41, 142*f*6.16,
      143*t*6.7, 144*f*6.17,
      145*f*6.18, 146*f*6.19,
      150*t*6.9
   quality summary, 121*t*6.3,
      141, 144, 146*t*6.8,
      147*f*6.20, 148*f*6.21,
      150*t*6.9
water and sewerage sectors,
      157–65, 166*t*7.5, 167*f*7.6,
      183*t*7.10, 298–99*t*A3.12

employment summary,
158*t*7.3, 165, 168*f*7.7,
169*f*7.6, 169*f*7.8,
183*t*7.10, 184*n*2
price summary, 158*t*7.3,
173–76, 177*f*7.15,
178*t*7.8, 183*t*7.10
productivity and efficiency
summary, 158*t*7.3,
166–67, 171–73, 174*t*7.7,
183*t*7.10
quality summary, 158*t*7.3,
176, 178–80, 181*f*7.18,
182*f*7.19, 182*t*7.9,
183*t*7.10
water distribution and
sewerage, 298–99*t*A3.12
See also empirical analysis
results; means and
medians analysis
Economic Commission for
Latin America and the
Caribbean (ECLAC), 66
economic opportunities, impact of
infrastructure on, 9–10
Ecuador, summary of power market
reforms in, 310–14*t*A4.1
efficiency, 228
electricity sector, 91*t*5.5,
101–06, 107*t*5.8, 111*n*12,
113*t*5.11
growth analysis, 264–
67*t*A3.2
levels analysis, 260–63*t*A3.1
improvement of, 49–50
telecommunications sector,
121*t*6.3, 132, 136–38,
150*t*6.9
growth analysis,
275–79*t*A3.5
levels analysis, 270–74*t*A3.4
water and sewerage sectors,
158*t*7.3, 166–67, 171–73,
174*t*7.7, 183*t*7.10
growth analysis,
293–97*t*A3.11
levels analysis, 288–92*t*A3.10

electricity sector, 18–19, 42*n*7, 45,
224
data sets, 3, 60, 65–67, 90,
115*n*4
econometric analysis of, 74*t*4.5,
268–69*t*A3.3
and employment, 91*t*5.5,
98–101, 113*t*5.11,
115*nn*8–11
employment in, 91*t*5.5, 98–101,
115*nn*8–11, 115*t*5.11
growth analysis, 264–67*t*A3.2
and labor productivity, 91*t*5.5,
101–06, 107*t*5.8,
113*t*5.11, 115*n*12
levels analysis of, 260–63*t*A3.1
literature review of, 241–42,
243–50*t*A1.1
methodologies used to study, 3–4
output and coverage summary,
90–98, 113*t*5.11,
115*nn*6–7, 268*t*A3.3
performance indicators and
evaluation, 58–60,
61–62*t*4.1, 63–64*t*4.2,
76*nn*2–3
coverage, 187, 188*f*8.1
labor productivity, 187, 190,
191*f*8.3, 192*f*8.4, 199,
201*f*8.11, 202*f*8.12
main findings overview,
186–87
operating performance, 190,
193*f*8.5, 203, 204*f*8.13
outputs, 187, 189*f*8.2, 199,
200*f*8.10
overview, 185, 206*n*1
quality of service, 195,
197*f*8.8, 198*f*8.9, 203,
205*f*8.14
tariffs, 190, 194*f*8.6, 195,
196*f*8.7, 206*n*2
privatization process of, 79–89,
114–15*nn*1–3
PSP in, 5*t*1.1
public finance in, 15–16
reforms in, 43–44, 50–54

summary statistics used for
sector variables,
63–64*t*4.2
trends in, 12, 13*f*2.5a
welfare gains in, 52, 53*f*3.6
See also econometric analysis;
Latin America and
the Caribbean (LAC)
countries; means and
medians analysis
Eletrobras, 88
El Salvador
summary of power reforms in,
304–06*t*A4.1
utility companies in, 318–19*t*A5
empirical analysis results
electricity sector
electricity distribution,
268–69*t*A3.3
growth analysis,
264–67*t*A3.2
levels analysis of, 260–
63*t*A3.1
regulatory and contract
variables, 300–01*t*A3.13
telecommunications sector,
280–81*t*A3.6
growth analysis,
275–79*t*A3.5
and instrumental variables,
286–87*f*A3.9
levels analysis, 270–74*f*A3.1
liberalization and
competition summary,
282–83*t*A3.7
mobile competition,
284–85*t*A3.8
water and sewerage sectors
growth analysis,
293–97*t*A3.11
levels analysis,
288–92*t*A3.10
water distribution and
sewerage, 298–99*t*A3.12
See also econometric analysis;
means and medians
analysis

employment
electricity sector, 91*t*5.5,
98–101, 113*t*5.11,
115*nn*8–11
impact of reform in utilities
service on, 44–45, 53*t*3.1
PSP study findings concerning,
224
and regulatory and contract
variables
autonomy of regulatory body,
211, 213*t*9.3
contract award criteria, 217,
218*t*9.6
duration of regulatory body
appointments, 212,
214*t*9.4
nationality of investors,
214–15, 216*t*9.5
tariff regulations, 219,
220*t*9.7
telecommunications sector,
121*t*6.3, 129–31, 132*t*6.5,
150*t*6.9, 152*n*7
water and sewerage sectors,
158*t*7.3, 165, 168*f*7.7,
169*f*7.8, 169*t*7.6,
183*t*7.10, 184*n*2
Empresa Nacional de Electricidad
S.A. (ENDESA), 85
Empresa Nacional de
Telecomunicaciones
(ENTel), 120
Empresa Social Eléctrica de Buenos
Aires (ESEBA), 87, 115*n*2
ENDE. *See* National Enterprise of
Electricity (ENDE)
ENDESA. *See* Empresa Nacional
de Electricidad S.A.
(ENDESA)
endogeneity, 74–76, 257–58
energy sector
energy per employee, 91*t*5.5,
102, 113*t*5.11
and investor types, 26–27
PPI in, 17–18, 41*n*6
See also electricity sector

energy sold, 90–93, 97, 113*t*5.11,
115*n*6, 187, 189*f*8.2
output and coverage, 97, 98*t*5.6
per employee, 101–02, 106,
192*f*8.4
public vs. private, 199,
200*f*8.10, 202*f*8.12
ENTel. *See* Empresa Nacional
de Telecomunicaciones
(ENTel)
ESEBA. *See* Empresa Social
Eléctrica de Buenos Aires
(ESEBA)
estimations, 256–57
Europe and Central Asia (ECA),
11, 20, 21*t*2.1
evaluation, 236–37
exclusivity periods, 120, 151*n*3

F

Feasible Generalized Least
Square (FGLS), 73, 76,
255
financial equilibrium, 231
financial solvency, 49–50, 54*t*3.1
fiscal flows, impact of
infrastructure reforms on,
48–49, 54*t*3.1, 230
fixed-line telecommunications, 19,
42*n*9
data analysis, 120–21
econometric analysis of,
280–81*t*A3.6
and instrumental variables,
286–87*f*A3.9
and liberalization,
282–83*t*A3.7
and mobile competition,
284–85*t*A3.8
employment summary, 121*t*6.3,
129–31, 132*t*6.5, 150*t*6.9,
152*n*7
growth analysis, 275–79*t*A3.5
labor productivity and efficiency,
121*t*6.3, 131–38, 150*t*6.9,
152*n*8

levels analysis, 270–74*t*A3.4
liberalization and competition
summary, 119–20,
124*t*6.2, 144, 147–50,
152*n*14, 282–83*t*A3.7
output and coverage summary,
121*t*6.3, 122–29, 150*t*6.9,
151–52*nn*4–6
performance indicators data
sets, 58–60, 61–62*t*4.1,
63–64*t*4.2, 76*nn*2–3
price summary, 121*t*6.3, 138–
41, 142*f*6.16, 143*t*6.7,
144*f*6.17, 145*f*6.18,
146*f*6.19, 150*t*6.9
privatization process, 118–21,
151*nn*1–3
quality of services, 121*t*6.3,
141, 144, 146*t*6.8,
147*f*6.20, 148*f*6.21,
150*t*6.9
trends in, 12, 14*f*2.5b
See also telecommunications
sector
foreign investors, 30

G

GDP. *See* gross domestic product
(GDP)
Generalized Least Square (GLS)
model, 257
generation sector, 18–19, 85
gigawatt hours (GWh), 93*f*5.2,
307*t*A4.1
GLS. *See* Generalized Least Square
(GLS) model
governments
and infrastructure service
delivery, 232
and modal distribution of PPI,
21, 23, 23*t*2.2
greenfield projects, 18, 23, 25–26,
41–42*n*6, 42*n*12
gross domestic product (GDP), 2
cross-regional gaps in, 7
and inventory costs, 7–8

PPI as share of, 19, 40, 42n15
rate of, 242
growth
   electricity sector
      electricity distribution,
         268–69tA3.3
      means and medians analysis
         of distribution,
         264–67tA3.2
      and infrastructure, 1–2, 7,
         8f2.1, 41n1
      telecommunications sector,
         275–79tA3.5
      water and sewerage sectors,
         293–97tA3.11
Guatemala
   summary of power market
      reforms in, 307–09tA4.1
   utility companies in, 319tA5
GWh. *See* gigawatt hours (GWh)

H

Honduras, summary of power
   market reforms in,
   310–14tA4.1
household earnings, impact of access
   to services on, 50–51

I

IEA. *See* International Energy
   Agency (IEA)
incomplete calls, 132, 136–38,
   150t6.9, 280tA3.6
   as efficiency variable, 121t6.3,
      135t6.6, 150t6.9
   growth analysis of, 276tA3.5
   levels analysis of, 271tA3.4
   and liberalization, 282tA3.7
independent power producers
   (IPPs), 43, 80–81
infrastructure, 1–2
   financing of, 19–21
   investment in by region, 12,
      12f2.4
   linked to growth, 7, 8f2.1, 41n1

literature review of privatization
   of, 239–50, 251nn1–3
operation and maintenance of,
   21–26, 42n12
reforms of, 48–49, 54t3.1, 230
sectoral distribution of projects,
   17–19, 17f2.8,
   41–42nn6–9
trends in financing of, 10–17,
   41nn4–5
and unit costs, 7–8
See also investments in
   infrastructure; private
   participation in
   infrastructure (PPI);
   specific sector
inputs
   electricity sector, 260–63tA3.1,
      264–67tA3.2
   telecommunications sector,
      270–74tA3.4,
      275–79tA3.5
   water and sewerage sectors,
      288–92tA3.10,
      293–97tA3.11
installations charges, 139,
   145f6.18, 146f6.19,
   150t6.9
institutions, and privatization
   programs, 233
instrumental variables (IVs),
   75–76, 257–58,
   286–87fA3.9
See also variables
Integrated Records and Information
   System (IRIS), 66
internal rate of return (IRR), 47,
   48f3.1
International Energy Agency
   (IEA), 66
International Telecommunication
   Union (ITU), 59, 122
interruptions of services, 91t5.5,
   110–14, 115nn15–16,
   195, 197f8.8, 198f8.9,
   203, 205f8.14
PSP study findings, 225, 226

inventories, and unit costs, 7–8
investments in infrastructure, 2, 12, 12*f*2.4
    canceled or distressed, 30, 31*t*2.3
    investment plans link to contract awards, 215–18
    in LAC, 15–17, 19–21
    See also private participation in infrastructure (PPI)
investors
    impact of reforms on, 47, 48*f*3.1, 54*t*3.1
    nationality of, 214–15, 216*t*9.5, 221
    sectoral variation by investor type, 26–27, 28, 29*f*2.15, 42*n*13
IPPs. *See* independent power producers (IPPs)
IRIS. *See* Integrated Records and Information System (IRIS)
IRR. *See* internal rate of return (IRR)
ITU. *See* International Telecommunication Union (ITU)
IVs. *See* instrumental variables (IVs)

K

Korea, Republic of, PPI as share of GDP in, 40, 42*n*15

L

labor productivity. *See* productivity
Latin America and the Caribbean (LAC) countries, 9, 13
    data sets for analysis of
        for contract and regulatory characteristics, 60, 65*t*4.3, 76–77*nn*4–9
        electricity sector, 60, 65–67, 90, 115*n*4

performance indicators, 58–60, 61–62*t*4.1, 63–64*t*4.2, 76*nn*2–3
        telecommunications sector, 120–21
        water and sewerage sectors, 155, 157, 158*t*7.3
    electricity sector
        impact on employment, 91*t*5.5, 98–101, 113*t*5.11, 115*nn*8–11
        impact on labor productivity and efficiency, 91*t*5.5, 101–06, 107*t*5.8, 111*n*12, 113*t*5.11
        prices summary, 91*t*5.5, 106–09, 110*t*5.9, 113*t*5.11, 115*nn*13–14
        privatization process of, 79–89, 90, 114–15*nn*1–4
        quality summary, 91*t*5.5, 109–14, 115*nn*15–16
    investment in infrastructure, 2, 15–17
    methodologies of privatization study
        distinguishing levels from trends, 68, 70, 77*n*11
        transition vs. long-run effects, 67–68, 69*f*4.2
    PPI in, 2, 12, 13, 41*n*5
        geographic distribution of, 19–21
        by investor type, 26, 28, 29*f*2.15, 42*n*13
        limitations of, 30–35
        modal distribution of, 23–26, 27*f*2.13, 42*n*12
        public opinion against, 32–35, 36–37*b*2.1, 38–39*b*2.2
        sectoral distribution of, 17*f*2.8, 18–19, 41–42*nn*6–9
        as share of GDP, 40, 42*n*15
    summary of power market reforms, 304–14*t*A4.1

telecommunications sector,
    17–18, 19, 41*n*6
  data analysis, 120–21
  labor productivity and
    efficiency summary,
    121*t*6.3, 131–38, 150*t*6.9,
    152*n*8
  liberalization and
    competition summary,
    119*t*6.2, 124*t*6.2, 144,
    147–50, 151, 152*nn*10–
    14, 282–83*t*A3.7
  outputs and coverage
    summary, 121*t*6.3, 122–
    29, 150*t*6.9, 151–52*nn*4–6
  price summary, 121*t*6.3,
    138–41, 142*f*6.16,
    143*t*6.7, 144*f*6.17,
    145*f*6.18, 146*f*6.19,
    150*t*6.9
  privatization process,
    118–21, 151*nn*1–3
  quality summary, 121*t*6.3,
    141, 144, 146*t*6.8,
    147*f*6.20, 148*f*6.21,
    150*t*6.9
water and sewerage sectors
  employment summary,
    158*t*7.3, 165, 168*f*7.7,
    169*f*7.6, 169*f*7.8,
    183*t*7.10, 184*n*2
  outputs and coverage
    summary, 153–65,
    166*t*7.5, 167*t*7.6,
    183*t*7.10, 298*t*A3.12
  price summary, 158*t*7.3,
    173–76, 177*f*7.15,
    178*t*7.8, 183*t*7.10
  privatization process,
    153–55, 156–57*t*7.2
  productivity and efficiency
    summary, 158*t*7.3,
    166–67, 171–73, 174*t*7.7,
    183*t*7.10
  quality summary, 158*t*7.3,
    176, 178–80, 181*f*7.18,
    182*f*7.19, 182*t*7.9,
    183*t*7.10

liberalization
  PSP study findings, 226
  See also reforms; *specific sector*
LIBOR. *See* London Interbank
    Offered Rate (LIBOR)
literature review
  and details of econometric
    framework, 253–58, 258*n*1
  impact of reform
    on access to services and
      coverage, 46, 53*f*3.6,
      54*t*3.1
    on asset ownership, 46–47,
      54*t*3.1
    on employment and wages,
      44–45, 53*t*3.1
    on fiscal flows, 48–49, 54*t*3.1
    on investors, 47, 48*f*3.1,
      54*t*3.1
    on prices of services, 45,
      53*f*3.6, 53*t*3.1
    on productivity and financial
      solvency, 49–50, 54*t*3.1
    on quality of services, 45–46,
      53*t*3.1
    on utilities service, 44–45,
      53*t*3.1
  of infrastructure privatization,
    239–50, 251*nn*1–3
logistics costs, 8–9, 9*f*2.2
London Interbank Offered Rate
    (LIBOR), 89
long-distance telecommunications
    market, 118–19

M

market-oriented reform, in
    electricity sector, 80–85
means and medians analysis
  electricity sector, 61–62*t*4.1,
    63–64*t*4.2
  growth analysis,
    264–67*t*A3.2
  impact on employment,
    91*t*5.5, 98–101,
    113*t*5.11, 115*nn*8–11,
    115*n*16

impact on labor productivity
and efficiency, 91t5.5,
101–06, 107t5.8, 111n12,
113t5.11
levels analysis, 260–63tA3.1
output and coverage, 90–98,
113t5.11, 115nn6–7,
260–63tA3.1, 264–
67fA3.2, 268tA3.3
quality summary, 91t5.5,
109–14, 115nn15–16
overview, 70–71, 72t4.4,
77nn13–14
telecommunications sector,
121t6.3, 122–29,
151–52nn4–6, 270–
74tA3.4, 275–79tA3.5
cellular telephone service,
149–50, 284tA3.8
employment summary,
121t6.3, 129–31, 132t6.5,
150t6.9, 152n7
growth analysis,
275–79tA3.5
labor productivity and
efficiency summary,
121t6.3, 131–38, 150t6.9,
152n8
levels analysis, 270–74fA3.4
liberalization and
competition summary,
119t6.2, 124t6.2, 144,
147–50, 151, 152nn10–
14, 282–83tA3.7
price summary, 121t6.3, 138–
41, 142f6.16, 143t6.7,
144f6.17, 145f6.18,
146f6.19, 150t6.9
quality summary, 121t6.3,
141, 144, 146t6.8,
147f6.20, 148f6.21,
150t6.9
variables, 61–62t4.1, 63–
64t4.2
water and sewerage sectors,
157–65, 166t7.5, 167f7.6,
183t7.10, 288–92tA3.10,
293–97tA3.11, 298tA3.12

employment summary,
158t7.3, 165, 168f7.7,
169f7.6, 169f7.8,
183t7.10, 184n2
growth analysis, 293–
97tA3.11
levels analysis, 288–92tA3.10
price summary, 158t7.3,
173–76, 177f7.15,
178t7.8, 183t7.10
productivity and efficiency
summary, 158t7.3,
166–67, 171–73, 174t7.7,
183t7.10
quality summary, 158t7.3,
176, 178–80, 181f7.18,
182f7.19, 182t7.9,
183t7.10
variables, 61–62t4.1, 63–
64t4.2
megawatt hours of energy
(MWhs), 90, 91t5.5,
92f5.1, 93, 113t5.11,
189f8.2
increase in, 190, 192f8.4
output and coverage, 98t5.6
and prices, 90, 91t5.5,
109, 195
PSP study findings, 226
and reforms, 307tA4.1
See also energy sold
MENA. *See* Middle East and
North Africa (MENA)
countries
Merchant projects, 41–42n6
methodologies
contribution of, 223–24
description, 3–4
to evaluate impact of
privatization
distinguishing levels from
trends, 68, 70, 77n11
transition vs. long-run effects,
67–68, 69f4.2
See also econometric analysis;
empirical analysis results;
means and medians
analysis

Mexico
    literature review of privatization
        in, 241–42, 243–50tA1.1
    summary of power market
        reforms in, 310–14tA4.1
    telecommunications sector, 131
Middle East and North Africa
    (MENA) countries, 9,
    21t2.1
minutes consumed per year, 121t6.3,
    124–26, 128–29, 131–36,
    150t6.9, 152n5, 152n8
mobile telecommunications, 19,
    42n9, 150
    competition of providers,
        123t6.1, 149–50,
        152nn13–14, 284–85tA3.8
monitoring, 236–37
monopolies, 24–25, 80, 81t5.1

N

National Enterprise of Electricity
    (ENDE), 87–88
National Telecommunications
    Company, 120
network digitization, 141, 150t6.9
network expansion, 124
Nicaragua, 245tA1.1
    summary of power market
        reforms in, 307–09tA4.1
    utility companies in, 319tA5

O

OECD. See Organisation for
    Economic Co-operation
    and Development (OECD)
    countries
OfWAT. See Water Services
    Regulation Authority
    (OfWAT)
OLADE. See Organización
    Latinoamericana de
    Energiá (OLADE)
OLS. See Ordinary Least Square
    (OLS)

Operador Nacional do Sistema
    Elétrico (ONS), 88
Ordinary Least Square (OLS), 73,
    256–57, 258
Organisation for Economic
    Co-operation and
    Development (OECD)
    countries, 8–9, 246tA1.1
Organismo Supervisor de
    Inversión en Energiá
    (OSINERG), 88
Organización Latinoamericana de
    Energia (OLADE), 59
OSINERG. See Organismo
    Supervisor de Inversión en
    Energia (OSINERG)
outcomes
    indicators of, 59–60, 61–62t4.1,
        63–64t4.2
    See also productivity
outputs
    electricity sector, 90–98,
        113t5.11, 115nn6–7, 187,
        189f8.2, 199, 200f8.10,
        268tA3.3
    means and medians analysis
        of, 260–63tA3.1, 264–
        67tA3.2
    PSP study findings, 226
    and regulatory and contract
        variables
        autonomy of regulatory body,
            211, 213t9.3
        contract award criteria, 216,
            218t9.6
        duration of regulatory body
            appointments, 212,
            214t9.4
        impact of sale method on
            output, 209–11, 220
        nationality of investors,
            214–15, 216t9.5, 221
        tariff regulations, 219,
            220t9.7
    telecommunications sector,
        121t6.3, 122–29, 150t6.9,
        151–52nn4–6

growth analysis of,
275–79*t*A3.5
levels analysis of,
270–74*t*A3.4
output indicators, 121*t*6.3,
122–29, 135
water and sewerage sectors,
157–65, 161, 166*t*7.5,
167*f*7.6, 183*t*7.10,
298*t*A3.12
growth analysis,
293–97*t*A3.11
levels analysis, 288–92*t*A3.10
ownership, link to productivity
growth, 240, 241–42

P

Panama, 245*t*A1.1
summary of power market
reforms in, 307–9*t*A4.1
utility companies in, 319*t*A5
performance
determinants of, 4–6
indicators of, 61–62*t*4.1,
63–64*t*4.2
Peru, 228
and access to markets in,
50–51
electricity sector, 87*t*5.4, 88,
89*b*5.1
impact of access to services
on household earnings,
51*f*3.3
literature review of privatization
in, 245–46*t*A1.1
public perceptions of PPI in,
38–39*b*2.2
summary of power reforms in,
304–06*t*A4.1
utility companies in, 319*t*A5
policies, considerations for private
sector participation in,
228–33
Pooled Ordinary Least Square
(POLS) estimators,
256–57, 258

postprivatization period
electricity sector
econometric analysis of
distribution, 268–69*t*A3.3
growth analysis of,
264–67*t*A3.2
impact on employment,
91*t*5.5, 98–101, 113*t*5.11,
115*nn*8–11
impact on labor productivity
and efficiency, 91*t*5.5,
101–06, 107*t*5.8,
111*n*12, 113*t*5.11,
187, 190, 191*f*8.3,
192*f*8.4, 199, 201*f*8.11,
202*f*8.12
impact on prices, 91*t*5.5,
106–09, 110*t*5.9,
113*t*5.11, 115*nn*13–14
labor productivity, 187, 190,
191*f*8.3, 192*f*8.4, 199,
201*f*8.11, 202*f*8.12
levels analysis of, 260–
63*t*A3.1
operating performance,
190, 193*f*8.5, 203,
204*f*8.13
output and coverage,
90–98, 113–14*t*5.11,
115*nn*6–7, 187, 188*f*8.1,
189*f*8.2, 199,
200*f*8.10
overview of evaluation of
performance, 185,
186–87, 206*n*1
quality of service, 91*t*5.5,
109–14, 115*nn*15–16,
195, 197*f*8.8, 198*f*8.9,
203, 205*f*8.14
tariffs, 190, 194*f*8.6, 195,
196*f*8.7, 206*n*2
literature review of performance
in, 241
methodological contributions of
performance study during,
223–24
PSP, 5*t*1.1, 224–28

and regulatory and contract
    variables
  autonomy of regulatory
    body, 211–12, 213*t*9.3,
    220–21
  award criteria, 215–18, 221
  changes disaggregated by,
    300–01*t*A3.13
  duration of regulatory body
    appointments, 212–14,
    221
  impact of sale method on
    output, 209–11, 220
  nationality of investors,
    214–15, 216*t*9.5, 221
  overview of determinants of
    impact on performance,
    207–09, 222*nn*1–2
  and tariff regulation, 218–19,
    220*t*9.7, 221
telecommunications sector
  data analysis, 120–21, 148
  econometric analysis of,
    280–81*t*A3.6
  employment summary,
    121*t*6.3, 129–31, 132*t*6.5,
    150*t*6.9, 152*n*7
  growth analysis of,
    275–79*t*A3.5
  and instrumental variables,
    286–87*f*A3.9
  labor productivity and
    efficiency summary,
    121*t*6.3, 131–38, 148,
    150*t*6.9, 152*n*8,
    282–83*t*A3.7
  levels analysis of, 270–74*t*A3.4
  liberalization and
    competition summary,
    119*t*6.2, 124*t*6.2, 144,
    147–50, 151, 152*nn*
    10–14, 282–83*t*A3.7
  mobile competition,
    284–85*t*A3.8
  output and coverage summary,
    121*t*6.3, 122–29, 150*t*6.9,
    151–52*nn*4–6

  price summary, 121*t*6.3, 138–
    41, 142*f*6.16, 143*t*6.7,
    144*f*6.17, 145*f*6.18,
    146*f*6.19, 150*t*6.9
  privatization process,
    118–21, 151*nn*1–3
  quality summary, 121*t*6.3,
    141, 144, 146*t*6.8,
    147*f*6.20, 148*f*6.21,
    150*t*6.9
transition versus long-run effects
    evaluation, 67–68, 69*f*4.2
water and sewerage sectors
  employment summary,
    158*t*7.3, 165, 168*f*7.7,
    169*f*7.6, 169*f*7.8,
    183*t*7.10, 184*n*2
  growth analysis of,
    293–97*t*A3.11
  levels analysis of,
    288–91*t*3.10
  output and coverage
    summary, 157–65,
    166*t*7.5, 167*t*7.6,
    183*t*7.10, 298*t*A3.12
  price summary, 158*t*7.3,
    173–76, 177*f*7.15,
    178*t*7.8, 183*t*7.10
  productivity and efficiency
    summary, 158*t*7.3,
    166–67, 171–73, 174*t*7.7,
    183*t*7.10
  quality summary, 158*t*7.3,
    176, 178–80, 181*f*7.18,
    182*f*7.19, 182*t*7.9,
    183*t*7.10
  water distribution and
    sewerage, 298–99*t*A3.12
potability of water, 158*t*7.3,
    178, 180, 181*f*7.18,
    182*f*7.19, 182*t*7.9,
    183*t*7.10
power markets, summary of
    reforms in, 304–14*t*A4.1
Power Purchase Agreements, 19
PPI. *See* private participation in
    infrastructure (PPI)

PPIAF. *See* Public–Private
    Infrastructure Advisory
    Facility (PPIAF)
preprivatization period
    electricity sector
        growth analysis,
            264–67tA3.2
        impact on employment,
            91t5.5, 98–101, 113t5.11,
            115nn8–11
        impact on labor productivity
            and efficiency, 91t5.5,
            101–06, 107t5.8, 111n12,
            113t5.11, 187, 190,
            191f8.3, 192f8.4, 199,
            201f8.11, 202f8.12
        impact on prices, 91t5.5,
            106–09, 110t5.9,
            113t5.11, 115nn13–14
        levels analysis of, 260–
            63tA3.1, 264–67tA3.2
        operating performance, 190,
            193f8.5, 203, 204f8.13
        output and coverage, 90–98,
            113–14t5.11, 115nn6–7,
            187, 188f8.1, 189f8.2,
            199, 200f8.10
        overview of evaluation of
            performance, 185,
            186–87, 206n1
        quality of service, 91t5.5,
            109–14, 115nn15–16,
            195, 197f8.8, 198f8.9,
            203, 205f8.14
        tariffs, 190, 194f8.6, 195,
            196f8.7, 206n2
    evaluation of, transition versus
        long-run effects, 67–68,
        69f4.2
    methodological contributions of
        performance study during,
        223–24
    PSP study findings, 224–28
    and regulatory and contract
        variables
        autonomy of regulatory body,
            211–12, 213t9.3, 220–21
        award criteria, 215–18, 221
        duration of regulatory body
            appointments, 212–14,
            221
        impact of sale method on
            output, 209–11, 220
        nationality of investors,
            214–15, 216t9.5, 221
        overview of determinants of
            impact on performance,
            207–09, 222nn1–2
        and tariff regulation, 218–19,
            220t9.7, 221
    telecommunications sector
        data analysis, 120–21
        employment summary,
            121t6.3, 129–31, 132t6.5,
            150t6.9, 152n7
        growth analysis of,
            275–79tA3.5
        labor productivity and
            efficiency summary,
            121t6.3, 131–38, 150t6.9,
            152n8
        levels analysis, 270–74fA3.4
        liberalization and
            competition summary,
            119t6.2, 144, 150,
            152n14, 282–83tA3.7
        output and coverage
            summary, 121t6.3, 122–
            29, 150t6.9, 151–52nn4–6
        price summary, 121t6.3,
            138–41, 142f6.16,
            143t6.7, 144f6.17,
            145f6.18, 146f6.19,
            150t6.9
        privatization process,
            118–21, 151nn1–3
        quality summary, 121t6.3, 141,
            144, 146t6.8, 147f6.20,
            148f6.21, 150t6.9
    water and sewerage sectors
        employment summary,
            158t7.3, 165, 168f7.7,
            169f7.6, 169f7.8,
            183t7.10, 184n2

growth analysis of,
  293–97tA3.11
levels analysis of,
  288–92tA3.10
output and coverage
  summary, 157–65,
  166t7.5, 167t7.6,
  183t7.10, 298tA3.12
price summary, 158t7.3,
  173–76, 177f7.15,
  178t7.8, 183t7.10
productivity and efficiency
  summary, 158t7.3, 166–67,
  171–73, 174t7.7, 183t7.10
quality summary, 158t7.3,
  176, 178–80, 181f7.18,
  182f7.19, 182t7.9,
  183t7.10
price-cap regulation, 218–19
prices of services, 45, 210
electricity sector
  and growth analysis,
    264–67tA3.2
  and levels analysis,
    260–63tA3.1
  summary of, 91t5.5, 106–9,
    110t5.9, 113t5.11,
    115nn13–14
impact of reform on, 45, 53f3.6,
  53t3.1
PSP study findings, 226
and regulatory and contract
  variables
  autonomy of regulatory body,
    212, 213t9.3
  contract award criteria, 217,
    218t9.6
  duration of regulatory board
    appointments, 213,
    214t9.4
  nationality of investors,
    214–15, 216t9.5
telecommunications sector,
  121t6.3, 138–41,
  142f6.16, 143t6.7,
  144f6.17, 145f6.18,
  146f6.19, 148–49, 150t6.9

and growth analysis,
  275–79tA3.5
and levels analysis,
  270–74tA3.4
water and sewerage sectors,
  158t7.3, 173–76,
  177f7.15, 178t7.8,
  183t7.10, 223
and growth analysis,
  293–97tA3.11
and levels analysis,
  288–92tA3.10
See also tariffs
private participation in
  infrastructure (PPI), 2–3,
  5t1.1, 12, 43
canceled or distressed
  investments, 30, 31t2.3
conclusions concerning, 35, 37,
  40–41
deficiencies of, 230–31
geographic distribution of,
  19–21
improving success of, 233–37
institutionality of, 233
by investor type, 26, 28,
  29f2.15, 42n13
limitations of, 28, 30–35,
  36–37b2.1, 38–39b2.2
modal distribution of, 21–26,
  42n12
public opinion against,
  32–35, 36–37b2.1,
  38–39b2.2
sectoral distribution of, 17–19,
  41–42nn6–9
trends in, 10–17, 41nn4–5
types of, 6n2
See also infrastructure;
  privatization; specific
  sector
private sector participation
  (PSP), 4
methodological contributions,
  223–24
policy considerations for,
  228–33

study findings concerning,
224–28
water sector, 155*t*7.1
private utilities, performance
evaluation of electricity
sector
coverage, 187, 188*f*8.1
labor productivity, 187, 190,
191*f*8.3, 192*f*8.4, 199,
201*f*8.11, 202*f*8.12
operating performance, 190,
193*f*8.5, 203, 204*f*8.13
outputs, 187, 189*f*8.2, 199,
200*f*8.10
overview, 185, 186–87, 206*n*1
quality of service, 195, 197*f*8.8,
198*f*8.9, 203, 205*f*8.14
privatization
Central Europe, 208
data sets for, 58, 76*n*1
contract and regulatory
characteristics, 60, 65*t*4.3,
76–77*nn*4–9
LAC electricity benchmarking
database, 60, 65–67
performance indicators,
58–60, 61–62*t*4.1,
63–64*t*4.2, 76*nn*2–3
literature review of
infrastructure
privatization, 239–50,
251*nn*1–3
methodologies to evaluate
distinguishing levels from
trends, 68, 70, 77*n*11
transition vs. long-run effects,
67–68, 69*f*4.2
Mexico, 208
and regulatory and contract
variables
autonomy of regulatory body,
211–12, 213*t*9.3, 220–21
award criteria, 215–18, 221
duration of regulatory body
appointments, 212–14, 221
impact of sale method on
output, 209–11, 220

nationality of investors,
214–15, 216*t*9.5, 221
overview of determinants of
impact on performance,
207–09, 222*nn*1–2
and tariff regulation, 218–19,
220*t*9.7, 221
See also private participation
in infrastructure (PPI);
specific sector
privatization paradox, 227–28, 229
productivity, 210
electricity sector, 187, 190,
191*f*8.3, 192*f*8.4, 199,
201*f*8.11, 202*f*8.12
econometric analysis of,
268–69*t*A3.3
impact on, 91*t*5.5, 101–06,
107*t*5.8, 111*n*12,
113*t*5.11
impact of infrastructure on,
1–2, 9
impact of reforms on, 49–50,
54*t*3.1
literature review of, 240
PSP study findings concerning,
224
and regulatory and contract
variables
autonomy of regulatory body,
211, 213*t*9.3
contract award criteria, 217,
218*t*9.6
duration of regulatory body
appointments, 212,
214*t*9.4
nationality of investors,
214–15, 216*t*9.5
tariff regulations, 219,
220*t*9.7
telecommunications sector,
121*t*6.3, 131–36, 138,
150*t*6.9, 152*n*8
econometric analysis,
280–81*t*A3.6
instrumental variables,
286–87*t*A3.9

and liberalization,
    282–83tA3.7
mobile competition,
    284–85tA3.8
water and sewerage sectors,
    158t7.3, 166–67, 171–73,
    174t7.7, 183t7.10
water distribution and
    sewerage, 298–99tA3.12
product value, logistics cost as
    share of, 8–9, 9f2.2
profits, 38b2.2, 49–50
PSP. *See* private sector participation
    (PSP)
public infrastructure investment,
    13, 15f2.6a
public opinion
against PPI in LAC, 32–35,
    36–37b2.1, 38–39b2.2
sources of, 228
Public–Private Infrastructure
    Advisory Facility (PPIAF),
    Working Database, 42n13
public–private partnerships, 232–33
public utilities
performance evaluation of
    electricity sector
    coverage, 187, 188f8.1
    labor productivity, 187, 190,
        191f8.3, 192f8.4, 199,
        201f8.11, 202f8.12
    operating performance, 190,
        193f8.5, 203, 204f8.13
    outputs, 187, 189f8.2, 199,
        200f8.10
    overview, 185, 186–87,
        206n1
    quality of service, 195,
        197f8.8, 198f8.9, 203,
        205f8.14
treatment of debt of, 48–49
See also specific utility sector

Q

quality indexes, 76n3, 141, 144,
    225

and autonomy of regulatory
    body, 212, 213t9.3
quality of services
electricity sector, 195, 197f8.8,
    198f8.9, 203, 205f8.14
growth analysis,
    264–67tA3.2
levels analysis, 260–63tA3.1
summary of, 91t5.5, 109–14,
    115nn15–16
impact of reforms on, 45–46,
    53t3.1
PSP study findings, 225, 226
and regulatory and contract
    variables
    autonomy of regulatory body,
        212, 213t9.3
    contract award criteria, 217,
        218t9.6
    duration of regulatory board
        appointments, 213,
        214t9.4
    nationality of investors,
        214–15, 216t9.5
    tariff regulations, 219,
        220t9.7
telecommunications sector,
    121t6.3, 141, 144,
    146t6.8, 147f6.20,
    148f6.21, 150t6.9
    growth analysis,
        275–79tA3.5
    levels analysis, 270–74tA3.4
water and sewerage sectors,
    158t7.3, 176, 178–80,
    181f7.18, 182f7.19,
    182t7.9, 183t7.10
    growth analysis,
        293–97tA3.11
    levels analysis, 288–92tA3.10

R

rate-of-return, 47, 48f3.1, 218–19
reforms
in electricity sector, 43–44,
    79–89, 114–15nn1–3

impact of
on asset ownership, 46–47,
53t3.1
on consumer welfare,
50–54
on coverage, 46, 53f3.6,
54t3.1
on distribution of services
and consumer welfare,
50–54
on employment and wages,
44–45, 53t3.1
on fiscal flows, 48–49,
54t3.1
on investors, 47, 48f3.1,
54t3.1
on prices of service, 45,
53f3.6, 53t3.1
on productivity, 49–50, 54t3.1
on quality of services, 45–46,
53t3.1
market oriented, 80–85
policy considerations for,
228–33
power markets reforms,
304–14tA4.1
in telecommunications sector, 44
in water and sewerage sector,
44, 153–55, 156–57t7.2
See also specific sector
regression analysis, 71, 73–76
regulatory bodies
autonomy of regulatory bodies,
211–12, 213t9.3
duration of appointments to,
212–14, 221
regulatory framework
and determinants of impact on
performance, 207–09,
222nn1–2
econometric analysis, 65t4.3,
73–74
changes disaggregated by
regulatory and contract
variables, 300–01tA3.13
details of, 255–57
improvement of, 235

and regulatory and contract
variables
autonomy of regulatory body,
211–12, 213t9.3, 220–21
award criteria, 215–18, 221
changes disaggregated by,
300–01tA3.13
data sets for, 60, 65t4.3,
76–77nn4–9
duration of regulatory body
appointments, 212–14, 221
impact of sale method on
output, 209–11, 220
nationality of investors,
214–15, 216t9.5, 221
and tariff regulation, 218–19,
220t9.7, 221
water and sewerage sectors, 154
weaknesses of, 230–31
regulatory instruments, 235–36
returns on equity, 47, 48f3.1
revenue guarantees, 31–32, 33t2.6

S

SA. *See* South Asia (SA) countries
sanitation sector, 30
SD. *See* standard deviation (SD)
sea ports, 19, 42n8
sectors
performance indicators data
sets, 58–60, 61–62t4.1,
63–64t4.2, 76nn2–3
PPI in
geographic distribution of,
19–21
investor type by geographic
location, 26, 28, 29f2.15,
42n13
modal distribution of, 21–26,
42n12
sectoral distribution of,
17–19, 41–42nn6–9
See also specific sector
SEGBA. *See* Servicios Eléctricos
de Gran Buenos Aires
(SEGBA)

selection bias, 75–76
services
    access to, 46, 50–54
    continuity of in water and
        sewerage sectors, 158*t*7.3,
        178, 179*f*7.16, 180*f*7.17,
        182*t*7.9, 183*t*7.10
    interruptions of, 110–14,
        115*nn*15–16, 195,
        197*f*8.8, 198*f*8.9, 203,
        205*f*8.14
        PSP study findings,
            225, 226
    See also prices of services;
        quality of services
Servicios Eléctricos de Gran
    Buenos Aires (SEGBA),
    87, 115*n*2
sewerage sector, 18
    data use in water and sewerage
        sectors study, 3, 155, 157,
        158*t*7.3
    econometric analysis of water
        distribution and sewerage,
        298–99*t*A3.12
    employment in, 158*t*7.3, 165,
        168*f*7.7, 169*f*7.8, 169*t*7.6,
        183*t*7.10, 184*n*2
    growth analysis of, 293–97*t*A3.11
    IRR in, 47
    levels analysis, 288–92*t*A3.10
    literature review of, 242
    outputs, 157–65, 166*t*7.5,
        167*f*7.6, 183*t*7.10,
        298*t*A3.12
    perfomance indicators,
        59–60, 61–62*t*4.1,
        63–64*t*4.2
    PPI in, 18
    price summary, 158*t*7.3, 173–76,
        177*f*7.15, 178*t*7.8,
        183*t*7.10
    privatization process, 153–55,
        156–57*t*7.2
    reforms in, 50
    variables in, 61–62*t*4.1,
        63–64*t*4.2
    See also water sector

social issues, 230, 236
    See also public opinion
SOEs. *See* state-owned enterprises
    (SOEs)
South Asia (SA) countries, PPI in,
    21*t*2.1
SSA. *See* Sub-Saharan Africa (SSA)
    countries
standard deviation (SD), 8
    See also means and medians
        analysis
state-owned enterprises (SOEs), 10,
    33, 80, 98
    financial losses of, 80
    literature review of, 241
Sub-Saharan Africa (SSA) countries,
    21*t*2.1
subsidies, targeting of, 230

T

tariffs
    electricity sector, 190, 194*f*8.6,
        195, 196*f*8.7, 206*n*2
    regulation of as determinant of
        impact, 218–19, 221
    See also prices of services
Telebras, 120, 149
telecommunications sector,
    135–36
    data used in study, 3
    employment in, 121*t*6.3,
        129–31, 132*t*6.5, 150*t*6.9,
        152*n*7
    growth analysis of, 275–79*t*A3.5
    and investor types, 28
    and liberalization, 282–83*t*3.7
    literature review of, 241–42,
        243–50*t*A1.1
    methodologies used to study,
        3–4
    PPI in, 17–18, 19, 30, 41*n*6
    private investment in, 15, 16*f*2.7
    PSP in, 5*t*1.1
    reforms in, 44, 50
    variables in, 61–62*t*4.1,
        63–64*t*4.2
    welfare gains in, 52, 53*f*3.6

See also fixed-line
    telecommunications;
    mobile
    telecommunications;
    prices of services; quality
    of services
TFP. *See* total factor productivity
    (TFP)
time trends, 3
    conclusions concerning, 223–24
    firm-specific, 100, 253, 256
    See also trends
toll roads, 19
total factor productivity (TFP), 9,
    41n2, 240
transition period, 3
    electricity sector
        econometric analysis of
            distribution, 268–69tA3.3
        and employment, 91t5.5,
            98–101, 113t5.11,
            115nn8–11
        growth analysis of,
            264–67tA3.2
        impact on prices, 91t5.5,
            106–09, 110t5.9,
            113t5.11, 115nn13–14
        and labor productivity
            and efficiency, 91t5.5,
            101–06, 107t5.8, 111n12,
            113t5.11, 187, 190,
            191f8.3, 192f8.4, 199,
            201f8.11, 202f8.12
        levels analysis of, 260–
            63tA3.1
        operating performance, 190,
            193f8.5, 203, 204f8.13
        outputs and coverage, 90–98,
            113–14t5.11, 115nn6–7,
            187, 188f8.1, 189f8.2,
            199, 200f8.10
        overview of evaluation of
            performance, 185,
            186–87, 206n1
        quality of services, 91t5.5,
            109–14, 115nn15–16,
            195, 197f8.8, 198f8.9,
            203, 205f8.14

        tariffs, 190, 194f8.6, 195,
            196f8.7, 206n2
        evaluation of transition vs.
            long-run effects of, 67–68,
            69f4.2
        literature review of privatization
            in, 240–41, 246tA1.1,
            250tA1.1
        and PSP, 5t1.1, 224–28
        and regulatory and contract
            variables
            autonomy of regulatory body,
                 211–12, 213t9.3, 220–21
            award criteria, 215–18, 221
            changes disaggregated by,
                 300–01tA3.13
            duration of regulatory body
                 appointments, 212–14, 221
            impact of sale method on
                 output, 209–11, 220
            nationality of investors,
                 214–15, 216t9.5, 221
            overview of determinants of
                 impact on performance,
                 207–09, 222nn1–2
            and tariff regulation, 218–19,
                 220t9.7, 221
        telecommunications sector
            data analysis, 120–21
            econometric analysis of,
                 280–81tA3.6, 282–83t3.7
            employment summary,
                 121t6.3, 129–31, 132t6.5,
                 150t6.9, 152n7
            growth analysis of,
                 275–79tA3.5
            and instrumental variables,
                 286–87fA3.9
            labor productivity and
                 efficiency summary,
                 121t6.3, 131–38, 150t6.9,
                 152n8
            levels analysis of, 270–74tA3.4
            liberalization and
             competition summary,
                 119t6.2, 124t6.2, 144,
                 148–50, 151, 152nn10–
                 14, 282–83tA3.7

mobile competition,
   284–85*t*A3.8
output and coverage
   summary, 121*t*6.3,
   122–29, 150*t*6.9,
   151–52*nn*4–6
price summary, 121*t*6.3,
   138–41, 142*f*6.16,
   143*t*6.7, 144*f*6.17,
   145*f*6.18, 146*f*6.19,
   150*t*6.9
privatization process,
   118–21, 151*nn*1–3
quality summary, 121*t*6.3,
   141, 144, 146*t*6.8,
   147*f*6.20, 148*f*6.21,
   150*t*6.9
water and sewerage sectors
   employment summary,
      158*t*7.3, 165,
      168*f*7.7, 169*f*7.6,
      169*f*7.8, 183*t*7.10,
      184*n*2
   growth analysis of,
      293–97*t*A3.11
   levels analysis of,
      288–92*t*A3.10
   output and coverage
      summary, 157–65,
      166*t*7.5, 167*t*7.6,
      183*t*7.10, 298*t*A3.12
   price summary, 158*t*7.3,
      173–76, 177*f*7.15,
      178*t*7.8, 183*t*7.10
   productivity and efficiency
      summary, 158*t*7.3,
      166–67, 171–73, 174*t*7.7,
      183*t*7.10
   quality summary, 158*t*7.3,
      176, 178–80, 181*f*7.18,
      182*f*7.19, 182*t*7.9,
      183*t*7.10
   water distribution and
      sewerage, 298–99*t*A3.12
transparency, 230, 236
transport sector, 18, 19, 23,
   248*t*A1.1

trends, 3–4, 223–25, 242, 254
   distinguishing levels from trends,
      68, 70, 77*n*11
   in electricity sector, 12, 13*f*2.5a,
      90, 97, 100, 102
   in fixed-line telecommunications,
      12, 14*f*2.5b, 122, 123*f*6.1,
      126–29, 135, 141, 149,
      280–81*t*A3.6, 282–83*t*A3.7
   in infrastructure financing,
      10–17, 41*nn*4–5
   in mobile competition,
      284–85*t*A3.8
   modal trends, 27*f*2.13
   PSP study findings, 186, 224–28
   versus long-run effects, 67–68,
      69*f*4.2
   in water and sewerage sectors,
      12–13, 14*f*2.5c, 157–59,
      165–67, 171, 183, 184*n*3
   See also time trends

U

unit costs, 708
Uruguay, summary of power market
   reforms in, 310–14*t*A4.1
utility companies, list, 315–19*t*A5

V

variables
   electricity sector, 90, 91*t*5.5
      growth analysis, 264–67*t*A3.2
      levels analysis,
         260–63*t*A3.1
      used for benchmarking in
         LAC, 60, 65–67
   fixed-line telecommunications,
      121*t*6.3, 286–87*t*A3.9
   IV procedures, 257–58
   means and medians analysis
      of, 70–71, 72*t*4.4,
      77*nn*13–14, 260–63*t*A3.1,
      264–67*t*A3.2
   and performance, 61–62*t*4.1
   of PPI, 23*t*2.2

and regulatory and contract
variables, 300tA3.13
autonomy of regulatory body,
211–12, 213t9.3, 220–21
award criteria, 215–18, 221
changes disaggregated by,
300–301tA3.13
duration of regulatory body
appointments, 212–14, 221
impact of sale method on
output, 209–11, 220
nationality of investors,
214–15, 216t9.5, 221
overview of determinants of
impact on performance,
207–09, 222nn1–2
and tariff regulation, 218–19,
220t9.7, 221
summary statistics used in study,
63–64t4.2
telecommunications sector
growth analysis of,
275–79tA3.5
levels analysis of,
270–74tA3.4
water and sewerage sectors,
158t7.3
growth analysis of,
293–97tA3.11
levels analysis of,
288–92tA3.10
See also specific variable
Venezuela, Républica Bolivariana de
summary of power market
reforms in, 310–14tA4.1

W

WACC. *See* weighted average cost
of capital (WACC)
wages, impact of reform in utilities
service on, 44–45
water sector, 18, 223
and child mortality, 10
data used in water and sewerage
sectors study, 3, 155, 157,
158t7.3

econometric analysis of,
298–99tA3.12
employment in, 158t7.3,
165, 168f7.7, 169f7.8,
169t7.6, 183t7.10,
184n2
growth analysis,
293–97tA3.11
and investor types, 26–27
IRR in, 47
levels analysis, 288–92tA3.10
literature review of, 242,
243–50tA1.1
methodologies used to study,
3–4
outputs, 157–65, 166t7.5,
167f7.6, 183t7.10,
298tA3.12
perfomance indicators, 58–60,
61–62t4.1, 63–64t4.2,
76nn2–3
PPI in, 23, 30
price summary, 45,
158t7.3, 173–76,
177f7.15, 178t7.8,
183t7.10
privatization process, 153–55,
156–57t7.2
and PSP in, 5t1.1, 224–25
reforms in, 44, 50
trends in distribution of, 12–13,
14f2.5c
water production, 158t7.1, 159,
161, 162f7.3, 163f7.4,
183t7.10, 184n1
welfare gains in, 52
See also sewerage sector
Water Services Regulation
Authority (OfWAT), 154
weighted average cost of capital
(WACC), 47, 48f3.1
welfare gains, 50–53
World Bank, databases, 17f2.8,
41n4, 41–42n6,
42n13, 66
World Wide Web, as data
source, 66